PENGUIN BOOKS

D. H. LAWRENCE: LIFE INTO ART

Keith Sagar is Reader in English Literature in the Extra-Mural Department of the University of Manchester. He was born in Bradford in 1934 and was educated at Bradford Grammar School and King's College, Cambridge. He took his Ph.D. at Leeds in 1962. Dr Sagar is the author of *The Art of D. H. Lawrence* (1966), *The Art of Ted Hughes* (1975 and 1978), *D. H. Lawrence: A Calendar of His Works* (1979), *The Life of D. H. Lawrence* (1980), *The Reef and Other Poems* (1980) and, with Stephen Tabor, *Ted Hughes: A Bibliography* (1983). He has also edited several books, including the Penguin *Selected Poems* of Lawrence and two of the Lawrence volumes in the Penguin English Library, *Sons and Lovers* and (with his wife, Melissa Partridge) *The Complete Short Novels*. He is now editing volume 7 of Lawrence's letters for the Cambridge edition, and working on a *magnum opus*, *Worshippers of Nature*.

Keith Sagar lives on Pendle Hill in the Ribble Valley. His main pursuits are gardening, photography and keeping marine tropical fish.

KEITH SAGAR

D. H. LAWRENCE:

LIFE INTO ART

PENGUIN BOOKS

Penguin Books Ltd, Harmondsworth, Middlesex, England
Viking Penguin Inc., 40 West 23rd Street, New York, New York 10010, U.S.A.
Penguin Books Australia Ltd, Ringwood, Victoria, Australia
Penguin Books Canada Ltd, 2801 John Street, Markham, Ontario, Canada L3R 1B4
Penguin Books (N.Z.) Ltd, 182–190 Wairau Road, Auckland 10, New Zealand

First published by Viking 1985
Published in Penguin Books 1985

Typeset, printed and bound in Great Britain by
Hazell Watson & Viney Limited,
Member of the BPCC Group,
Aylesbury, Bucks.

Typeset in Palatino

Of poems of the third or fourth class, (perhaps even some of the second,) it makes little or no difference who writes them – they are good enough for what they are; nor is it necessary that they should be actual emanations from the personality and life of the writers. The very reverse sometimes gives piquancy. But poems of the first class, (poems of the depth, as distinguished from those of the surface,) are to be sternly tallied with the poets themselves, and tried by them and their lives.

Walt Whitman

It seems to me that no poetry, not even the best, should be judged as if it existed in the absolute, in the vacuum of the absolute. Even the best poetry, when it is at all personal, needs the penumbra of its own time and place and circumstance to make it full and whole. If we knew a little more of Shakespeare's self and circumstance how much more complete the Sonnets would be to us, how their strange, torn edges would be softened and merged into a whole body!

D. H. Lawrence

I think there ought to be a new approach to criticism, you can't separate a man from his work! Nothing is said about L[awrence]'s integrity.

Frieda Lawrence, 1956

CONTENTS

INTRODUCTION

In 1966 I published my first book, *The Art of D. H. Lawrence*. It was a work of orthodox criticism, consisting largely of textual analysis, a study of language, form and themes. In 1980 *The Life of D. H. Lawrence* appeared. My aim there was to write a documentary biography, to get as close as possible to Lawrence the man by telling his story with, as far as possible, the same degree of immediacy and authenticity as the photographs, letters and contemporary first-hand accounts. I felt that the rhythms and shape of that life would emerge more clearly if I did not attempt to relate it to the work in any developed way.

My intention now is to get as close as I can to Lawrence the creative writer, again by grounding the book in Lawrence's letters and manuscripts, and in other primary documents. I knew from the start that this third book would be needed, to tackle a subject more important and more difficult than either criticism or biography – the relationship between the life and the art, the genesis of the art in the life. More important and difficult because it involves an attempt to describe the miracle, the creative act itself. The gap between the raw material of experience and the accomplished work of art is the arc the charge of imagination must leap, or, in Lawrence's image, the ark of the covenant, the rainbow, symbol of man's ability to discover living truth in the world's chaos.

Criticism which does not get beyond the words on the page sterilizes and emasculates literature. Each published work is only the latest bulletin of the writer's battle to achieve and articulate a vision of life adequate to his experience. Each work is part of an œuvre, which is part of a life, which is part of an age, a culture and a tradition; part, above all, of the continuing human struggle to discover man's true relation to the world by the discipline of imaginative thought.

Lawrence's preeminence as a novelist has worked against the recognition of his achievement in other genres. He was by no means simply a novelist who happened occasionally to dabble in other forms. His imagination flowed into whatever he wrote, even casual letters. There were several phases of his life when his main imaginative effort went into works other than full-length novels. One of the questions to which I address myself here is why, at a certain point in his life, his imagination should have chosen to express itself in one genre rather than another. Certainly, no attempt to assess Lawrence's total achievement can ignore the great body of non-fictional writings.

The works I have selected for close attention are those which seem to me to constitute new stages in the development of Lawrence's essential vision. I have not given much space to the full-length novels after *Women in Love*. Most of what I want to say about them I have already said in *The Art of D. H. Lawrence*. *The Plumed Serpent* certainly develops Lawrence's vision of leadership, but, though impressive, it is a forced and to some extent phony performance which Lawrence himself soon saw to be a cul-de-sac from which he retreated to reaffirm some of his basic human commitments in *Lady Chatterley's Lover*. But here again there does not seem to me to be any significant imaginative breakthrough, rather a final statement of the love ethic and phallic vision he had been developing for many years. The genesis of *The Plumed Serpent* has been thoroughly described by L. D. Clark in *The Dark Night of the Body*; and many critics have discussed the evolution of *Lady Chatterley's Lover*.

My concern is not, primarily, to trace the evolution of the selected works through the surviving manuscript drafts (though I refer to these where it seems appropriate), so much as to trace the genesis of them in Lawrence's mind before he put pen to paper. Lawrence wrote so rapidly, such large chunks came all in a rush, that it is obvious that most of the creation and shaping went on during that pre-writing stage. It was commonplace for Lawrence in full flow to produce several thousand words a day. Only the mechanical limit to his speed of writing and the shortage of hours in a day prevented him from writing yet more. The real work, the imagining, had already been done.

There is no way I or anyone else can 'explain' the genius of Lawrence. What I can hope to do is to describe some of the forces, both external and internal, which determined that the work before us should be as it is, and something of what great imaginative writing costs – costs the writer in suffering and self-exposure to let that fire burn through him, for the sake of his countrymen, and of the human race.

ACKNOWLEDGEMENTS

I am, of course, by no means the first to approach Lawrence in the way I have outlined in the Introduction. Emile Delavenay extended biography in this direction in *D. H. Lawrence: L'Homme et la Genèse de son Œuvre: Les Années de Formation: 1885–1919* (1969). There have been studies of the major novels using this approach in varying degrees by George H. Ford, Mark Kinkead-Weekes, Charles Ross and John Worthen; of the poems by Sandra Gilbert and Christopher Pollnitz; and of the plays by Sylvia Sklar. Closest to my own approach (and, I believe, the best study of Lawrence) is L. D. Clark's *The Minoan Distance* (1980). I should like to acknowledge my debt to these, and to the authors of all the books listed in my bibliography and articles referred to in my notes. I owe a particular debt to Sandra Gilbert for my title, first used by her as a chapter title in *Acts of Attention*.

I should like also to thank the following for their generous help: Professor J. T. Boulton, Brian Finney, W. Forster, R. A. Gekoski, Dennis Jackson, Mark Kinkead-Weekes, Donald McFarlan, Charles Ross, Michael Squires, Lindeth Vasey and John Worthen.

My thanks are due to Laurence Pollinger Ltd and the Estate of Frieda Lawrence Ravagli for permission to quote freely from Lawrence's writings; to the Cambridge University Press for permission to quote from the volumes of their edition of Lawrence's *Complete Works* which were published at the time of going to press; to the Executors of the Jessie Chambers Estate; and to the *D. H. Lawrence Review* for permission to incorporate into this book parts of several essays which first appeared there.

I am grateful to those libraries which have given me access to original manuscripts and permission to quote from them, particularly the Harry Ransom Humanities Research Center of the University of Texas at Austin, the Bancroft Library of the University of California at Berkeley, and the University of Nottingham Library.

Finally, I should like to thank my severest critic, my wife Melissa Partridge.

ONE

THE YOUNG MAN AND
THE DEMON

It was probably a Miss Matthews, a teacher at Beauvale Board School, who first fired Lawrence's love of poetry. At the age of about six, he told a school-friend, Mabel Thurlby: 'When I grow up, I will write poetry like Miss Matthews reads to us' [CB I 29]. Five years later Mabel had become Bert's childhood sweetheart, and he wrote for her his first recorded poem:

> We sit in a lovely meadow
>   My sweetheart and me
> And we are oh so happy
>   Mid the flowers, birds, and the bees.   [32]

An innocent augury of *Birds, Beasts and Flowers*? (Or even of *Lady Chatterley's Lover*!) Certainly Lawrence never lost the habit of setting love and happiness in a context of flora and fauna. But surely even an eleven-year-old with half an ear should have winced at that appalling half-rhyme. Lawrence's rhyming remained inert, ponderous. Many an adult poem falls on its face even more bathetically than this.

The utter conventionality of that childish trifle is, of course, inevitable. The same conventionality of expression is less easy to forgive in the next poems of Lawrence's to have survived, and Lawrence himself was later scathing about them:

> The first poems I ever wrote, if poems they were, was when I was nineteen: now twenty-three years ago. I remember perfectly the Sunday afternoon when I perpetrated those first two pieces: 'To Guelder-Roses' and 'To Campions'; in springtime, of course, and, as I say, in my twentieth year. Any young lady might have written them and been pleased with them; as I was pleased with them.   [CP 27]

It is not strictly true that any young lady might have written them, since the poems are covert, symbolic attacks upon the young ladies of his acquaintance. Of all the flowers he knew, he chooses

1

campions and guelder roses to represent the heroes on either side in the battle Lawrence was himself deeply involved in in the spring of 1905, the battle between male and female, body and spirit, vitality and death.

Lawrence always wrote, consciously or unconsciously, to explore, clarify, objectify and generalize his own most pressing problems and most vivid experiences. In the spring of 1905 his most urgent problems centred on his relationship with Jessie Chambers. Their friendship had begun when he was fifteen. At first it was a friendship for the whole Chambers family; but soon the possessive Jessie monopolized him. For a few years their relationship was sustained by their shared interests, particularly in literature, but by 1905 Lawrence's sexual needs drove him to make demands on Jessie which it was not in her nature to fulfil. Again and again her beauty and her closeness stimulated his desire; again and again her fierce purity killed it. A passage in *Sons and Lovers* records the beginning of this phase. Miriam wants to show Paul a wild rose-bush she has discovered. The roses are 'pure white':

> Point after point the steady roses shone out to them, seeming to kindle something in their souls . . . It was the communion she wanted. He turned aside, as if pained . . . There was a cool scent of ivory roses – a white, virgin scent. Something made him feel anxious and imprisoned . . . She walked home slowly, feeling her soul satisfied with the holiness of the night. He stumbled down the path. And as soon as he was out of the wood, in the free open meadow, where he could breathe, he started to run as fast as he could. It was like a delicious delirium in his veins. [SL 210]

By the time we reach the fourth and fifth lines of 'Campions':

> Though the purple dreams of the innocent spring have gone
> And the glimmering dreamlets of the morning are pallid and wan

we have probably lost the ability or the will to attend seriously to the next line:

> Though the year is ripening like a woman who has conceived

or to anything in the rest of the poem.

> The Campions drift in fragile, rosy mist,
> Draw nearer, redden and laugh like young girls kissed
> Into a daring, short-breath'd confession
> Which opens earth and Heaven to Love's fugitive, glowing
>   progression

Again, the kernel of serious meaning – 'Which opens earth and Heaven to Love' – is lost between the coyness of the preceding lines and the appalling rhyme which follows. That the campions should be made to redden like blushing girls undermines Lawrence's subsequent attempt to make them the masculine love-fire which wildly attacks the prim bugle and virginal guelder rose:

Love-fire is drifting, though the bugle is prim and demure,
Love-light is glowing, though the guelder-rose is too chaste and pure
Ever to suffer love's wild attack,
For with the redness of laughter the battle is waging in the Campions'
      rosy wrack.   [CP 853]

Again, 'Guelder Roses', with its 'massèd green', its 'pale dreamy chaplets' and its 'pearled zones', has lost the reader before it reaches its point – 'the nothingness purity brings'. In its original ending the poem moved towards a certain authenticity in its bitterness towards the 'dreaming woman' and the sterility of her purity:

At the end of a sweet spring day they will vanish;
Eloquent purity voiceless in the dust;
Utterly dead; who lived but to banish
The quick, kindling spark of a generous trust.

In the autumn I'll look for immortal fruit,
Heavy nodding clusters of crimson red,
Not on the stems of virginity, lovely and mute
But of those life-loving, careless of their rank among the
      dead.   [B E317]

But Lawrence rewrote these stanzas, possibly in response to criticism from Jessie,[1] and in the process drained them of what authenticity they had. The interesting line 'Eloquent purity voiceless in the dust' is replaced with the cliché 'Forgotten, like last year's linnet song'. 'The quick, kindling spark of a generous trust' goes. And 'careless of their rank among the dead' collapses into 'who could hope for no rank among the pallid dead' [CP 854]. The revision seems to be a deliberate muffling, emasculating, to make the poem milder and nicer; an exorcizing of the demon at the first whiff of him; perhaps the first instance of what Lawrence meant when he said, of Jessie, 'she let down my demon till he howled' [850].

*

As Lawrence himself recalled: 'I was very green and unsophisticated at twenty' [CP 849]. He was also priggish, narcissistic and puritanical. When he went to college in September 1906, he had hardly begun to get clear of his mother's influence and expectations, and of the repressive religion and morality she mediated to him. Indeed, he was still prepared to consider a career in the ministry. It was the same month as his twenty-first birthday. The photographs he had taken that day are, in his own words, of a 'clean-shaven bright young prig in a high collar like a curate' [FS 159]. This is the 'young man' [CP 28] who put his hand over the demon's mouth, and was ashamed of the demon. From the vantage-point of 1928 Lawrence remembered

half-furtive moments when I would absorbedly scribble at verse for an hour or so, and then run away from the act and the production as if it were secret sin . . . I used to feel myself at times haunted by something, and a little guilty about it, as if it were an abnormality. Then the haunting would get the better of me, and the ghost would suddenly appear, in the shape of a usually rather incoherent poem. Nearly always I shunned the apparition once it had appeared. From the first, I was a little afraid of my real poems – not my 'compositions', but the poems that had the ghost in them. They seemed to me to come from somewhere, I didn't quite know where, out of a me whom I didn't know and didn't want to know, and to say things I would much rather not have said: for choice. But there they were. [849]

They were written in college notebooks so that his mother would think he was working.

It is significant that Lawrence should here speak of his early poems in language appropriate to masturbation. It is the same demon being denied expression, and for the same reasons, in either poetry or sex. The self Lawrence is ashamed of and doesn't want to know is, among other things, his sexual self. What fuels many of the early poems, the poems Lawrence was later to group together as Rhyming Poems, is the torment of baffled desire, desire baffled by form, that is the proprieties, what is permitted and approved within that culture. But the expression of that bafflement is equally baffled by form, proprieties of language, what is permitted and approved in verse. The demon is let down both ways, and can only howl.

'Virgin Youth' is one of the poems which expresses this:

Then I tremble, and go trembling
Under the wild, strange tyranny of my body,
Till it has spent itself . . . [850]

If his mother had caught him writing this poem, her disgust would have been much the same as if she had caught him committing the secret sin. It violates the first puritan commandment: thou shalt not do anything which anyone else might regard as not respectable.

4

'The chapel system of morality is all based upon "Thou shalt not" ',
Lawrence said to Jessie. 'We want one based upon "Thou shalt" '
[PR 85–6].

According to Jessie:

Lawrence entered College in a mood of wistful anticipation. He felt it
might be a step into a fuller life; he hoped for a lead of some kind, for
contact with things that were vitally alive. In this he was acutely
disappointed.   [76]

Lawrence was mortified at being treated 'like a school-kid':

There was nothing adult about life in College, and there was a decided
atmosphere of repression . . .   [79]

So college, too, stifled his demon. As he put it at the end of a poem
('Study') wisely rejected by the college magazine:

>   making friends of the brainy dust
> Of ancient swotters long since dead.
> Don't I wish I was only a bust
>   All head.   [B E317]

Lawrence's Congregational background had been by no means
simply repressive. Among other things, it had fostered a spirit of
independence – 'Dare to be a Daniel. Dare to stand alone.' If college
could give Lawrence nothing, he could at least take the time he
needed for his own pursuits. He transferred from the degree course
to the less demanding 'normal' course, so that he could read during
lectures and write in his own time, not just poems now, but also
short stories and the first drafts of his first play, *A Collier's Friday
Night*, and his first novel *Laetitia* (which became *The White Peacock*).

*

Lawrence had begun *Laetitia* in the spring of 1906, and finished
the first version in June 1907. Nothing remains of this draft but
Jessie's recollection that it was 'story-bookish and unreal':

The upright young farmer, hopelessly in love with the superior young
lady (very conscious of her social superiority) who had been served
shabbily by a still more socially superior young man, married her after a
puritanical exposition of the circumstances by her mother, and a highly
dubious conjugal life began in the melancholy farmhouse, with, one
imagined, Letty always in the parlour and George in the kitchen . . . I
think Lawrence despised the story from the bottom of his heart, for he
immediately started to rewrite it.   [PR 116–17]

It seems that at this time Jessie's critical standards were rather
higher than Lawrence's, if she remembered them accurately in

1935, for she was also unimpressed by his 'sentimental little story',
'A Prelude to a Happy Christmas', which Lawrence persuaded her
to submit in her name for the *Nottinghamshire Guardian* Christmas
story competition in 1907 [113]. Another girl-friend, Louie Burrows, agreed to submit another equally sentimental story, 'The
White Stocking'.² Lawrence himself submitted 'Legend', an early
version of 'A Fragment of Stained Glass'. 'A Prelude' won the competition and became Lawrence's first appearance in print, though
under Jessie's name. Indeed, like the earliest poems, 'any young
lady' might have written it.

The second version of *Laetitia* was written during Lawrence's
second year at college, between July 1907 and April 1908. Shortly
after finishing it, Lawrence described this version in the first of his
many letters about it to Blanche Jennings:

all about love – and rhapsodies on spring scattered here and there –
heroines galore – no plot – nine-tenths adjectives – every colour in the
spectrum descanted upon – a poem or two – scraps of Latin and French –
altogether a sloppy, spicy mess.   [L I 44]

The eighty-five pages of surviving manuscript confirm this
description. It is, indeed, 'cloyed with metaphoric fancy' [92]. A
rhapsodic, adjective-laden description of daffodils ends:

I felt inclined to hug them, I wanted desperately to know their language
perfectly so that I might talk out my heart to them.   [DB 5]

A few years later, in *Sons and Lovers*, Lawrence was to present the
desire to hug daffodils as a manifestation of Miriam's abnormality:

He watched her crouching, sipping the flowers with fervid kisses. 'Why
must you always be fondling things!' he said irritably . . . 'Can you never
like things without clutching them as if you wanted to pull the heart out
of them? . . . You don't want to love – your eternal and abnormal craving
is to be loved. You aren't positive, you're negative. You absorb, absorb, as
if you must fill yourself up with love, because you've got a shortage
somewhere . . .'   [SL 273–4]

The mature Lawrence sought to understand the language of
flowers, but in order to learn their secrets, not tell them his. The
writing here is excruciatingly self-conscious and narcissistic:

I am inclined to blush for myself – I know there is such a lot of crude
sentimentality in it, and youthful gusty sighing, bungling insupportable.
                                                                    [L I 55]

He could defend it only in terms of 'some rather fine scenes and
effects'.

The whole story is mediated to the reader through the sensibility of the narrator, Cyril. And Lawrence, despite the fact that Cyril was very much himself (the 'young man' in him) could see that Cyril would not do:

> he is a young fool at the best of times, and a frightful bore at the worst. Moreover, the first person allows of whimsicality in treatment. [61]

Whimsicality, judging from the letters, seems to have been Lawrence's dominant mode of writing at this time, fanciful rather than imaginative. Fancy is invariably sentimental, since it is the projection of purely subjective feelings and ideas onto an unresisting world. It pays no debts to reality, but finds its 'objective correlatives', if at all, in other fictions. 'The sex group of chords', for example, he defines as 'beautiful aesthetics, poetry and pictures, and romance' [66]. Much easier thus than to wrestle with his actual needs as he was to do, retrospectively, in *Sons and Lovers*. He dare not develop the relationship between Cyril and Emily, which was at the centre of his real life. It begins as something marginal, then fades away altogether. It is hard to recognize Cyril and Paul Morel as the same person; but all too easy to recognize Cyril in Lawrence's letters to Blanche Jennings; Cyril's narcissism, for example:

> As I was rubbing myself down in the late twilight a few minutes ago, and as I passed my hands over my sides where the muscles lie suave and secret, I did love myself. I am thin, but well skimmed over with muscle; my skin is very white and unblemished; soft, and dull with a fine pubescent bloom, not shiny like my friend's. [65]

This is the same letter which ends:

> I will write the thing again, and stop up the mouth of Cyril – I will kick him out – I hate the fellow . . . I *will* leave out Cyril, the fool. [69]

But Cyril remained the narrator. For though Lawrence could stand apart from Cyril long enough to curse him, he had no alternative vision to offer. The whimsicality, sentimentality and coyness would have been there with or without Cyril. Lawrence was afraid of being 'a laughingstock'. Cyril he could to some extent hide behind.

Again we are largely dependent on Jessie for an account of the differences between the first and second versions of *Laetitia*:

> In the second writing the story was radically altered and the characters became more like flesh and blood, except Cyril, who remained as he began, old-maidish. Lawrence concentrated upon George, and the figure of Annable emerged, at first only cynically brutal, but later developing into symbolic stature. I was horrified at Annable's first appearance and remonstrated with Lawrence, but he shook his head decisively, and said:

'He *has* to be there. Don't you see why? He makes a sort of balance. Otherwise it's too much one thing, too much *me*,' and grinned. [PR 117]

Thus it seems that Lawrence conceived Annable as a counterweight to Cyril, to give the demon his say through the mouth of a character who stands outside Cyril's world, the world of 'art', of carefully cultured sensibility, of the proprieties, almost outside the human world. But this means that he stands outside the fanciful world of the rest of the novel, or drives destructively through it. His few scenes are out of key. He looms out of the darkness like a 'devil of the woods'. His significance has to be forced into the novel by external description (his 'magnificent physique, his great vigour and vitality, and his swarthy, gloomy face'), by emblematic anecdote (his story of Lady Crystabel), by mythological reference ('like some malicious Pan'), and by sheer assertion ('Be a good animal'). Even in a rural community, even with the job of gamekeeper, he cannot survive. The demon is exorcized, leaving Cyril feeling bereft and reduced, but once more at the centre, the 'sort of balance' gone.

When he had finished the second version of *Laetitia* in April 1908, Lawrence told Jessie: 'Everything that I am now, all of me, so far, is in that' [82]. The 'so far' reveals how aware he was of passing through a phase of change and growth. The first version had been 'a mosaic of moods' [104]; the second had 'some rather fine scenes and effects'. One reason for Lawrence's dissatisfaction must have been the lack of any coherent view of life ('metaphysic' as he was later to call it) informing and unifying the whole book, and that he could not yet provide, beyond a mood of fashionable fin-de-siècle pessimism.

*

His voracious reading during those two college years took Lawrence further and further from his mother and his up-bringing.

He resented the tone of authority adopted by the conventionally religious people, including his mother. He said, 'Even mother doesn't like me when I'm different. I've got to be as they are, or else I'm all wrong.' He used to complain that in chapel one had to sit still and seem to agree with all that the minister said. He would have liked to be at liberty to stand up and challenge his statements. It was a matter of grief to him, too, that whoever opposed the orthodox teaching was cast out of the church, which claimed to have a monopoly of the right way of living. Lawrence had an idea of writing to our minister telling him of the agnostic authors he had read, particularly J. M. Robertson, T. H. Huxley and Haeckel, and asking him to define his position with regard to the standpoint of these writers . . . Probably the thought of his mother held him back, for the letter was never sent to the minister.   [84–5]

But Jessie was wrong. Lawrence kept even from her that he wrote two such letters to the Rev. Robert Reid in October and December 1907. As well as raising these questions, provoked by his reading, about evolution, original sin, heaven and hell, the problem of suffering, Lawrence told Reid that he could no longer believe in a *'personal, human* God'. He gave Reid his new credo – 'this is the first time I have ever revealed myself':

> A man has no religion who has not slowly and painfully gathered one together, adding to it, shaping it; and one's religion is never complete and final, it seems, but must always be undergoing modification.   [L I 40–41]

That credo was to serve him well. And both 'life' and 'art' could be substituted for 'religion'. At last Lawrence was coming into a belated independence and maturity: 'I had a devil of a time, getting a bit weaned from my mother, at the age of 22'.

The next stage in this process, during his second year at college, was, according to Jessie, his avid reading and absorption of materialist philosophy:

> The materialist philosophy came in full blast with T. H. Huxley's *Man's Place in Nature*, Darwin's *Origin of Species*, and Haeckel's *Riddle of the Universe*. This rationalistic teaching impressed Lawrence deeply. He came upon it at a time of spiritual fog, when the lights of orthodox religion and morality were proving wholly inadequate, perplexed as he was by his own personal dilemma. My feeling was that he tried to fill up a spiritual vacuum by swallowing materialism at a gulp. But it did not carry him far. He would tell me with vehemence that nature is red in tooth and claw, with the implication that 'nature' included human nature. Yet when he heard the cry of a rabbit tracked by a weasel he would shiver in pain. His dominant feeling seemed to be a sense of hopelessness.   [PR 112]

This hopelessness carried over into the novel, as Lawrence, it seems, deepened the 'sad odors' towards a fatalistic view of life, with nature, as in Hardy, a tragic chorus.

But materialism, particularly that of Haeckel, took Lawrence further than Jessie, in her own transparent hostility to it, allowed. Haeckel's monism, grounding spirit in substance, offered Lawrence a way forward in the gathering together and shaping of his new religion, and a release from the sterility of dualism. In the spring of 1908 Lawrence gave a talk on 'Art and the Individual' to a 'gathering of the Eastwood "intelligentsia" ' [DHLR 12 82]. Perhaps the most interesting passage in the whole talk (which is otherwise sentimental, precious and decadent) is one which seems to be expressing his response to Haeckel:

when this extended sympathy is directed to the history (origin) and destiny of mankind, when it reverentially recognises the vast scope of the laws of nature, and discovers something of intelligibility and consistent purpose working through the whole natural world and human consciousness, the religious interest is developed, and the individual loses for a time the sense of his own and his day's importance, feels the wonder and terror of eternity with its incomprehensible purposes. This, I hold it, is still a most useful [and] fruitful state.   [STH 224]

This, too, carried over fruitfully into the novel. It was the beginning of what was to become one of Lawrence's most characteristic strengths; as he was later to put it, speaking of Hardy and all the greatest writers:

this setting behind the small action of his protagonists the terrific action of unfathomed nature, setting a smaller system of morality, the one grasped and formulated by the human consciousness within the vast, uncomprehended and incomprehensible morality of nature or of life itself, surpassing human consciousness.   [29]

                    *

In October 1908 Lawrence left home for the first time, to teach in Croydon. After the Christmas break he got down to writing again:

Since coming back I have set down to write in earnest – now verses – now Laetitia: I am astonished to find how maudlin is the latter. It needed to come out here to toughen me off a bit; I am a fearful, sickly sentimentalist.   [L I 106]

The 'verses' were both new poems about London, schoolteaching, and Hilda Mary, his landlord's baby, and rewritings of older poems. According to Lawrence's recollection in 1928, he had written the first version of 'The Wild Common' – the first of the 'subjective poems with the demon fuming in them smokily' [CP 850] – as early as 1905. But the earliest surviving manuscript dates from the Croydon period. It is, as Lawrence says, confused and incoherent, with such poeticisms as 'my fond and fluctuant soul' and 'where were the marigolds and the songs of the brook' [PP 164], but it does not seem to belong to the same phase of Lawrence's life as 'To Guelder Roses' and 'To Campions'; rather to the phase when he came under the influence of Haeckel.

The theme is, by the standards of the young man brought up with a dualistic consciousness and transcendental religion, heretical. His spirit, he imagines, would prefer to 'bereave' him and wander free as the wind. But his 'insolent soul', could it do so, would be lost, and would quickly wither, since the soul is to the body only as blossom to a flower, as the gold to the gorse; it needs flesh and blood as a flower needs earth and 'pulsing waters'. But the poem is not merely theoretical. It works through strong images, beginning with that of the poet standing naked looking at his own reflection in a deep pond. His reflection quivers as if it would leave him, but must cleave to his flesh. It is as though this going naked in imagination frees the young man from some of his usual constraints, both of thought and expression. The penultimate stanza rises to an ecstatic atonement with the natural world:

> Over my sunlit skin the warm clinging air
> Rich with songs of seven larks singing at once goes kissing me glad.

And the final stanza translates this intercourse into frankly sexual terms:

> Oh but the water loves me and folds me
> Plays with me, sways me, lifts me and sinks me as though it were
> living blood
> Blood of a heaving woman who holds me
> Owning my supple body a rare glad thing, supremely good.   [164]

Jessie Chambers tells us that Lawrence used to call some of his early poems 'Whitmanesque'; perhaps this poem, with its long arms of verse embracing the world, is the first of them. But the truly Whitmanesque poems are all too few, and untypical. Whitman spoke directly to Lawrence's demon, probably more directly than any other poet he had yet read, but his voice was largely drowned out by the many other voices calling Lawrence in other directions. There was nothing yet in Lawrence's baffled life to justify anything approaching the relaxed poise and confidence of Whitman.

The monism of this poem comes close to that of Haeckel:

> Monism recognizes one sole substance in the universe, which is at once 'God and Nature'; body and spirit it holds to be inseparable . . . Our scientific experience has never yet taught us the existence of forces that can dispense with a material substratum, or of a spiritual world over and above the realm of nature. Like all other natural phenomena, the psychic processes are subject to the supreme, all-ruling law of substance . . . The idea of God is identical with that of nature or substance.
>
> [*The Riddle of the Universe*]

'Substance' is the key word in Haeckel's philosophy. When Lawrence rewrote 'The Wild Common' in 1928, he introduced the word five times, culminating in the purely Haeckelian:

All that is right, all that is good, all that is God takes substance! [CP 34]

as if rewriting the poem had reminded him of Haeckel.

Lawrence's first poems to be published were those sent by Jessie to the *English Review* in June 1909. They included one of the most revealing of the new Croydon poems, 'Dreams Old and Nascent'. The *English Review* published this poem in November 1909, but two earlier manuscript drafts have survived. The first version is a single poem called 'A Still Afternoon in School'. 'The afternoon/Is full of dreams'; the poem drifts through them, musing. The dreams are literary – of Lorna Doone or Dora Copperfield, or cloudy and wistful:

> Far-off, hollow pleasure-domes, where forgotten music sings.

The scene is dominated by the frail blue dome of the Crystal Palace and Norwood Hill:

> the hill and the gleam
> Of glass open the doors of the years that now lie still.

The word 'hollow' is the only hint so far that there is anything wrong with these dreams, but the next stanza, the last about the old dreams, makes clear that their seductiveness lures towards a distorted, rose-tinted view of the world:

> I can see no hill aright, for the snows of yesteryear
> Still cover the slopes with memories and soft
> Warm reflections from the sunsets of glowing souls that were here
> Once, and are here for ever.

These beautiful but passive ghosts and the reveries they spin are roughly shunted aside by 'active figures of men', railway workers, apparently, who are 'creators – the rest are dreams, the finished, the created'. They have nothing to do with the 'fixed and finite' dreams of the past. In them 'the dream-stuff is molten and moving mysteriously . . . like a heartbeat moves the blood'. Now the poem, confused and inept so far, moves into an impressive, rapturous coda:

> Oh the great mystery and fascination of the unseen shaper,
> Oh the power of the melting, fusing force
> Heat, light, colour, everything great and mysterious in One swelling
> and shaping the dreams in the flesh
> Oh the terrible ecstasy of the consciousness that I am life
> Oh the unconscious rapture that moves unthought with Life
> Oh the miracle of the whole, the wide spread labouring concentration
> of life

That makes the whole of mankind at once one bud to bring forth the
      fruit of a dream
Oh the terror of lifting the innermost I out of the sweep of the impulse
      of Life
And watching the Great thing labouring through the whole round
      flesh of the world
And striving to catch a glimpse of the shape of the coming dream
And the scent and colour of the coming dream
Then to fall back exhausted into the molten unconscious life
                                          [PP 167–8]

The second version, which follows immediately in the same
exercise book, adds the subtitle 'Dreams Old and Unborn', with
'Unborn' crossed out and replaced with 'Nascent'. The new word
exactly describes the urgency, wonder, freshness and formlessness
of that coda. Lawrence obviously felt that the ending of the part of
the poem about the old dreams was not clear or strong enough, not
sufficiently contrasted with what was to follow. Perhaps it was
only while writing the poem that he realized how disabling such
nostalgia could be.

And the sweet live dream of the old time fills
With colour, the sketch of my own world's form.
My world is a painted fresco of the past
Where the old lives linger blurred and warm
Obscuring my own world's substance to the last.   [B E317]

These lines were revised again to appear in the *English Review* in
November 1909 as follows:

Through the coloured iridescence that swims in the warm
Wake of the hushèd tumult now spent and gone
Drifts my boat, wistfully lapsing after
The mists of receding tears, and the echo of laughter.

My world is a painted fresco, where coloured shapes
Of old ineffectual lives linger blurred and warm:
An endless tapestry the past has woven, drapes
The halls of my life, and compels my soul to conform.   [CP 909]

The development is striking. Lawrence now introduces deliberate
archaisms, 'hushèd', and 'half-acquaint' earlier, as if pushing the
old dreams back into a dead past where they belong. The image of
the drifting boat is new, and is surely a conscious echo of the
Prologue to Wordsworth's 'Peter Bell', where the little Boat of
Fancy invites the poet:

'Or we'll into the realm of Faery,
Among the lovely shades of things;

13

The shadowy forms of mountains bare,
And streams, and bowers, and ladies fair,
The shades of palaces and kings!'

But the poet knows that 'Temptation lurks among your words', the temptation to escape into a dream world and forget 'what on the earth is doing'. The 'warm reflections from the sunsets of glowing souls' in the first draft have become now merely 'coloured shapes /Of old ineffectual lives', smothering him and putting a compulsion upon him to allow his vision to be coloured and his voice muffled by them.

Lawrence could not, in his first revision, improve significantly on the poem's close; but in the *English Review* version he apparently got cold feet about its rhapsodic tone, about exposing himself so nakedly in public. He cut the final section to half its length, and drained it of most of its enthusiasm and energy. When the poem was revised again for *Amores* in 1916, he restored the original ending.

*

'Dreams Old and Nascent' is, in a sense, a commentary on *The White Peacock*, a clear indication of the nature of Lawrence's growing dissatisfaction with it. On beginning the third version in January 1909 he wrote: 'I want to write live things, if crude and half formed, rather than beautiful dying decadent things with sad odors' [L I 108]. *Nethermere* was finished in October 1909 and sent to Hueffer. There was further intermittent revision over the next six months, partly in response to Hueffer's suggestions. Hueffer placed the novel with Heinemann, who did not like the title *Nethermere*, and selected *The White Peacock* from the many alternatives Lawrence came up with (including such appalling ones as *The Talent in the Napkin* and *Outreach of Tendrils*!). The publisher also required the removal or rewriting of certain passages which might have given offence to some readers. Lawrence complied: 'It is now all quite suitable even for the proverbial jeune fille – a kind of exquisite scented soap, in fact' [158]. The novel was published in January 1911.

We know from elsewhere what Lawrence's most urgent concerns were at the time of the writing of *The White Peacock*. For the most part they are conspicuously absent from the novel. There is nothing of his home and family, or of the pressures and poverty of life in a mining community. Indeed, the world of the novel seems to have been conceived as an escape from that world:

Pity to hunt out the ugly side of the picture when nature has given you an eye for the pretty, and a soul for flowers, and for lounging in the lozenge lighted shade of a lilac tree.   [57]

That Lawrence was perfectly capable of understanding and objectifying as art the complex tensions of his real world he had already demonstrated in *A Collier's Friday Night*. But the play was written in ignorance of the theatre, and without a thought of any possible audience or readership. There were no motives behind the writing of it beyond the desire to set down the truth. But fiction was a different matter. Here was a known audience, the fiction-reading public, and the novel was an art form with which he was very familiar: 'The usual plan is to take two couples and develop their relationships. Most of George Eliot's are on that plan' [PR 103]. It is not that there is anything wrong with such a structure – Lawrence was to make wonderful use of it in *Women in Love*; rather that Lawrence was never again to choose a 'plan' first and then write a novel to fit it.

Probably the first thing Lawrence wrote after finishing *The White Peacock* was 'Odour of Chrysanthemums'. Though this story was to be much improved in later revision,[3] Lawrence could not improve on the marvellous opening paragraph which so impressed Hueffer. The locomotive engine is given the dignity of a number; the woman 'insignificantly trapped' by it remains anonymous [PO 181; SSS 88]. It is an almost ludicrously crude and inefficient machine – clanking, stumbling and jolting 'with loud threats of speed' – which the colt can easily outdistance; yet all living things which cannot flee from it are subject to it, including the human beings who are dependent on the pit for their 'living'. Nature in this place seems to have given up the struggle against pollution, as though succumbing to some hellish corruption spreading from the pit-bank, 'flames like red sores licking its ashy sides'. The locomotive is only a small extension of the larger machine, 'the clumsy black headstocks of Brinsley Colliery'. The 'little spasms' of the winding engine signify that the miners are being turned up. We do not need to be told that they are often turned up maimed or dead. The paragraph is far more than just background or scene painting. Like an overture, it contains the seeds of all that follows.

Hueffer claims that he was able to accept the story for the *English Review* without reading beyond that first paragraph [CB I 106–9]. He saw, quite rightly, that this was the territory Lawrence should also have been exploring in his novels:

I was inclined to prescribe to him a course of workingman novels, the

15

idea of which he found oppressive. He wanted to try his hand at something more romantic and with more polished marble and gold and titled people among its furnishings . . . A young man brought up in his circumstances would be less than human if he was not determined to have for himself two thousand a year and footmen and the intimacy of lords and, particularly, ladies.   [116]

We must make allowances for hindsight, and for Hueffer's habitual exaggeration and embroidery, but there must be some truth in this, and Lawrence's determination to earn two thousand a year is confirmed by the much more reliable Jessie [PR 168].

If Lawrence was already well aware of the relationship between personal tragedies, the economics and mechanics of coal-mining, and the blighting of the landscape, why is that awareness so conspicuously absent from *The White Peacock*? Only once does Lawrence there approach the world of 'Odour of Chrysanthemums' or the opening of *Sons and Lovers*:

> We came near to the ugly rows of houses that back up against the pit-hill. Everywhere is black and sooty: the houses are back to back, having only one entrance, which is from a square garden where black-speckled weeds grow sulkily, and which looks on to a row of evil little ash-pit huts. The road everywhere is trodden over with a crust of soot and coal-dust and cinders.   [WP 180;247⁴]

The language here is pedestrian, against the grain, quite lacking the vitality of the more typically romantic impression of the same scene a few lines earlier:

> As you walk home past Selsby, the pit stands up against the west, with beautiful tapering chimneys marked in black against the swim of sunset, and the head-stocks etched with tall significance on the brightness.

The miners and their families hardly appear at all. Everything is transposed upwards socially, and from town to country.

There is nothing, either, of the other major concern of Lawrence at the time, the difficulties of his relationship with Jessie Chambers, despite the fact that he puts both himself and Jessie into the novel. He cannot transmute his sexual frustration into anything more balanced and self-aware than a bitter resentment against women, especially idealistic women who destroy their men. The theme, focusing on Lettie, is not convincing because not sufficiently grounded in the particularity of a real relationship, and because of Lawrence's squeamishness when he approaches sexual matters. Lawrence is trying to write about tragedy while by-passing his own limited experience of it, so that Cyril stands outside the rather manufactured tragedies he witnesses.

Within a few years, Lawrence's experience was to flow strongly into his work. But at this stage he could not recognize his own experience as fit material for a novel. The characters and situations are not fully realized because they are too literary, second-hand, imported from George Eliot, Meredith, Hardy, and, most directly, from *Wuthering Heights*, which Lawrence forbade Jessie to read in the spring of 1906:

> I said I meant to read it anyhow, and then he became serious and made me promise I wouldn't. His mother had read it, and I remember hearing her say with comic exaggeration what she would like to do to 'that Heathcliff'. [PR 102]

Presumably Lawrence anticipated that Jessie would react to Heathcliff with the same horror that his own Annable was shortly to provoke in her. Lettie, after she has married Leslie for the sake of wealth, security, elegance and adoration, is very like Catherine at Thrushcross Grange:

> She seemed to live, for the most part contentedly, a small indoor existence with artificial light and padded upholstery. Only occasionally, hearing the winds of life outside, she clamoured to be out in the black, keen storm. She was drawn to the door, she looked out and called into the tumult wildly . . . [WP 291; 371]

There are also similarities between Cyril and Lockwood, another first-person narrator. But whereas Emily Brontë is able to establish, largely by savage comedy, the total inadequacy of the effete Lockwood's conventional interpretation of what he sees and hears, Lawrence is unable to transcend Cyril's vision, so that the novel becomes symptomatic of the decadence it describes.

Aldous Huxley was to speak, after Lawrence's death, of 'that marvellously rich and significant landscape which is at once the background and the principal personage of all his works' [H xxx]. It is, perhaps, on this ground that the largest claims for *The White Peacock* have been made. Some of the best passages in the novel are certainly about the natural world; for example, the splendid evocation of the simultaneous sadness and exultation of the lapwings:

> Then I heard the lapwings in the meadow, crying, crying. They seemed to seek the storm, yet to rail at it. They wheeled in the wind, yet never ceased to complain of it. They enjoyed the struggle, and lamented it in wild lament, through which came a sound of exultation. All the lapwings cried, cried the same tale 'Bitter, bitter, the struggle – for nothing, nothing, nothing' – and all the time they swung about on their broad wings, revelling. [WP 83–4; 135]

17

There are moments when nature seems miraculous, ecstatic, demonic or, most frequently, tragic, but again and again the hints of serious meanings peter out in coyness or affectation. None of the characters seems able to relate to it other than sentimentally. Despite the attention lavished on it, nature is hardly there, since it is so overlaid with ornament – literary effects, self-conscious poeticality, echoes of Lawrence's favourite poets at the time – Tennyson, Rossetti, Swinburne, even Rachel Annand-Taylor. All these contrivances of style and the prevalence of the pathetic fallacy make nature seem more like a painted backcloth than a determining influence, touchstone of normality, or tragic chorus.

Even the spirit of place, whose centrality was indicated by Lawrence's preferred title *Nethermere*, seems inauthentic, being so largely a romanticism of place derived from Fenimore Cooper and Thoreau. Jessie Chambers reports that Lawrence became 'wildly enthusiastic over Thoreau's *Walden*, especially the essay on "The Ponds" ':

> It was a still, sunless morning, with a brooding light over the landscape, and the atmosphere he conveyed in his description seemed to tally perfectly with that particular morning. [PR 101]

Or perhaps the idea of using a lake, Nethermere, to act as a focal point of a landscape and a community came from Cooper's Glimmerglass, which years later had not lost its romantic appeal for Lawrence:

> The world – the pristine world of Glimmerglass – is, perhaps, lovelier than any place created in language: lovelier than Hardy or Turgenev, lovelier than all the lands in ancient poetry or in Irish verse. [SM 106]

*

Towards the end of *The White Peacock* there occurs an episode which Lawrence was later to use as a short story, 'A Modern Lover', probably written at the end of 1909, just after finishing *The White Peacock*. In December 1911, he completely rewrote it as 'The Soiled Rose'; and in July 1914 revised it and changed the title to 'The Shades of Spring'. These four versions of essentially the same material provide a paradigm of Lawrence's remarkable development over those five years.

The episode in *The White Peacock* is typical of the novel as a whole. Cyril, having deserted his sweetheart Emily, a farmer's daughter, some years earlier, returns unexpectedly to Nethermere, and finds, to his chagrin, that he has been supplanted in Emily's affections by another man, a man quite different from himself –

non-intellectual, and therefore, by his own standards, inferior. And no standards other than Cyril's are brought to bear on the situation. What the episode cries out for is irony, but irony is stylistically impossible within the restricted personal focus, the self-consciousness, that Lawrence's first-person narrative involves:

> The daffodils under the boat-house continued their golden laughter, and nodded to one another in gossip, as I watched them, never for a moment pausing to notice me.   [WP 305; 387]

The reflections of the daffodils tremble as they tell haunted tales in the gloom. The shadows are peopled with 'dryads' who are looking out for Cyril. There is an almost childish anthropomorphism: 'A robin sat and asked rudely "Hello! Who are you?"' Lawrence backs up his claim to hear 'the whole succession of chords' with a series of experimental effects:

> The trees caught the wind in their tall netted twigs; and the young morning wind moaned at its captivity. As I trod the discarded oak-leaves and the bracken they uttered their last sharp gasps, pressed into oblivion. The wood was roofed with a wide young sobbing sound, and floored with a faint hiss like the intaking of the last breath. Between, was all the glad out-peeping of buds and anemone flowers and the rush of birds. I, wandering alone, felt them all, the anguish of the bracken fallen face-down in defeat, the careless dash of the birds, the sobbing of the young wind arrested in its haste, the trembling, expanding delight of the buds.
>
>   [306; 388]

There is plenty of life in the writing, but nothing to resist the continual pull towards whimsy. The style is an end in itself, narcissistic; and the content is equally self-indulgent. Cyril claims that Nethermere had cast him out many years ago. While he believed it cherished him in memory, it had, in fact, forgotten him, and now treats him as an intruder. At the farm he patronizes his rival, reasserts his old power over Emily – 'I saw a last flicker of the old terror' [308; 391] – and enjoys playing the part of the rejected lover.

In 'A Modern Lover', which must have been written very soon after this, the young man, still called Cyril but now in the third person, returns to a winter landscape where 'only the unopposed wind and the great clouds mattered, where even the little grasses bent to one another indifferent of any traveller'. This indifference in the landscape is sustained, in ironic contrast with Cyril's desire to re-enter the past:

> Cyril Mersham [mere sham?] stopped to look round and to bring back old winters to the scene, over the ribbed red land and the purple wood.

The surface of the field seemed suddenly to lift and break. Something had startled the peewits, and the fallow flickered over with pink gleams of birds white-breasting the sunset. Then the plovers turned, and were gone in the dusk behind.   [WWR 225]

The suggestion here is subtly made that Cyril himself, without realizing it, is the unwanted intruder. The fact that he has become a stranger here is conveyed indirectly and economically: 'The road was heavy with mud . . . The abandoned road used to seem clean and firm'. Mersham's struggle to recapture the past sinks into the mud – 'the earth sucking and smacking at his feet'. If he cannot appropriate the scene to himself, at least he can, in a grand gesture, see it as a timeless reality to set against the unreal world of civilized activity: 'Here, on the farther shore of the sunset, with the flushed tide at his feet, and the large star flashing with strange laughter, did he himself naked walk with lifted arms into the quiet flood of life' [226]. In *The White Peacock* we should have had to take this at face value, but here we have already been put on our guard – 'It was all very wonderful and glamorous here'. The language becomes even more rhapsodical:

Surely, surely somebody could give him enough of the philtre of life to stop the craving which tortured him hither and thither, enough to satisfy for a while, to intoxicate him till he could laugh the crystalline laughter of the star, and bathe in the retreating flood of twilight like a naked boy in the surf, clasping the waves and beating them and answering their wild clawings with laughter sometimes, and sometimes gasps of pain.

He rose and stretched himself. The mist was lying in the valley like a flock of folded sheep; Orion had strode into the sky, and the Twins were playing towards the West. He shivered, stumbled down the path, and crossed the orchard, passing among the dark trees as if among people he knew.

He came into the yard. It was exceedingly, painfully muddy. He felt a disgust of his own feet, which were cold, and numbed, and heavy.

[226–7]

There is a marked discrepancy between Orion striding into the sky and Cyril stumbling down the path; between the laughter of the naked boy in the surf and the disgust of Cyril squelching through the mud with numbed and heavy feet. His soul is 'open like a foolhardy flower in the night'. We know that he is in for a disappointment, expecting, as he does, a 'fine broad glow of welcome' matching his own intensity: 'His disappointment rose as water suddenly heaves up the side of a ship. A sense of dreariness revived, a feeling, too, of the cold wet mud that he had struggled through'. This method, creating a rapturous but false epiphany (or expectation of epiphany) which is soon brought down to earth with its exposure to harsh reality, is exactly the method Joyce had already used in some of the stories in *Dubliners,* and was shortly to develop into the main structural device of his *Portrait of the Artist as a Young Man,* in order to solve exactly the same problem, the problem of finding an ironic perspective from which to judge objectively a narcissistic young man to whom he would otherwise be much too close.

The collier boys, Muriel's brothers, embody what Cyril seeks:

Now they stood wiping themselves, the firelight bright and rosy on their fine torsos, their heavy arms swelling and sinking with life. They seemed to cherish the firelight on their bodies. Benjamin, the younger, leaned his breast to the warmth, and threw back his head, showing his teeth in a voluptuous little smile. Mersham watched them, as he had watched the peewits and the sunset.

That last sentence puts an immense distance between him and them. He retreats into an easy cynicism and priggishness:

He felt how irrevocably he was removing them from him, though he had loved them. The irony of the situation appealed to him, and added brightness and subtlety to his wit. [229]

But the irony of the situation is not what Cyril takes it to be. There is a photograph of a man unknown to him on the mantelpiece, looking 'a bit of a clown beside the radiant, subtle photos of himself; he smiled broadly at his own arrogance'.

The rival, Tom Vickers, arrives. Cyril immediately takes his measure:

He was classifying his rival among the men of handsome, healthy animalism, and good intelligence, who are children in simplicity, who can add two and two, but never xy and yx. His contours, his movements, his repose were, strictly, lovable. 'But,' said Mersham to himself, 'if I were blind, or sorrowful, or very tired, I should not want him. He is one of the men, as George Moore says, whom his wife would hate after a few years for the very way he walked across the floor. I can imagine him with a family of children, a fine father. But unless he had a domestic wife –' [237–8]

In *The White Peacock* the reference to George Moore would have been a token of Cyril's and Lawrence's culture and real superiority. Here it helps to establish the hollowness of Cyril's pose of superiority. His triumph, too, is a hollow one. Cyril's classification of Vickers may, nevertheless, be broadly right. Lawrence still has strong reservations about such men. When Vickers is classed among men 'such as have been found the brief joy and unending

21

disappointment of a woman's life', we think of Walter Morel in *Sons and Lovers*. But we can also already sense the grudging admiration and envy of such men which was to produce the apotheosis of the father first clearly seen, perhaps, in the figure of Alfred Durant in 'Two Marriages' (1911), an early version of 'Daughters of the Vicar'.

In a letter of 13 May 1908, Lawrence had defended *Laetitia* as '*not* romantic . . . not Meredithian' [L I 52]. The title 'A Modern Lover' is clearly an ironic reference to Meredith's *Modern Love*, a sequence of sonnets in which Meredith imposes his own overblown emotions on the natural world. The very title, then, prepares us for the controlling ironic tone which enables Lawrence to distance himself from Cyril and his sentimental egotism. But Cyril is far from being a merely comic figure. We feel that his vitality has been drained from him partly by Muriel's cowardice, her fear of love. The irony undermines Cyril's values, but alternative values are merely gestured towards by such words as 'vitality' or 'lustihood'. The strongest presence in the story is the landscape, which provides, in such phrases as 'the quiet flood of life', sanctions which Lawrence himself does not sufficiently understand to be able to embody them in human relationships.

Lawrence's mother died in December 1910. A few months earlier his relationship with Jessie Chambers had finally collapsed. 'The sick year after', 1911, saw the bitterness of two more failed relationships, with Helen Corke and Louie Burrows, and the end, through illness, of Lawrence's career as a schoolteacher:

> Then, in that year, for me, everything collapsed, save the mystery of death, and the haunting of death in life. I was twenty-five, and from the death of my mother, the world began to dissolve around me, beautiful, iridescent, but passing away substanceless. Till I almost dissolved away myself, and was very ill: when I was twenty-six. Then slowly the world came back: or I myself returned: but to another world. [CP 851]

That experience burned away much of Lawrence's callowness. One of the first fruits of it was 'The Soiled Rose'. On 30 December 1911 Lawrence wrote to Edward Garnett:

> I think I'll send you this story. My sense of beauty and of interest comes back very strong. I wrote this story last week, in bed – before I could sit up much. You'll find it, perhaps, thin – maladif. I can't judge it at all – one reason why I send it. [L I 343]

'The Soiled Rose'[5] is indeed thin in comparison with the best stories Lawrence had yet written, but it marks a significant advance on 'A Modern Lover'.

In this third version of the story, the lover, now called Syson, has been away in London for several years and has recently married. He returns to a valley still very familiar to him: 'It was a mile nearer through the wood. Mechanically, Syson turned up by the forge and lifted the field-gate' [BR 6]. But he is no longer recognized as belonging: 'The blacksmith and his mate stood still, watching this self-assured trespasser. But Syson, dressed in stylish tweeds, looked too much a gentleman to be accosted'.[6] We are back in the spring setting of the first version, but there is no attempt now to attribute hostile or ironic intentions to it: 'There was not the least difference between this morning and those of the bright springs, six or eight years back'. The difference, therefore, must be in Syson himself; and the responsibility for his alienation: 'This was his past, the country he had abandoned, in which he was now only a visitor' [9]. He has also, we learn, abandoned his sweetheart, whom he is on his way to see. But standing between Syson and his attempt to reclaim that past, barring his way, is the gamekeeper Pilbeam, Hilda's new suitor. Pilbeam challenges Syson's right to prolong Hilda's attachment to him, especially now that he is married. Syson admits to himself that he has been a dog in the manger, and resolves to do his best on the keeper's behalf. He takes for granted that it is Hilda's love for him which has prevented her from marrying.

But Hilda has changed, not only from Syson's image of her, but also from the heroines of the earlier versions, Emily and Muriel. Even before we meet her, Lawrence associates her with fruition (ironically, Syson had sown the seeds) and rich colour:

> With many pangs, Syson noted the plum blossom falling on the daffodils and on the profuse, coloured primroses, which he himself had brought here and set. How they had increased! There were thick tufts of scarlet, and pink, and pale primroses, under the plum trees.   [10]

The place and the people embody a maturity and composure which force Syson into a defensive irony. Hilda's new surety overwhelms him with both ecstasy and fear:

> He was dumb and stupid, and at the bottom, afraid. If he were going to fall in love with this old lover, whose youth had marched with his as stately, religious nights march beside reckless days, then it would be a love that would invade many lives and lay them waste.   [14]

We are given little information about their earlier love and parting. It seems that Hilda had sent Syson away too young, first to Cambridge, then into business in London. His success has taken him out of her sphere, to which she has been unable to lure him back. He believes that she still worships at the highest altar, the one she worshipped at with him; but in a low, husky tone, and with averted face, she admits that she has 'turned away' – that in order to 'keep pace' with him, to 'understand', she had slept with her gamekeeper on the night of Syson's wedding [16]. She has not regretted it. Syson's pride is wounded, and he accuses her of opportunism.

The emphasis here is clearly very different not only from the earlier versions, but also from *Sons and Lovers*, which Lawrence was then in the middle of writing. The very name of Hilda Millership suggests an altogether more independent and robust woman than Miriam, Muriel or Emily. It seems that it is Syson, not Hilda, who has kept their relationship on a 'high' intellectual or spiritual plane. He had been too pure to sow any wild oats:

> He was shocked that she could sneer at their young love, which had been the greatest thing he had known. Certainly he had killed her love at last, as he had often wished he could. Now he felt a great sense of desolation. [20]

The changes in this version all make for greater objectivity. The keeper is clearly intended to embody everything Syson lacks:

> The strong forward thrust of his chest, and the perfect ease of his erect, proud carriage gave one the feeling that he was taut with life, like the thick jet of a fountain balanced at ease. [7]

But the thinness of the story shows in the way Pilbeam's animal vitality is not subsequently dramatized, except for the moment when, in his absence, Hilda laughs at Syson in the keeper's hut from out of her 'barbaric mantle' [17] of rabbit and stoat skins. The word 'barbaric', however, seems to have little to do with the man who later fusses about whether they are to be married 'at church, or chapel or what –' [23]. Apart from that isolated incident Lawrence does not make it matter that Pilbeam should be a gamekeeper. In the original manuscript Lawrence had overtly identified Pilbeam with Pan:

> 'Here, as a creature of Pan, I love him truly,' she said . . . 'Iacchos, Iacchos!' she cried, a sort [of] ecstasy burning dark in her eyes.
> [B E359.4a]

But, realizing that the story could not sustain such weight, Lawrence took out all the references to Pan in the March revision.

The intention is to relate Hilda's new womanliness, her reserve and surety, her pride of bearing, to her relationship with Pilbeam. But that intention is undermined by Lawrence's inability to give substance to whatever it is Pilbeam offers. At crucial points he reverts to the theme of the earlier versions, where the new lover has been taken up as merely second best: the point, for example, where Hilda's composure is described as 'calm acceptance of sorrow'. After Syson's departure, she weeps. Her sudden decision to marry Pilbeam is very much on the rebound. The story leaves her 'not watching him, but looking south over the sunny counties towards London, far away' [23].

Helen Corke must have read 'The Soiled Rose' when it was published in the spring of 1913, and written to Lawrence praising it, for on 29 May 1913 Lawrence replied:

Perhaps you are a little bit mistaken about the 'Soiled Rose'. I wrote it while I was still in Croydon – still in bed after the last illness. Don't you think it a bit affected? It is a bit stiff, like sick man's work. – So that the philosophy which is in the 'Soiled Rose' didn't hold good for me long after the writing of the story. I had not really seen the best, when I left Croydon . . . You see, I have been married for this last year . . . And this is the best I have known, or ever shall know. [L I 558]

Lawrence was then already working on *The Sisters* (later to become *The Rainbow* and *Women in Love*). By the time he came to revise 'The Soiled Rose' for inclusion in *The Prussian Officer* in July 1914, *The Rainbow* had become 'a big and beautiful work' embodying all the 'great blind knowledge and suffering and joy' that his marriage had brought him [L II 164].

The revisions Lawrence made in 'The Soiled Rose' seem at first glance to be slight, but they completely transform the story, informing it again and again with Lawrence's new-found insights. The change of title is significant, for this is to be in no sense the story of a soiled rose. Perhaps the new title 'The Shades of Spring' suggests, among other things, that Syson is a ghostly insubstantial presence out of a dead past. He is no longer 'self-assured' but 'like an uneasy spirit'. It is now Pilbeam who is 'self-sufficient'. In the unrevised version his encounter with the gamekeeper had left Syson merely in a bad temper that his 'sacred' claim upon Hilda should have been so rudely challenged. Now the encounter leaves him humiliated, 'bitterly self-contemptuous': 'What a fool he was! What a god-forsaken folly it all was!' The 'ironic' spirit now becomes the 'tormented' spirit.

Hilda is transformed in the opposite way: 'He felt foolish, almost unreal beside her'. What had been her 'calm acceptance of sorrow' becomes now her 'calm acceptance of herself and triumph over him':

There was about her the same manner, the same intonation in her voice, now as then, but she was not what he had known her to be. He knew quite well what she had been for him. And gradually he was realising that she was something quite other, and always had been . . . She saw the scales were fallen from him, and at last he was going to see her as she was. It was the thing she had most dreaded in the past, and most needed, for her soul's sake. Now he was going to see her as she was. He would not love her, and he would know he never could have loved her. The old illusion gone, they were strangers, crude and entire. But he would give her her due – she would have her due from him.   [PO 104–5; SSS 166]

This is prose which Lawrence could not have written in 1911. It is neither narrative nor interior monologue. It is Lawrence's careful articulation of deep feelings just on the point of emerging into consciousness. It is a language which became possible for Lawrence only as, with Frieda's help, he learned to see into and understand himself, and to understand and respect 'the living, striving *she*' in a woman [L II 151]. Hilda is now a free soul, freed by finding her own soil to grow in, by being her own self and serving her own god. She no longer admits, pathetically, with averted face, to having turned from the altar at which they had worshipped together, but 'looking full at him' says: 'There are no old ones. I was always looking for this' [PO 105; SSS 167]. Pilbeam, she admits, cannot make things *wonderful* as Syson could; 'but I have them all for myself now' [107; 169]. Syson had considered her 'all spirit'. Pilbeam does not bully her by reshaping her according to an image which exists only in his own mind. He respects her otherness. Syson 'knew it had never been true, that which was between him and her, not for a moment. The truth had stood apart all the time' [110; 172].[7] That truth is present in the story not so much in the gamekeeper's own person as in the marvellous natural world, eternal and forever new, with which he is associated. And the woman has become even more part of that world than her lover, even more free of the constraints of conventionality. It is Pilbeam, not Hilda, who needs the security of marriage. She says to him: 'What more would you have, by being married? It is most beautiful as it is.' As the two men depart, she looks after neither of them, but 'over the sunny country' [112; 173].

It seems that Syson had treated Hilda in much the same way that Lawrence, both in life and in *Sons and Lovers*, had treated Jessie. Syson is startled 'to see his young love, his nun, his Botticelli angel, so revealed' [110; 171]. This final version of the story involves a full recognition of his own inadequacy in that relationship, which had not been possible to the author of *Sons and Lovers*.

*

The transformation which took place in Lawrence's poetry in 1912 was even more sudden and dramatic. Lawrence met Frieda Weekley in mid-March 1912 and they became lovers almost at once. They spent the last weekend in April together at the Cearne, Edward Garnett's house in Kent. It was there that Lawrence wrote his first poems to Frieda. In most of these half-dozen poems, Lawrence's powerful new emotions are still caged in artificial and inappropriate verse forms:

> Happy am I, a naked sprig,
> In my bursting and budding; I feel
> My joy-blossoms shaping, am big
> With gladness, reel
> Prolific; I am a blossoming twig.   [CP 893]

'At the Cearne' has a splendid stanza:

> No, I am not here, I am not here.
> Life twisting its crazed machinery
> Has conveyed this thing that sits and writes
> Hither, has taken away to that hell
> In the city, something of you.
> But you and I, you and I
> On the little bank where bluebells droop
> Sit and make love to each other.   [891]

But it lapses at the end back into conventionality and inept rhyming. One poem, however, 'The Chief Mystery', is almost wholly successful in finding its appropriate form. The speaker wakes after lovemaking in a field, and does not know who he is or where he is. All his old bearings have gone. But his tentative questioning, rippling outwards in widening circles, reveals to him that he has been reborn into an altogether larger and richer world:

> I do not know where I had been
> Nor what had become of me
>   But I had not slept . . .
> I only know that like a sod
> In a meadow lost I lay,
> And that a peewit called . . .
>   But whether it called in my soul,
>   Or whether it rang in the air,
>   Or whether its heart was my nest,
>   I do not know.
> I was there, that was all . . .
> And like a sod in a meadow
> I was embedded in the rest of things

Along with the moon.
    For the full moon shone: but whether
    It lay on me as on water,
    Or whether I was the darkness with arched wings
    Hovering over it
    To fold in a shining concave the pale night,
    I do not know.   [886]

*

The following week Lawrence and Frieda left for Germany together. This was a clean break with the past, which brought an amazing belated maturing in Lawrence, both as man and artist.

> In 1912, when I was still twenty-six, the other phase commenced, the phase of *Look! We Have Come Through!* – When I left teaching, and left England, and left many other things, and the demon had a new run for his money.   [CP 851]

It is as though Lawrence left behind, among all those 'other things', the 'young man'.

Look! We Have Come Through! is a record of the first years with Frieda, up to the war. It reveals, as the Foreword says, 'the intrinsic experience of a man during the crisis of manhood when he marries and comes into himself' [191]. It is also an epithalamium, a celebration of marriage and sexual love, not omitting the conflict and occasional misery. Marriage, he claimed, 'sort of keeps me in direct communication with the unknown, in which otherwise I am a bit lost' [L I 503]. Of their honeymoon by the Isar Frieda wrote: 'Everything he met had the newness of a creation just that moment come into being' [NI 53]. His poems had to re-enact that communion and recreate that newness. Spontaneously, he began to write free verse:

> You are the call and I am the answer,
> You are the wish, and I the fulfilment,
> You are the night, and I the day.
>   What else? it is perfect enough.
>   It is perfectly complete,
>   You and I,
>   What more – ?
> Strange how we suffer in spite of this!   [CP 203]

The first night of the honeymoon may have been 'a failure', but the poem which records and transcends that failure is the finest Lawrence had yet written. The opening of the poem mimes the failure, with its blind groping and striving, its inability to generate any rhythmic impetus, any point of balance, any perspective beyond the dark bedroom:

In the darkness
with the pale dawn seething at the window
through the black frame
I could not be free,
not free myself from the past, those others –
and our love was a confusion,
there was a horror,
you recoiled away from me.   [204]

The previous week Lawrence had written to Frieda:

It's a funny thing, to feel one's passion – sex desire – no longer a sort
of wandering thing, but steady, and calm. I think, when one loves, one's
very sex passion becomes calm, a steady sort of force, instead of a
storm.   [L I 403]

No single failure or quarrel could now shake that calm. The
following morning the steady force, the sense of atonement with
the rest of life which his love had brought him, reasserts itself, with
a sense of being, in Whitman's words, 'a hub for the wheel'd
universe':

Now, in the morning
As we sit in the sunshine on the seat by the little shrine,
And look at the mountain-walls,
Walls of blue shadow,
And see so near at our feet in the meadow
Myriads of dandelion pappus
Bubbles ravelled in the dark green grass
Held still beneath the sunshine –
It is enough, you are near –
The mountains are balanced,
The dandelion seeds stay half-submerged in the grass;
You and I together
We hold them proud and blithe
On our love.
They stand upright on our love,
Everything starts from us,
We are the source.

Such a poem does not only record Lawrence's sense of himself as
a man who is loved; it implies also his discovery of his vocation as
a poet. For Lawrence was to be from now on exactly the kind of
visionary and sacramental poet defined by Whitman:

His analogy the earth complete in itself enfolding in itself all processes
of growth effusing life and power for hidden purposes.
                    ['Outline Sketch of a Superb Calm Character']

To me the converging objects of the universe perpetually flow,
All are written to me, and I must get what the writing means. [WW 82]

This whole new world to which Frieda had given Lawrence access depended, it seemed to him, on the permanence of their relationship, which, in the first months, was by no means certain. To lose her would be a mutilation, a severing of his connection with the universe:

I think, if they told me so
I could convulse the heavens with my horror.
I think I could alter the frame of things in my agony.
I think I could break the System with my heart.
I think, in my convulsion, the skies would break. [CP 213]

This agony forces him, for the first time, to conceive of his own demon not simply as his own manhood, his authentic free self, his repressed sexuality, but also, primarily, as that part of himself, that innermost ghost, which was part of, and could communicate with, the legions of spirits and powers at work in the world, given different names in different mythologies, but to be called by Lawrence, henceforth, the dark gods:

Night folk, Tuatha De Danaan, dark Gods, govern her sleep,
Magnificent ghosts of the darkness, carry off her decision in sleep,
Leave her no choice, make her lapse me-ward, make her,
Oh Gods of the living Darkness, powers of Night.

I have suggested that these developments in Lawrence's poetry took place spontaneously. There is, of course, no way of proving that. But it is not until August 1913 that we find Lawrence attempting, not very coherently, to explain in his letters the nature of the improvement:

I think you will find my verse smoother – not because I consciously attend to rhythms, but because I am no longer so criss-crossy in myself. I think, don't you know, that my rhythms fit my mood pretty well, in the verse. And if the mood is out of joint, the rhythm often is. I have always tried to get an emotion out in its own course without altering it. It needs the finest instinct imaginable, much finer than the skill of the craftsmen . . . Sometimes Whitman is perfect. [L II 61]

In a later letter to Edward Marsh (18 November 1913), Lawrence struggled a little further:

It is the hidden *emotional* pattern that makes poetry, not the obvious form . . . It doesn't depend on the ear, particularly, but on the sensitive soul. And the ear gets a habit, and becomes master, when the ebbing and lifting emotion should be master, and the ear the transmitter . . . I don't write for your ear. This is the constant war, I reckon, between new

expression and the habituated, mechanical transmitters and receivers of
the human constitution . . . I find it frightfully easy to theorise and say all
the things I don't mean, and frightfully difficult to find out even for
myself, what I do mean.   [104–5]

These are Lawrence's first faltering steps towards the marvellous
analysis of Whitman's free verse in his 1918 essay on Whitman,
and his definitive apologia for free verse in 'Poetry of the Present'
(1919), which, Lawrence says, 'should have come as a preface to
Look! We Have Come Through!' [CP 186].

In his theorizing about poetry, Lawrence is, as usual, general-
izing from his own needs. It is, of course, untrue that, as Lawrence
claimed, 'skilled verse is dead in fifty years' [L II 61]; nor is it true
that any verse which is not free verse is necessarily habituated and
mechanical. But for Lawrence it was certainly true. Every poet
needs a discipline to help him to focus and concentrate his
attention, to clarify his vision and release his energies. For some
poets, Yeats, for example, among Lawrence's contemporaries,
formal constraints can provide that discipline. But what Lawrence
needed from verse was a vehicle to enable him to articulate not so
much discoveries as revelations, meanings inherent in the world
and in human experience being transmitted through him whenever
he could be spontaneous and open and attuned enough:

Free verse is, or should be, direct utterance from the instant, whole
man. It is the soul and the mind and the body surging at once, nothing left
out . . . We can get rid of the stereotyped movements and the old
hackneyed associations of sound or sense. We can break down those
artificial conduits and canals through which we do so love to force our
utterance. We can break the stiff neck of habit. We can be in ourselves
spontaneous and flexible as flame, we can see that utterance rushes out
without artificial form or artificial smoothness.   [CP 184]

The poem in which this theory is most triumphantly justified is
the poem whose first line Frieda unerringly chose as the title of
her book about their relationship, 'Song of a Man Who Has Come
Through', written on or shortly after the day of their marriage, 13
July 1914. It is a poem simultaneously about life and art, about
Lawrence the married man and Lawrence the poet. The poem
consists almost entirely of images – wind, chisel, fountain, and
angels.

Not I, not I, but the wind that blows through me!
A fine wind is blowing the new direction of Time.
If only I let it bear me, carry me, if only it carry me!
If only I am sensitive, subtle, oh, delicate, a winged gift!   [CP 250]

Whatever the wind is, it is the opposite of the 'I'. The 'I', the self-conscious, self-centred, self-protective ego, must be yielded to it. The wind is the 'not-I', the other, the invisible wandering energies of the world. In a poem so full of echoes of the Bible and the nonconformist hymns, it suggests also the Holy Spirit, the breath of God; which is also, of course, poetic inspiration.

> If only, most lovely of all, I yield myself and am borrowed
> By the fine, fine wind that takes its course through the chaos of the
>   world
> Like a fine, an exquisite chisel, a wedge-blade inserted;
> If only I am keen and hard like the sheer tip of a wedge
> Driven by invisible blows,
> The rock will split, we shall come at the wonder, we shall find the
>   Hesperides.

Lawrence wants to be borrowed by the wind in order that it might use him as a chisel to split a rock – a rock which must be split to release the wonder, the fountain of fresh water in the desert, to find the Hesperides, a divine garden where a tree grows bearing the golden apples of Aphrodite guarded by a serpent. What Lawrence is describing here is a return to Paradise (there is a poem called 'Paradise Re-Entered' a few pages earlier), but a Paradise which has as much to do with pagan fertility religions as with Genesis, a Paradise to which we are denied entry not by the serpent, but by the rock, which is, surely, the 'I' again, the closed ego hardened into a thick shell of callousness, of insulation against the unknown and potentially dangerous. This shell seals people off from each other, from the non-human and superhuman, natural and supernatural worlds, reducing them to insentient monads incapable of love, wonder or worship. The splitting of this shell can be a painful, even tragic experience, but it is a necessary prelude to rebirth.

> Oh, for the wonder that bubbles into my soul,
> I would be a good fountain, a good well-head,
> Would blur no whisper, spoil no expression.

The fountain is life itself, the free flowing of all that sustains it, fertility, creativity. Again it is impossible to tell whether Lawrence is thinking of his art or his life. The distinction disappears.

> What is the knocking?
> What is the knocking at the door in the night?
> It is somebody wants to do us harm.
>
> No, no, it is the three strange angels.
> Admit them, admit them.

The three strange angels are those who came to Abraham and Sarah to announce that they had been chosen to bear the seed of the future – the 'new direction of Time' – while all in nearby Sodom perished. Lawrence felt that his marriage was an ark in which he and Frieda might be saved, while Europe rushed towards the abyss of the First World War. When the angels knock on his door, the defensive ego fears to open. They are dangerous. They make all-or-nothing demands. But it is only by total exposure to the angels and acceptance of their demands that blessedness can be achieved.

What had happened in those first months with Frieda, which had made the writing of such poems possible, was that Lawrence had, partly by completing and publishing *Sons and Lovers*, exorcized the young man, leaving the demon free to become no longer the writhing repressed half of a split psyche, but Lawrence's newborn self, his new wholeness and courage, the self which can recognize and respond to the sacred.

TWO

THE BIRTH AND EARLY DEATH OF A DRAMATIST

It was Saturday ... and the lads ran off to the little travelling theatre that had halted at Westwold ... They sat open-mouthed in the theatre, gloriously nicknamed the 'Blood-Tub', watching heroes die with much writhing, and heaving, and struggling up to say a word, and collapsing without having said it. [WP 63–4; 111–12]

This was Teddy Rayner's 'Star Theatre', touring the midlands with one-night stands in an old tent lighted with coal oil flares. The staple fare was melodrama – *Sweeney Todd, the Demon Barber of Fleet Street* and *Maria Marten, or Murder in the Red Barn* – but they occasionally rose to Shakespeare. This was Lawrence's introduction to the theatre:

When I was a child I went to the twopenny travelling theatre to see *Hamlet*. The Ghost had on a helmet and a breastplate. I sat in pale transport.
' 'Amblet, 'Amblet, I *am* thy father's ghost.'
Then came a voice from the dark, silent audience, like a cynical knife to my fond soul:
'Why tha arena, I can tell thy voice.' [TI 82]

Neither that experience nor growing up spoiled Lawrence's capacity to be transported by plays, and by *Hamlet* in particular. Jessie Chambers recalled:

We went to the theatre occasionally. I saw *Hamlet* for the first time with Lawrence and my brother. Lawrence was intensely excited. He went through Hamlet's soliloquy afterwards in our kitchen – 'To be, or not to be ...' And it was the same when we had seen *Macbeth* – 'Is this a dagger I see before me, the handle towards my hand ...?' grasping at an imaginary dagger. It was his characteristic blending of the serious with the comic ... Going to the theatre was the same as reading, Lawrence identified himself with the play, and for the time being lived in its atmosphere. [PR 108–9]

But the period Jessie is discussing here is Lawrence's college days. It seems quite possible that when Lawrence wrote his first play, *A Collier's Friday Night* (if, indeed, he wrote it 'when I was twenty-one, almost before I'd done anything'), he had never set foot in a proper theatre. His note on the manuscript continues 'It is most horribly green' [B E74a].

Ernest, the Lawrence-figure in *A Collier's Friday Night*, is, we are told, twenty-one, and the action takes place six weeks before Christmas. This might seem to confirm the claim that the play was written in or shortly after November 1906. However, the only surviving manuscript cannot have been written earlier than the spring of 1909, for it refers to the deaths of Meredith and Swinburne. Jessie Chambers, who is a major character in the play (Maggie Pearson), claims that Lawrence never mentioned the play to her before September 1909, and 'certainly wrote it that autumn' [DHLR 12 105]. Lawrence may, of course, have revised in 1909 a play begun in 1906. It seems that the play existed in some form in May 1908 when Lawrence wrote to Blanche Jennings describing his experiences when he first went to college in terms almost identical to those of the play. Both the play and the letter speak of Lawrence's disillusionment when he found that his college teachers were 'no better' than himself, and his boredom with their twenty-year-old lectures, especially on Langland. This passage in the play ends:

> By Jove, if you once lose your illusion of 'great men', you're pretty well disillusioned of everything – religion and everything.   [CPL 496]

The corresponding passage in the letter ends:

> So I lost my reverence, and my reverence was a big part of me – and having lost my reverence for men, my religion rapidly vanished.   [L I 49]

It seems unlikely, that, if Jessie were correct and the play written for the first time in the autumn of 1909, Lawrence could have got so close to the wording of a letter written a year and several months earlier.

Even by the autumn of 1909 Lawrence's experience of the theatre was still minimal. Before his departure to London in October 1908, there is evidence, apart from *Hamlet* and *Macbeth*, of only one visit to the theatre by Lawrence, to see Sarah Bernhardt in *La Dame Aux Camélias* at the Theatre Royal Nottingham on 15 June 1908. Her performance (at the age of sixty-four) disturbed him so much that he battered at the doors to be let out. He warned Blanche Jennings not to see Bernhardt 'unless you are very sound':

> Sarah Bernhardt was wonderful and terrible. She opened up the covered tragedy that works the grimaces of this wonderful dime show. Oh, to see her, and to hear her, a wild creature, a gazelle with a beautiful panther's

fascination and fury, laughing in musical French, screaming with true panther cry, sobbing and sighing like a deer sobs, wounded to death, and all the time with the sheen of silk, the glitter of diamonds, the moving of men's handsomely groomed figures about her! She is not pretty – her voice is not sweet – but there she is, the incarnation of wild emotion which we share with all live things, but which is gathered in us in all complexity and inscrutable fury . . . When I think of her now I can still feel the weight hanging in my chest as it hung there for days after I saw her. Her winsome, sweet, playful ways; her sad, plaintive little murmurs; her terrible panther cries; and then the awful, inarticulate sounds, the little sobs that fairly sear one, and the despair and death; it is too much in one evening. [59]

Teaching at Davidson Road School, Croydon, from 1908 to 1911 allowed Lawrence to develop his interest in theatre by teaching Shakespeare in a way which was, in those days of chalk and talk, unusually dramatic. In *The Tempest* he sent several boys to a far corner of the classroom to wail the sea-choruses from under a blackboard. For *As You Like It*, he told Louie Burrows, 'we act as if the front of the class were a stage: good fun' [245]. For a school production of *Ali Baba and the Forty Thieves* Lawrence revised and extended the text and painted all the scenery. The headmaster, Philip Smith, recalled:

Lawrence was greatly interested in a section of boys who attended the school from the English Actors' Home. Some of these pupils bore well-known names connected in the past with the English stage . . . After the initial rehearsals [Lawrence] remarked, 'These actor boys know more than we do about this kind of thing. We can't teach them the beginnings of play acting. Let them run this show as they think fit'. We agreed, with beneficial results. [CB I 87]

In London Lawrence was able to see several operas and plays. The latter included Justin McCarthy's *Proud Prince* ('never saw such rot in my life' [L I 138]) at the Lyceum in September 1909; Rudolf Besier's *Don* ('jolly good!' [143]) at the Haymarket in October 1909; and Alfred Sutro's *Making a Gentleman*, which he saw with Jessie at the Garrick on 27 November 1909.

Lawrence explained to me that the theatre existed mainly in the interests of fashion, and that the leaders of Society came not for the play (which was obviously rubbish) but to observe the varied and beautiful dresses worn by the leading ladies. [PR 165–6]

After the performance Lawrence took Jessie back to his lodgings and showed her his new play 'that was about his home on a Friday night. Sitting there in the tiny suburban room, it troubled me deeply to see his home put before me in his vivid phrases'.

If Lawrence's home in Eastwood was a world away from the middle-class suburban semi-detached in which he now lodged, it was still further, immeasurably further, from the world of the Garrick Theatre, stage or auditorium. The commercial theatre had not seen, and did not wish to see, anything resembling *A Collier's Friday Night*. It is difficult now to credit the degree of ignorance, philistinism, snobbery, callousness and hypocrisy of almost everyone connected with the Edwardian commercial theatre, the theatre dominated by Sir Arthur Wing Pinero and Henry Arthur Jones. Society drama existed to support a lie. Jones was only voicing one of its central assumptions when he said that working-class life 'does not matter'. Not only were working-class characters thought to be unworthy of dramatic presentation, except occasionally as rogues or louts; they were not thought to be human beings at all.

There was the honourable exception of the Royal Court Theatre, where the socialist dramatists, Shaw, Galsworthy and Granville-Barker, were challenging the great lie. But as far as working-class life went, they had no first-hand knowledge of it, and tended to sentimentalize the workers or present them as types. Class, for them, was part of the mechanism of contrived and tendentious plots. Jessie says that she saw Galsworthy's latest play, *Strife*, with Lawrence; perhaps they saw its opening production at the Duke of York's in 1909. Certainly Lawrence knew the play by 1919 when he wrote, of the strike situation: 'Mr Galsworthy had a peep, and sank down towards bathos' [P II 291].

Had he lived near Manchester, Lawrence might have been taken up by Miss Horniman, who staged Stanley Houghton's first play at the Gaiety Theatre in 1908 and Harold Brighouse's in 1909. Later she founded the Manchester Repertory Theatre, with its emphasis on the realistic, the regional and the working-class. But even such influential friends as Hueffer and Edward Garnett could do nothing for Lawrence in London. As late as 1934, when Garnett published *A Collier's Friday Night*, he still found it 'a bit too artless and diffuse, too lacking in concentration and surprise' for the theatre.

Lawrence was an avid reader, and wrote to Blanche Jennings in December 1908: 'I put out my hands passionately for modern verses, and drama' [L I 103]. There was, indeed, little modern drama available to him at that time. We can be sure that he knew some Ibsen, who figured prominently in the play-readings Lawrence organized at Haggs Farm during his college years:

He admired Ibsen tremendously, and recommended my brother to give me a volume of his plays on my birthday, so we read *Rosmersholme*, which was Lawrence's favourite, and *The Lady from the Sea*, of which he gave us a full description in advance, saying it was the most poetical of Ibsen's plays that he had read. Finally we read *Hedda Gabler* which he thoroughly disliked. [PR 108]

By 1909, when he gave Louie Burrows two volumes of Ibsen, including this one, Lawrence had changed his standards: '*Hedda Gabler* is subtlest, profoundest – and, I think, truest; least imaginary' [L I 114]. Apparently Lawrence was by now committed to the realistic rather than the 'poetical' in modern drama, though he hated Strindberg – 'he's rotten' [464] – when he read *Miss Julia* and *There Are Crimes and Crimes* in 1912.

Lawrence seems to have known enough of Shaw to describe him, in May 1908, as 'a jester, a motley to tap folks on the head fairly smartly with a grotesque stick' [L I 53] and in December as 'one of those delightful people who give one the exquisite pleasure of falling out with him wholesomely' [103].

In November 1909 Lawrence claimed to know the volume which contained Synge's *Riders to the Sea* and *In the Shadow of the Glen*. In the same letter he wrote: 'I have been out a good bit lately: to the theatre and so forth . . . Have you got any of Synge's plays – the *Playboy of the Western World* –' [141–2]. If he had not read *Playboy*, perhaps his desire to read it, and other Synge plays, had been fired by seeing the Abbey Theatre production at the Royal Court in June. The following year he wrote: 'As for Synge, his folk are too bodiless, mere spirits, but nevertheless he is a great dramatist and I love him' [183].

Chehov has been frequently mentioned as an influence on Lawrence's early plays, but no Chehov was available in England until Calderon's translations of *The Seagull* and *The Cherry Orchard* in 1912. By 22 April 1912 Lawrence had read them and registered Chehov's importance: 'Tchekhov is a new thing in drama' [385].

In none of his surviving letters does Lawrence mention his work in progress on his first play to anyone. We know nothing of his motives for taking up the dramatic form. In December 1910 he wrote to Violet Hunt: 'But what am I to do with these plays [*A Collier's Friday Night* and *The Widowing of Mrs Holroyd*]? Do tell me. I want some money to get married' [199]. But the plays brought no income, then or later. Of his eight completed plays only three were published and two performed in his lifetime. *A Collier's Friday Night* was first published in 1934 and first performed in 1965.

*

The title *A Collier's Friday Night*, with its ironic allusion to Burns's sentimental *The Cotter's Saturday Night*, announces, almost belligerently, that this is a naturalistic play, a 'slice of life'. Never before had working-class life in all its vital or stifling intimacy been presented in a play with such immediacy and authenticity. There is little in the way of a plot. Nothing very 'dramatic' happens. Yet the continual play of love and hate, the living process of young lives being moulded by the domestic and social and economic environment, and asserting themselves against these pressures, controls the movement of the play and holds the attention of a sympathetic audience far better than any plot would do. The immediacy and authenticity are such that, if we are aware of the play having been 'written' at all, we feel it must have been written on the Saturday morning. Indeed, the first draft may have been; but, as we have seen, Lawrence must have worked on the play at intervals over a period of at least three years.

The play is highly autobiographical, but is by no means a slavish attempt to reproduce an actual Friday night. The closeness to fact is evident from passages in Jessie Chambers's *A Personal Record*:

It was arranged that I should call at his home for my French lesson on Friday evenings as I returned from the Centre [Ilkeston Pupil-teacher Centre]. Friday was the night when the little market was held in the open space in front of the Sun Inn, and we were often left alone while Mrs Lawrence went to the market. The father I rarely saw. He was always out in the evenings . . .   [56]

Our Friday evening lessons were not always undisturbed. Occasionally, one or other of the girls who drifted so casually in and out of the house would come in and sit watching us quizzically, and the atmosphere would become charged with curious cross-currents of feeling. There was one girl in particular [Alice Hall; Beatrice in the play] who delighted to create this electric atmosphere. She had a ready wit and a caustic tongue, and her gibes flew like arrows. Lawrence would sit with his head lowered over the book, trying to let the storm pass over him, and making short rejoinders only when he was directly appealed to. His mother went about with a subtle smile, half-amused, half-ironic. The mark for all the sly innuendo was of course myself. I was too confused to speak.   [59]

The play uses all this, but not with strict autobiographical accuracy, for the Friday night French lessons ceased before Lawrence went to college.

Friday was always a significant night. No doubt everything which happens in the play really happened, and happened on a Friday night. Ernest comes home from college for the weekend. He needs yet more books his mother can ill-afford to buy him. His girl-friend Maggie, whom his family dislikes and of whom his mother is intensely jealous, visits him. It is baking night for the weekend; and shopping night, for Mrs Lambert has just received her week's housekeeping money from her husband, who, after sharing out the week's wages with his fellow butties, retires to the pub with them. While his mother is at the market, Ernest must mind the baking bread. Preoccupied with Maggie and distracted by the taunts of Beatrice, he lets it burn. Ernest's sister, Nellie, has finished a week's drudgery schoolteaching and must see her boy-friend, who works late on a Friday. She will be late home, to the annoyance of her mother. Mr Lambert will also be late home, tipsy and aggressive. Ernest will be even later, having walked Maggie home. No doubt all these things happened, and happened much as they do in the play; but they certainly did not all happen on the same Friday. Lawrence has, with amazing dramatic skill, concentrated several Fridays into one, to give us a distillation of the essence of Friday night, drawing together to this common centre, this room on this night, all the family tensions, which, separately, could be lived with, kept beneath the surface, so that they flare into open crisis.

What, then, is the core of the play, its central theme? Obviously it is the story of Ernest. His mother's favouritism towards him alienates both father and sister. He cannot be normal with Maggie because of his mother's disapproval. He feels he has betrayed his mother doubly when he burns the bread entrusted to him. After Maggie has gone he accepts his role as his father's rival for the affections of his mother. The play ends with a tearful reconciliation of mother and son, reaffirming the primacy of their relationship in both their lives. But the *Times* reviewer of the 1965 production would disagree:

Ernest, the young student, is not even the dominant figure: it is the *collier's* night, and the shape of the play is determined by his movements: coming home from the pit to eat and get his back scrubbed; climbing into his suit and holding a club share-out; storming back from the pub for a shouting match with his long-suffering genteel wife. Ernest hates the sight of him, but the play treats him tenderly as he bends grimly over his plate shovelling down his supper, miserably conscious that the rest of the family are ashamed of him. Even in the midst of his desperately inarticulate harangues, he is inclined to stop and say something generous or ask humbly for a bit of pudding. [LH 302]

Yes; but Sylvia Sklar sees the mother at the centre of the dramatic pattern:

We find the acts themselves to be divided in accordance with the stages

in the baking process . . . The thematic function of the bread baking
becomes even more evident when we notice how much of the play's
realistic detail is devoted to illustrating Mrs Lambert's nourishment of her
family . . . It is, of course, the most 'natural' thing in the world for a mother
to be concerned about feeding her family; so natural that, in this most
naturalistic of plays, we scarcely notice the way in which these details are
used to bind the play together, giving it a structural and thematic unity so
indissolubly connected that the resultant picture appears to be a seamless
rendering of life.   [SK 43–5]

All three views are right as far as they go; each of the three main
characters does give the play a structure or dimension. Then, with
highly developed craftsmanship (or instinctive sureness of touch),
they are superimposed, dovetailed, fused.

The whole play takes place in one room, the hot living-
room/kitchen where all the life of the family is concentrated. Here
the mother cooks, the family eats, the father conducts his pit
business, the daughter gossips with her friends, the son studies or
reads Baudelaire to his girl. Yet we know the rest of the house.
There are sounds of washing and washing-up from the draughty
scullery, of a piano from the little-used front room. The father's
clean trousers, brought down from upstairs, steam when he holds
them to the fire.

The life of the family is continuous with the life of the neigh-
bourhood and the whole mining community. All the meticulous
detail is there not to fool an audience into believing that it is
watching real life, but to bring real life onto the stage, life much
more real than one could have seen by actually visiting the
Lawrence home on a Friday night in 1906, because more essential,
concentrated and revealing. The props are there to be used, and
used in such a way that every household task implies a culture, a
whole way of life, testifies to the infinite adjustments these people
have evolved to the exigencies of life in this community. They
testify not only to the life-sapping labour of the mother, for whom
the burning of a loaf is a major catastrophe, but also to the
indomitable human spirit which has created, out of suffering and
conflict, a family life which gives us no sense of deprivation for the
young: the tensions frequently giving way to both hope and gaiety.
Routine becomes ritual; the action grows out of it and drops back
into it.

I have not yet mentioned the play's greatest strength, which is
to remain Lawrence's greatest strength as a dramatist: the quality
of the dialogue – and of the silences. The spontaneous family
silence which greets the father on his return from work conveys as

much as a page of *Sons and Lovers*. The mother says little, but her presence and character is strongly felt, even when she is out of the house. Her stillness centres on her suffering. Every terse understatement implies a personal history, meanings both speaker and hearer are too familiar with to labour or even fully articulate. And beneath the surface lies the history of the whole community, the patterns of speech corresponding to patterns of life, of survival and dignity, generated by the conditions of mining life. The dialect, the regional rhythms, the salty proverbs, have all the characteristics of a living, rooted speech. But they are just sufficiently rich and strange to a theatre audience to charge the dialogue with poetic force, in, for example, such potent unfamiliar words as 'sluthering' and 'slikey', or such phrases as 'Ah dun, if you dunna'.

Beyond this, each character has his or her own distinctive speech habits and rhythms which can be raised, at the crises, to the level of poetry. When Mrs Lambert finds the scorched loaf she says to herself:

> So this is it, is it? It's a nice thing! – And they put it down there, thinking I shouldn't see it. It's a nice thing! I always said she was a deep one. And he thinks he'll stop out till his father comes! – And what have they done with the other? – Burnt it, I should think. That's what they've done. It's a nice thing – a nice thing! [CPL 518; TP 66]

After the confrontation of father and son, which has almost come to blows, the father speaks out of the depths of his humiliation:

> But don't think I'm going to be put down in my own house! It would take a better man than you, you white-faced jockey – or your mother either – or all the lot of you put together! (*He waits awhile.*) I'm not daft – I can see what she's driving at. (*Silence.*) I'm not a fool, if you think so. I can pay you yet, you sliving bitch! (*He sticks out his chin at his wife.*)
>   ERNEST *lifts his head and looks at him.*
> (*Turns with renewed ferocity on his son*): Yes, and you either.
> I'll stand no more of your chelp. I'll stand no *more*!
> Do you hear me?
> MOTHER: Ernest!
>   ERNEST *looks down at his book.*
>   The FATHER *turns to the* MOTHER.
> FATHER: Ernest! Ay, prompt him! Set him on – you know how to do it – you know how to do it!
>   There is a persistent silence.
> I know it! I know it! I'm not daft, I'm not a fool!
> (*The other boot falls to the floor.*) [522; 70–71]

A page of such dialogue has more life in it than a whole play of Galsworthy or Granville-Barker.

Mrs Lambert loves her son Ernest with a deep possessive love against which he is beginning to strain, though he loves her deeply. She has taught her children to reject and despise the father, who struggles pathetically to maintain an authority and dignity only he believes in. These conflicts, just under the surface, set all their lives on edge. Any triviality can trigger an explosion. Again and again there is an adjustment, a reconciliation, a crisis averted; but the conflict is only shifting its ground around its real, unacknowledged (until the end) centre.

In *The White Peacock*, the novel Lawrence was writing at the same time as *A Collier's Friday Night*, these problems, which we know to have been uppermost in his consciousness at that time, are not faced. The novel conspicuously avoids not only Lawrence's home life, but the whole mining background he knew so well. Not until the later drafts of *Sons and Lovers* did Lawrence return to the theme of *A Collier's Friday Night*, and even there we may doubt whether he entirely recaptured the amazing objectivity and insight of the play in relation to the central problem. Sympathy is not here deliberately withheld from the father, as it seems to be at times in *Sons and Lovers*. We see that his coarseness is his only defence against the denial and exclusion of him by his family. How warmly he responds when someone treats him with ordinary decency, as a human being:

> The FATHER *stands warming his trousers before the fire.*
> GERTIE: Are they cold, Mr Lambert?
> FATHER: They are that! Look you, they steaming like a sweating hoss.
> MOTHER: Get away, man! The driest thing in the house would smoke if you held it in front of the fire like that.
> FATHER (*shortly*): Ah, I know I'm a liar. I knowed it to begin wi'.
> NELLIE (*much irritated*): Isn't he a nasty-tempered kid!
> GERTIE: But those front bedrooms are clammy.
> FATHER (*gratified*): They h'are, Gertie, they h'are.
> GERTIE (*turning to avoid* NELLIE's *contempt*): I know the things I bring down from ours, they fair damp in a day.
> FATHER: They h'are, Gertie, I know it. And I wonder how 'er'd like to clap 'er arse into wet breeches. [479; 25–6]

His aggression towards Ernest is clearly to a large extent frustrated love.

It would be possible to play the ending as a happy reconciliation of mother and son. The stage directions, however, make clear that this is not intended; that, indeed, we are to see in their embrace a 'moment of abnormal emotion and proximity' [527; 76], and in their tones 'a dangerous gentleness – so much gentleness that the

43

safe reserve of their souls is broken' [530; 79]. The vindication of the mother in *Sons and Lovers* allows for no such stress on abnormality and danger. *A Collier's Friday Night* was not written to vindicate anybody. The dramatic medium imposes its own discipline of objectivity. The author is not required to excuse or blame. He is required by the kind of naturalistic play that he had virtually invented to present these people, their relationships, their world, in such a way that the play yields its own moral significance, which an honest author must let stand. It seems that at this point in his life, such a discipline was particularly valuable to Lawrence.

*

Lawrence sent *A Collier's Friday Night* to Hueffer, who lost it for a year or so, then returned it with the comment that it was interesting but formless, and the suggestion that Lawrence should try to get it published with Garnett's help. Lawrence sent it to Garnett at the beginning of April 1912. The previous year Garnett's own play *Lords and Masters* had been produced by Ben Iden Payne at the Gaiety Theatre in Manchester. Payne was now touring with his own repertory company. Garnett discussed Lawrence's plays (he also had *The Widowing of Mrs Holroyd* and *The Merry-Go-Round*) with Payne. Payne invited Lawrence to meet him in London.

> It is huge to think of Iden Payne acting me on the stage: you are like a genius of Arabian Nights, to get me through. Of course I will alter and improve whatever I can, and Mr Payne has fullest liberty to do entirely as he pleases with the play – you know that. And of course I don't expect to get money by it. But it's ripping to think of my being acted.   [L I 384]

But nothing came of their meeting. In this same letter, Lawrence told Garnett that he had met 'the finest woman I've ever met' – Frieda Weekley. Within three weeks, Lawrence and Frieda were in Germany together, and Lawrence had forgotten about *A Collier's Friday Night*. So, it seems, had Garnett, who found it, and published it, in 1934.

Sean O'Casey, reviewing the play in the *New Statesman*, found it 'saturated with an intense and accurate feeling in the vision of the life of the family he seeks to set upon the stage'. He saw in it Lawrence's potential greatness as a dramatist:

> . . . a play that was worth production when it was first written, and it is worth production now. Had Lawrence got the encouragement the play called for and deserved, England might have had a great dramatist.

The blame for this he placed squarely on the theatre of the time:

> There never was a chance of him moving behind the curtain, and so

getting into intimate touch with the hidden life of the theatre . . . He came into the theatre, and the theatre received him not.[1]

The theatre in 1934 was no more receptive to Lawrence than it had been in 1911–12. *A Collier's Friday Night* had to wait until 1965 for its first performance, and even that was by accident. Peter Gill at the Royal Court Theatre wanted to do a Sunday night production without decor of *The Widowing of Mrs Holroyd*, wrote off for a copy, and was sent in error *A Collier's Friday Night*. This successful and well-received production laid the foundation of Peter Gill's dedication to Lawrence's plays, and the famous Lawrence season at the Royal Court in 1968 of *A Collier's Friday Night*, *The Daughter-in-Law* and *The Widowing of Mrs Holroyd*. The productions were splendid, but some reviewers praised them at the expense of the plays. The same complaints that Lawrence was already losing patience with in 1912, with the same assumptions behind them about the nature of theatre, as if Chehov and Beckett had never lived, were still being voiced in 1968: 'nothing really happens'; 'little notion of how a play should develop and resolve itself'; 'no clear shape, little sense of an ending . . . It's simply a slice out of the life of a family'. But Benedict Nightingale wrote: 'There is continual action, reaction and re-reaction; they are the least static plays one could imagine. In short they are tremendously alive'. And Irving Wardle wrote of *A Collier's Friday Night*: 'It would be a big mistake to dismiss the play as artless . . . One is left to discern the complex family bonds under the daily traffic of eating, washing, gossiping and sharing out the pay packet . . . [It] reawakens one to what naturalism should be: the art of riveting the attention by telling the truth about ordinary life' [LH 318–20].

*

Lawrence sent the first draft of his second play, *The Widowing of Mrs Holroyd*, to Grace Crawford on 17 November 1910:

Here is the MSS. I shudder to think of its intruding like a muddy shaggy animal into your 'den', sacred to the joss-stick and all vaporous elegantly-wreathed imaginations of literature . . . Give the thing to Miss Hunt, please. Tell her I hope she may consider the work fit for staging, after necessary clipping and tinting . . . Don't let Mrs Crawford read the thing – it's too common. Mothers like stuff to be decently high-falutin. [L I 188]

Lawrence's own mother was on her death-bed. By the time he heard from Violet Hunt on 13 December, his mother was dead.

Lawrence was saddened to hear that Hueffer accused him of 'Dostoieffskyism':

I was trying to persuade myself that I had really got the tones flat enough for an act-able play . . . so I thought these Holroyd folk were nicely levelled down. Woe is me!

I don't know what Holroyd suffered. He was my uncle, and his name was Lawrence. I heard my Grandmother say, 18 years ago 'Like a blessed smiling babe he looked – he did that.' But my mother looked beautiful, dead – like a maiden dreaming – yet the past fortnight has been unutterable. So we shall never know.   [199]

At least Hueffer had thought enough of *The Widowing of Mrs Holroyd* to forward it to Harley Granville-Barker at the Royal Court. But Granville-Barker simply sent Lawrence a standard rejection note. In October 1911, Lawrence sent the play to Garnett, describing it as the least literary and least unified of his plays: 'I tried to write for the stage – I tried to make it end up stagily . . . The first scenes are good' [309]. This was the first play of Lawrence's that Garnett had seen, and he was sufficiently impressed to offer to try to get all three published in one volume. Nothing came of this. Garnett kept the manuscript for 'nearly two years', then found Lawrence a publisher, Mitchell Kennerley. Lawrence wrote to Garnett:

I have been very busy reading the play to Frieda. It wants *a lot* of altering. I have made it heaps better . . . What a jolly fine play it is, too, when I have pulled it together.   [L II 58]

The nature of the revision is made clearer in a letter to Kennerley:

Particularly I hated it in the last act, where the man and woman wrangled rather shallowly across the dead body of the husband. And it seemed nasty that they should make love where he lay drunk. I hope to heaven I have come in time to have it made decent.   [71]

These revisions (which Lawrence made on the typescript of the earlier draft) delayed publication, but, as Kennerley wrote to Garnett: 'This hardly matters, as a play can only sell a few copies at most' [72]. Only 1,000 copies were printed.

The opening of 'Odour of Chrysanthemums', as we saw, shows a woman 'insignificantly trapped between the jolting black wag-gons and the hedge'. In the play Lawrence can hardly bring a colliery engine onto the stage, but he goes as far as he can, specifying in the opening stage-directions, as Mrs Holroyd brings her laundry basket in, that 'the colliery rail can be seen not far from the threshold, and, away back, the headstocks of a pit'. Mrs Holroyd is trapped by the mine and by her marriage. The location of her home and the drudgery that causes are consequences of both the tyranny of the mine and the waywardness of the husband:

This vile hole! I'd never have come to live here, in all the thick of the pit-grime, and lonely, if it hadn't been for him, so that he shouldn't call in a public-house on his road home from work. And now he slinks past on the other side of the railway, and goes down to the New Inn instead of coming in for his dinner. I might as well have stopped in Bestwood.

[CPL 15–16; TP 154]

Although on the surface Holroyd is coarse and brutal and unworthy of his wife, we do not need to look far below it to see what has provoked him to it. Her assumption of superiority, her real superiority in certain respects, drives him to strike out, to mask his humiliation with outrageous behaviour. The wife cannot but despise dirt, drunkenness and brutality. Holroyd, in his manhood, knowing himself despised, cannot but retreat into still more coarseness, drunkenness and brutality. He has known from the first that she had taken him – 'the first man that turned up' – only to escape from an intolerable situation. His vulnerability is rarely seen now; only when he is asleep or drunk, or, in its purest form, when he is dead. In spite of everything he is still the more open of the two, the less unbending. Her pride and self-righteousness make it impossible for him to apologize or initiate a reconciliation. The stage-direction at the end of Act I deftly establishes that without a word spoken: 'He turns to look at her. She turns herself still farther away, so that her back is towards him. He goes.' Lizzie Holroyd lacks the courage and patience it would need to meet him half-way, to elicit his love without destroying his manhood. She has the easier option of giving herself and her children to another man, a man already gentle and understanding. Holroyd's accident is his unconscious revenge on her for despising him and preferring Blackmore.

It is not until they bring his body home that she is able to open herself to him. There are elements of recrimination and guilt and sorrow in her final keening over his body, but these are subsumed by a purer, less self-directed emotion, by compassion for this man she had never known, this man with a body whiter than hers under the pit-dirt, in his final helplessness:

My dear, my dear – oh, my dear! I can't bear it, my dear – you shouldn't have done it. You shouldn't have done it. Oh – I can't bear it for you. Why couldn't I do anything for you? The children's father – my dear – I wasn't good to you. But you shouldn't have done this to me. Oh, dear, oh dear! Did it hurt you? – oh my dear, it hurt you – oh, I can't bear it. No, things aren't fair – we went wrong, my dear. I never loved you enough – I never did. What a shame for you! It was a shame. But you didn't – you didn't try. I *would* have loved you – I tried hard. What a shame for you! It was so cruel for you. You couldn't help it – my dear, my dear. You couldn't help it. And I can't do anything for you, and it hurt you so!

[CPL 58–9; TP 198]

Much depends on the actress, but this can be one of the great moments of modern theatre.

Synge had been greatly moved by the keening of the women of the Aran Islands, who had to cope with the loss of many sons to the sea:

Each old woman, as she took her turn in the leading recitative, seemed possessed for the moment with a profound ecstasy of grief, swaying to and fro, and bending her forehead to the stone before her, while she called out to the dead with a perpetually recurring chant of sobs . . . In this cry of pain the inner consciousness of the people seems to lay itself bare for an instant, and to reveal the mood of beings who feel their isolation in the face of a universe that wars on them with winds and seas.[2]

He had given his dramatic rendering of this at the end of *Riders to the Sea*, which Lawrence considered 'about the genuinest bit of dramatic tragedy, English, since Shakspere' [L I 260–61]. The women of his own community were well acquainted with such grief, the loss of sons and husbands to the pit:

GRANDMOTHER (*wailing*): Eh, they'll bring 'im 'ome, I know they will, smashed up an' broke! An' one of my sons they've burned down pit till the flesh dropped off 'im, an' one was shot till 'is shoulder was all of a mosh, an' they brought 'em 'ome to me. An' now there's this . . .

[CPL 50; TP 189]

At the end of *The Widowing of Mrs Holroyd* Lawrence too was able to tap a depth of tragic feeling rare in the drama of his time.

*

On the recommendation of Arnold Bennett, the Stage Society asked to see the play. Lawrence could not wait for copies to arrive from Kennerley, and sent them the proofs. When the first copy arrived, he forwarded it at once to Eddie Marsh, who had hinted that a friend might produce it. The publication of the English edition by Duckworth in April 1914 more or less coincided with Lawrence's completion of *The Wedding Ring* (the penultimate version of *The Rainbow*). This 'magnum opus', this 'big and beautiful work', now had all his attention, and *The Widowing of Mrs Holroyd* seemed small beer beside it. 'I don't set great store by it', he wrote to Murry on 8 May [L II 171]; and on the following day he expressed surprise at the enthusiasm of the *Times* review:

The play has the qualities of finished craftsmanship . . . The dialogue is packed with significance and suggestion. As to the form of the play as a single work of art, it is finely built and perfectly shaped. It rises to a great height of emotion, and sinks from it swiftly into a quiet and mournful close.   [L II 173]

Nevertheless, on his return to England that summer to get married and to see about the publication of *The Rainbow*, Lawrence also resumed his efforts to get the play staged. On 24 July he went to see Lena Ashwell, a well-known actress who was also the manager of the Kingsway Theatre. She recalled:

> I only met him once when he wanted me to act in a very tragic play of his . . . It was terribly tragic, and I felt if I acted in it I would make the part unbearable for even the toughest audience.   [C B I 598]

On 23 August 1915 Lawrence went to see Esmé Percy, 'who talks of producing my play in Edinburgh and Glasgow and Manchester. That will be rather good fun, seeing what the thing looks like on the stage' [L II 382]. Ten days later, he was still negotiating with Percy, who had suggested dropping Manchester. Lawrence was disappointed – 'As a matter of fact, a good many people in Manchester care about my work' [384]. Nothing came of this. The war was now beginning to disrupt things. Four months later Percy enlisted. He did eventually direct *The Widowing of Mrs Holroyd*, but not until 1926.

Lawrence tried again in 1919, when he decided that Douglas Goldring's wife Betty would make a perfect Mrs Holroyd. The first production, when it came the following year, was by a group of experienced amateurs, the Altrincham Garrick Society in Cheshire. Lawrence, now back in Italy, was unable to get back to see it, but was so anxious to have a reliable account of it that he sent his friend Catherine Carswell £5 for her fare to Cheshire and back. In fact she did not need the money, for she had obtained a commission from *The Times*. In her review she described it as a straightforward, unforced production which showed up the play's defects as well as its qualities:

> Here we have an every-day situation stripped, as only a master can strip it, of all inessentials, developing and coming to a crisis of clear statement by means of every-day action and every-day speech, yet in its simplicity making an intense impression on the mind and the emotions . . . The weakness emerging in the acted play is that we are not given enough knowledge of what Holroyd had meant to his wife in the early days of their marriage.   [LH 285]

According to the review which appeared on the same day in the *Altrincham Guardian*, the audience had been unworthy of the production:

When the body of Jack Holroyd is brought home and placed on his hearth before a sorrowing mother and weeping wife, the bulk of the audience accepted the situation as funny and utterly destroyed the work of author and players.

The reviewer blamed author more than players for their failure to reach 'the sublime height':

The play is badly constructed as drama, the act endings being weak and the finale inconclusive. Nevertheless, the cast did their best, and often succeeded in rising to great heights of pathos, but never quite achieved tragedy.   [286]

Catherine Carswell's review had been much cut by *The Times*. They had taken out much of her praise of the play. In *The Savage Pilgrimage* (1932) she set the record straight. She had felt that the closing scene, where the dead miner's body is washed by his women, was 'theatrically unacceptable' unless the whole production could be 'lifted into a plane beyond realism with movements that were classically simplified':

To read, the scene is simple and tragic. Outside the Irish People's Plays I reckon we can hardly match it in English with any other scene of dramatic dialogue having working folk as the protagonists. And the play holds its own against the Irish plays. Yet, as things are, it does not quite 'do', and I believe the reason lies in the fact that the theatre itself was antipathetic to Lawrence, so much so that even when writing for it he maintained his antipathy. 'Here is drama,' one imagines him to say – 'here is prose drama as authentic as any the English theatre can show. It is not "good theatre!" Then the English theatre must change itself to accommodate a living contemporary English play.'   [SP 135]

Lawrence was again in Italy when *The Widowing of Mrs Holroyd* received its next production, by the amalgamated 300 Club and Stage Society at the Kingsway Theatre in December 1926. He begged his friends to send him reports of it. On 13 December Rolf Gardiner wrote to him:

I have just come back from seeing 'Mrs Holroyd.' It was a very good performance and Esmé Percy had produced it in the right way. Mrs Holroyd [Marda Vanne] herself was perfect, and Blackmore [Colin Keith-Johnston] and the children and all the subsidiary characters, quite splendid. But the man who played Holroyd [Peter Earle] wasn't fine or big enough, I thought; not that touch of fire and physical splendour that I feel was the hidden ore in the body of him as you meant him perhaps. The atmosphere was right and you were in the play right through; only of course they couldn't talk the Derbyshire vernacular. Bernard Shaw, who was there, said the dialogue was the most magnificent he had ever heard, and his own stuff was "The Barber of Fleet Street" in comparison! The actors loved the play; one felt that. The bulk of the audience? I can't tell. But anyway the audiences at these shows are mostly bloody. [C B III 121]

Esmé Percy remembered Shaw's words rather differently: 'Compared with that, my prose is machine-made lace. You can hear the typewriter in it' [LH 288]. Shaw himself later wrote:

In my ignorance, I attached no importance to Lawrence until one afternoon at the Stage Society, when I saw a play by him which rushed through in such a torrent of profuse yet vividly effective dialogue, making my own seem archaic in comparison, that I was strongly interested technically. [LH 288]

Lawrence was delighted with Shaw's praise: 'He ought to know about dialogue, it's very generous of him' [FL 147].

On 19 December Lawrence wrote to Esmé Percy:

Mrs Whitworth sent me photographs and press-cuttings of your production of *The Widowing of Mrs Holroyd*. I dearly wish I could have been there. You seem to have done the thing so well, and the actors, especially Miss Vanne, seem to have put such heart into it. What a bore that the audience and the critics didn't like it! – Anyhow they all say plainly it was my fault – which no doubt it was: for an audience and a critic is always the same perfection unto itself. – Why do they never have the grace to say: But alas, perhaps I was an inefficient listener!

I have to confess it's years since I read the play myself. I wrote it fifteen years ago, when I was raw. Perhaps they're quite right when they say that the last act is too much taken up with washing the dead, instead of getting on a bit with life. I bet that would be my present opinion. If you've a moment to spare, tell me, will you, what you think – and what Miss Vanne thinks. – And then, if ever the play were to be done again, I'd re-model the end. I feel I should want to.

I should be really grateful for your criticism, and for that of any of the actors who wouldn't mind telling me how they feel.

Meanwhile many thanks to you and Miss Vanne and Colin Keith-Johnston and the others who did what they could, and evidently made the play live, even if there was no making it please the audience. [CL 953–4]

Marda Vanne wrote: 'I felt all the time that I was failing Lawrence. My own country, South Africa, has in it something of the doom-like quality. Perhaps that is why *Mrs Holroyd* is so real to me.'

Lawrence wrote to Gertie Cooper:

I believe most of the people found it too gloomy. I think, if it were being done again, I should alter the end, and make it more cheerful. Myself, I hate miserable endings, now. But it's so long since I wrote that play.

[EL 148]

When he wrote that letter, Lawrence was in the middle of writing *Lady Chatterley's Lover*, a novel flawed by its willed refusal of tragic possibilities. Several critics had indeed found the play gloomy, especially its ending. One called it 'a sombre but insignificant picture of life in a pit village near Nottingham'. Another 'stagnant and tormented; it lies like a burden on the mind'. But the criticisms of the ending suggest that it was done without conviction, and that it was disliked for being inconclusive and for denying the audience the expected dramatic climax between Mrs Holroyd and Blackmore:

> The curtain fell before a bewildered audience which could with difficulty be persuaded to believe that the play was over. (St J.E.)

> [Lawrence] allowed himself to be obsessed by the idea of the corpse, and left the emotional core of the play unresolved.
> (*Nation and Athenaeum*)

> It is a good situation from which the dramatist has bolted in a way disastrous to his piece. How will the lovers face that shadow, how avoid or dispel it? The question is not answered. (Ivor Brown)

Hubert Griffith saw exactly what was happening:

> The chief interest about Mr D. H. Lawrence's sombre play, *The Widowing of Mrs Holroyd* – and of very powerful and unusual interest it is – is that Mr Lawrence has dared to make his characters uncertain of what they want. They are doubtful. They have, on the top, a current of desire, and they have, underneath, an opposing undercurrent of instinct. It is extremely like life. Dramatically, of course, this is all wrong. It is outside the tradition. A perfectly simple love story should run perfectly simply.

It was certainly not true to say that 'the critics didn't like it'. Griffith called it 'an achievement . . . The interest of the play remains and grows'; Desmond MacCarthy found it 'remarkable for the vigour and credibility of its passions'; the *Nation* critic wrote:

> The bare life is filled with that astonishing vitality Mr Lawrence can put into his best work. This is not realism, but reality shorn of everything irrelevant to the emotional issue. These acts, crisp yet weighted, have that real literary quality which comes of fidelity to the truth imaginatively grasped: they are dramatic and moving.

And H.H. in *The Outlook* called it 'a masterpiece':

> Mr Lawrence expressed character by means of dialogue that is too intense to be merely realistic, too richly charged with significance to permit of the rustling of chocolate wrappings. [LH 290–94]

Despite this critical success, *The Widowing of Mrs Holroyd* was not to be performed again for thirty-five years. An excellent adaptation on Granada Television in 1961 indirectly inspired the whole series of Lawrence plays at the Royal Court in the mid-sixties. Of these, *The Widowing of Mrs Holroyd* was the most enthusiastically received.

This time it was the final scene which elicited the most striking tributes. Simon Gray wrote of it:

It is as if Lawrence were rediscovering the source of those great choric threnodies in Greek tragedy. For a short time at least, the separate members of the audience become one, not only with the mourning widow, but also with the pathetic and still vulnerable body in her arms. The wretched, wearying battle between husband and wife is over, the division between the stage and the spectators vanishes, and something like a community is created out of the shared recognition of the race's tragedy.   [320–21]

*

When, with his mother's final illness and his own 'sick year' in 1911, Lawrence's life became almost unbearable, and such creative energy as he could muster was going into *Paul Morel*, he began to use plays for a new, therapeutic purpose. Four days after the death of his mother he wrote to Violet Hunt:

I began, in the interminable watches of the bedroom, still another play – which *shall* be playable. It is high comedy. When things get too intolerably tragic one flies to comedy, or at least romance – and is cured, I hope, of heavy heroics and Jeremiahishness.   [L I 200]

The play was *The Merry-Go-Round*. It is, in intention, an Eastwood *As You Like It*. Here, for the first time, Lawrence forsakes naturalism, or rather attempts just such a mixture of the real and the fantastic, the natural and the formal, the serious and the comic, as we find in Shakespeare's comedies. His previous plays had obeyed the classical unities, taking place in a single room on a single day. Now he feels free to move his scene around the village and the surrounding countryside, to extend the action over several days, and to introduce several colourful minor characters not really necessary to the action.

The comic perspective enables Lawrence to see his own situation with ironic clarity, a clarity conspicuously absent in real life. In the same letter to Violet Hunt (virtually a stranger) in which he told her about *The Merry-Go-Round*, he wrote: 'We buried my mother yesterday: and there is gone my love of loves' [199]. Yet in the play the dying mother, Mrs Hemstock, is presented as unambiguously harmful to her whole family, especially to her thirty-year-old son Harry, who is 'nowt but a baby' and 'scared to death of a wench' [CPL 397]. In his desperation he turns for comfort to Nurse Broadbanks in a way which offers a sharp comment on Lawrence's own proposal to Louie Burrows while writing the play:

I want motherin', Nurse. I feel as if I could scraight. I've been that worked
up these last eight month – An' after my mother's gone – what am I to
do? . . . I've lived by my mother. What am I to do, Nurse?   [426]

It was predictable that in order to help him to cope with the
almost unbearable strains of that period, Lawrence should turn not
merely to comedy, but to a highly formal, artificial and mannered
type of comedy. It must have been a great relief to him to see his
own tragedy as yet another enacting of the eternal human comedy,
another spin of life's merry-go-round, amenable, perhaps, to comic
resolution. Lawrence actually attempted to impose such a resolution in real life. Marriage to Louie Burrows would be, he decided,
the instant gateway to happiness. Neither in art nor life could he
make the contrived pairings work. 'It's "As You Lump It" ' says
the play's last line; and that tells all.

The wry, anti-romantic tone which Shakespeare reserves for
such minor characters as Touchstone and Audrey, overtakes the
whole play at the end of *The Merry-Go-Round*. Shakespeare's artifice
in *As You Like It* finally releases forces we recognize as wholly
natural; contrived, as it were, by the powers of nature, embodied
in Hymen. The final pairings are the opposite of arbitrary:

Then is there mirth in heaven,
When earthly things made even
    Atone together . . .

Peace ho! I bar confusion.
'Tis I must make conclusion
    Of these most strange events.
Here's eight that must take hands
To join in Hymen's bands,
    If truth holds true contents.

The six who join hands in the confusion which ends *The Merry-
Go-Round* receive no such blessing. Their sudden arbitrary pairing-
off is as strange as any of the play's events. It is a conclusion
which, failing to resolve anything, tips the play from comedy into
farce.

The Merry-Go-Round has its comic moments, but Lawrence's gift
was not really for 'high comedy'.[3] The plot is clumsy, the wit
laboured, the characterization not strong or subtle enough. When
it was eventually staged by Peter Gill at the Royal Court in 1973,
Gill not only took many liberties with the text, but imposed on the
first four acts a uniformly realistic style, of a piece with his earlier
productions, which made the broader, more stylized farce of the
last act quite unacceptable, and left the audience longing for a

wholly serious resolution of problems the production had presented far too seriously.

*

Most of 1911 Lawrence spent working on *Paul Morel*, with no excursions into drama. April 1912 was the most important month of his life. It began with the finishing, as he thought, of his 'colliery novel': 'It's by far the best thing I've done' [L I 381], and ended with his decision to leave England with Frieda a few days later. We may doubt whether this third draft of *Paul Morel* was in fact his best work to date. His own subsequent dissatisfaction with it was amply justified. The best of the early short stories, such as 'Odour of Chrysanthemums' and 'Daughters of the Vicar', existed only in versions much inferior to the 1914 revisions. The considerable body of verse contained nothing to guarantee that Lawrence was to become a great poet. *A Collier's Friday Night* and *The Widowing of Mrs Holroyd* seem to me at least as good as anything Lawrence had done at the end of this, the first phase of his career.

*

In 1912 Lawrence wrote two 'impromptus', *The Married Man* and *The Fight for Barbara*. *The Married Man* was suggested by the experiences of a Don Juanish friend, George Neville, whose sexual adventures finally brought him low. Lawrence described it as a 'middling good' comedy [L I 386]. It is a short play, possibly unfinished, but its four acts of coy flirting, arch conversations, leaden wit and callow moralizing are more than enough. It has never been performed. Written in April 1912, its main interest is in giving us some idea of the impact Frieda Weekley had just had on Lawrence. She appears in the play as Elsa Smith, to rescue her fiancé, the Lawrence-figure William Brentnall, from the round of compulsive but half-hearted seductions and sexual manoeuvrings in which he and his friend George Grainger seem to be trapped. She is the dea ex machina who resolves the moral impasse with her liberating philosophy of openness and tolerance:

> Well, I, who am a woman, when I see other women who are sweet or handsome or charming, I look at them and think: 'Well, how can a man help loving them, to some extent? Even if he loves *me*, if I am not there, how can he help loving them?' . . . I think a man ought to be fair. He ought to offer his love for just what it is – the love of a man married to another woman – and so on. And, if there is any strain, he ought to tell his wife – 'I love this other woman.' [CPL 198]

One of the girls comments: 'It's worse than Mormons', and Brentnall leaps to Elsa's defence: 'But better than subterfuge, bestiality, or starvation and sterility'. While writing the play, Lawrence had written to Edward Garnett:

> Mrs Weekley is perfectly unconventional, but really good – in the best sense. I'll bet you've never met anybody like her, by a long chalk . . . Oh but she is the woman of a lifetime. [L I 384]

Though the timely arrival of Frieda in Lawrence's life may indeed have saved him as a man and made him as an artist, the arrival of Elsa in the play with all the answers, renders it unnecessary for the comedy to develop through plot and character towards a resolution of the problems it has raised, and leaves the play with nowhere to go.

The Married Man confirms that Lawrence's infatuation was in no small measure due to Frieda's unconventionality. It reflects his sense that his long struggle with intractable problems had been mere groping in the dark, blinkered by the limitations of his class, culture and experience. Frieda offered him a new, liberating, startlingly simple perspective. He responds to her as a fount of spontaneous wisdom, a new pragmatic morality which would have seemed wicked to his mother.

Yet we can hardly recognize the Elsa of the play, with her upper-class suavity and hauteur – 'How perfectly lovely!', 'How awfully nice!', her motor-car, her lady and gentleman friends in dinner dress, as the Frieda who was shortly to scandalize Nottingham society by running off with a miner's son. In the play it even seems that it is from this very class superiority that her moral authority derives.

Perhaps this is an extreme manifestation of the discomfort, the awkwardness Lawrence felt in writing high comedy. At the back of all his attempts at comedy is his sense of what constituted the theatre audience of the day, and of the need, in comedy, to establish a ground of common values with that audience. But there was no way in which Lawrence could speak with his true voice to the audiences for Pinero or Henry Arthur Jones (or even for *Man and Superman*).

By October 1912, when he wrote *The Fight for Barbara*, Lawrence had learned that you could not disown the past, and even in Gargnano, envelopes full of English morality fell frequently through his letter box. Nor, he and Frieda found, was it possible to love without possessiveness and jealousy. Their relationship was under great strain, as several poems testify:

> Behind me on the lake I hear the steamer drumming
> From Austria. There lies the world, and here
> Am I. Which way are you coming? [CP 231]

Again things were getting 'too intolerably tragic', and again Lawrence flew to comedy to get them in perspective and laugh himself out of despair. Thus the three greatest crises of Lawrence's life so far, the dying of his mother, the decision to commit himself to Frieda, and the fight to keep her, are all dramatized as comedies.

But in *The Fight for Barbara* there is no serious attempt to write high comedy or at popular theatricality, and with it the brief experiment with comedy is over.

*

In January 1913 Lawrence wrote to Garnett:

> I am going to send you a new play I have written. It is neither a comedy nor a tragedy – just ordinary. It is quite objective, as far as that term goes, and though no doubt, like most of my stuff, it wants weeding out a bit, yet I think the whole thing is there, laid out properly, planned and progressive. If you don't think so, I am disappointed.
>
> I enjoy so much writing my plays – they come so quick and exciting from the pen – that you mustn't growl at me if you think them waste of time. At any rate, they'll be stuff for shaping later on, when I'm more of a workman. And I look at the future, and it behoves me to keep on trying to earn money somehow. [L I 500–501]

The new play was *The Daughter-in-Law*. It seems that Lawrence was disappointed by Garnett's response to it, and by his lack of enthusiasm for the three comedies, which he returned to Lawrence at this time. On 1 February Lawrence wrote to him again:

> I believe that, just as an audience was found in Russia for Tchekhov, so an audience might be found in England for some of my stuff, if there were a man to whip 'em in. It's the producer that is lacking, not the audience. I'm sure we are sick of the rather bony, bloodless drama we get nowadays – it is time for a reaction against Shaw and Galsworthy and Barker and Irishy (except Synge) people – the rule and measure mathematical folk. But you are of them and your sympathies are with your own generation, not with mine. [509]

But Lawrence did not find his Stanislavsky. Neither *The Daughter-in-Law* nor any of the three comedies was produced (or published) in his lifetime.

Certainly there is nothing bloodless about *The Daughter-in-Law*. Its strengths are those of *A Collier's Friday Night* and *The Widowing of Mrs Holroyd*. The first line plunges us into that same vivid world. Mrs Gascoigne greets her son Joe with the words: 'Well, I s'd ha' thought thy belly 'ud a browt thee whoam afore this'. Mrs Gascoigne's speech throughout has the flavour of proverbs substantiated by experience: 'Marriage is like a mouse-trap, for either man or woman. You've soon come to the end o' th' cheese' [CPL 210; TP 86].

The main theme is the effort of Minnie Gascoigne, a young woman of great character and some refinement, to 'wriggle a place out for hersen', and to give back to her husband, Luther, the manhood lost at his mother's apron strings, out of which he will then, she hopes, be able to give her the love she needs. Minnie brings £120 to her wedding, but comes to realize that the independence this gives her undermines her husband's self-esteem. In desperation she goes to Manchester and spends it all on a ring and two prints. She wins the grudging admiration of her mother-in-law; but the husband takes the prints (which are actually an investment) as a further sneer at his lack of refinement, and thrusts them into the fire. This ending of Act III is masterly:

MINNIE (*with a cry*): Ah! – that's my ninety pounds gone.
(*Tries to snatch them out.*)
MRS GASCOIGNE (*beginning to cry*): Come, Joe, let's go; let's go, my lad. I've seen as much this day as ever my eyes want to see. Let's go, my lad. (*Getting up, beginning to tie on her bonnet.*)
MINNIE (*white and intense, to* LUTHER): Should you like to throw my ring after them? It's all I've got left. (*She holds out her hand – he flings it from him.*)
LUTHER: Yi, what do I care what I do! (*Clenching his fists as if he would strike her.*) – what do I! – what do I –!
MRS GASCOIGNE (*putting on her shawl*): A day's work – a day's work! Ninety pound! Nay – nay, oh, nay – nay, oh, nay – nay! Let's go, Joe, my lad. Eh, our Luther, our Luther! Let's go, Joe. Come.
JOE: Ah, I'll come, Mother.
MRS GASCOIGNE: Luther!
LUTHER: What?
MRS GASCOIGNE: It's a day's work, it is, wi' thee. Eh dear!
Come, let's go, Joe. Let's go whoam.
LUTHER: An' I'll go.
MRS GASCOIGNE: Dunna thee do nowt as ter'll repent of, Luther – dunna thee. It's thy mother axes thee. Come, Joe.
MRS GASCOIGNE *goes out, followed by* JOE. LUTHER *stands with face averted from his wife; mutters something, reaches for his cap, goes out.* MINNIE *stands with her hand on the mantelpiece.*

CURTAIN

Joe, the younger brother still at home, has little to say here, but his mother's refrain: 'Let's go, Joe' invests him with a dramatic importance as great as the other three. Mrs Gascoigne has lost Luther and her battle with Minnie:

MINNIE: It was your fault. You held him, and persuaded him that what he wanted was *you*. You kept him, like a child, you even gave him what money he wanted, like a child. He never roughed it – he never faced out anything. You did all that for him.

MRS GASCOIGNE: And what if I did! If you made as good a wife to him as I made a mother, you'd do.

MINNIE: Should I? You didn't care what women your sons went with, so long as they didn't love them . . . All you cared about was to keep your sons for yourself. You kept the solid meal, and the orts and slarts any other woman could have. But I tell you, I'm *not* for having the orts and slarts, and your leavings from your sons. I'll have a man, or nothing, I will. [CPL 255–6; TP 134]

Whether Minnie can make a man of Luther remains doubtful. The ending, with Luther weeping in his wife's arms, is open. Minnie has done all that a woman, with courage and tenderness, can do. But it may be that Luther will simply transfer his dependence from his mother to her.

Meanwhile, Joe remains with his mother, talking of Australia, flirting with Minnie. He is in a worse case than his brother and knows it. 'How is a woman ever to have a husband, when the men all belong to their mothers?' Minnie cries. And Joe adds:

Nay, Mother, tha knows it's right. Tha knows tha's got me – an'll ha'e me till ter dies – an' after that – yi . . . And sometimes, Mother, I wish I wor dead, I do . . . Tha knows I couldna leave thee, Mother – tha knows I couldna. An' me, a young man, belongs to thy owd age. An' there's nowheer for me to go, Mother. For tha'rt gettin' nearer to death an' yet I canna leave thee to go my own road. An' I wish, yi, often, as I wor dead. [257–8; 136–7]

It was, perhaps, a mixed blessing that Lawrence could not find a producer for his plays. Had he done so, he might well have had to witness and struggle against the same kind of humiliating treatment that *The Daughter-in-Law* suffered when it turned up after his death among various manuscripts he had left with his sister-in-law in Germany in 1913. In 1933 Curtis Brown, Lawrence's agent, sent it to a theatrical impresario, Leon M. Lion. Lion decided that it was insufficiently theatrical, and would have to be 'adapted'. Frieda objected strongly to this, but Laurence Pollinger assured her that 'it was necessary that the Play should be revised in certain places if it were ever to be produced. Please don't lose sight of the fact that Lawrence wrote it many, many years ago, and times and conditions have considerably changed since then'.

Conditions governing the difficulty of getting a good play staged had changed not at all.

Richard Hughes, the author of *A High Wind in Jamaica*, was commissioned to do the adaptation, but he failed to come up with anything after eighteen months, and the job was given to Walter Greenwood, author of *Love on the Dole*. The press releases suggested that the play as found had lacked a final act, which Greenwood had written. In fact he produced only three pages of new dialogue, and diluted the dialect. He also produced more 'theatrical' curtain lines for three earlier scenes. The title was changed to *My Son's My Son*, and the play was advertised as 'An Unrevised Play by D. H. Lawrence Completed by Walter Greenwood'. Still, as one reviewer of the 1936 production charmingly wrote: 'Walter Greenwood has more of the theatre in one of his little fingers than Lawrence could muster from a whole life's suppressed eructation' [LH 299]. Greenwood's dialect coaching seems not to have been wholly successful, since the reviewers reported accents ranging from Oxford to Blackpool, and one referred to the 'passages of pure Kensington which crept persistently in, and into which Miss Sarah Erskine, as Luther's wife, at last frankly relapsed'. Little care seems to have been taken with the costumes. At one point Luther, returned from work, sat down, and displayed to the audience the virgin white soles of his brand new pit boots.[4]

In 1967 the play finally came into its own, first at the Traverse in Edinburgh, then at the Royal Court. Reviewing the Royal Court production, Ronald Bryden wrote:

> Lawrence feared, correctly, that his contemporaries would find his plays too naturalistic and slow, but he was right and they were wrong. *The Daughter-in-Law* may not compare with his novels, but it makes most of our post-war essays in working-class drama look flimsy. [304]

Lawrence wanted to create a dramatic form which would embody, in the words of Raymond Williams, 'the detail and closeness of fiction . . . the flow of experience and the sympathy with ordinary life and speech'. What he came up against was

> the habits of theatre, and of most traditional drama, in which posture, rhetoric, formality and presentation, had been the ordinary means. That this problem is still unsolved is evident from the movement of so much of our best drama away from ordinary experience and away from the flow of sympathy; the counter-movement, in part in the theatre, but mainly in film and in television, has only just begun. [TP 13]

Since 1969, when Raymond Williams wrote this, that counter-movement in television has come a long way. Perhaps Lawrence was the perfect television dramatist.

*

Although Lawrence was to write two more plays, *Touch and Go* in 1918 and *David* in 1925, his brief career as a dramatist was virtually over by 1913. The later plays were occasional, out of the mainstream of Lawrence's creative effort. The early plays were not. If Synge could make genuine dramatic tragedy out of the culture and speech of the Aran Islands, why could not Lawrence out of the culture and speech of the Nottinghamshire coalfields? Speaking of his new novel, *The Insurrection of Miss Houghton*, Lawrence told Garnett that he thought he had inside him 'a sort of answer to the *want* of today: to the real, deep want of the English people, not to just what they fancy they want' [L I 511]. He saw his plays also as part of his effort for England, describing them as 'plays about people' [P II 290]; but for an audience for such plays he would have needed a People's Theatre, and, as he wrote in his Preface to *Touch and Go*: 'There's no such thing in existence as a People's Theatre: or even on the way to existence, as far as we can tell' [289]. Real people, in Lawrence's sense, either did not go to the theatre, or did not go expecting or desiring to see real people and their suffering; they went to *Chu Chin Chow*.

What was the point of writing more such plays, when those he had written already, and been peddling for two years, had no prospect of production? Yet, however successful these plays had been, it is difficult to see where Lawrence could have gone from here as a dramatist. All the plays he had yet written except the 'impromptus' had been on the same theme, the emasculating effect of an over-possessive mother on her sons. It seems that Lawrence could only tap this vein of dramatic energy and authenticity at this one point, the point where the life of that mining culture coincided with his own rawest autobiographical concern. He could not have written many more variations on that theme. In any case, the writing of *Sons and Lovers* had enabled him to shed that particular sickness, and write FINIS under that stage of his life from which the colliery plays had drawn their life-blood.

The break represented by the completion of *Sons and Lovers* was not merely biographical. Lawrence needed to make a new start in his fiction, to forge new fictional forms and a new language which would enable him to explore new and deeper territory. *The Insurrection of Miss Houghton* was the beginning of this process:

– so new, so really a stratum deeper than I think anybody has ever gone, in a novel . . . It is all analytical – quite unlike *Sons and Lovers*, not a bit visualised.   [L I 526]

The process was to continue, and to occupy most of Lawrence's attention, for the next four years, as he struggled to get out clean from the marble of *The Sisters* those perfect statues *The Rainbow* and *Women in Love*. By 'visualised' one assumes that Lawrence meant that the method of *Sons and Lovers* had been essentially realistic 'in that hard, violent style, full of sensation and presentation' [L II 132]. 'Presentation', where characters and relationships are concerned, implies a dramatic mode. Much of *Sons and Lovers* could have been, some of it was, equally well presented as drama. There is no way that *The Rainbow* or *Women in Love* could have been done other than as prose fiction. In those four years Lawrence developed his prose as a supreme instrument for probing the depths of the human psyche. Once he had broken away from the 'rules of construction' arbitrarily laid down for the novel by such conservative practitioners as Arnold Bennett, the medium itself offered almost limitless opportunities for experiment. The limitations were those of the imagination of the artist, not his medium. The same could hardly have applied to non-poetic drama.

*

In the spring of 1918 the Lawrences were poverty-stricken and virtually homeless. The war dragged on. Lawrence's health suffered. Then his sister Ada found them a cottage at Middleton-by-Wirksworth, some twenty miles from Eastwood. It was the first time since 1912 that Lawrence had lived near his birthplace, his family, the mining country. On 18 June he wrote to Amy Lowell:

We are here in Derbyshire, just near my native place – come home, in these last wretched days – not to die, I hope. Life is very wretched, really, in the outer world – and in the immediate world too, such a ghastly stress, a horrid pressure on one, all the time – and gnawing anxiety. The future seems utterly impenetrable, and as fathomless as the Bottomless Pit, and about as desperate.   [L III 254]

Lawrence renewed his friendship with his old friend and mentor, the Eastwood socialist Willie Hopkin, who visited Mountain Cottage several times. No doubt they argued politics. Lawrence's own thinking at this juncture had moved far to the right. He was inspired by his reading of Gibbon to write a school-book of European history. Lawrence told Cecil Gray at the outset what the controlling theme would be:

The chief feeling is, that men were always alike, and always will be, and one must view the species with contempt first and foremost, and find a few individuals, if possible – which seems at this juncture not to be possible – and ultimately, if the impossible were possible, to *rule* the species. It is proper ruling they need, and always have needed. But it is impossible, because they can only be ruled as they are willing to be ruled: and that is swinishly or hypocritically.   [262]

Lawrence suffered worst from his sense of helplessness. On 12 September he wrote to Lady Cynthia Asquith:

It is time I had an issue. And one can do nothing from here. As for the people – Labour itself – it is hopeless, as hopeless as Lloyd George or Balfour – just the green half of the same poisonous apple.   [283]

Lawrence felt like an exile in his home land, like Ovid in Thrace as he put it in several letters, cut off from the possibility of finding associates and from the centres of power. In spite of his declared hopelessness about the Labour movement, the disdain of the proletariat he expressed in his Education essays, and the fascist programme of *Movements in European History*, he could think of no movement other than the Labour movement with which he could conceivably associate himself. He wrote to a London friend, S. S. Koteliansky, that he felt he must come to London:

I want to know Robert Smillie and Snowden and Mary Macarthers [*sic*] and Margaret Bondfield. I must find somebody to bring me to them. It is no good, one cannot wait for things to happen. One must actually move.
                                                                                    [284]

Philip Snowden was to be Chancellor of the Exchequer in the first Labour government in 1924. Margaret Bondfield was to be the first woman Cabinet member and the first chairwoman of the Trades Union Council. Smillie and Mary Macarther were also trade-union leaders.

On 26 September Lawrence was summoned to Derby for a second humiliating medical examination. On his return to Mountain Cottage he wrote to Lady Cynthia Asquith:

I've had enough of the social passion. Labour and military can alike do their dirty business to the top of their bent. I'm not going to squat in a cottage feeling their fine feelings for them, and flying for them a flag that only makes a fool of *me*. I'm out on a new track – let humanity go its own way – I go mine. But I *won't* be pawed and bullied by them – no.   [288]

In October Lawrence did go to London for a fortnight, but it is not known whether he contacted or attempted to contact any Labour leaders. The Lawrences both went down with influenza in London, and went to Berkshire to recuperate. There Lawrence wrote *Touch and Go.* On 28 October he offered to send the play – 'which *might* be acted' – to Lady Cynthia:

> But no, truly, I am ashamed in daylight to confess it, I have written a play out of my deep and earnest self, fired up my last sparks of hope in the world, as it were, and cried out like a Balaams ass. I believe the world yet might get a turn for the better, if it but had a little shove that way. And this is my attempt – I believe the last I am capable of – or the first, perhaps – at a shove. [293]

*

Touch and Go and *David* differ from the earlier plays in that their themes are public, not private. The lives of the leading characters are important not so much in themselves as in embodying, typifying or affecting the life of the community or the nation. *Touch and Go* is about industrial conflict, but industrial conflict is itself only symptomatic of all human conflict based on money and power. The violence in the play is a contained local outbreak of the obscene violence of the war. We are reminded of the fact that men are actually capable of killing one another (as Sylvia Sklar has pointed out) by the war memorial which the stage-directions specify should be the focal point of the market-place in the opening and closing scenes of the play. Although strike action figured in *The Daughter-in-Law*, it was part of a world 'out there' which was not directly the play's concern. The life of the community was important in the early plays, but only as it affected the life of the family. Everything was drawn in to the invariably domestic setting. Now personal relationships are of interest mainly insofar as they affect the community. The play continually moves outwards from private dialogue to public arena. Even sexual relationships are dragged into the market-place because they prove inseparable from larger responsibilities. Anabel cannot love Gerald and at the same time turn a blind eye to his behaviour towards his employees. This is not to say only that she cannot escape the obligation to be aware and make her own judgements, but also that Gerald's manhood and humanity are tested and defined in the play more fully and clearly in the industrial crisis than in the sexual crisis.

The structure of the play has something in common with that of *Aaron's Rod*, which Lawrence was writing at the same time. After the intensely familial novels, *Sons and Lovers* and *The Rainbow*, and the transitional *Women in Love*, where relationships have to be fought for in a disintegrating society, comes a novel which begins with the breaking up of a family and continues to move, in fits and starts, in terms of failed relationships and dispersion, which has its public manifestation in simmering and eventually exploding violence. In the play, nearly all the relationships are forms of antagonism. The mediator, the reasonable humane man, Willie Houghton (a portrait of Willie Hopkin), only brings down on himself the wrath of both sides. Natural ties of family, love and friendship seem to have been superseded by economic exploitation and dependency, by an arbitrary mechanical system which sets man against man. The title, *Touch and Go*, means that it is touch and go whether the conflict will lead to bloodshed or even killing; but it may also be taken literally to mean that human contacts are more likely to produce division than relationship.

The play is avowedly didactic, Lawrence's first attempt in the drama to give the world a little shove. It is a problem play in which each of the major characters voices a different answer to the problem, which is: how to prevent the industrial system leading to dehumanization and social breakdown. Old Mr Barlow stands for Christian philanthropy, the morality of the soup-kitchen. His son Gerald stands for the perfecting of the system at whatever human cost, mechanization, with himself as the god of the machine. His antagonist Job Arthur Freer stands for the simple reversal of roles, the masters being replaced by union leaders. Willie Houghton is a deeply committed socialist arguing for nationalization of the industry. Anabel simply wants to get on with being an artist, making her little models of animals. But she is dependent on the patronage of the industrial aristocracy for the security she needs. There is no such thing as a 'sanctum the world cannot invade' [CPL 340]. Gerald's friend Oliver Turton is the mouthpiece for Lawrence and voices what we are presumably meant to take as the true answer and the play's message.

If it is Lawrence's intention to create a balance of sympathies, he quite fails to do so. Nowhere in the play does he give the audience an opportunity to sympathize with Gerald in any way. He is a snob and a bully who redirects the violence of his inner life against his employees. It is impossible to understand Willie's claim that the men would be 'far more degraded' with Job Arthur as their boss than with Gerald Barlow, who has 'one tiny little spark of decency left' [378]. The audience has not seen it. They have not seen in what way he is supposed to have deserved the friendship of Oliver or the love of Anabel; nor why Job Arthur should be so deserving of contempt. Gerald's sudden claim at the end that he wants a 'better way' as much as anyone and doesn't care about money is quite unprepared for and unconvincing. He is in a position to change the system, but has shown no inclination to do so. On the contrary, he has shown himself to be the ruthless champion of the system, with nothing but contempt for his father's efforts to humanize it.

The hitherto ineffectual Oliver steps forward at the end with his utopian solution:

> We're all human beings, after all. And why can't we try really to leave off struggling against one another, and set up a new state of things . . . Why can't we have the decency to agree simply about money – just agree to dispose of it so that all men could live their own lives . . . If you want what is natural and good, I'm sure the owners would soon agree with you.
> [384–5]

One cannot imagine his audience, on or off stage, being moved by this. Dramatically, it is anticlimax. The real climax of the play was Anabel's cry 'He's a man as you are', a raw appeal to common humanity which, on this occasion at least, prevents bloodshed. It can be a powerful moment in the theatre.

If we compare these characters with their equivalents in *Women in Love*, or with those in the early plays, we have to say that they are lacking in authentic life. But perhaps it is unfair to ask for that here. What looks like a lack of authenticity is rather an attempt to portray a community where authentic living has become almost impossible. Anabel's cry is her protest against the final triumph of the machine, the ultimate dehumanization, the iron entering the soul. As such, it is similar to moments in several Arthur Miller plays – to Joe Keller's 'I guess to him they were all my sons'; to Linda Loman's 'But he's a human being, and a terrible thing is happening to him. So attention must be paid'. What looks like failed naturalism is probably an attempt to get beyond naturalism, something Lawrence had attempted before only in the direction of farce. Miller had learned from Ibsen and Brecht techniques for escaping the limitations of naturalism. Lawrence, though familiar enough with Ibsen, lapses back here towards 'the rule and measure mathematical folk' [L I 509] he had rejected earlier. *Touch and Go* is in no way an improvement on Galsworthy's *Strife*.

*

Lawrence was anxious that the play should be performed. At the beginning of December he sent it to Lady Cynthia Asquith, asking her to read it and show it to Mrs Patrick Campbell. He received a dusty answer, and affected indifference: 'Don't bother a bit about the play – the hour isn't ripe' [L III 333]. A few months later, however, Lawrence met Douglas Goldring, who had just started the People's Theatre Society. Goldring proposed that *Touch and Go* should be the first play to be performed by the society, and the first to be published in his series *Plays for a People's Theatre*. On this understanding Lawrence let him have the play free, and wrote a preface for it. In his preface Lawrence tried to define a People's Theatre. His first point is that the seats are cheap; his second that 'the plays of A People's Theatre are plays about people' [P II 290]. If there are still a few 'living individuals' among the miners and among the masters, then the strike situation becomes potentially tragic.

> The essence of tragedy, which is creative crisis, is that a man should go through with his fate, and not dodge it and go bumping into an accident. And the whole business of life, at the great critical periods of mankind, is that men should accept and be one with their tragedy. Therefore we should open our hearts. For one thing, we should have a People's Theatre. Perhaps it would help us in this hour of confusion better than anything.
>
> [293]

In the event, the first play to be published in the series was Goldring's own *The Fight for Freedom*, which Lawrence despised. *Touch and Go* was second. But much more disappointing for Lawrence was the fact that Goldring's attempts to secure a production of *Touch and Go* were thwarted by a reactionary majority on the theatre committee. It was not to be produced until 1973.

*

As soon as he was able to leave England after the war, Lawrence headed for Italy. In Florence he felt himself to be at the point where the influences from northern Europe, the cold and the wet elements of the soul, self-consciousness, meet and marry the dark and fiery Dionysian influences from the south, the Mediterranean. For a moment, at the Renaissance, they were held in perfect balance, 'pure pride of life' [P 63]; and the supreme embodiment of that balance was Michelangelo's *David*. The balance was soon lost, the fire overwhelmed by a sweep of waters from the north – morality, chastity, equality, democracy: 'Christ-like submissiveness which, once it bursts its bounds, floods the face of the earth with such devastation'. His intense desire to redeem that 'inestimable loss' drove Lawrence, in the years which followed, to throw his weight entirely behind the dark gods. When he returned to Florence in 1926 he could see *David* as nothing more than 'the incarnation of the modern self-conscious young man, and very objectionable' [P 124].

In February 1925, shortly after finishing *The Plumed Serpent*, Lawrence suffered an almost fatal attack of malaria. From Mexico City the following month he wrote that he was 'struggling through the days with some difficulty, feeling done in by this dirty sickness' [CB II 396]. Nevertheless, on the same day he announced to Ida Rauh that he had begun a play. This was the unfinished *Noah's Flood*.

Noah's Flood is a mere fragment of ten pages in manuscript. It exists in two drafts. Part of the first draft was revised, and it is this shorter version which has been published in *Phoenix*. Here there are only three characters who appear, called simply First, Second and Third Man. They are plotting to steal fire from Noah and his sons. The sons of men are no longer cowed by the mere size and power and mystical knowledge of the demi-god sons of Noah. They regard themselves as more intelligent: 'Big is the bull by the river, but a boy leads him by the nose' [P 811]. Men are makers, and, if they only had the secret of fire, they could be free; they could kill the demi-gods:

If we had the red bird in our hand, we could force the sun to give himself up in answer; yea, even the Great White Bird would answer in obedience. So we could unleash the waters from the ice, and shake the drops from the sky, in answer to our demand.   [815]

The demi-gods know that the little red bird of fire is only a feather from the yellow bird of the sun, which is itself only a feather of the Great White Bird which nests in the middle of the tree of darkness, and which is the source of all freshness and creativity on earth. But the sons of men say: 'We are ourselves the Great White Birds of the Universe' [814]. The published fragment goes no further. But the first draft has a little more, ending with Noah's prophecy that if man does steal fire or is given fire and attempts to live by it forever, he will at last 'drown it in blood, and quench it in tears' [DB 126].

This is obviously much closer to the Prometheus myth than to the Biblical myth of the flood. Prometheus, by the gift of fire, seeks to make men independent of the gods. He can foresee that fire will lead to the development of science, but sees no reason to question men's competence to handle such power. In Aeschylus, the Chorus tells Prometheus that he respects 'too highly the race of mortals':

Did you not note the helpless infirmity,
Feeble as a dream,
Which fetters the blind tribes of men?
For human purposes shall never trespass
Outside the harmony of Zeus's government.

He cannot foresee, as Noah can, that man will ultimately destroy both himself, and, perhaps, the source of life and harmony of the universe with that same fire.

Perhaps Lawrence felt that this myth did not have sufficient theatrical potential. Certainly the part we have is more like a semi-dramatized essay than anything which could conceivably be staged. He was keen to create a big part for Ida Rauh, an actress friend of Mabel Luhan's, who, according to Brett, bore 'an amazing resemblance to Sarah Bernhardt' [LB 49]. He returned to an idea which had first come up a year earlier. Lawrence had asked Ida what kind of plays she liked best. When she replied that she liked stories from the Bible, he asked if she knew the story of David's wife, Michal. She did not. Lawrence told her that when David came back from the wars, Michal said 'I'll never live with you again,' and never did. Ida thought the story perfect, and Lawrence said that he would write a play about it for her [60]. In November 1924 he had written to Ida that he was still thinking about a play, which would be 'either Aztec or Jewish – King David or Moses: or else Montezuma' [MD 342]. In mid-March 1925, he abandoned *Noah's Flood* and began *David*. Composition was interrupted while Lawrence dragged himself back to the Kiowa ranch. For most of April he lay on a camp bed on the porch in the 'wonderful sunny days' [CL 839], and finished *David* early in May.

David is quite unlike any of Lawrence's other plays. The plot is very close to the Biblical account of David's early life – his relationship with his brothers, with Samuel, Saul, and Saul's children Jonathan and Michal. Almost every word of direct speech in 1 Samuel 15–20 is in the play, and these quotations are incorporated seamlessly into Lawrence's own dialogue. This forces Lawrence to create language of great distinction and poetic power, which, nevertheless, does not strike us merely as pastiche, for it combines the authentic Biblical mode with the characteristics of a living spoken language. The subject matter of the play is ineluctably archaic. It is about men standing in the fire of God, existing solely to carry out his inscrutable purposes. Failure to do so brings instant and total rejection, and to be rejected by God is to be damned; all that is not God is evil. Samuel and the prophets transmit God's decisions, but are as ignorant of his reasons as anyone else. God orders Saul to annihilate the Amalekites, including their women, children, cattle and goods. Saul defeats the Amalekites, but reserves some prisoners and booty, seeing no reason why he should not have some share in the glory. This attempt to reserve an area of selfhood aside from God is fatal. Despite the intercession of

Samuel, God drops Saul into the abyss of knowledge of the self-apart-from God, and turns to David as his instrument. Saul's great powers, no longer in the service of God, churn upon themselves, turn black and destructive. Fits of depression alternate with fits of homicidal madness. Lawrence has no interest in modernizing the story in any way, for example by giving it a psychological interpretation. It is precisely 'that feeling of primitive religious passion' that he sets himself to get across 'to a London audience' [CL 941]. No English dramatist had attempted it since Shakespeare. Even outside the theatre it had disappeared from English literature by the end of the seventeenth century. Blake had signally failed to revive it in his prophetic books. Drama in the 1920s had become a supreme expression of that very cult of the individual – 'Hamlet in a smoking jacket' [1016] – against which Lawrence struggled.

The story is highly dramatic, with the conflict of Saul and David at its centre. I cannot share George Panichas' interpretation of this conflict as 'the eternal quarrel between purity and innocence on the one side, and treachery and debasement on the other'.[5] Lawrence had always associated himself with his Biblical namesake. Humanly speaking, David is a very sympathetic figure. Lawrence clearly identifies with him, particularly in his relationships with Michal and Jonathan, where he creates a lovely balance between sexual love and male comradeship. But the relationship between David and Saul is not so crude as Panichas suggests. There is far more to Saul than 'treachery and debasement'. He is like a father to David, and there is much in him for David to respect and love. He is a great-souled man, and his very treachery is the helpless symptom of baffled magnanimity. Lawrence had seen his own father for the last time at the beginning of 1924. Arthur Lawrence's death in September forced Lawrence to a reassessment:

> He had come to respect his father much more than when he wrote *Sons and Lovers*. He grieved having painted him in such a bitterly hostile way in that book. He could see now that his father had possessed a great deal of the old gay male spirit of England, pre-puritan, he was natural and unruined deep in himself. [CB III 276]

David rises through the fall of two giants, Goliath and Saul, but is not himself a giant. Saul is the last representative of the old titanic world age, when God burned in every bush. David inaugurates a new, more humane and self-conscious age, as men become more self-sufficient, manipulating the fire of God, the sacred energies of the world, to their own purposes, and living by cunning rather than blind faith. The anointing of David is the beginning of God's withdrawal from men.

It was an attitude to David that Lawrence had adumbrated as early as 1915, in 'The Crown':

These warrior kings seek to pass beyond all relatedness, to become absolute in might and power. And they fall inevitably. Their Judas is a David, a Brutus: the individual who knows something of both flames, but commits himself to neither. He holds himself, in his own ego, superior either to the creative dark power-flame, or the conscious love-flame. And so, he is the small man slaying the great. He is virtuous egoistic Brutus, or David: David slaying the preposterous Goliath, overthrowing the heroic Saul, taking Bathsheba and sending Uriah to death: David dancing naked before the Ark, asserting the oneness, his own oneness, the one infinity, *himself*, the egoistic God, I AM. And David never went in unto Michal any more, because she jeered at him. So that she was barren all her life.

But it was David who really was barren. Michal, when she mocked, mocked the sterility of David. For the spirit in him was blasted with unfertility; he could not become born again, he could not be conceived in the spirit. Michal, the womb of profound darkness, could not conceive to the overweak seed of David's spirit. David's seed was too impure, too feeble in sheer spirit, too egoistic, it bred and begot preponderant egoists. The flood of vanity set in after David, the lamps and candles began to gutter.

Power is sheer flame, and spirit is sheer flame, and between them is the clue of the Holy Ghost. But David put a false clue between them: the clue of his own ego, cunning and *triumphant*. [P II 380]

In *Noah's Flood* the sons of men who conspired against Noah would have been drowned in the flood, so that Noah's prophecy could only refer to another theft of fire in a later age. In *David* our own age of human intelligence and materialism is inaugurated, and we are in a position to witness the fulfilment of Saul's prophecy:

And the world shall be Godless, there shall no God walk on the mountains, no whirlwind shall stir like a heart in the deeps of the blue firmament. And God shall be gone from the world. Only men there shall be, in myriads, like locusts, clicking and grating upon one another, and crawling over one another. The smell of them shall be as smoke, but it shall rise up into the air, without finding the nostrils of God. For God shall be gone! gone! gone! And men shall inherit the earth! [CPL 117]

At one point in his prophecy, Saul seems to be seeing the effects of the neutron bomb:

And man is his own devourer, and the Deep turns away, without wish to look on him further. So the earth is a desert, and manless, yet covered with houses and iron.

Samuel certainly does not see David as embodying nothing but purity and innocence:

The Lord is all things. And Saul hath seen a tall and rushing flame and hath gone mad, for the flame rushed over him. Thou seest thy God in thine own likeness, afar off, or as a brother beyond thee, who fulfils thy desire. Saul yearneth for the flame: thou for thy tomorrow's glory. The God of Saul hath no face. But thou wilt bargain with thy God . . . So shalt thou at last have the kingdom and the glory in the sight of men. I anointed thee, but I would see thee no more, for my heart is weary of its end. [145]

At the end of the play, Jonathan, left alone, looks forward with trepidation to the new age:

I would not see thy new day, David. For thy wisdom is the wisdom of the subtle, and behind thy passion lies prudence. And naked thou wilt not go into the fire. Yea, go thou forth, and let me die. For thy virtue is in thy wit, and thy shrewdness. But in Saul have I known the magnanimity of a man. [153]

Jonathan takes comfort in the fact that the new era will at last run its course, and men will turn again towards the fire:

In the flames of death where Strength is, I will wait and watch till the day of David at last shall be finished, and wisdom no more be fox-faced, and the blood gets back its flame. [154]

Lawrence hoped, with *David*, to fan that flame in the blood of a London theatre audience.

'It is a good play, and for the theatre', Lawrence wrote to his agent Curtis Brown. 'Someone ought to do it' [CL 845]. Curtis Brown did not agree, and sent it to Knopf for publication. But Lawrence wrote to Knopf:

I don't want it published unless it is produced. Curtis Brown thinks it would be better if it appeared first as 'literature'. Myself, I am a bit tired of plays that are only literature. If a man is writing 'literature', why choose the form of a play? And if he's writing a play, he surely intends it for the theatre. Anyhow I wrote this play for the theatre, and I want the theatre people to see it first. Curtis Brown says it is full of long speeches that call for a whole company of Forbes-Robertsons. There might be a whole company of even better men. I believe there might be found Jews or Italians or Spaniards or Celts to do the thing properly: not Teutons or Scandinavians or Nordics: it's not in their blood – as a rule. And if the speeches are too long – well, they can be made shorter if necessary. But my God, there's many a *nigger* would play Saul better than Forbes-Robertson could do it. And I'd prefer the nigger. Or men and women from that Jewish theatre. – Curtis Brown says it's not a 'popular' play. But damn it, how does he know even that? Playgoing isn't the same as reading. Reading in itself is highbrow. But give the 'populace' in the theatre something with a bit of sincere good-feeling in it, and they'll respond. If you do it properly. [845–6]

When Robert Atkins agreed to produce *David* for the 300 Club and Stage Society in October 1926, Lawrence, who was in England that summer, postponed his return to Italy in order to help; but when the production was postponed until December, he returned to the Villa Mirenda. From there he wrote to Atkins:

I enclose the music I have written out for *David*. It is very simple – needs only a pipe, tambourines, and a tom-tom drum. I hope it will do. Let me know when you get the thing going a bit. I hope I can come to London and help, later, if you think it really worthwhile. If only one can get that feeling of primitive religious passion across to the London audience. If not, it's no good. [941]

Then the 300 Club decided to do *The Widowing of Mrs Holroyd* in December, and postpone *David* until March. Lawrence could not face a London winter for the sake of *Mrs Holroyd*, 'but I feel I must go and give a helping hand to *David*' [950]. In the new year, his enthusiasm for returning to England faded rapidly: 'I feel an infinite disgust at the idea of having to be there while the fools mimble-pimble at the dialogue' [963–4]. By 8 March he had finally decided against it: 'I won't go to London for *David*. I simply won't go, to have my life spoilt by those people. They can maul and muck the play about as much as they like' [968].

In the event, it was probably just as well that he had not gone. The reviewer in the *Nation and Athenaeum* wrote that 'this particular production was of such an uninspired nature that one hesitates to blame the author entirely for the resultant fiasco' [LH 297]. The *Times* reviewer said that the play was 'neither drama nor poetry', and that there were only two scenes in it which tempted him to lose his detachment. Lawrence wrote to Earl Brewster: 'My business is a fight, and I've got to keep it up. I'm reminded of the fact by the impudent reviews of the production of *David*. They say it was just dull. I say they are eunuchs, and have no balls' [CL 980].

In October 1927 Lawrence's friend Max Mohr made some attempts to get *David* produced in Berlin. But Lawrence was no longer in a fighting mood:

And of course the whole play is too literary, too many words. The actual technique of the stage is foreign to me. But perhaps they – and you – could cut it into shape. I shall be very much surprised if they *do* play it in Berlin. The public only wants foolish realism: Hamlet in a smoking jacket. [1016]

That was Lawrence's last word on the theatre of his time.

There has never been another production of *David*. Yet surely the theatre today would be much more receptive to it. There is an audience now for non-realistic and poetic drama, an audience capable of paying close attention to heightened language. We no longer think of technique solely in terms of the well-made three-act play. As Sylvia Sklar has pointed out, *David*, with its great sweep of action in time and space, its sixteen short and self-contained scenes, its refusal to aim at 'foolish realism', its techniques for preventing identification with a single hero and for helping us to retain our detachment, answers closely to Brecht's definition of epic theatre. There are actors now with 'enough *inside* to them' [979], directors capable of evoking 'primitive religious passion', major national companies with the resources to 'do the thing properly'. Indeed, 'someone ought to do it.'

*

It is quite untrue, as must by now be evident, that Lawrence did not care about the production of his plays in the theatre. He was abroad on all three occasions his plays were produced in his lifetime; but the difficulties of getting home could have been overcome had there not been also the more fundamental difficulty of Lawrence's fear of the theatre world, a world which was very much part of the England he had chosen to cut himself off from. As Michael Marland has suggested, 'dramatist' and 'exile' are almost mutually exclusive terms. Lawrence very understandably felt a strong distaste for the whole business of negotiating with impresarios, of putting his works, which were always like children to him, into the hands of producers and actors who were not his kind of people, and of exposing himself to audiences and reviewers he knew would be unsympathetic. Publishing was less intimate, less nerve-wracking, more like casting one's bread upon the waters.

After *David* Lawrence did not again expose himself to the impudence of the public and the press. There were no more productions of his plays in his lifetime. He never saw a play of his on the stage.

THREE

'A GREAT TRAGEDY': THE GENESIS OF *SONS AND LOVERS*

At the end of 1909, shortly after Lawrence had finished *The White Peacock*, Hueffer, on the strength of 'Odour of Chrysanthemums', had prescribed for him 'a course of workingman novels'. But his next novel, *The Trespasser*, is even further from his family experience and mining background than *The White Peacock*, being about a tragic love-affair between middle-class people in London and the Isle of Wight.

Early in 1910, Helen Corke, a London friend, showed Lawrence her diary of her experiences at Freshwater, Isle of Wight, the previous summer. She had gone there with her lover, an older married man, who had hanged himself shortly after his return, leaving her derelict. Lawrence tried to revive her interest in life. He persuaded her to help with the final revision of *The White Peacock*. Then he suggested that she should help him to turn her diary into a novel.

In four months the first draft of *The Saga of Siegmund* (Lawrence's original title for *The Trespasser*) was finished. Helen Corke was amazed that Lawrence, never having met her lover, and with so little help from her, could enter so deeply into that relationship. Lawrence was able to identify so closely with Siegmund not only because he was falling in love with Helen, but also because the pressures which had driven Siegmund to his death were primarily the same sexual frustrations Lawrence was suffering at the hands of all his girl-friends, Agnes Holt, Jessie Chambers, and now Helen herself. On 31 July Lawrence wrote to Helen (who, still living in the past, had returned to Freshwater):

[Jessie] came to see me yesterday. She kisses me. It makes my heart feel like ashes. But then she kisses me more and moves my sex fire. Mein Gott, it is hideous . . . I must tell her . . . that we ought finally and definitely to part . . . I am a rather despicable object. But can I hurt her so much. I wish I had not come home. I wish fate wouldn't torture one with these conjunctions – and you in Freshwater.   [L I 173]

Helen was a much more extreme example than Jessie of 'the dreaming woman':

> My early religious training had divided soul and body, and presented the body as the inferior, rightly subordinate to the soul. The literary patterns of the period mostly enhanced this teaching. They tended to exhibit physical passion as a gross manifestation, linking man with the animal, but, in the case of man, properly controlled by reason and the will. Love was either divine or human. Religion imposed no prohibition against *spiritual* intimacy, for which it claimed complete essential detachment from bodily functions. [HC 162–3]

Therefore she had tried to impose on her lover a purely spiritual relationship, forcing him always to struggle against the demands of a passionate nature. She had made him hate his own ungovernable body to the point where, 'in an extremity of mental torture', he had destroyed it.

Lawrence was putting himself into Siegmund not only on paper. In real life he knew that he was merely 'filling the place of a ghost with warmth' [T 227], and that if he could eventually make Helen aware of him as a living man, history could only repeat itself. As for Helen, she knew that he would ultimately make an impossible demand upon her:

> Since the early summer of this year I have been increasingly aware of the demand that he, instinctive man, makes upon me as a woman. I cannot definitely ignore it, but there is no physical response from my own body. My desire is not towards him. I do not want either to marry him and bear him children, or to be his mistress. [HC 191]

*

On 4 August 1910 Lawrence announced to Grace Crawford that he had just finished his second novel. The same letter contains a remarkable passage which suggests that Lawrence may have been pondering the implications of Hueffer's advice, and the difficulties he might expect to encounter if he attempted to write a novel about his home life for readers such as Miss Crawford:

> Here I am at home. You may as well know what it's like: even though you may not be interested. – My father is a coal miner: the house has eight rooms: I am writing in the kitchen, or the middle parlour as it would be called if my mother were magniloquent – but she's not, she's rather scornful. It is cosy enough. There's a big fire – miners keep fires in their living rooms though the world reels with sun-heat – a large oval mahogany table, three shelves of study-books, a book-case of reading-books, a dresser, a sofa, and four wooden chairs. Just like all other small homes in England. [L I 174]

He cannot assume that a typical novel-reader would know anything about 'small homes'; still less about miners. Perhaps this knowledge dictated his decision (constant through the surviving drafts) to open *Sons and Lovers* with a socio-economic history of Eastwood, followed by a meticulous placing of the Morel household within the industrial landscape.

Lawrence must have begun *Paul Morel* (his title for *Sons and Lovers* until the final draft) very soon after this, for on 18 October he wrote to Sydney Pawling of Heinemann about 'my third novel, Paul Morel, which is plotted out very interestingly (to me), and about one-eighth of which is written . . . It interests me very much. I wish I were not so agitated just now, and could do more' [184].

The agitation which was preventing Lawrence from getting on with *Paul Morel* was presumably the failure of the final attempt with Jessie, and the continuing difficulties with Helen. There was soon to follow the illness and slow death of his mother. In his desperation Lawrence became engaged to Louie Burrows:

> You will be the first woman to make the earth glad for me: mother, J[essie] – all the rest, have been gates to a very sad world. But you are strong & rosy as the gates of Eden. [195]

It did not take him long to discover that Louie could only be to him the

> Betrothed young lady who loves me, and takes good care
> Of her womanly virtue and of my good name. [CP 129]

But he could not see how he could honourably extricate himself. The impasse in his life produced an impasse in his work. On 11 February 1911 he wrote to Frederick Atkinson of Heinemann:

> The third novel 'Paul Morel', sticks where I left it four or five months ago, at the hundredth page. I've no heart to tackle a serious work just now . . . When I can get some money I shall marry and settle down to steady work. [L I 230]

But the idea of marriage was coming to seem to him more and more like a doom. He turned again to Helen Corke, was again rejected, and announced to her, in consecutive sentences, the end (for the moment) of their struggle, and the resumption of *Paul Morel*:

> There, Helene – let's have done. It is sickening, this cats-pawing. I have begun 'Paul Morel' again – glory, you should see it. The British public will stone me if ever it catches sight. [239]

'Let's have done': 'I have begun'. Only in the impersonality of art could Lawrence escape his personal dilemma.

The previous day (13 March 1911) Lawrence had written to Louie:

I have begun Paul Morel again. I am afraid it will be a terrible novel. But, if I can keep it to my idea and feeling, it will be a great one.   [237]

A month later he had made little progress:

I have just done one folio, a dozen MSS pages, of Paul Morel. That great, terrible but unwritten novel, I am afraid it will die a mere conception.

[258]

By 4 May he had done 90 pages; three days later 112. By the end of the month he had reached 200. On 4 July Lawrence told Louie that he had 'done a fair amount of Paul' [281], but this seems to be the last work on this draft, since a fortnight later he wrote 'No, I've not done any Paul lately' [289], and in October 'I haven't done a stroke of Paul for months' [310].

In October Lawrence sent the manuscript to Jessie for her comments. This manuscript has survived (with some gaps); the last page is numbered 353.[1] Jessie's description of it is very accurate:

He had written about two thirds of the novel and appeared to have come to a standstill. In reading the MS. I felt oppressed by a sense of strain, as though he had had to force himself to write it. There was no spontaneity, no sparkle. It was his mother's story, told rather sentimentally; a young non-conformist minister whose sermons she composed was there as a set-off to the brutal husband. Our household of Willey Farm was not there at all, and the character he calls Miriam was placed in a suburban atmosphere in Eastwood. In my reply to Lawrence I suggested that he should relate the story of his mother's married life as it had actually happened, and include his brother Ernest, whose story was omitted in the first draft. It seemed to me that the reality was so much more poignant and interesting than his semi-fictitious account. Not only that, I felt that if he could work out art-istically, and *within himself* all the issues of his mother's life and their implications, not only would he write a magnificent novel, but he would rid himself of his obsession with regard to his mother, and be a free and whole man.   [DHLR 12 65–6]

A sentence which impressed Jessie particularly was: 'Perhaps he wanted Miriam to rise and conquer his mother in him' [PM 268]. If Jessie had been unable to 'conquer' Mrs Lawrence in real life, she certainly wanted Lawrence to lay her ghost in the novel. After all, had not Lawrence, in the thick of writing *Paul Morel*, written to Jessie: 'They [meaning his mother and sisters] tore me from you, the love of my life. It was the slaughter of the foetus in the womb' [L I 268]. If Lawrence really believed that, Jessie had every right to expect to find some vindication in the novel. Only five months before writing that letter, Lawrence had described his mother to Louie Burrows (to whom he had been engaged for just three days) as 'my first, great love' [195]. A week later he wrote to Violet Hunt: 'We buried my mother yesterday: and there is gone my love of loves' [199]. His ambivalence towards his mother is perfectly captured in a letter Lawrence wrote to the poetess Rachel Annand Taylor on the very day he had proposed to Louie Burrows, where he gives what is virtually a synopsis of the novel in progress:

My mother was a clever, ironical delicately moulded woman, of good, old burgher descent. She married below her. My father was dark, ruddy, with a fine laugh. He is a coal miner. He was one of the sanguine temperament, warm and hearty, but unstable: he lacked principle, as my mother would have said. He deceived her and lied to her. She despised him – he drank.

Their marriage life has been one carnal, bloody fight. I was born hating my father: as early as ever I can remember, I shivered with horror when he touched me. He was very bad before I was born.

This has been a kind of bond between me and my mother. We have loved each other, almost with a husband and wife love, as well as filial and maternal. We knew each other by instinct . . . We have been like one, so sensitive to each other that we never needed words. It has been rather terrible, and has made me, in some respects, abnormal. [190]

The attitude to the father is correspondingly ambivalent. In this letter, Lawrence is reasonably fair to him. 'Warm and hearty', he is almost a standard of normality. But a month later Lawrence was writing to the Congregational minister in Eastwood that his father was 'disgusting, irritating, and selfish as a maggot' [220].

Jessie wanted *Paul Morel* to be Lawrence's effort to objectify, confront, and thus cure himself of that abnormality, which would have involved the most rigorous autobiographical truthfulness. But this was not at this stage Lawrence's 'idea and feeling' at all. Three days before his mother's death Lawrence wrote to Louie Burrows:

Mother has had a devilish married life, for nearly forty years – and this is the conclusion – no relief. What ever I wrote, it could not be so awful as to write a biography of my mother. But after this – which is enough – I am going to write romance – when I have finished Paul Morel, which belongs to this . . .

She was a wonderful, rare woman – you do not know; as strong, and

steadfast, and generous as the sun. She could be as swift as a white whip-
lash, and as kind and gentle as warm rain, and as steadfast as the
irreducible earth beneath us . . .

She hated J[essie] – and would have risen from the grave to prevent my
marrying her.   [195, 197]

So we see that Lawrence felt that *Paul Morel* must be his tribute to
his mother, his attempt to compensate her for that 'devilish married
life', and assuage her ghost. The last thing he could do was to call
her to account for his own abnormality, or to vindicate Jessie.

Another passage in the manuscript which particularly impressed
Jessie was one in which it seems that Lawrence *must* recognize the
destructiveness of the mother's jealousy, but manages somehow to
evade such a recognition:

If once Miriam was able to win Paul's sex sympathy and service, then
he was lost indeed to his mother. Mrs Morel felt that her life was
meaningless once her son was really withdrawn from her. She could have
given him up to another woman for passion; she could have borne even
that he should love and marry some woman weaker than herself, because
then she would not have lost him: but that this intense girl, who had set
herself with a fervour almost terrible to win the brilliant, blind-eyed lad,
– that Miriam, the woman of inaction, the woman of deep, half-swooning
rhapsodic dreams, should win the son from her who had fought so
heroically all the way through life, was horrible.   [PM 245–6]

So Mrs Morel is vindicated as 'the woman who lives to make heroic
men', upon whom, in their helpless larval stage, such women as
Miriam are parasitic.

In a sense, Lydia Lawrence did rise from the grave, as Gertrude
Morel, and Lawrence handed her the laurels of victory over Miriam,
as he had handed his mother the laurels of victory over Jessie in
real life. How could he do otherwise if she were sun, rain and earth
to him, and he had loved her 'like a lover'? If his mother is to be
revealed to the world as a 'wonderful, rare woman', then her faults
must be hidden, not least from Lawrence himself.

By this time Lawrence had already handled this theme 'as it had
actually happened', in *A Collier's Friday Night*. But he had no
intention of making *Paul Morel* a fictional expansion of the play. He
was obliged to make his own home in Eastwood the focal point of
the novel, and to make Paul a much more autobiographical
character than Cyril in *The White Peacock*. Jessie had to be there as
the defeated 'other woman'. But in many ways, the story was to be
highly fictionalized. Jessie wrote:

Since he had elected to deal with the big and difficult subject of his family, and the interactions of the various relationships, I felt he ought to do it faithfully – 'with both hands earnestly', as he was fond of quoting.

[PR 192]

It is difficult to imagine artistic motives for most of Lawrence's departures from the facts. Perhaps he unconsciously feared that it would be difficult to reconcile doing it faithfully, keeping it 'true to life' in Jessie's sense, with the 'idea and feeling' from which he had started out regarding the role of Mrs Morel.

First, Walter Morel must bear the blame for that 'devilish married life'. There are scenes in *Paul Morel*, as in *Sons and Lovers*, where Lawrence cannot avoid showing him as 'warm and hearty', but for the most part, the novel's moral perspective is that of Mrs Morel. Mrs Lawrence had taught young Bert to pray that his father would either become a chapel man or die. In the novel Lawrence can play God and make that prayer come true. Paul plans to poison his father slowly with verdigris in his tea, but is saved from having to carry out his plan when Walter, whose outbursts have become more and more violent, throws a steel at Paul's younger brother, Arthur, killing him, is then imprisoned, and dies of grief shortly after his release. (Such an incident actually happened to an uncle of Lawrence's.)

By Lydia Lawrence's standards, Arthur Lawrence was simply irresponsible. He had, for example, before their marriage, described himself to her as a mining contractor. This was strictly true, since 'mining contractor' was the official term for a butty, who sub-contracted work to the day-men, but was just as much a face-worker. He knew, however, that Lydia would take it to be something rather grand. The first time he returned home from work, in his pit-dirt, she did not recognize him. She loved reading and talking more than anything else, but she could not talk to him. He could hardly write, and his reading never went beyond the newspapers, of which he understood very little. Mrs Lawrence disapproved of the dialect he spoke, when he spoke at all. She thought she could make him teetotal, but he could not keep it up for long. She conditioned her children to regard drunkenness as an extreme form of moral degradation. In *Sons and Lovers* Lawrence himself occasionally lapses into the language of the temperance tracts: 'She knew that the man who stops on the way home from work is on a quick way to ruining himself and his home.'

There were two Arthur Lawrences. The one known to his friends was gentle, generous, easy-going, good-humoured – the ideal workmate or drinking companion. A miner loses several pints of body fluid every shift. If he did not replenish it he would die. That particular culture dictated that it should be replenished with beer, and that the intense comradeship built up between the men underground should be continued in the pub. Hence the need for all that intense temperance activity in the mining areas. Since he was treated as a stranger in his own house, the pub was Arthur Lawrence's home from home. He was not, by the standards of his workmates, a heavy drinker, and was even more convivial when slightly tipsy. This Arthur Lawrence was generally respected and loved, but his family saw little of him.

It is difficult to remain genial when confronted by systematic ostracism. The transformation when Arthur arrived home has been vividly described by Ada Lawrence:

> Mother would wait up for him at night, her rage seething, until on his arrival it boiled over in a torrent of biting truths which turned him from his slightly fuddled and pleasantly apologetic mood into a brutal and coarse beast. [C B I 11]

Unable to match his wife in verbal abuse, he would occasionally resort to violence. The children blamed the beer, not their mother. No one outside the family ever saw this Arthur Lawrence. People were outraged when they heard toffee-nosed Bert, who would never make half the man his father was, insult his father in public.

Both *Paul Morel* and *Sons and Lovers* contain several scenes where our sympathy goes out to Walter Morel, as he tells stories to his children, makes fuses, cooks his rasher of bacon in the early morning when he has the kitchen to himself. In several other scenes, where he behaves badly, we can still sympathize, given the provocation he receives. As long as Lawrence gives us scenes without interpretation, there is usually a balance kept, but when he passes judgement on Morel, his condemnatory tone is close to that of Mrs Morel. The standards by which Morel is judged are largely those of his wife, because Lawrence's were still largely those of his mother. A more mature Lawrence would have been able to analyse the failure of the marriage in terms of the completely different values and attitudes which each had inherited through class and culture. Instead we are simply given the mother as right, the father as wrong.

Lawrence dare not, at this stage, tell the whole truth about his brother William Ernest. He must have known, in his heart of hearts, that William, who had died at twenty-one, had been his mother's sacrifice to the Great Goddess of Getting On. So William's presence in *Paul Morel* is so perfunctory as to be pointless. His career and marriage occupy a single paragraph, and he does not die:

> Mrs Morel had not lost, would never lose, her eldest son. She loved him dearly, and still extended to him her shelter. [PM 285]

The mother must bear no blame for the failure of Paul's relationship with Miriam. On the contrary, she is praised for providing him with standards of normality and wholeness by which he can judge Miriam and find her wanting. Though Miriam, in her relationship with Paul, is clearly based on Jessie Chambers, in other respects she is not. In *Paul Morel* she is not Miriam Leivers of Willey Farm, but Miriam Staynes of Belfast House. The Stayneses are modelled on the Cullen family of London House, who disappear altogether from *Sons and Lovers* but reappear in Lawrence's next novel, *The Insurrection of Miss Houghton* (an early draft for *The Lost Girl*) as the Houghton family of Manchester House. The Stayneses are tradespeople, and Miriam, who is given some of the experiences of Flossie Cullen, is a sort of foundling in their house. Miss Wright, the Cullen family governess, whom Lawrence much admired, is a major character in the novel, Miss May, who marries Mr Revell, the incompetent Congregational minister, when Mrs Morel has tired of him. They go to live at Herod's Farm (which is Haggs Farm), taking Miriam with them. When her father dies she inherits some money. She proposes to become a nurse, but becomes a peripatetic music teacher instead. All this was to go.

The evasions extended to the handling of Paul himself. Why is he presented as an artist rather than a writer? Why does his brother, not he, go to university? These were sensitive areas. Mrs Lawrence had taken an interest in Bert's painting; it was a harmless enough recreation, conventional and second-hand. But his creative writing had to be hidden from her, written in college notebooks so that she would think he was 'working'. She had scrimped and saved to send him to college to work hard and pass examinations and get a good job and get on in the world, not to fritter away his time writing about things he could not possibly understand. By 1911 Lawrence had lost his mother's admiration for learning and 'getting on', so that area of discord had to be avoided.

*

On 3 November 1911 Lawrence wrote to Louie: 'Tonight I am going to begin Paul Morel again, for the third and last time. I shall need all your prayers if I'm to get it done' [L I 321]. A week later he told Louie that he could not get on with *Paul*, was tired of school, and would have to leave. He spent the weekend of 18–19 November at the Cearne, Edward Garnett's house in Kent. Waiting for trains on the way home he caught a chill which rapidly developed into pneumonia. He was confined to bed for over a month and never returned to school. After convalescing in Bournemouth for the whole of January 1912, followed by a week at the Cearne, Lawrence returned to Eastwood on 9 February, and went to see Jessie. He had accepted her suggestions about the novel, and asked her to write down what she could remember of their early days. Now she gave him the notes she had been writing for three months, and this must have stimulated him to resume work on the novel, for on 23 February he wrote: ' "Paul Morel" is going pretty well, now I have once more tackled it' [367]. According to Jessie, he incorporated her notes into this next version.

The novel continued to go well, and Lawrence passed the manuscript to Jessie a few pages at a time as he wrote it. The early pages delighted her:

Here was all that spontaneous flow, the seemingly effortless translation of life that filled me with admiration. His descriptions of family life were so vivid, so exact, and so concerned with everyday things we had never even noticed before. There was Mrs Morel ready for ironing, lightly spitting on the iron to test its heat, invested with a reality and significance hitherto unsuspected. It was his power to transmute the common experiences into significance that I always felt to be Lawrence's greatest gift. He did not distinguish between small and great happenings; the common round was full of mystery, awaiting interpretation. Born and bred of working people, he had the rare gift of seeing them from within, and revealing them on their own plane. [PR 197–8]

But as the pages came which dealt with their relationship, Jessie felt more and more deeply betrayed. It was a double betrayal, in life and art. Lawrence's mother, the great obstacle between them hitherto, was gone. Lawrence had just broken his engagement to Louie. His involvement with Helen Corke was over. His health was gone, his career as a teacher prematurely ended. He seemed to Jessie to be in a state of hopelessness, 'like a man with a broken mainspring' [199]. Jessie could see no reason why they should not now come together finally:

We were together again, and outwardly there was nothing to keep us apart, but his mother's ban was more powerful now than in her lifetime . . . It was a bond that definitely excluded me from the only position in which I could be of vital help to him. We were back in the old dilemma, but it was a thousand times more cruel because of the altered circumstances . . .

The novel was written in this state of spirit, at a white heat of concentration . . . The mother had to be supreme, and for the sake of that supremacy
every disloyalty was permissible.   [200]

Lawrence could no longer face Jessie, but began sending the
manuscript by post.

It was at this moment, probably on 17 March 1912, that Lawrence
met Frieda Weekley and began the affair which was to lead to their
elopement only six weeks later. Lawrence and Jessie met at her
sister's house on 31 March. She returned the manuscript, with
some notes in which she accused Lawrence of writing 'First Love'
from 'the standpoint of twentysix instead of that of seventeen':

At this stage Paul and Miriam were in sympathy: giving and taking
unconsciously. There was no thought of the distinction between body and
spirit because each was perfectly pure. That note of purity must dominate.
Miriam never thought of kisses. It was her pride that no constraint of sex
came between her and Paul: that was one great delight. *Paul was not more
virgin than Miriam.* This chapter must be white: not smudged with a
thought of sex: because at seventeen such things are bound to be rather
smudgy. All that was forced on us from outside – mostly from the strife of
your people; because my folk were generous to a fault. Constraint and
misery only came with interference from outside; with all the inexplicable
things of sex dragged in train.   [B E373 b]

They did not discuss the novel at this meeting, or at their last, a
month later, when Lawrence was 'tongue-tied' except when he
talked 'with forced brightness about his going to Germany'
[PR 215]. Three weeks later Lawrence wrote to her from the
Rhineland:

I am going through Paul Morel. I'm sorry it turned out as it has. You'll
have to go on forgiving me.   [L I 408]

But Jessie could not forgive him: 'The shock of Sons and Lovers gave
the death-blow to our friendship'. Lawrence later sent her the
proofs of Sons and Lovers, with a letter she found both priggish and
off-handed. She read enough of the proofs to find 'both story and
mood alike unchanged' [PR 220], and returned the letter. That was
the end of their relationship.

*

It is a sad story that Jessie Chambers tells in *A Personal Record*. It is
no doubt a truer account, in some respects, than *Sons and Lovers*. It
is an invaluable book in other ways too, particularly as a first-hand
record of that remarkable culture, whose pivots were the Congregational Church and Mechanics' Institute Library, at that moment

in history. It tells us what the young Lawrence was reading and discussing and painting and singing, and what these things meant to him. It is where *A Personal Record* is most personal that it is least reliable – in its account of the relationship between herself and Lawrence. Her record cannot be used, as many critics have tried to use it,[2] as a totally accurate 'control' against which Lawrence's distortions of the truth can be measured. Jessie's version of events is given in good faith, but she cannot help putting herself always at the centre of the stage, sometimes excluding the rest of her family completely; giving the impression that she and Lawrence were alone on several occasions when her sisters or brothers were also there. She casts herself in the role of betrayed maiden, tragic heroine. Jessie's elder sister May also left a record of many of the same incidents which are described by her sister in *A Personal Record* and by Lawrence in *Sons and Lovers*. Since May was not emotionally involved, her account is much more objective. Often it is nearer to Lawrence's than to Jessie's.[3]

Nevertheless, one's sympathy goes out to Jessie. She loved Lawrence deeply. Given her upbringing, the moral climate of the time, Lawrence's own psychological problems, it is hard to see how she could have behaved otherwise than she did. It is true that, in the novel, Lawrence did not do justice to 'the years of devotion to the development of his genius – devotion that had been pure joy' [PR 203]. And it seems grossly unfair to load so much of the responsibility for the failure of Paul and Miriam onto Miriam. Several critics have chivalrously leapt to the defence of Jessie/Miriam against Lawrence/Paul and his mother. But it seems to me that in doing so they have distorted the novel as much as Lawrence, in the opposite direction. Let us suppose that Mrs Morel had been not at all possessive and had positively encouraged his relationship with Miriam. Can we imagine that the novel could have ended with Paul and Miriam happily married? These critics seem to be suggesting that every normal man should marry his first love.

Lawrence and Jessie Chambers shared much of real value, but it is clear that a marriage would have been disastrous. Years later Lawrence said:

> It would have been a fatal step. I should have had too easy a life, nearly everything my own way, and my genius would have been destroyed.
>
> [C B I 71]

He needed a woman not only free herself from that puritanical inheritance, but also strong enough to shake him out of his own narcissistic priggishness and puritanism. He needed Frieda. If his mother ensured that in 1912 he was not married to Jessie Chambers or Louie Burrows, but free and ready for Frieda, then he had much to thank her for. Mrs Lawrence's dislike of Jessie did not spring entirely from selfish possessiveness. Lawrence would have found aspects of Jessie's character irritating without any prompting from his mother. Jessie was not well liked, even within her own family. Her brother David wrote of her 'rhapsodical moods' and 'inflexible will':

> She knew what was right – in taste as well as in conduct; she did what was right and expected to receive what was due to her for her universal rightness. [CB III 537]

Jessie recorded one occasion when she visited the Lawrence home:

> The talk was lively, and Mrs Lawrence seemed to be the pivot on which the liveliness centred. She struck me as a bright, vivacious little woman, full of vitality and amusingly emphatic in her way of speaking. [PR 24]

Such a tribute, by someone who had every reason to resent Mrs Lawrence, indicates that the qualities Lawrence ascribed to her were not entirely in his own imagination.

Lawrence had once told Jessie that George Borrow 'had mingled autobiography and fiction so inextricably in *Lavengro* that the most astute critics could not be sure where the one ended and the other began' [110]. Judged as autobiography (and Jessie could hardly have judged it otherwise) *Sons and Lovers* was indeed a cruel betrayal of her, and a travesty of the truth. Starting from the assumption that at the centre of the novel was 'a recognizable picture of our friendship' [203], and that the character called Miriam was herself, she could only explain why Lawrence had presented so distorted a picture in one way: 'so that the martyr's halo might sit becomingly on his mother's brow'. But the critic should beware of making these same assumptions. Jessie tried hard to remind herself 'that after all *Sons and Lovers* was only a novel':

> I could hear in advance Lawrence's protesting voice: 'Of course it isn't the truth. It isn't meant for the truth. It's an adaptation from life, as all art must be. It *isn't* what I think of you; you know it isn't.' [204]

Of course, this was no consolation to Jessie. But it was a real problem for Lawrence, one which was to exacerbate his relationships for the rest of his life.

All Lawrence's fiction draws heavily on his own experience and relationships. He did not see the point of inventing anything if he could draw on first-hand reality. Many of his characters are amalgams of two or three real people, and also aspects of himself. Often his friends would recognize themselves in unsympathetic characters and feel betrayed. Two of them, Philip Heseltine and Compton Mackenzie, even threatened legal action. Yet Lawrence could create his fictional characters in no other way than by adaptation from life. Usually he refused to accept that his characters were 'portraits', insisting that, though certain immediately recognizable features of real people might have been incorporated into his characters, their inner significance was quite different from his real-life judgement of those people. Sometimes this defence was disingenuous. Sometimes there was a good deal of truth in it. For example, the figure of Hermione in *Women in Love* was already created in her essentials before Lawrence had ever met Lady Ottoline Morrell, who took it to be a travesty of herself.

Jessie Chambers was well aware that Lawrence used this method:

> The character of Clara is a clever adaptation of elements from three people, Miss Burrows, Miss Corke, and Mrs Dax. The external resemblance to Mrs Dax is the strongest. At any rate, she regarded herself as the original because I received a letter from her some years after the publication of *Sons and Lovers* in which she said – 'I have read *Sons and Lovers* and I *swear* that it is not true.' [DHLR 12 67]

After Lawrence's death, Alice Dax wrote to Frieda saying, virtually, that it *was* true. But there is little of Louie Burrows and less of Helen Corke in Clara. What Jessie did not see, could hardly have seen given the strong 'external resemblance' between Miriam and herself, was that Miriam also was an adaptation of elements from at least three people, herself, Louie Burrows, Helen Corke, and, perhaps, Agnes Holt.

Lawrence's creative motivation was always a matter of trying to deal imaginatively with urgent and immediate problems. When he began *Paul Morel* his relationship with Jessie, his engagement to her and full involvement with her, was over. But the problems of that relationship were by no means over, since he was to experience very similar problems with all his subsequent girl-friends. What Lawrence wrote to Blanche Jennings in January 1910 about his latest girl-friend, Agnes Holt, he might equally have said of any of them:

> She still judges by mid-Victorian standards, and covers herself with a woolly fluff of romance that the years will wear sickly. She refuses to see that a man is a male, that kisses are the merest preludes and anticipations, that love is largely a physical sympathy that is soon satisfied and satiated. She believes men worship their mistresses; she is all sham and superficial in her outlook, and I can't change her. [L I 153]

He had entered upon that relationship fatalistically, with a weary, cynical generalization: 'I can't help it: the game begins, and I play it, and the girl plays it, and – what matter what the end is!' [141]. Helen Corke drove Lawrence into 'an extremity of mental torture':

> How we hate one another to-night, hate, she and I
> To numbness and nothingness; I dead, she refusing to die.
> The female whose venom can more than kill, can numb and then
> nullify.   [CP 98]

The same doomed struggle was resumed with Louie. On 3 November 1911, for example, he wrote to her, on the day after visiting her in Leicester:

> I've now got to digest a great lot of dissatisfied love in my veins. It is very damnable, to have slowly to drink back again into oneself all the lava and fire of a passionate eruption.   [L I 321]

Many of the letters and poems of this period, to different girl-friends, are interchangeable.

All Lawrence's hatred of the dreaming woman, his sense of her destructiveness, went into his work. In *The White Peacock* it was Lettie, in *The Trespasser* Helena. In *Sons and Lovers* it is Miriam. Miriam must bear the blame for the whole generation of young ladies who had so tormented Lawrence. In the fight for Paul's soul, she, not the mother, is the evil angel. Lawrence seemed to Jessie, in February 1912, to be 'fixed in the centre of the tension, helpless, waiting for one pull to triumph over the other' [PR 201]. She assumed that the two pulls were loyalty to herself and loyalty to the dead mother. But Lawrence was also caught between two needs, the need to 'tell the truth' in Jessie's sense, and avoid hurting her yet again, and the need to produce art rather than reproduce life, to attempt a wider significance than the exclusively personal, to speak for a whole generation of young men. His theme was no longer the vindication of the mother, it was the tragedy of the young man:

> It is a great tragedy, and I tell you I've written a great book. It's the tragedy of thousands of young men in England . . . I think it was Ruskin's, and men like him. – Now tell me if I haven't worked out my theme, like life, but always my theme.   [L I 447]

To do this Lawrence had to draw on *all* his experience, not just the triangle of himself, his mother and Jessie.

The form he now had in mind for the novel was that the mother would function as a stable centre, pivot, source of vitality and standards of normality and wholeness. It had hardly yet dawned on Lawrence that she too might belong to the class of destructive women. Paul would be baptized into life by her. As a young man he would begin to move away from her, but would keep her standards to prevent him from throwing himself away like his elder brother. He has two relationships, one with a dreaming or spiritual woman, one with a passionately physical woman. These women objectify the dualistic split within himself.

Though the symbolism of names in *Sons and Lovers* is largely the invention of American critics, Lawrence himself calls attention to the significance of Paul's name by having his brother call him 'Postle as a child. The apostle Paul is associated with just such puritanical dualism as cripples Paul in adolescence:

> For the flesh lusteth against the spirit, and the spirit against the flesh: and these are contrary the one to the other; so that ye cannot do the things that ye would. [Galatians 5:16]

Neither woman proves satisfying in the long run because neither meets the standard of wholeness set by the mother. The physical relationship is good as far as it goes, but limited; the spiritual relationship is deadly. That, presumably (the manuscript of this intermediate version has not survived), is the form the novel still took when Lawrence met Frieda in March 1912.

*

Lawrence and Frieda left for Germany together on 3 May 1912. As soon as Lawrence had a breathing space, in Waldbröl a fortnight later, while Frieda visited her family, he began to revise the novel:

> I am eating my heart out, and revising my immortal Heinemann novel 'Paul Morel', in this tiny village stuck up in the Rhineland. [L I 409]

The work was virtually finished by the time he left Waldbröl twelve days later, and so can have been little more than a tidying up of the manuscript before sending it to Heinemann on 9 June. On 1 July William Heinemann replied, declining the novel:

> I feel that the book is unsatisfactory from several points of view; not only because it lacks unity, without which the reader's interest cannot be held, but more so because its want of reticence makes it unfit, I fear, altogether for publication in England as things are . . . one has no sympathy for any character in the book . . . Even, after a while, one's interest in Paul flags, – while, in the early part, the degradation of his mother, supposed to be of gentler birth, is almost inconceivable. [421]

There may have been good reasons for rejecting the novel, but not these. It is no wonder that Lawrence immediately wrote to Garnett of Heinemann: 'may his name be used as a curse and an eternal infamy'. But the enemy was not really Heinemann. These were the first salvoes in the lifelong battle between Lawrence and England, where the truth could be neither conceived nor published in the literary world.

So Lawrence had to reconcile himself to writing *Paul Morel* yet again. He sought advice from Garnett:

> I will make what alterations you think advisable. It would be rather nice if you made a few notes again. I will squash the first part together – it is too long. [423]

The novel came back from Garnett, together with his notes, on 22 July, and Lawrence was anxious to get to work at once. But he and Frieda were about to embark on their long walk from Bavaria, over the Tyrolese Alps, to Sterzing am Brenner. It was not until they settled on Lake Garda in early September that he was able to begin in earnest.

By this time, Lawrence had been exposed to six months of Frieda's influence. From the first they had discussed Lawrence's attitude to women, and Frieda had flown straight to Freud:

> He said he had finished with his attempts at knowing women. I was amazed at the way he fiercely denounced them. I had never before heard anything like it. I laughed, yet I could tell he had tried very hard, and had cared. We talked about Oedipus and understanding leaped through our words. [NI 4]

He read bits of *Paul Morel* to her and they fought 'like blazes over it'. Frieda wrote to Garnett:

> I think L. quite missed the point in 'Paul Morel'. He really loved his mother more than any body, even with his other women, real love, sort of Oedipus. [L I 449]

Freud's theories were unknown in England at that time, but Frieda's previous lover had been Otto Gross, a disciple of Freud. Elsewhere she recorded:

> Towards the end of *Sons and Lovers*, I got fed up and turned against all this 'house of Atreus' feeling, and I wrote a skit called: 'Paul Morel, or His Mother's Darling'. He read it and said, coldly: 'This kind of thing isn't called a skit'. [NI 74]

Lawrence's acknowledgement of the truth of Frieda's analysis was registered in his decision, in October, to change the name of the novel to *Sons and Lovers*.

This final draft of the novel was finished and sent to Duckworth on 18 November. The following day Lawrence tried to preempt any further criticism from Garnett, who would read it for Duckworth:

> I want to defend it, quick. I wrote it again, pruning it and shaping it and filling it in. I tell you it has got form – *form*: haven't I made it patiently, out of sweat as well as blood. [L I 476]

He went on to give Garnett his well-known synopsis of the novel:

> It follows this idea: a woman of character and refinement goes into the lower class, and has no satisfaction in her own life. She has had a passion for her husband, so the children are born of passion, and have heaps of vitality. But as her sons grow up she selects them as lovers – first the eldest, then the second. These sons are *urged* into life by their reciprocal love of their mother – urged on and on. But when they come to manhood, they can't love, because their mother is the strongest power in their lives, and holds them . . . As soon as the young men come into contact with women, there's a split. William gives his sex to a fribble, and his mother holds his soul. But the split kills him, because he doesn't know where he is. The next son gets a woman who fights for his soul – fights his mother. The son loves the mother – all the sons hate and are jealous of the father. The battle goes on between the mother and the girl, with the son as object. The mother gradually proves stronger, because of the tie of blood. The son decides to leave his soul in his mother's hands, and, like his elder brother, go for passion. He gets passion. Then the split begins to tell again. But, almost unconsciously, the mother realises what is the matter, and begins to die. The son casts off his mistress, attends to his mother dying. He is left in the end naked of everything, with the drift towards death. [476–7]

In fact the novel does not follow this idea at all closely. Had it done so Jessie would have been mollified, and could not have found in the proofs 'both story and mood alike unchanged'. The novel is much more ambivalent than this account suggests. This 'split' theory oversimplifies the death of William. The battle takes place more between Paul and Miriam than between Miriam and Mrs Morel. The ending is much more complex than 'the drift towards death' suggests. Lawrence is here describing not so much the novel he has written as the novel he would prefer to have written, or the novel he would write if he were to begin again from scratch. His new insights were too fundamentally different from those which had informed *Paul Morel* for Lawrence to be able to accommodate them in a mere revision of that novel. He would have had to start again on a different basis. But, at the outset of his marriage and his career as a professional writer, penniless, he was not in a position to jettison all the work he had already put into the novel. Better to do what he could with it in terms, more or less, of the old idea, then turn to the new novel he was itching to begin.

In January 1913 Lawrence wrote:

> The old son-lover was Oedipus. The name of the new one is legion. And if a son-lover take a wife, she is only his bed. And his life will be torn in twain, and his wife in her despair shall hope for sons, that she may have her lover in her hour.   [H 102]

In that same month he wrote *The Daughter-in-Law*, which dramatizes that same situation far more clearly than the novel. As the years passed, his position hardened against the mother. In the 'Parent Love' chapter of *Fantasia of the Unconscious* he summed up, in 1921, his mature position:

> The son gets on swimmingly for a time, till he is faced with the actual fact of sex necessity. He gleefully inherits his adolescence and the world at large, without an obstacle in his way, mother-supported, mother-loved. Everything comes to him in glamour, he feels he sees wondrous much, understands a whole heaven, mother-stimulated. Think of the power which a mature woman thus infuses into her boy. He flares up like a flame in oxygen. No wonder they say geniuses mostly have great mothers. They mostly have sad fates.   [F 127]

According to Frieda, Lawrence said in later life: 'I would write a different *Sons and Lovers* now; my mother was wrong, and I thought she was absolutely right' [NI 74]. A *Sons and Lovers* in which the mother was presented as simply 'wrong' would seem to me a lesser *Sons and Lovers* than the one we have, where, almost by accident, the mother cannot be so easily judged. The version we have holds in creative tension his opposing attitudes. His love and gratitude towards his mother had not yet turned to resentment and bitterness ('all self-righteous women ought to be martyred' [RC 255]), though there are intimations of his embryonic awareness that she had damaged him, broken his father, given Jessie no chance. The relationship between Paul and his mother is not rendered uncritically, as it would have been in 1910, nor is it distorted to make it fit a crude psychological theory, as it might have been in 1913; it is ambivalent and complex, and hence true to the essential paradox of all mother-son relationships.

Lawrence himself soon realized the crudity of psychoanalytic interpretations of literary works when the Freudians got hold of *Sons and Lovers*:

> You know I think 'complexes' are vicious half-statements of the Freudians: sort of can't see wood for trees. When you've said Mutter-complex, you've said nothing . . . A complex is not simply a sex relation:

far from it. – My poor book: it was, as art, a fairly complete truth: so they carve a half lie out of it, and say 'Voila'. Swine! [L II 655]

Despite Lawrence's precautions, Garnett was still not satisfied with the novel. He saw that it still needed extensive cutting, not only because it was too long to suit the publishers, but because there were still many passages of irrelevant, slack, sometimes embarrassingly bad writing. Apparently his letter pulled no punches, for Lawrence replied:

I sit in sadness and grief after your letter. I daren't say anything. All right, take out what you think necessary – I suppose I shall see what you've done when the proofs come, at any rate. I'm sorry I've let you in for such a job – but don't scold me too hard, it makes me wither up. [L I 481]

Lawrence had by this time had enough of *Sons and Lovers*. He wanted to write FINIS under the part of his life it represented, and to embark on a new novel 'purely of the common people – fearfully interesting' [431] (probably the never-to-be-written *Scargill Street*). He was glad to be able to leave to Garnett such 'pedgilling' work as still needed to be done on *Sons and Lovers*.

Garnett removed about a tenth of the novel. He did his work very skilfully, as can be seen from the published facsimile of the manuscript. In his introduction to the facsimile Mark Schorer writes:

Every deletion that Garnett made seems to me to have been to the novel's advantage. Nothing important is lost, ineptitudes disappear, and the novel emerges as tighter and more smoothly paced than it would otherwise have been. A final interesting fact about these deleted passages, a fact that suggests that they were indeed extraneous, is that they could simply be lifted out, almost never involving Lawrence in the necessity of writing in little transitional bridges. [SLF 9]

Garnett was not in any way censoring the novel. Of the seventy-odd cuts he made, only one can have had anything to do with propriety. Much of the deleted material is about Paul's insufferable elder brother William – his athletic prowess, his irresistible knees (in a kilt), and the succession of 'brazen hussies' who are 'gone on him'. There are also several passages where Lawrence tells us again and again in almost identical terms why Paul cannot kiss Miriam. These passages had been much revised already by Lawrence himself without making much difference, as though he were nervously picking at a sore.

When Lawrence saw the proofs, he wrote to Garnett:

You did the pruning jolly well, and I am grateful. I hope you'll live a long long time, to barber up my novels for me before they're published. I wish I weren't so profuse – or prolix.   [L I 517]

He did not restore any of Garnett's cuts. He dedicated the novel to Garnett. When he received his first copy on 19 May 1913 he was 'fearfully proud' of it, and wrote to Garnett: 'Thanks a hundred times' [551]. He was soon to leave Garnett behind, as he left behind every other critic except Frieda, but he could hardly have found a better barber for Sons and Lovers.

*

Sons and Lovers was published on 29 May 1913. Lawrence and Frieda were in Germany at the time. A friend sent Lawrence an unsigned review from the Standard, which was so favourable that Lawrence thought it must be by Garnett:

> In description of incident, even more than in revelation of character, Mr Lawrence shows that he is a master, and in reading his book we feared always to miss a line containing the touch which shows the mark of genius and inspiration as distinct from that of talent and invention. No other English novelist of our time has so great a power to translate passion into words, but that is neither the beginning nor the end of his art.   [CH 58]

Garnett did not, in fact, review the book, but published his assessment of it in 1916, when he compared it as a family epic and social history with Balzac and Flaubert:

> This novel is really the only one of any breadth of vision in contemporary English fiction that lifts working-class life out of middle-class hands, and restores it to its native atmosphere of hard veracity.   [117]

In mid-June Lawrence and Frieda returned to England and went straight to Garnett's house in Kent. There waiting for Lawrence was a batch of reviews which delighted him. The Standard was by no means alone in acclaiming him as a major writer. Nearly all the reviewers recognized and praised the sincerity, authenticity, vividness and vitality of the novel. There was almost universal admiration for his rendering of the early married life of the Morels. Several reviewers felt that he had succeeded in making the mother admirable without always being likeable. The father too, they thought, escaped easy judgements. The Nation reviewer commented perceptively: 'Our sympathy with the sentimental, violent miner-husband is deeper than (we imagine) it was intended to be' [70]. Lascelles Abercrombie concluded his review in the Manchester Guardian:

> Life, for Mr Lawrence, is a coin which has both obverse and reverse;

so it is for most people, but his unusual art consists in his surprising ability to illuminate both sides simultaneously. The scope and variety of the life he describes, his understanding and vivid realizing of circumstances and his insights into character, and chiefly his power of lighting a train of ordinary events to blaze up into singular significance, make *Sons and Lovers* stand out from the fiction of the day as an achievement of the first quality. [68]

Some reviewers detected a falling away in the second half. The *Westminster Gazette* reviewer thought it would have been better if Lawrence had been able to keep the whole of his story 'within the bounds of Mrs Morel's experience'. He found 'an implicit acquiescence in Paul's super-human selfishness in his relations with the two women whom he tries to love' [60]. Harold Massingham in the *Daily Chronicle* thought that Paul could 'never get far enough away from his creator to solidify into a self-sufficient person' [63].

Several reviewers complained at the lack of plot or obvious formal shaping; but the *Nation* reviewer saw the lack of plot as an advantage: 'How would a "plot" have torn through this fine web of poetry, realism, and shrewd or tender analysis!' [69]. Others, though feeling that by all the rules they ought to be bored, admitted that they were not, but could not account for what held them and gave the book its coherence except by vague gestures towards something 'poetic'. Some meant by this simply that the novel had lyrical passages, but some were clearly groping towards some expression of the way in which they felt Lawrence was able to handle apparently realistic scenes in such a way that they acquire a resonance and significance far beyond mere scene-painting. Apparently the word 'symbolism' had not yet entered the vocabulary of novel reviewers. We had to wait until the 1950s before criticism evolved a language adequate to the discussion of Lawrence's major novels as dramatic poems.[4]

At the outset Lawrence had defined the style he wanted for *Paul Morel* rather negatively. All that was clear to him was that he must avoid the excesses of *The White Peacock* and *The Trespasser*:

Paul Morel will be a novel – not a florid prose poem, or a decorated idyll running to seed in realism: but a restrained, somewhat impersonal novel. [L I 184]

He successfully purged his style of all its florid, poetical and self-indulgent elements, but, finding no other way to charge his prose with his own very personal vitality and vision, was left with something rather too 'restrained' and 'impersonal'. This was the first thing that struck Jessie Chambers when she read it:

It was extremely tired writing ... I could not help feeling that his treatment of the theme was far behind the reality in vividness and dramatic strength.   [PR 190]

If, as Jessie said, the final version had not significantly changed the novel in 'story' or 'mood', the hard work Lawrence did on it, 'shaping it and filling it in', giving it 'form', must have been largely stylistic, developing and strengthening the sub-text, the pattern of images which give the novel so much of its coherence and wider meaning.

Many of the characters in the novel are inarticulate, taciturn, or paralysingly self-conscious. This placed severe limits on what could realistically be conveyed by dialogue. A stream of authorial commentary would have deprived the novel of all objectivity. Lawrence therefore developed what was to become, in *The Rainbow*, his characteristic stylistic device, the organic symbol. He creates numerous scenes and incidents which are perfectly realistic, natural, appropriate, on the surface, but are rendered in such a way that, without our realizing it, they reverberate, open out into larger significance, and link up with other such symbols to provide a matrix of images and resonances which is both a formal grid for the novel, and, often, a source for its value judgements.

There is nothing in the surviving *Paul Morel* drafts corresponding to the series of night-communions[5] which begins with Mrs Morel, pregnant with Paul, looking out from her garden into the rich world he is to inherit:

The night was very large, and very strange, stretching its hoary distances infinitely. And out of the silver-grey fog of darkness came sounds vague and hoarse: a corncrake not far off, sound of a train like a sigh, and distant shouts of men.   [SL 60]

She smells the lilies, and returns to the house with a blessing of dusky pollen on her face. Every element in this memorable scene, night, moonlight, darkness, white, silver and gold, flowers, lilies, bird-calls, distant manifestations of human activity, is to surface again, in different contexts, accumulating meanings, at later crises in the novel.

In *Paul Morel* Paul touches flowers with his fingers, 'a thing he liked to do' [PM 223]. In *Sons and Lovers* this is made exclusively a characteristic of Miriam, so that Paul, Miriam and Clara can each be given a way of responding to flowers which is emblematic of their characters. In *Paul Morel* we have:

They came to the wood-gate. He helped her over the fence, laughing because she gripped his hands so tight. She sprang beside him, rather heavily, laughing in a peculiar low fashion; she had so nearly fallen on his breast. He was quite oblivious. [226]

In *Sons and Lovers* this becomes:

But she was physically afraid. If they were getting over a stile, she gripped his hands in a little hard anguish, and began to lose her presence of mind. And he could not persuade her to jump from even a small height. Her eyes dilated, became exposed and palpitating. [SL 203–4]

Not only is this an improvement in itself; it enables Lawrence to contrast Miriam's fear with his mother's cautious, but independent and determined climbing of a stile earlier in the novel, and Clara's careless abandon later:

She stood on top of the stile, and he held both her hands. Laughing, she looked down into his eyes. Then she leaped. Her breast came against his; he held her, and covered her face with kisses. [371]

The crucial scenes of the swing and the wild rose bush have no equivalent in *Paul Morel*.

Our interpretation of the ending of *Sons and Lovers* depends entirely on our precise response to words and images which have accumulated such meanings and resonances and function as poetry. The last paragraph of the novel reads:

But no, he would not give in. Turning sharply, he walked towards the city's gold phosphorescence. His fists were shut, his mouth set fast. He would not take that direction, to the darkness, to follow her. He walked towards the faintly humming, glowing town, quickly. [492]

Without the poetic overtones the passage would be simple. Paul overcomes the temptation to commit suicide and follow his mother into the darkness of death, accepting instead the challenge to live, to join the quick rather than the dead, to answer the call to find a place for himself within the world of creative human activity represented by the city which glows with promise on the horizon. But the imagery introduces much more complex ideas. Darkness has not, until the last chapter, been an image for death, rather for the unknown, out of which all life comes. Gold has been consistently an image of that life, life with a blessing. Gold has been associated both with Mrs Morel, who, in the night-communions, seemed to be baptizing Paul into a life rich with potentialities, and with Mr Morel, whose warmth had so captivated Gertrude Coppard:

Therefore the dusky, golden softness of this man's sensuous flame of life, that flowed off his flesh like the flame from a candle, not baffled and gripped into incandescence by thought and spirit as her life was, seemed to her something wonderful, beyond her.   [45]

Here too, gold is associated with darkness, the darkness of underground:

This was a new tract of life suddenly opened before her. She realized the life of the miners, hundreds of them toiling below earth and coming up at evening. He seemed to her noble. He risked his life daily, and with gaiety.   [46]

This is a theme which Lawrence in later years would have developed much more fully:

Under the butty system, the miners worked underground as a sort of intimate community, they knew each other practically naked, and with curious close intimacy, and the darkness and the underground remoteness of the pit 'stall', and the continual presence of danger, made the physical, instinctive, and intuitional contact between men very highly developed, a contact almost as close as touch, very real and very powerful. The physical awareness and intimate *togetherness* was at its strongest down pit . . . And if I think of my childhood, it is always as if there was a lustrous sort of inner darkness, like the gloss of coal, in which we moved and had our real being.   [P 135]

This is only hinted at in *Sons and Lovers*, but there is enough to make clear that Walter Morel's darkness is quite different from Mrs Morel's, which is merely the obscurity of the future and distance of a wide world waiting for her son to shine in it. Even the golden pollen on Mrs Morel's face in the first night-communion has come from madonna lilies. As the novel progresses we become aware, retrospectively, that it had been a false epiphany. The intense whiteness of the full moon and the lilies had signalled the entry of Paul not into a rich unknown, but into an all-encompassing mother-love, which becomes a weight upon him, at adolescence, a barrier to his further maturing. The blanched white light symbolizes the possession of his soul by women who, as mother and virgin, cannot foster the life of the body and the development of a strong, self-sufficient masculinity.

Clearly the ending of the novel is affirmative, in so far as Paul resists the attractions of suicide or a Schopenhauer-like nihilism. He sets off in quest of life, taking as his beacon a golden glow on the horizon. But Lawrence does not allow us to take the desire for the accomplishment. What is that glow, that 'gold phosphorescence', but an emanation of the mechanized life of an industrial city? He had already written, in 'Parliament Hill in the Evening':

The hopeless, wintry twilight fades,
  The city corrodes out of sight
As the body corrodes when death invades
  That citadel of delight.

Now verdigris smoulderings softly spread
  Through the shroud of the town, as slow
Night-lights hither and thither shed
  Their ghastly glow.   [CP 142]

The word 'phosphorescence' was shortly to become one of Lawrence's jargon words, always expressing corruption and decay. In *Twilight in Italy* he associates it with Hamlet's diseased consciousness, and with Aphrodite:

She is the gleaming darkness, she is the luminous night, she is goddess of destruction, her white, cold fire consumes and does not create. [TI 42]

Lawrence himself, by the time he finished *Sons and Lovers*, had found his way to freedom and fulfilment with Frieda in Italy. But we leave Paul at the end of the novel on the threshold of no such new life. Had the novel followed him further, in autobiographical terms, it would have been into the 'sick year' of 1911, when 'everything collapsed, save the mystery of death, and the haunting of death in life' [CP 851].

The ending is another false epiphany,[6] very like the ending of *Portrait of the Artist as a Young Man*, which Joyce was writing at the same time as Lawrence was writing *Sons and Lovers*. The device is used much more systematically in the *Portrait*. At the end of every chapter Stephen feels that he has solved his problems, come into his own as Stephen Hero, or made some transfiguring discovery about life. Each time the style is ironically inflated. Each time the beginning of the next chapter punctures the illusion with an injection of sordid reality, revealing the epiphany to have been false, or at least inadequate. The novel ends with Stephen, after the death of his mother, turning his back on Ireland and the past. The moonlit distance beckons him:

The spell of arms and voices: the white arms of roads, their promise of close embraces and the black arms of tall ships that stand against the moon, their tale of distant nations . . . Welcome, O life! I go to encounter for the millionth time the reality of experience and to forge in the smithy of my soul the uncreated conscience of my race.   [P A 252–3]

This epiphany, since it comes at the end, cannot be undermined in the next chapter. But it is undermined in the next book, *Ulysses*: 'You flew. Whereto? Newhaven-Dieppe steerage passenger. Paris and back' [U 210].

Sons and Lovers, like so many of Lawrence's novels, ends with an incomplete or ambivalent resolution, an open question which the next novel can then take as a point of departure. It is left for Ursula in *The Rainbow* to discover that life is to be found in sunshine or in darkness, but not in sterile moonlight or the stagnant gleaming and fuming of cities:

'The stupid, artificial, exaggerated town, fuming its lights. It does not exist really. It rests upon the unlimited darkness, like a gleam of coloured oil on dark water, but what is it? – nothing, just nothing.'   [R 498]

Skrebensky, bereft in London after 'the first deadly anguish' in his relationship with Ursula, 'the first sense of the death towards which they were wandering' [507], is Lawrence in London after his mother's death, or Paul in whatever city he is walking towards:

Now he found himself struggling amid an ashen-dry, cold world of rigidity, dead walls and mechanical traffic, and creeping, spectre-like people. The life was extinct, only ash moved and stirred or stood rigid, there was a horrible, clattering activity, a rattle like the falling of dry slag, cold and sterile. It was as if the sunshine that fell were unnatural light exposing the ash of the town, as if the lights at night were the sinister gleam of decomposition.   [508]

Given the decision to live, and to move away from things gone dead, be they one's old split personality, one's ties of family, class, culture and religion, England, a whole false inheritance and metaphysic, the question is in what direction to set out, towards what, in the effort to discover how the life that is in you wants to be lived. This is Ursula's problem in *The Rainbow*, Birkin's in *Women in Love*, Alvina's in *The Lost Girl*, Aaron's in *Aaron's Rod*, Somers's in *Kangaroo*, Lou's in *St Mawr*, Kate's in *The Plumed Serpent*, Connie's in *Lady Chatterley's Lover*. Each finds an incomplete resolution until the last of Lawrence's fictional protagonists and alter egos, the man who had died in *The Escaped Cock*, finds himself and his place in the world.

FOUR

'NEW HEAVEN AND EARTH':
THE GENESIS OF *THE RAINBOW*

On 3 May 1912 Lawrence and Frieda eloped to Germany together. Frieda was ostensibly visiting her family, and Lawrence was left on his own for much of the first three weeks. As he became more and more assured of the rightness and permanence of his relationship with Frieda, he was able to work 'quite hard' at revising *Paul Morel*. But his experience of 'real love' was bringing him new insights which that novel could not possibly accommodate: 'I am realising things that I never thought to realise' [L I 403]. The letters he wrote to Frieda at this time reveal the extent to which he was to draw on this experience when describing Tom's courtship of Lydia in *The Rainbow*:

> Can't you feel how certainly I love you and how certainly we shall be married . . . Do you know, like the old knights, I seem to want a certain time to prepare myself – a sort of vigil with myself. Because it is a great thing for me to marry you, not a quick, passionate coming together. I know in my heart 'here's my marriage'. It feels rather terrible – because it is a great thing in my life – it is *my life* . . . It's the very strength and inevitability of the oncoming thing that makes me wait, to get in harmony with it. Dear God, I am marrying you, now, don't you see. It's a far greater thing than ever I knew. [403]

In *The Rainbow* we find:

> The facts and material of his daily life fell away, leaving the kernel of his purpose clean. And then it came upon him that he would marry her and she would be his life . . . So he sat small and submissive to the greater ordering . . . And if it should be so, that she should come to him! It should be so – it was ordained so. [R 75–6]

The 'honeymoon' in Beuerberg a week later confirmed Lawrence's assurance:

> The world is wonderful and beautiful and good beyond one's wildest imagination. Never, never, never could one conceive what love is, beforehand, never. Life *can* be great – quite god-like. It *can* be so. God be thanked I have proved it. [L I 414]

Even the first year with Frieda, a year of terrible strain, could not diminish this conviction: 'This is the best I have known, or ever shall know' [553].

Lawrence felt that this experience constituted a kind of tragedy (the only kind that really interested him) – death to the old life and rebirth into a greater life after the pangs of marital conflict: 'I think the real tragedy is in the inner war which is waged between people who love each other, a war out of which comes knowledge . . .' [419]. It seemed to him strictly a religious experience, a confirmation of human participation in a permanent creative process: 'A woman I love sort of keeps me in direct communication with the unknown, in which otherwise I am a bit lost' [503]. It is this communication with the unknown through human relationships, particularly marital love, that the rainbow of the title is to symbolize.

*

Life was, however, running ahead of art. It was not until several months and several false starts later that Lawrence's marital experience took over the shaping of a novel. As early as 9 May 1912 Lawrence wrote to Frieda that he had 'thought of a theme' [396] for his next novel. Our only clue to what he might have had in mind is that two days later he wrote his only surviving letter to Flossie Cullen: 'Ada says you are cross with me – no, don't be so – pray forgive me' [398]. Whatever Lawrence wanted to be forgiven for, Ada's letter reminded him of Flossie, whose character and life-story had always fascinated him. In March 1911, when Lawrence was putting a good deal of Cullen family history into Paul Morel (though Flossie herself was surprisingly absent),[1] he had written to Ada: 'I often think of Flossie . . . I know what she's had to go through, and has: and I think of her very often, with sympathy' [234]. In the same letter Lawrence had written: 'I hate Eastwood abominably, and I should be glad if it were puffed off the face of the Earth.' Perhaps Lawrence's hatred of Eastwood and sympathy for Flossie were parts of a common theme, for when his novel based on her, The Lost Girl, was finally completed in 1920, its major theme was to be the need for the heroine, Alvina Houghton, to die to a false, sordid 'reality' embodied in Woodhouse (Eastwood) in order to be reborn to a new and vital consciousness by taking a foreign lover, abandoning everything, and starting a new life on the continent with him. Still in the throes of Paul Morel, Lawrence might have been attracted to the idea of a sequel which would enable him to deal with the larger issues of the rejection of Eastwood and England and of psychic rebirth without the pressures and limitations of autobiography. A protagonist of the opposite sex would involve still greater objectivity. Flossie Cullen was the perfect alter ego.

There is no further mention of a new novel in Lawrence's letters until August 1912, when, in the same letter in which he announces to Garnett that he is 'going to write Paul Morel over again', he also tells him that he has 'thought of a new novel – purely of the common people – fearfully interesting' [430–31]. The next four months were spent working very hard on *Paul Morel*, and we hear nothing more of the next novel until 30 October, when Lawrence tells Garnett that *Paul Morel* will be done in a fortnight, 'then I start "Scargill Street" ' [466]. He seems to expect Garnett to know what he is talking about, though he has never mentioned such a title before. Lawrence's birthplace was at the junction of Victoria Street and Scargill Street, Eastwood, and in *Sons and Lovers* Walker Street, where Lawrence lived from six to nineteen, is called Scargill Street. So Lawrence was certainly still thinking of another Eastwood novel.

At the beginning of the month Lawrence had read Arnold Bennett's *Anna of the Five Towns*. It was almost the first English print he had read in five months, and the contrast between the world of the novel in the industrial midlands, and Lake Garda where he now lived, struck him hard:

I don't know where I am. I am so used to the people going by outside, talking or singing some foreign language, always Italian now: but today, to be in Hanley, and to read almost my own dialect, makes me feel quite ill. I hate England and its hopelessness. I hate Bennett's resignation. Tragedy ought really to be a great kick at misery. But *Anna of the Five Towns* seems like an acceptance – so does all the modern stuff since Flaubert. I hate it. I want to wash again quick, wash off England, the oldness and grubbiness and despair. [459]

Anna, in Bennett's novel, allows her better nature, her independent spirit and her womanliness to wither as she accepts the dehumanizing materialism of Hanley. It is as though the grime of the place clogs her very soul. Lawrence must have seen at once how he could make the story of Flossie Cullen into his answer to *Anna of the Five Towns* – 'a great kick at misery'. When he wrote *The Insurrection of Miss Houghton* in the New Year, he gave his heroine the name Anna [546].

Lawrence sent the manuscript of *Paul Morel* off to Duckworth on 18 November, but did not immediately begin another novel. For a month he wrote nothing but a handful of poems, and sketched in water-colours on the quayside at Villa di Gargnano: 'It is such healing work, I find, to paint a bit' [491]. He also read Lockhart's

Life of Robert Burns, and when he did begin to write seriously again, it was not to take up the Flossie Cullen theme, but to explore the possibility of using Burns as another alter ego, transposed to 'the hills of Derbyshire':

> I've thought of a new novel I'm keen on. It's a sort of life of Robert Burns. But I'm not Scotch. So I shall just transplant him to home . . . I have always been fond of him, as a sort of brother. [489]

> He seems a good deal like myself – nicer in most ways. I think I can do him almost like an autobiography. [487]

It seems Lawrence wrote no more than a few pages. But they are enough to reveal how like the young Tom Brangwen in *The Rainbow* the hero, Jack Haseldine, was to be. He is a farmer's son, set apart from his father and brother by his restlessness, his need to 'grasp something'. After supper they 'returned to the fire to half-sleep,' as, at the beginning of *The Rainbow*, 'the men sat by the fire and their brains were inert' [R 42]. But Jack went out into the night:

> There was something he wanted, out of the glittering night. He stood quite still, fronting it all. He ought to be going back to the house, but he did not want to. He wanted to get away from something – he wanted something. Turning swiftly, he set off across the fields up hill. After walking about a mile he saw the lights of the quarry cottages, the farms, the inn at Underwood. He did not want to go to the 'Brick and Tile'. Keeping along the rutty road, he descended the hill on the other side, into Jacksdale that lay in the dark hollow. But he went past the inn and the houses. On the stone bridge he halted. Set back there was the row of cottages where the girl lived. He guessed she lived in the end house. There was a dim light in the window. [CB I 191]

It is like a first draft of Tom's half-unconscious walk to the vicarage to propose to Lydia. And the first coming together of Tom and Lydia is also prefigured in the Burns fragment:

> He was breathless and astonished in all his being. Holding her fast, he moved his lips over her face, her cheeks, her shut eyes, her brows. The discovery was amazing. The whole secret of the night and the stars was in these soft, smooth grooves and mounds and hollows. It was her face! Yet it seemed to include big distances and wonderful things. The flashing lights overhead were no further off than the strange roughness of her eyebrows under his lips, the arched, dark sky didn't frighten him more than the firm domes of her eyes under the softly closed eyelids. And she was breathing against him, live and warm like the rabbit. And it was the darkness he was kissing, discovering. It was the night he had his mouth upon. [192–3]

It seems that Lawrence's enthusiasm for the Burns project did not last more than a few days or take him beyond a dozen pages. By 23 December he was again thinking of what he could do with a female protagonist; he wrote to Sallie Hopkin, who was active in the campaign for women's rights (the Commons had rejected women's franchise earlier that year): 'I shall do a novel about Love Triumphant one day. I shall do my work for women, better than the suffrage' [L I 490]. A week later he wrote to Garnett:

> I've stewed my next novel inside me for a week or so, and have begun dishing it up. It's going to have a bit of a plot, and I don't think it'll be unwieldy, because it'll be further off from me and won't come down on my head so often. [496]

This, it seems, was Lawrence's first attempt at the Flossie Cullen novel – an abandoned twenty-page opening, written in the first person, in which the heroine was called Elsa Culverwell. It was a false start, but Lawrence tried again, and wrote to Garnett on 12 January:

> I'm simmering a new work that I shall not tell you about, because it may not come off. But the thought of it fills me with a curious pleasure – venomous, almost. I want to get it off my chest. [501]

The venom was, no doubt, his hatred of Eastwood and England. This time Lawrence was launched, and by 17 January he had written eighty pages of *The Insurrection of Miss Houghton*: 'a most curious work, which gives me great joy to write, but which, I am afraid, will give most folk extreme annoyance to read; if it doesn't bore them' [505].

What Lawrence was so much enjoying getting off his chest was presumably some fictional equivalent of the 'great religion' he outlined in his famous letter to Ernest Collings that same day:

> My great religion is a belief in the blood, the flesh, as being wiser than the intellect... All I want is to answer to my blood, direct, without fribbling intervention of mind, or moral, or what not. [503]

This is often quoted as an example of Lawrence at his most facile, extreme, and irresponsible. It was natural enough that Lawrence, having just got out from under the stifling weight of his inherited culture, should feel that every aspect of that culture was false and deadly, and that the truth could easily be found by turning that culture on its head and believing the opposite of everything he had been taught to believe. Every subsequent work was to be a testing, maturing and refining of that 'religion'.

We are dealing with a letter, not an essay written for publication; a letter to a man Lawrence felt he could speak freely to, without reservations. Collings seemed to Lawrence 'too onesided . . . *afraid* of the female element' [503]; so Lawrence throws all his weight on the other side, with deliberate outspokenness: 'I am a great bosher, and full of fancies that interest me'. Moreover, it soon becomes clear that by 'blood' he means something much more than bodily appetites and animal instincts. He uses the word three times in the first six sentences, then abandons it entirely in favour of the word 'flame', and by 'flame' he means the mysterious selfhood, the innermost ghost, 'the mystery of the flame forever flowing, coming God knows how from out of practically nowhere, and being *itself*'. The Englishman's mind is so intent on amassing knowledge and pursuing shadowy ideals that he cannot *be*: 'So he goes in for Humanitarianism and such like forms of not-being'. The Italians around him provided living proof that it need not be so:

> And instead of chasing the mystery in the fugitive, half lighted things outside us, we ought to look at ourselves, and say 'My God, I am myself!' That is why I like to live in Italy. The people are so unconscious.   [504]

The new novel, therefore, would be about a young woman who comes to realize the atrophy of England (and especially of East-wood), who has the courage to rebel against it, to make her bid for free and healthy sex and selfhood, presumably in Italy.

On 1 February 1913 Lawrence wrote to Garnett:

> I have done 100 pages of a novel. I think you will hate it, but I think, when it is re-written, it might find a good public among the Meredithy public. It is quite different in manner from my other stuff – far less visualised. It is what I *can* write just now, and write with pleasure, so write it I must, however you may grumble. And it is good too. I think, do you know, I have inside me a sort of answer to the *want* of today: to the real, deep want of the English people, not to just what they fancy they want. And gradually, I shall get my hold on them.   [511]

Over the next six weeks Lawrence wrote another hundred pages, 'rather more than half' the novel in all. Not a word of it has survived. We are entirely dependent on Lawrence's own descriptions of it in his letters, and on our knowledge that it was a first draft for *The Lost Girl*.

> It's all crude as yet, like one of Tony's clumsy prehistorical beasts – most cumbersome and floundering – but I think it's great – so new, so really a stratum deeper than I think anybody has ever gone, in a novel. But there, you see, it's my latest. It is all analytical – quite unlike *Sons and Lovers*, not a bit visualised . . .
>
> The novel is *not* about Frieda and me, nor about a Baroness neither.
>
>   [526–7]

107

It was, we gather, an attempt to get inside his characters, into their unconscious, rather than simply to visualize and present them. Frieda's most telling criticism of *Sons and Lovers* was in precisely these terms:

> You see I dont really believe in *Sons and Lovers* it feels as if there were nothing *behind* all those happenings as if there were no 'Hinterland der Seele' only intensely felt fugitive things – I who am a believer though I dont know in what, to me it seems an irreligious book – It does not seem the deepest and last thing said, if for instance a man loves in a book the pretty curl in the neck of 'her', if he loves it ever so intensely and beautifully, there is some thing behind that curl, *more* than that curl, there is *she*, the living, striving *she*. [L II 151]

Perhaps *The Insurrection of Miss Houghton* was Lawrence's first attempt to create a 'living, striving *she*', and to plumb the depths of consciousness, the hinterland of the soul.

But the deeper Lawrence went in this sense, especially in sexual matters, the more certain that 'nobody will ever dare to publish it' [L I 526]. Even Frieda found *The Insurrection* 'improper!' [549]. Though Lawrence found it 'fearfully exciting', and it lay next to his heart for months, he could not afford to spend his time on unpublishable work. Reluctantly, he decided to set it aside in order to write 'another, shorter, absolutely impeccable – as far as morals go – novel . . . or else what am I going to live on, and keep Frieda on withal' [526].

*

The new novel, which Lawrence called *The Sisters*, was frankly intended to be a money-spinner, a 'pot-boiler', 'meant to be for the "jeunes filles" ' [546]. But by 5 April, when Lawrence had reached page 110, it had 'developed into an earnest and painful work' [536]. After breaking off to correct the last proofs of *Sons and Lovers*, Lawrence wrote to McLeod on 23 April:

> I am doing a novel which I have never grasped. Damn its eyes, there I am at page 145, and I've no notion what it's about. I hate it. F. says it is good. But it's like a novel in a foreign language I don't know very well – I can only just make out what it is about. [544]

In a letter to Garnett probably written on 2 May, Lawrence wrote:

> I have written 180 pages of my newest novel 'The Sisters'. It is a queer novel, which seems to have come by itself. I will send it you. You may dislike it – it hasn't got hard outlines – and of course it's only first draft – but it is pretty neat, for me, in composition . . . Already it has fallen from

grace. I can only write what I feel pretty strongly about: and that, at present, is the relations between men and women. After all, it is *the* problem of today, the establishment of a new relation, or the re-adjustment of the old one, between men and women.   [546]

Apparently Garnett did dislike it, for when he received Garnett's comments, Lawrence replied:

I was glad of your letter about the Sisters. Don't schimpf, I shall make it all right when I re-write it. I shall put it in the third person. All along I knew what ailed the book. But it did me good to theorise myself out, and to depict Friedas God Almightiness in all its glory. That was the first crude fermenting of the book. I'll make it into art now. I've done 256 pages, but still can't see the end very clear. But it's coming. Frieda is so cross, since your letter came, with the book. Before that she was rather fond of her portrait in straight pleats and Athena sort of pose.   [550²]

Garnett had called the sisters, Ella and Gudrun, 'remarkable females'. Frieda went further, calling them 'superior flounders': 'The worst, it's like his impudence, they are *me*, these beastly, superior, arrogant females!' [549]. But she was honest enough to admit to 'Ellaing' from time to time. She compared Ella to Goethe's Iphigenie. Lawrence commented:

Iphegenie [*sic*], according to Frieda, is a noble statue to the frosty Frau von Stein; – noble, but done in hate; the cruelest thing a man can do to a woman is to portray her as perfection.   [549]

By the beginning of June, Lawrence had nearly finished the novel, having reached page 283. He finished it a few days later, and sent the second half to Garnett. He had fallen just four pages short of the 300 he had prophesied at the outset. Only the last six have survived.

The characters in this fragment are Gerald Crich, his mother and sister Winifred, Gudrun Brangwen, and Loerke. The first page has the end of a chapter about Mrs Crich:

She had almost lost her touch with conventional life, but lived alone, a blind, unconscious existence . . . More and more she kept to her rooms, where she lay passive, or where she read . . .

This comes very close to the description of her in 'The Industrial Magnate' chapter of *Women in Love*:

As the years went on, she lost more and more count of the world, she seemed rapt in some glittering abstraction, almost purely unconscious . . . She only sat in her room like a moping, dishevelled hawk, motionless, mindless.   [WL 289–90]

The following chapter in *Women in Love* is 'Rabbit', in which Gerald is scratched by, and almost kills, a pet rabbit. This may derive from Gerald's recollection, later in this fragment, of a rabbit running to a groom for protection from a cat, as no creature had ever run to him for protection or tenderness.

The remainder of the fragment is the final chapter, in which Gerald goes to ask Gudrun, who is pregnant by him, to marry him. They have recently returned from Switzerland. He finds the German sculptor Loerke already there on the same errand, having been sent for from Germany by Gudrun. There are threats of violence, but Loerke eventually leaves, his face broken in an agony of emotion. Gerald and Gudrun are reconciled. Beginning to weep, almost for the first time in his life, he holds her, her face buried in his shoulder:

> And he felt himself giving her shelter, relief, and ease, and his heart grew hot with a trembling joy. He was something he had feared he never could be: he had got something he had pretended to disbelieve in. And, breathing hard, he knew this was his life's fulfilment, and a wave of faith, warm, strong, religious faith went over him.

The fragment ends:

> There was still a good deal that hurt still, between them. But he was humble to her. Only, she must love him – She must love him, or else everything was barren. This aloofness of hers – She came to him as the father of her child, not as to a lover, a husband. Well, he had had a chance, and lost it. He had been a fool. Now he must make the best of it, and get her again. But it hurt that she did not seem to want him very much. It hurt keenly.
> Then while he was thinking, with his forehead hard with pain, she kissed him, drawing him to her, murmuring 'My love!'.

Thus the first *Sisters* seems to have been very similar, in plot and characters, to *Women in Love*, but with a happy ending which is somewhat story-bookish. There is no reason to suppose that this *Sisters* contained anything at all which was subsequently to be part of *The Rainbow*.

*

Lawrence spent most of July 1913 at Broadstairs, revising and vastly improving his short stories. In August he and Frieda returned to Irschenhausen, where he made 'two false starts' at the second *Sisters*. By 4 September he had got going, and wrote to Garnett: 'The Sisters has quite a new beginning – a new basis altogether' [L II 67]. By the middle of the month he had done a hundred pages. But at the end of the month the Lawrences moved to Lerici, and it took Lawrence until the beginning of November to settle down to the novel again:

> I am writing my novel slowly – it will be a beautiful novel – when it's done. But here, it is so beautiful, one can't work. I was out rowing on the sea all afternoon . . . [118–19]

Not until 6 January did Lawrence send 'the first half' of *The Sisters*, now 're-christened' *The Wedding Ring*, to Garnett, predicting that he would finish it in six or eight weeks:

> You will see the whole scheme of the book is changed – widened and deepened. But, I think you will be able to gather how it is going on. There may be some small weeding out to do – but this will be the final form of the book. [134]

A fortnight later Lawrence wrote to Henry Savage:

> I have done 340 pages of my novel. It is very different from *Sons and Lovers*. The Laocoon writhing and shrieking have gone from my new work, and I think there is a bit of stillness, like the wide, still, unseeing eyes of a Venus of Melos . . . There is behind every woman who walks, and who eats her meal, a Venus of Melos, still, unseeing, unchanging, and inexhaustible. And there is a glimpse of it everywhere, in somebody, at some moment – a glimpse of the eternal and unchangeable that they are. [137–8]

Shortly after this Lawrence must have written the only surviving fragment of this version, which is numbered 373–80. The fragment begins with another proposal scene, Birkin's visit to Ella while her parents are away on holiday. The equivalent scene in *Women in Love* is only half-way through the novel. In the last page of the fragment, Ella and Gudrun on holiday are walking on the shore at Filey when they see Ella's former lover, Ben Templeman. Ella almost loses consciousness: 'A wave of terror, deep, annihilating, went over her'. It is clear that a good deal of the earlier part of this draft must have been devoted to Ella's relationship with Ben Templeman, before she meets Birkin.

On 29 January Lawrence received Garnett's hostile reponse to the first half of the manuscript:

> I am not very much surprised, nor even very much hurt by your letter – and I agree with you. I agree with you about the Templeman episode. In the scheme of the novel, however, I *must* have Ella get some experience before she meets her Mr Birkin. – I also felt that the character was inclined to fall into two halves – and gradations between them. It came of trying to graft on to the character of Louie the character, more or less, of Frieda.

111

That I ought not to have done . . . Tell me whether you think Ella would be possible, as she now stands, unless she had some experience of love and men. I think, impossible. Then she must have a love episode, a significant one. But it must not be a Templeman episode.   [142]

The original *Sisters* had begun with Ella's meeting Birkin, 'the School Inspector and so on' [164]. Ending with the return from Switzerland, it had therefore covered almost exactly the same ground as *Women in Love*. The 'new beginning' and 'new basis' of the second version had obviously been a result of Lawrence's feeling that he could not do justice to Ella and her relationship with Birkin without giving her a past. But the scheme of the book had been 'widened and deepened' in more senses than that; the style was also different, especially as applied to characterization and relationships. The fragment shows him continuing to develop what he calls his 'exhaustive method', his attempt to go deeper than 'object and story' will take you, to the 'eternal and unchangeable' in character. There is hardly any dialogue between Birkin and Ella. Her response to him is extreme, hardly realistic. She is giving physical expression to feelings she can neither understand nor control, to her very being at a moment of great stress and turmoil:

Her womb, her belly, her heart were all in agony. She crouched together on the floor, crying like some wild animal in pain, with a kind of mooing noise, very dreadful to hear, a sound she was unaware of, that came from her unproduced, out of the depths of her body in torture. For some wild moments the paroxysm continued, when she crouched on the ground with her head down, mad, crying with an inarticulate, animal noise . . .

He walked away, feeling as if the heavens had fallen, and he were not himself, he were somebody else, walking in a different life. In one crash, the whole form of his life, the whole conception of himself, which he had, was gone: he did not know what he was, who he was: he did not know what he knew or what he did not know. Reduced to an elementary chaos, he drifted to his rooms, to sit till dawn by the fire, stunned, motionless . . .

She did not yet know quite where she was. She only knew that her fate was bringing her closer and closer into connection with this man, that something was taking place, implicating her with him, which she could never revoke or escape. And blindly, almost shrinking, she lapsed forward.

It was probably this kind of writing that Garnett found hard to take, and his criticism of it which most upset Lawrence, for it struck at the heart of his enterprise:

Then about the artistic side being in the background. It is that which troubles me most. I have no longer the joy in creating vivid scenes, that I had in *Sons and Lovers*. I don't care much more about accumulating objects in the powerful light of emotion, and making a scene of them. I have to write differently . . . I shall go on now to the end of the book. It will not take me long. Then I will go over it all again, and I shall be very glad to hear *all* you have to say. But if this, the second half, also disappoints you, I will, when I come to the end, leave this book altogether. – Then I should propose to write a story with a plot, and to abandon the exhaustive method entirely – write pure object and story.   [142]

There followed a second, even more critical letter from Garnett, which Lawrence could not swallow: it seemed to insult not what he had been able to do, but what he wanted to do:

> You know how willing I am to hear what you have to say, and to take your advice and to act on it when I have taken it. But it is no good unless you will have patience and understand what I *want* to do. I am not after all a child working erratically. All the time, underneath, there is something deep evolving itself out in me. And it is *hard* to express the new thing, in sincerity. And you should understand, and help me to the new thing . . .
> [164–6]

After receiving that second letter, Lawrence did not write to Garnett again for three months. It was the beginning of the end of their relationship.

*

On 9 February Lawrence wrote to McLeod:

> I have begun my novel again – for about the seventh time. I hope you are sympathising with me. I had nearly finished it. It was full of beautiful things, but it missed – I knew that it just missed being itself. So here I am, must sit down and write it out again. I know it is quite a lovely novel really – you know that the perfect statue is in the marble, the kernel of it. But the thing is the getting it out clean. I think I shall manage it pretty well. You must say a prayer for me sometimes.   [146]

Frieda attributed the failure to her own non-cooperation:

> If he denies my life and suffering I deny his art, so you see he wrote without me at the back of him. The novel is a failure, but you must feel something at the back of it struggling, trying to come out – I am going to throw myself into the novel now and you will see what a 'gioia' it will be.
> [151]

Lawrence agreed with her:

> I am sure of this now, this novel. It is a big and beautiful work. Before, I could not get my soul into it. That was because of the struggle and the resistance between Frieda and me. Now you will find her and me in the novel, I think, and the work is of both of us.   [164]

113

If the first *Sisters* was entirely, and the second largely, composed of material destined for *Women in Love*, this third draft, *The Wedding Ring*, is much closer to *The Rainbow*. Lawrence spoke of it as a new novel: 'In the Sisters was the germ of this novel: woman becoming individual, self-responsible, taking her own initiative' [165]. Frieda's contribution was very much more than general moral support. The new emphasis on Ella's girlhood and adolescence drew heavily upon Frieda's, as we can see from her autobiographical novel *'And the Fullness Therof . . .'*:

'I am not only a pretty young thing; I am also myself. What is going to become of this unknown "myself"?' She was scared. At the bottom, this whole elaborate society was meaningless for her. What was it all about? It had nothing to do with genuine living. [FL 67]

Moreover, Frieda had now become Lawrence's only constructive critic. She had long since recognized that 'any new thing must have a new shape, then afterwards one can call it art' [185]. But what fundamentally united Lawrence and Frieda against Garnett and the whole literary establishment was their joint conviction that literature must be religious, 'the deepest and last thing said':

But primarily I am a passionately religious man, and my novels must be written from the depth of my religious experience. [L II 165]

By religious experience he meant his contact with the sources of life in the unknown; and it was through his marriage that he felt he had the most direct contact:

I think the only re-sourcing of art, re-vivifying it, is to make it more the joint work of man and woman. I think *the* one thing to do, is for men to have courage to draw nearer to women, expose themselves to them, and be altered by them: and for women to accept and admit men. That is the only way for art and civilisation to get a new life, a new start – by bringing themselves together, men and women – revealing themselves each to the other, gaining great blind knowledge and suffering and joy, which it will take a big further lapse of civilisation to exploit and work out. [181]

This is, perhaps, what generates the symbolism of the rainbow which may have come into the novel at this writing, a beautiful and fertilizing fusion of opposites, and a token of a covenant between man and God: 'the source of all living is in the interchange and the meeting and mingling of these two.'

The Wedding Ring was 'on its legs and going strong' [153] by 7 March 1914, and two-thirds done by 3 April. Surviving from this version are sixty-three pages of typescript (numbered 219–75 and 279–84) which were inserted into the manuscript of *The Rainbow*. These must have been written in late March. They deal with

Ursula's career as a teacher at Brinsley Street School, and correspond to most of Chapters 13 and 14 of *The Rainbow*. In *The Rainbow* manuscript they were renumbered 548–604 and 608–13, which tells us that half-way through *The Wedding Ring* Ella/Ursula reaches a stage which in *The Rainbow* she reaches only three chapters from the end.

By 22 April Lawrence had 'only some 80 pages more to write' [164]; and by 16 May he had finished *The Rainbow* ('a better title than the Wedding Ring, for the book as it is' [174]). The rainbow imagery, with its associated images of arches and colours, is so pervasive throughout *The Rainbow* and central to its structure that, for the title to have been thought appropriate at this stage, we must assume that a great deal of the novel as we know it was already there in this version. Moreover, Lawrence was later to speak of his work on the final version as 'revising *The Rainbow*' [255]. We know that in the second *Sisters* Ella had still contained aspects of Louie Burrows. In *The Rainbow* Ursula's father, Will Brangwen, is still recognizably based on Louie's father, Alfred Burrows, a handicrafts teacher, who designed the oak reredos and a stained-glass window in Cossall church (Cossethay in *The Rainbow*). Presumably he had come into the novel while Ella was still closely associated in Lawrence's mind with Louie.

In his pioneering essay 'The Marble and the Statue', Mark Kinkead-Weekes sums up the likely contents of *The Wedding Ring*:

> *The Wedding Ring* may have included, then, the story of Ella's parents, her childhood and youth, the first girlish affair, Brinsley Street School, the Schofields, University and the second affair with Skrebensky, a return to schoolteaching, and the final finding of themselves of Ella and Birkin. Of the episodes that may have caused the banning of *The Rainbow*, we can say definitely that the last relationship between Anna and Will, and Ursula's relationship with Winifred Inger, were not in the novel; and that the handling of the affair with Skrebensky had not struck Lawrence as indiscreet. [IW 379–80]

Lawrence sent the completed *Wedding Ring* to Garnett. Predictably, he did not like it. In the last letter he wrote before leaving Italy, 5 June 1914, Lawrence made a final effort to explain himself to Garnett:

> I don't think the psychology is wrong: it is only that I have a different attitude to my characters, and that necessitates a different attitude in you, which you are not as yet prepared to give. [L II 182]

He had been reading the Futurists, especially Marinetti. A few months earlier, he had been encouraged in his new mode, and, no doubt, predisposed in favour of the Futurists, by Jane Harrison's *Ancient Art and Ritual*:

Modern life is *not* simple – cannot be simple– ought not to be; it is not for nothing that we are heirs to the ages. Therefore the art that utters and expresses our emotion towards modern life cannot be simple; and, moreover, it must before all things embody not only that living tangle which is felt by the Futurists as so real, but it must purge and order it, by complexities of tone and rhythm hitherto unattempted.   [232]

Although Lawrence found Futurism 'the most self conscious, intentional, pseudo scientific stuff on the face of the earth' [L II 181], and had no desire to follow the Futurists 'down the purely male or intellectual or scientific line', he had some sympathy with their 'applying to emotions of the purging of the old forms and sentimentalities' [180], which was just what Lawrence saw himself as attempting in the field of fictional psychology. Garnett wanted him, he felt, 'to conceive a character in a certain moral scheme and make him consistent'), but for Lawrence that 'certain moral scheme' was 'dull, old, dead'. To write about socially-determined colliding egos implies a world-view Lawrence did not share. He claimed not to care what a character feels ('according to the human conception'), but only 'what she *is* as a phenomenon (or as representing some greater, inhuman will)'. The new title, *The Rainbow*, implies this belief that man can only be understood in relation to the non-human world, and to whatever we understand by God. It is significant that the next project Lawrence conceived should have been 'a little book on Hardy's people' [198], for what seemed to Lawrence of most importance at this crucial stage of his own development, was 'the quality Hardy shares with the great writers, Shakespeare or Sophocles or Tolstoi, this setting behind the small action of his protagonists the terrific action of unfathomed nature, setting a smaller system of morality, the one grasped and formulated by the human consciousness within the vast, uncomprehended and incomprehensible morality of nature or of life itself, surpassing human consciousness' [STH 29]. His defence of Hardy's characters is equally a defence of the characters he was himself creating:

They are people each with a real, vital, potential self, . . . and this self suddenly bursts the shell of manner and convention and commonplace opinion, and acts independently, absurdly, without mental knowledge or acquiescence.   [20]

Such an attitude to character must also affect the shape and dynamics of the entire novel:

Again I say, don't look for the development of the novel to follow the lines of certain characters: the characters fall into the form of some other rhythmic form, like when one draws a fiddle-bow across a fine tray delicately sanded, the sand takes lines unknown.   [L II 184]

Lawrence must have seen photographs of some of Chladni's figures, where vibrations from a fiddle-bow have moved random grains of sand into the most intricate, balanced and beautiful patterns.[3] These patterns are always concentric. Two of the chapters in *The Rainbow* are entitled 'The Widening Circle'. The same title would have been appropriate for other chapters, too, or even for the whole novel.

*

In June 1914 Lawrence and Frieda returned to England, in order to get married (Frieda's divorce having come through at last) and to search for a publisher for *The Rainbow*, which Lawrence now considered to be finished. He appointed J. B. Pinker as his agent, and the first thing Pinker did for him was to obtain an advance of £300 on *The Rainbow* from Methuen. To placate Garnett, Lawrence offered Duckworth, through him, a book of short stories, and spent the whole of July 'forging them up' [198]. In August came the declaration of war:

What a miserable world. What colossal idiocy, this war. Out of sheer rage I've begun my book about Thomas Hardy. It will be about anything but Thomas Hardy I am afraid – queer stuff – but not bad.   [212]

His rage was no doubt compounded by the news that Methuen had returned *The Rainbow* saying that it was unpublishable as it stood, presumably because of 'flagrant love passages', though the passages which were subsequently to offend the reviewers and lead to the banning of the book were yet to be written. Lawrence could not bring himself to begin to mutilate his novel. For the next three months he worked exclusively on the Hardy book, which he decided to call 'Le Gai Savaire' (published as the 'Study of Thomas Hardy').

Though Lawrence may have known something of the origin of his title among the troubadours of fourteenth-century Provence, his more immediate reference is to Nietzsche's *Die fröhliche Wissenschaft*. Lawrence had probably read or reread Thomas Common's translation, *The Joyful Wisdom*, that summer, since the first line of 'Song of a Man Who Has Come Through', written in July:

Not I, not I, but the wind that blows through me!   [CP 250] clearly derives from Nietzsche's 'Not I! Not I! but a *God* through my instrumentality!' [JW 179]. The quotation comes from a section on polytheism which must have seemed to Lawrence particularly appropriate to his own joyful thinking:

> In polytheism man's free-thinking and many-sided thinking had a prototype set up: the power to create for himself new and individual eyes, always newer and more individualised: so that it is for man alone, of all the animals, that there are no *eternal* horizons and perspectives.   [180]

In 'Le Gai Savaire' Lawrence was to write in similar rhythms:

> So on and on till we get to naked jelly, and from naked jelly to enclosed and separated jelly, from homogeneous tissue to organic tissue, on and on, from invertebrates to mammals, from mammals to man, from man to tribesman, from tribesman to me: and on and on, till, in the future, wonderful, distinct individuals, like angels, move about, each one being himself, perfect as a complete melody or a pure colour.   [STH 43]

Hardy may seem, from our perspective, a long way behind Lawrence. But *Jude the Obscure* had been published only fourteen years when Lawrence read it in 1910. Certainly among English novelists Hardy felt closer to him than any other, particularly in the degree to which his novels lent themselves to analysis in terms of what Lawrence calls (probably having picked up the term from Lascelles Abercrombie's book on Hardy) a metaphysic:

> Because a novel is a microcosm, and because man in viewing the universe must view it in the light of a theory, therefore every novel must have the background or the structural skeleton of some theory of being, some metaphysic.   [91]

'Le Gai Savaire' 'turned out as a sort of *Story of My Heart*: or a Confessio Fidei' [L II 243] because it offered Lawrence the irresistible opportunity to clarify his own metaphysic in order that his novel in progress should have a 'structural skeleton'. It is the first of many such efforts – what Lawrence was later to call his 'pollyanalytics' (a reference to Tolstoy's estate, Yasnaya Polyana, from which issued a stream of eloquent propaganda for Tolstoy's eccentric ideas):

> This pseudo-philosophy of mine – 'pollyanalytics', as one of my respected critics might say – is deduced from the novels and poems, not the reverse. The novels and poems come unwatched out of one's pen. And then the absolute need which one has for some sort of satisfactory mental attitude towards oneself and things in general makes one try to abstract some definite conclusions from one's experiences as a writer and as a man.   [F 15]

Yet in the very next paragraph he writes:

Men live and see according to some gradually developing and gradually withering vision. This vision exists also as a dynamic idea or metaphysics – exists first as such. Then it is unfolded into life and art.

In 1914 there was no metaphysic to be abstracted from already written novels; but we can watch the vision of 'Le Gai Savaire' unfolding into The Rainbow. For example, Mark Kinkead-Weekes has shown how the as-yet-unwritten Lincoln Cathedral scene in The Rainbow was to evolve from this passage in the essay:

So through the Middle Ages went on in Europe this fight against the body, against the senses, against this continual triumph of the senses. The worship of Europe, predominantly female, all through the mediaeval period was to the male, to the incorporeal Christ, as a bridegroom, whilst the art produced was the collective, stupendous emotional gesture of the Cathedrals, where a blind, collective impulse rose into concrete form. It was the profound, sensuous desire and gratitude which produced an art of architecture, whose essence is in utter stability, of movement resolved and centralised, of absolute movement, that has no relationship with any other form, that admits the existence of no other form, but is conclusive, propounding in its sum, the One Being of All.   [STH 65]

This is what Lincoln Cathedral means to Will Brangwen, though in the novel Lawrence's art enables us to share Will's experience, so that there is no need of this tortuous abstraction. However, the next paragraph of 'Le Gai Savaire', finding its appropriate symbols, moves much closer to the language of art:

There was, however, in the Cathedrals, already the denial of the Monism which the Whole uttered. All the little figures, the gargoyles, the imps, the human faces, whilst subordinated within the Great Conclusion of the Whole, still, from their obscurity, jeered their mockery of the Absolute, and declared for multiplicity, polygeny.

Whereas Lawrence has a protracted struggle to render Will's experience in novelistic terms, Anna's reaction is perfectly expressed in the language already to hand from 'Le Gai Savaire':

So she caught sight of the wicked, odd little faces carved in stone, and she stood before them arrested. These sly little faces peeped out of the grand tide of the cathedral like something that knew better. They knew quite well, these little imps that retorted on man's own illusion, that the cathedral was not absolute. They winked and leered, giving suggestion of the many things that had been left out of the great concept of the church.   [R 246]

The 'Cathedral' chapter is a wonderful example of an incident in a marital relationship enlarged, through its cathedral setting, to

119

become also a manifestation of the largest and most permanent forces at work in the world. These Lawrence interprets as the conflict of great opposites which he calls female and male, God the Father and Christ the Son, Law and Love.

His terms are confusing, since male and female are not always identified with man and woman, God the Father is female, and Law and Love do not have the meanings we should ordinarily give them. Nor is Lawrence's deployment of these terms always consistent. But we can follow the main thrust of his argument if we recognize that Law and Love relate to each other as peace to struggle, stasis to movement, continuity to change, rootedness to freedom, completeness to perfection, fulfilment to aspiration, the senses to the mind, body to spirit, nature to heaven, time to eternity, experience to knowledge. The conflict between them is permanent, though in different historical epochs one or other will gain the ascendancy. Our own era, it seemed to Lawrence, had gone far in the direction of Love. The Lawrence of a year or two earlier would certainly have deplored this, and thrown his weight unreservedly behind the Law. But in 'Le Gai Savaire' Lawrence steadfastly refuses to make value judgements. Though his thinking is as dualistic as ever, he now recognizes that the problem for modern man is not that he has simply made the wrong choice, but that he has seen life as a matter of making a choice at all. Dualistic thinking is itself the sickness as soon as we begin to attach more value to one side than the other:

If a man find incomplete satisfaction in the body, why therefore shall he renounce the body and say, it is of the devil? And why, at the start, shall a man say, 'The body, that is all, and the consummation, that is complete in the flesh, for me.'

Must it always be, that a man set out with a worship of passion and a blindness to love, and that he end with a stern commandment to love and a renunciation of passion?

Does not a youth now know that he desires the body as the via media, that consummation is consummation of body and spirit, both?

How can a man say 'I am this body', when he will desire beyond the body tomorrow? And how can a man say 'I am this spirit', when his own mouth gives lie to the words it forms? [STH 81]

To resolve this dilemma Lawrence introduces a third element, which he calls the Holy Ghost or Reconciler.

What Lawrence at this stage understands by 'reconciliation' is simply the recognition that Law and Love are equally true and necessary, that humanity defines itself and draws its energies from the permanent conflict between them, not only in eras and races, but in every human relationship, especially in marriage, and within every human psyche, for Law and Love are the systole, diastole of the human heart.

In his determination to make his metaphysic all-inclusive Lawrence recklessly subdues history, particularly the history of art, to it. The method is exasperating, but does produce startling occasional insights. Though he plays fast and loose with Renaissance art, the use he makes of Turner, the incandescence and insubstantiality of his late paintings, is both apt and convincing. Hardy's novels, too, become grist to the mill, but here there is less forcing, the insights are more consistent, culminating in an interpretation of *Jude the Obscure* which, once we have made allowances for Lawrence's jargon, seems the only interpretation that can satisfactorily account for the essentials of that novel. The events of Hardy's later novels cannot be explained in terms of traditional novelistic psychology. For example, the deaths of the children of Jude and Sue are merely grotesque and gratuitous unless we have already interpreted the relationship between their parents in some such way as Lawrence's.

'Le Gai Savaire' was probably finished in early December 1914. Its relevance to *The Rainbow* is particularly striking in the concluding pages:

> We start from one side or the other, from the female side or the male, but what we want is always the perfect union of the two. That is the Law of the Holy Spirit, the law of Consummate Marriage. That every living thing seeks, individually and collectively. Every man starts with his deepest desire, a desire for consummation of marriage between himself and the female, a desire for completeness, that completeness of being which will give completeness of satisfaction and completeness of utterance. No man can as yet find perfect consummation of marriage between himself and the Bride, be the bride either Woman or an Idea, but he can approximate to it, and every generation can get a little nearer.   [127]

That perfect union and completeness in the novel is the rainbow itself, towards which all the protagonists strive. Tom Brangwen achieves satisfaction in his marriage; but he cannot go through his marriage into utterance. Marriage is, for him, 'what we're made for', and his only 'utterance' is his befuddled speech at his daughter's wedding when he insists that 'a married couple makes one Angel' [R 176–7].

In the second generation it seems that Anna will travel much further, but on the very threshold she lapses back:

> With satisfaction she relinquished the adventure to the unknown. She was bearing her children.

There was another child coming, and Anna lapsed into vague content. If she were not the wayfarer to the unknown, if she were arrived now, settled in her builded house, a rich woman, still her doors opened under the arch of the rainbow, her threshold reflected the passing of the sun and moon, the great travellers, her house was full of the echo of journeying.

She was a door and a threshold, she herself. Through her another soul was coming, to stand upon her as upon the threshold, looking out, shading its eyes for the direction to take.   [238]

Though Lawrence is sympathetic towards Anna here, he is also disappointed in her.[4] His attitude to procreation had been clearly stated in 'Le Gai Savaire':

That she bear children is not a woman's significance. But that she bear herself, that is her supreme and risky fate: that she drive on to the edge of the unknown, and beyond. She may leave children behind, for security.

[STH 52]

In the next chapter Lawrence is less sympathetic and more succinct – 'If her soul had found no utterance, her womb had' [R 249].

Her husband Will finds his perfect utterance, his consummation and Absolute, in Lincoln Cathedral:

Here the stone leapt up from the plain earth, leapt up in a manifold, clustered desire each time, up, away from the horizontal earth, through twilight and dusk and the whole range of desire, through the swerving, the declination, ah, to the ecstasy, the touch, to the meeting and the consummation, the meeting, the clasp, the close embrace, the neutrality, the perfect, swooning consummation, the timeless ecstasy. There his soul remained, at the apex of the arch, clinched in the timeless ecstasy, consummated.

And there was no time nor life nor death, but only this, this timeless consummation, where the thrust from earth met the thrust from earth and the arch was locked on the keystone of ecstasy.   [244]

But it is a false, or partial rainbow, for it excludes too much. It repudiates earth, time, life and death in its quest for purity, perfection. It is pure Love repudiating Law. It repudiates woman, and his own body. It appropriately uses the language of orgasm, for it is a kind of spiritual masturbation. Will cannot find any lasting satisfaction in it, and swings from it to its opposite, the attempt to set up woman, physical beauty and sexual passion as an alternative Absolute. Will must experience both extremes before he can come to rest finally in a life of limited utterance and satisfaction:

His intimate life was so violently active, that it set another man in him free. And this new man turned with interest to public life, to see what part he could take in it. This would give him scope for new activity of a kind

for which he was now created and released. He wanted to be unanimous
with the whole of purposive mankind.   [280–81⁵]

Thus the three-generation structure of The Rainbow takes on a
significance far beyond the simple need to give Ursula a past; and
the recurring theme of marriage becomes far more than a testimony
to the joy and knowledge Lawrence had gained from his own
recent marriage. The opening sentence – 'The Brangwens had lived
for generations on the Marsh Farm . . .' – announces the larger
theme. The Biblical language makes the early Brangwens seem like
Old Testament patriarchs. The hypnotic pulse of the prose won-
derfully mimes the heat and repetitiveness of a life which takes its
rhythms entirely from the seasons and the cycles of birth and
death. It is a rich life, in perfect harmony with the earth and the
non-human world. It is a life lived wholly according to the Law,
unleavened by Love. The loss of this rootedness, harmony and
continuity is painful and disabling to the later generations. But the
early Brangwens are spiritually and mentally inert, and therefore
not fully human. Their lives are undifferentiated, ploughed back
into the land. They 'lived full and surcharged, their senses full fed,
their faces always turned to the heat of the blood, staring into the
sun, dazed with looking towards the source of generation, unable
to turn round . . . the Brangwen men faced inwards to the teeming
life of creation, which poured unresolved into their veins' [43]. It
is the women, at this stage, who look outwards to the world of
activity and aspiration, away from the horizontal land towards the
buildings on a distant hill, church, school and hall.

Each generation sets its sights upon what it takes to be a
rainbow, a shining doorway to completeness. Each turns out to be
false or inadequate. The hall stands for all the privileges of birth,
wealth and leisure. What first arouses Tom Brangwen from his
stupor is his encounter in Matlock with 'a small, withered foreigner
of ancient breeding' and his 'voluptuous' woman companion:

> He began to imagine an intimacy with fine-textured, subtle-mannered
> people such as the foreigner at Matlock, and amidst this subtle intimacy
> was always the satisfaction of a voluptuous woman. He went about
> absorbed in the interest and the actuality of this dream. His eyes glowed,
> he walked with his head up, full of the exquisite pleasure of aristocratic
> subtlety and grace, tormented with the desire for the girl.   [60]

The church stands for purely spiritual aspiration. Will thinks he
has found his rainbow in the 'jewelled gloom' of Lincoln Cathedral.
In the third generation, Ursula seeks her fulfilment through
education, but is repeatedly disillusioned:

Always the shining doorway ahead; and then, upon approach, always the shining doorway was a gate into another ugly yard, dirty and active and dead. Always the crest of the hill gleaming ahead under heaven; and then, from the top of the hill only another sordid valley full of amorphous, squalid activity.   [487]

The structure of *The Rainbow* is in this respect very like that of Joyce's *Portrait of the Artist as a Young Man* (which Joyce was at that moment hawking round the publishers), where each chapter ends with an impressive 'epiphany', an experience of apparently complete harmony, which the beginning of the next chapter ruthlessly exposes as illusory.[6]

The truest rainbow is that produced by the creative conflict of marriage. The actual marriages of the novel, Tom and Lydia, Will and Anna, Ursula and Birkin, both embody this conflict and symbolize the larger struggle to reconcile Law and Love. 'Le Gai Savaire' ends with Lawrence's statement of faith that out of this 'final knowledge' shall grow a 'supreme art':

There shall be the art which recognises and utters his own law; there shall be the art which recognizes his own and also the law of the woman, his neighbour, utters the glad embrace and the struggle between them, and the submission of one; there shall be the art which knows the struggle between the two conflicting laws, and knows the final reconciliation, where both are equal, two-in-one, complete. This is the supreme art, which yet remains to be done.   [STH 128]

*

On 29 October 1914, while in the middle of writing 'Le Gai Savaire', Lawrence told Pinker that he did not feel in the humour for tackling the novel, but would 'go over the whole thing thoroughly' [L II 228] in about a month's time. When he did resume work on it at the end of November, it is clear that he no longer thought of this as a piece of drudgery – simply expurgating to suit Methuen – but as an opportunity to rewrite, adding much new material (including the whole of the first-generation story), and bringing the novel into conformity with the now clarified metaphysic. On 3 December he wrote to his new friend S. S. Koteliansky ('Kot') that he was 'working *frightfully* hard – rewriting my novel' [239]. Two days later he sent the first hundred pages to Pinker:

It needs the final running through. It is a beautiful piece of work, really. It will be, when I have finished it: the body of it is so now.   [240]

Once 'Le Gai Savaire' was out of the way (at least for the time being, since Lawrence already wanted to rewrite it) he threw himself into the novel with real joy. The second batch of a hundred pages was sent to Pinker on 18 December. Lawrence had now written the first four chapters, and effectively ended the first-generation story.

At this point Lawrence took a short break from the novel to read Mrs Henry Jenner's *Christian Symbolism*. With his usual remarkable instinct he had chosen a book which put him 'more into order' [250] and fed directly into the novel. To Gordon Campbell, himself an aspiring novelist, Lawrence wrote:

> I think there is a dual way of looking at things: our way, which is to say *'I* am all. All things are but radiations out from me.' – The other way is to try to conceive the Whole, to build up a Whole by means of symbolism, because symbolism avoids the I and puts aside the egotist; and, in the Whole, to take our decent place. That was how man built the Cathedral. He didn't say 'out of my breast springs this cathedral'. But 'in this vast Whole I am a small part, I move and live and have my being' . . . The old symbols were each a word in a great attempt at formulating the whole history of the Soul of Man . . . They mean a moment in the history of my soul, if I must be personal . . . It is necessary to grasp the Whole. At last I have got it, grasping something of what the mediaeval church tried to express . . . It is very dangerous to use these old terms lest they sound like Cant. But if only one can grasp and know again as a new truth, true for one's own history, the great vision, the great, satisfying conceptions of the worlds greatest periods, it is enough. Because so it is made new. [248–9]

It is the beginning of Lawrence's realization that symbolism is not an aesthetic matter like visual imagery, nor a method of achieving some local heightening, like metaphor, but is rather an alternative language, alternative, that is, to the language of individualism, the language of our normal discourse or of science, which is analytical, atomic, specialized for reducing the world to smaller and smaller units. The language of traditional religion having lapsed into cant, for want of being made new, it is left to the imaginative writer, through his symbolism, to preserve or revive an older language, which tries 'to conceive the Whole', that is to perceive relation-ships, patterns, continuities and essentials, so that every human being is a representative of his or her sex, race, species; and every moment in every man or woman's life is a moment in the history of that species; and that species cannot escape its dependence upon the whole non-human world, and the obligation to strive towards a new conception of God.

A single symbol, like a single word, has very limited meaning, but the matrix of symbols which can be developed in a full-length novel, which can grow organically from the rich and multifarious life of such a novel, is capable of expressing a 'new truth', of making new the 'great vision'. And already, in his early chapters, Lawrence could see the emergence of potent symbols which he knew he could develop in the later generations.

In this same letter to Campbell, Lawrence further develops ideas which will find their fullest expression in the 'Cathedral' chapter:

> But do, for God's sake, mistrust and beware of these states of exaltation and ecstasy. They send you, anyone, swaying so far beyond the centre of gravity in one direction, there is the inevitable swing back with greater velocity to the other direction, and in the end you exceed the limits of your own soul's elasticity, and go smash, like a tower that has swung too far.
> Besides, there is no real truth in ecstasy. All vital truth contains the memory of all that for which it is not true: Ecstasy achieves itself by virtue of *exclusion*; and in making any passionate exclusion, one has already put one's right hand in the hand of the lie.   [246–7]

Will's ecstasy in Lincoln Cathedral is achieved by passionate exclusion of everything outside; and inevitably he swings in reaction to seek ecstasy in the flesh.

Perhaps the most important of the symbols Lawrence found in *Christian Symbolism* was the phoenix, which he immediately adopted as the badge of the 'Order of the Knights of Rananim' [252]. It is a symbol of resurrection after self-immolation. It seemed to Lawrence that the war might even be a good thing if out of its ashes could arise a new life. He felt that it was up to him to build an ark against the flood, in the hope of a new covenant with God when the flood had subsided. And this would take the form of his 'pet scheme', Rananim:

> I want to gather together about twenty souls and sail away from this world of war and squalor and found a little colony where there shall be no money but a sort of communism as far as necessaries of life go, and some real decency. It is to be a colony built up on the real decency which is in each member of the Community – a community which is established upon the assumption of goodness in the members, instead of the assumption of [. . .] badness.   [259]

Though the phoenix itself does not appear in *The Rainbow*, there are several other resurrection symbols, including the rainbow itself. There were floods at Chesham in the New Year, so that Lawrence had to wade from his cottage to the high-road. Perhaps this gave him the idea for the flood at Marsh Farm in which Tom Brangwen would be drowned. We do not know how long the

Biblical flood had been in Lawrence's mind, with its ensuing rainbow:

And God said; This is the token of the covenant which I make between me and you and every living creature that is with you, for perpetual generations;
I do set my bow in the cloud, and it shall be a token of a covenant between me and the earth.
And it shall come to pass, when I bring a cloud over the earth, that a bow shall be seen in the cloud;
And I will remember my covenant, which is between me and you and every living creature of all flesh, and the waters shall no more become a flood to destroy all flesh.   [R 371]

By 5 January Lawrence had written 300 pages, reaching the end of the long chapter 'Anna Victrix'. He was about to begin 'The Cathedral', and could see that although he had now reached, chronologically, the beginning of *The Wedding Ring*, most of what he had already written there would have to be rewritten, and, no doubt, extended, in order to follow through his new grand design. Therefore Lawrence had to make the decision 'to split the book into two volumes: it was so unwieldy' [L II 256]. And so what had been his theme for 'the original Sisters', the contrasting marriages of Ursula/Birkin and Gudrun/Gerald, is pushed out of what has become his Brangwensaga.

On 20 January Lawrence sent Pinker what pages he had ready (presumably less than a hundred) 'because tomorrow we are leaving this cottage to go to one in Sussex' [260]. This was Viola Meynell's cottage at Greatham, where the Lawrences were to live for the next six months. It was a period in which Lawrence developed many new and important friendships, with John Middleton Murry and Katherine Mansfield, Lady Ottoline Morrell and Lady Cynthia Asquith, Bertrand Russell and E. M. Forster. All his friends, new and old, were candidates for Rananim. All failed the test:

And they make me tired, these friends of mine. They seem so childish and greedy, always the immediate desire, always the particular outlook, no conception of the whole horizon wheeling round.   [266]

Lawrence's preoccupation at this time with 'the mediaeval men' led him to conceive his colony as a monastic community composed of married couples, a human ark, and to seek to exercise the same control over his friends as over the characters in his novel; or, it may be, to find some compensation for the recalcitrance of his friends in the total control he could exercise in his fictional world.

127

He demanded of Forster, for example, that he should 'yield himself up to his metamorphosis, his crucifixion, and so come to his new issuing, his wings, his resurrection, his whole flesh shining like a mote in the sunshine, fulfilled and now taking part in the fulfilment of the Whole'.

Many of the letters of this period, such as this to Forster on 28 January 1915, are virtually rough drafts of passages in the novel, or echoes of what he had just written. For example, on the previous day Lawrence had described Fra Angelico's *Last Judgement* to Lady Ottoline as 'a whole conception of the existence of Man – creation, good, evil, and its return to the eternal source' [263]. And to Forster he wrote:

It is time to gather again a conception of the Whole: as Plato tried to do, and as the mediaeval men – as Fra Angelico – a conception of the beginning and the end, of heaven and hell, of good and evil flowing from God through humanity as through a filter, and returning back to god as angels and demons. [265–6]

Within a day or two he must have written this passage about Will Brangwen:

He loved the early Italian painters, but particularly Giotto and Fra Angelico and Filippo Lippi. The great compositions cast a spell over him. How many times he had turned to Raphael's 'Dispute of the Sacrament' or Fra Angelico's 'Last Judgement' or the beautiful, complicated renderings of the Adoration of the Magi, and always, each time, he received the same gradual fulfilment of delight. It had to do with the establishment of a whole mystical, architectural conception which used the human figure as a unit. Sometimes he had to hurry home, and go to the Fra Angelico 'Last Judgement'. The pathway of open graves, the huddled earth on either side, the seemly heaven arranged above, the singing progress to paradise on the one hand, the stuttering descent to hell on the other, completed and satisfied him. He did not care whether or not he believed in devils or angels. The whole conception gave him the deepest satisfaction, and he wanted nothing more. [R 322–3]

Without the letters we could not know just how much of himself Lawrence put into Will Brangwen, a character towards whom many commentators have assumed him to be unsympathetic.

The resurrection symbolism, too, had a deeply personal meaning for Lawrence. On the last day of January he wrote to Lady Cynthia Asquith that he had spent the last five months, since the declaration of war, in the tomb: 'The War finished me: it was the spear through the side of all sorrows and hopes' [L II 268]. But now he felt newly risen:

I feel hopeful. I couldn't tell you how fragile and tender the hope is – the new shoot of life. But I feel hopeful now about the war. We shall all rise again from this grave – though the killed soldiers will have to wait for the Last Trump . . . Being risen from the dead, I know we shall all come through, rise again and walk healed and whole and new, in a big inheritance, here on earth. [269]

In the poem 'New Heaven and Earth', written at this time, Lawrence spoke of awakening 'to a new earth, a new I, a new knowledge, a new world of time'. All this could be contained by his rainbow symbol. The language of both the letter and the poem comes close to that of the closing paragraph of The Rainbow. If the novel could not now follow Ursula through to her marriage, it could at least take her through to a resurrection of this kind. Lawrence now had an ending before him towards which he could direct what remained to be written.

In fact, Lawrence had now done 450 pages, well into Ursula's story. He estimated that the whole would come to about 600. In the event the third-generation story must have required much more new material than he anticipated, for the manuscript was to come to over 700 pages.[7]

Lawrence asked Pinker to assure Methuen that there would be 'no very flagrant love passages in it' [270]. But as he completed 'First Love' and moved on to 'Shame' (the chapter to be singled out as particularly disgraceful in the court proceedings against The Rainbow) he became anxious on this score: 'I hope the publishers will not think it impossible to print as it stands' [280].

*

At the beginning of February Forster sent the Lawrences two of his books, The Celestial Omnibus, which Lawrence had asked for, saying he knew only one or two of Forster's short stories, and Howards End, which Lawrence had read at the time of its publication in 1910, but which Frieda now wanted to read. Lawrence began immediately with the first story in the book, 'Story of a Panic', and took Forster to task for his use of Pan: 'You with your "Only Connect" motto, I must say that you reach the limit of splitness here' [266]. In his previous letter Lawrence had spoken of 'good and evil flowing from God through humanity as through a filter, and returning back to god as angels and demons'. Apparently Forster had, in his reply, objected to this terminology as one-sidedly, exclusively, metaphysical. If we are still thinking of Lawrence as the Lawrence who announced his belief in the blood and the instincts in 1912, we shall be surprised to find him now turning against that position, as represented by Forster:

My angels and devils are nothing compared with your Pan. Don't you see Pan is the undifferentiated root and stem drawing out of unfathomable darkness, and my Angels and Devils are old-fashioned symbols for the flower into which we strive to burst. No plant can live towards the root. That is the most split, perverse thing of all.   [275]

It is a Lawrence hardly to be distinguished from Will Brangwen who says: 'I am just in love with mediaeval terms, that is all – Fra Angelico and Cimabue and the Saints'.

Shortly after this Lawrence must have read the third story, 'The Celestial Omnibus' itself, whose title had already provoked his curiosity. There he would have found Forster's rainbow, taken straight from Wagner, as a bridge between earth and heaven – and a rainbow closely associated with one of the other primary symbols of *The Rainbow*, horses:

And in widening curves a rainbow was spreading from the horses' feet into the dissolving mists . . . The rainbow spanned an enormous gulf . . . The horses moved. They set their feet upon the rainbow.   [CSS 49]

Lawrence may also have looked again at the crucial passage in *Howards End* from which its epigraph, 'Only Connect', is taken. There Margaret hopes she might be able to help her husband 'to the building of the rainbow bridge that should connect the prose in us with the passion':

Without it we are meaningless fragments, half monks, half beasts, unconnected arches that have never joined into a man. With it love is born, and alights on the highest curve, glowing against the grey, sober against the fire . . . By quiet indications the bridge would be built and span their lives with beauty.   [HE 174]

Surely Lawrence was affected by this passage, consciously or unconsciously, when he conceived his own rainbow. He comes particularly close when he describes Tom as 'like a broken arch thrust sickeningly out from support' [R 101]. But by the time of Forster's visit to Greatham on 10 February, Lawrence was so committed to his rainbow as a symbol of Wholeness, inclusiveness, reaching the heavens at its apex, but with both feet firmly in this world, or as the doorway to that fulfilment, that he could only have been impatient with Forster's use of it as a bridge, simply connecting opposites in the hope that they would then cease to exist, leaving only the bridge. Towards the end of his life Forster could not remember whether they discussed rainbows at Greatham, only that he got 'a good deal scolded while Frieda wailed'. Lawrence scolded Forster so much because, believing him to be 'not dead yet', he wanted to galvanize him into activity: 'I hope to see him pregnant with his own soul' [L II 282]. Lawrence could not spiritually impregnate Forster, but pregnant with her own soul is exactly how we leave Ursula at the end of *The Rainbow*.

The rainbow symbol is by no means all *The Rainbow* shares with *Howards End*. The conclusion has much in common with Forster's where Margaret, despite the red rust of London creeping over the Downs, and the Imperialist-destroyers seeming to inherit the earth, believes that all this 'may be followed by a civilization that won't be a movement, because it will rest on the earth':

> All the signs are against it now, but I can't help hoping, and very early in the morning in the garden I feel that our house is the future as well as the past.   [HE 316]

She could be speaking of the early Brangwens when she sees England's hope in men whose 'hours were ruled, not by a London office, but by the movements of the crops and the sun':

> Clumsily they carry forward the torch of the sun, until such time as the nation sees fit to take it up. Half-clodhopper, half board-school prig, they can still throw back to a nobler stock, and breed yeomen.   [301]

Lawrence surely has this at the back of his mind when Ursula, in spite of all the signs of 'a dry, brittle, terrible corruption spreading over the face of the land', 'knew that the sordid people who crept hard-scaled and separate on the face of the world's corruption were living still, that the rainbow was arched in their blood and would quiver to life in their spirit, that they would cast off their horny covering of disintegration, that new, clean, naked bodies would issue to a new germination, to a new growth, rising to the light and the wind and the clean rain of heaven' [R 548].

*

In spite of 'working gallantly' [L II 276] at the novel, Lawrence also found time and energy to talk or write at great length to all his friends from his overflowing heart. Inevitably, with so little feedback from them, he began to feel drained. While Forster was at Greatham he wrote:

> We have talked so hard – about a revolution – at least I have talked – it is my fate, God help me – and now I wonder, are my words gone like seed spilt on a hard floor, only reckoned an untidiness there.   [280]

He told Barbara Low that she was one of the very few people who listened to him:

> You see I do believe some things . . . It is not *I* who matter – it is what

is said through me . . . My heart feels like a swelling root that quite hurts.
[280]

One new friend who listened was Bertrand Russell:

He is infallible. He is like Ezekiel or some other Old Testament prophet, prophesying. Of course, the blood of his nonconformist preaching ancestors is strong in him, but he sees everything and is always right. [O 273]

Both Forster and another novelist friend, Gilbert Cannan, had seen that Lawrence was expecting far too much of his novel, of the novel-reading public, and was setting himself up for a bitter disappointment. Now, with the end of the great work in sight, Lawrence was assailed by doubts: 'What is the use of giving books to the swinish public in its present state' [L II 276]. To Russell he wrote more compassionately of that public:

An explorer is one sent forth from a great body of people to open out new lands for their occupation. But my people cannot even move – it is chained – paralysed.   [284]

Hence Lawrence's new interest in 'revolution', which he understood as the social equivalent of personal resurrection. Ursula's resurrection is expressed through the symbol of a nut breaking from its shell:

And again, to her feverish brain, came the vivid reality of acorns in February lying on the floor of a wood with their shells burst and discarded and the kernel issued naked to put itself forth.   [R 545]

In the letters to Russell we have the same image as a symbol of revolution:

There comes a point when the shell, the form of life, is a prison to the life. Then the life must either concentrate on breaking the shell, or it must turn round, turn in upon itself, and try infinite variations of a known reaction upon itself.   [L II 285]

Lawrence's vision had widened yet again: 'Any big vision of life must contain a revolutionised society, and one must fulfil ones visions, or perish' [292]. His first draft of Ursula's final rainbow vision emphasizes its revolutionary aspect:

. . . the vast forest of mankind should spring up urgent and young out of the brittle, marshy foulness of the old corruption.   [CR 71–2]

But the new emphasis had come too late to be adequately incorporated into the novel as a whole. In any case, by the time Lawrence revised the passage in proof in August, his belief in the possibility of a political revolution was already on the wane.

But at the end of February, Lawrence's enthusiasm was high. Russell had promised to take him to Cambridge, where he hoped to recruit several important figures to the revolutionary cause. And he could hardly wait to begin rewriting 'Le Gai Savaire':

> It is my revolutionary utterance. I take on a very important attitude of profundity to it, and so feel happy. Also I feel frightfully important coming to Cambridge – quite momentous the occasion is to me. I don't want to be horribly impressed and intimidated, but am afraid I may be. I only care about the revolution we shall have. [L II 300]

A wave of high optimism carried Lawrence through to the visionary conclusion of his novel. On 1 March he wrote to Lady Ottoline:

> It makes me quite glad to think how splendid it will be, when more and more of us fasten our hands on the chains, and pull, and pull, and break them apart . . . Don't think that *I* am important. But this thing which is of all of us is so important and splendid that the skies shiver with delight when it is mentioned. [297]

The following day he wrote to Viola Meynell: 'I have finished my *Rainbow*, bended it and set it firm' [299].

Life and art could not be closer. His art in the novel was, Lawrence felt, but the 'final expression' of 'that piece of supreme art, a man's life' [299].

*

If Lawrence had taken a week longer to finish *The Rainbow* it might have had a very different ending. The visit to Cambridge, instead of initiating 'the great and happy revolution', was one of the greatest disappointments of his life. On the first evening, 6 March, Lawrence had dined in hall at Russell's college, Trinity. He had sat next to the great philosopher G. E. Moore, but they had hardly spoken, largely because Lawrence was shy, and Moore did not know who Lawrence was. After dinner Lawrence was happy enough holding forth about the revolution in Russell's rooms. Among his listeners he particularly impressed and liked G. H. Hardy, the mathematician.[8] But the following morning Russell took him to meet the economist John Maynard Keynes. Lawrence knew at first sight that Keynes was homosexual. He had, of course, met homosexuals before, and reacted with mild distaste; but on this occasion it was as though he had had a vision of evil. He felt he could not possibly ally himself with such people. To Russell he wrote:

> It is true Cambridge made me very black and down. I cannot bear its smell of rottenness, marsh-stagnancy. I get a melancholic malaria. How can so sick people rise up? They must die first.

I was too sad to write my 'philosophy' (forgive the word) any more. I
can't write it when I am depressed or hopeless.   [L II 309]

The imagery Lawrence was driven to use here about his Cambridge
experience is much more characteristic of the next work of
'philosophy', 'The Crown', and the next novel, *Women in Love*, than
of 'Le Gai Savaire' and *The Rainbow*. When he did resume work on
his 'philosophy' in April, Lawrence wrote to Kot: 'I will not tell the
people this time that they are angels in disguise. I will tell them
they are dogs and swine, bloodsuckers':

> I have been fighting the powers of darkness lately. Still they prevail
> with me . . . How one has to struggle, really, to overcome this cursed
> blackness. It would do me so much good if I could kill a few people. [313]

Lawrence was physically and mentally sick. He appealed for help
from the psychiatrist David Eder. Nevertheless, he was able, in
April and May, to make significant improvements as he revised
the typescript of *The Rainbow*. On 23 April he wrote to Pinker:

> I'm afraid there are parts of it Methuen wont want to publish. He must.
> I will take out sentences and phrases, but I won't take out paragraphs and
> pages. So you must tell me in detail if there are real objections to printing
> any parts.
> You see a novel, after all this period of coming into being, has a definite
> organic form, just as a man has when he is grown. And we don't ask a
> man to cut his nose off because the public won't like it: because he must
> have a nose, and his own nose too.   [327]

The reason for Lawrence's renewed concern on this score was that
he had just that day forwarded to Lady Ottoline a batch of
typescript to which he had added extensive new material – Will's
attempted seduction of the girl he picks up at the cinema, and the
violent sensuality of his subsequent relationship with his wife.
These additions had the effect of making Will's swing from a
metaphysical to a physical absolute more realistic and psychologi-
cally convincing, and made a little clearer why the burning out of
sensual shame in his marriage should free both himself and his
wife for more purposive and creative living; but they did involve
a good deal of sexual explicitness. Lawrence remained true to his
resolve, tinkering with phrases which Methuen objected to, but
refusing to make any larger cuts or alterations. He added, prophetically, in his letter to Pinker: 'Oh God, I hope I'm not going to have
a miserable time over this book, now I've at last got it pretty much
to its real being'.

Lawrence also at this stage altered and extended 'The Cathedral'.
He realized that he had given Anna too strong a case against Will,

so that it could be read as implying simply that she was right and he wrong. In the revised version, Lawrence refrains from judging. Will's position in the first draft had been a striving 'away from time, always away from life'. Lawrence's revision of that manuscript had transformed it into something much more positive, with the new image of a seed 'containing birth and death, potential with all the noise and transition of life, . . . containing the secret of all folded between its parts' [IW 387]. Now, revising the typescript, Lawrence gives Will's vision a new poetic intensity suggesting all-inclusiveness:

> Spanned round with the rainbow, the jewelled gloom folded music upon silence, light upon darkness, fecundity upon death, as a seed folds leaf upon leaf and silence upon the root and the flower, hushing up the secret of all between its parts, the death out of which it fell, the life into which it has dropped, the immortality it involves, and the death it will embrace again.   [R 244]

Anna's response is also changed, to become more malicious and destructive, jealous of Will's rainbow and blaming him for having failed to reach her own.

In July Lawrence heavily revised his proofs, adding some of the novel's most memorable sentences. He added the last sentence of the second chapter, after Tom has taken Anna to the cowshed: 'There was the infinite world, eternal, unchanging, as well as the world of life' [118]; and Will's discovery of his vocation as a handicraft teacher is given a new dimension by adding the sentence: 'He wanted to be unanimous with the whole of purposive mankind' [281].

And the novel acquired a new conclusion. At the end of July, the Lawrences visited the Asquiths in Littlehampton. He was deeply affected by the contrast between the purity of the surrounding 'original world' and 'this Littlehampton dark and amorphous like a bad eruption on the edge of the land':

> It is a dragon that has devoured us all: these obscene, scaly houses, this insatiable struggle and desire to possess, to possess always and in spite of everything, this need to be an owner, lest one be owned. It is too horrible. One can no longer live with people: it is too hideous and nauseating. Owners and owned, they are like the two sides of a ghastly disease. One feels a sort of madness come over one, as if the world had become hell. But it is only super-imposed: it is only a temporary disease. It can be cleaned away.   [L II 375]

The vision of hell has become stronger than the belief in rebirth. This last sentence carries no conviction, only desperation. Many critics have noted a similar desperation, with its reliance on the abstraction 'Truth', in the new final sentence of the novel:

> She saw in the rainbow the earth's new architecture, the old, brittle corruption of houses and factories swept away, the world built up in a living fabric of Truth, fitting to the over-arching heaven.   [R 548]

Lawrence himself must have felt this, for in the copy of *The Rainbow* he gave to his sister Ada he replaced the whole of the last paragraph with this lame conclusion:

> And the rainbow stood on the earth. She knew that the fight was to the good. It was not to annihilation, but at last to newness. She knew in the rainbow that the fight was to the good.   [MW 381]

*

Lawrence's first use of the term 'metaphysic' had been in April 1913:

> And I am so sure that only through a readjustment between men and women, and a making free and healthy of the sex, will she [England] get out of her present atrophy. Oh Lord, and if I don't 'subdue my art to a metaphysic', as somebody very beautifully said of Hardy, I do write because I want folk – English folk – to alter, and have more sense.   [L I 544]

Lawrence was well aware that, as he put it in 'Le Gai Savaire', 'the metaphysic must always subserve the artistic purpose beyond the artist's conscious aim. Otherwise the novel becomes a treatise' [STH 91]. Though Lawrence's complex metaphysic no longer has much room for anything as straightforward as propaganda for free and healthy sex, the very fact that it has become so complex, theoretical, abstract, jargon-ridden, so close to philosophy or theology, increased the danger that unconscious artistic purposes might be subdued to its all-too-conscious demands.

There are places in the novel where Lawrence the essayist takes over, losing touch with his characters for a while. There are passages of tiresome jargon. And, most damaging, there are scenes where he seems less interested in the inner logic of human relationships than in forcing them into conformity with his structural skeleton. But for the most part, the novel is far removed from a treatise. If the larger artistic purpose of a novel is to tell the truth about people and relationships, then Lawrence's metaphysic did subserve that purpose to a surprising degree.

Lawrence's particular metaphysic had two great advantages for the novelist. In 'Le Gai Savaire' he claims that 'the degree to which the system of morality, or the metaphysic, of any work of art is submitted to criticism within the work of art makes the lasting value and satisfaction of that work' [89]. Since Lawrence's theory is that all the great conflicting opposites which motivate human beings are equally valid, all the beliefs and life-modes embodied in the novel have their countervailing opposites. It is a 'dynamic idea' [F 15] which naturally translates into the dynamics of a novel, a novel's pattern of stresses and balances, gains and losses, within individuals, between individuals, between generations, between individuals and their society, between man and God.

The experience which lends itself most perfectly to these purposes is marriage. Though Lawrence's metaphysic had developed almost beyond recognition in the two years from the conception to the completion of *The Rainbow*, it had, in fact, retained marriage as its nucleus, its determining source and symbol:

> It needs that a man shall know the natural law of his own being, then that he shall seek out the law of the female, with which to join himself as complement. He must know that he is half, and the woman is the other half; that they are two, but that they are two-in-one.   [STH 128]

Though the first-generation story was the last to be written, the marriage of Tom and Lydia has nothing of the treatise in its sensitive realization. Tom Brangwen is no illustration of a theory. In forging his links between people, and between innermost and outermost, Lawrence is working from knowledge hard-won from deeply felt and pondered experience, with a grounding in common experience and a depth of apprehension which gives him the right to claim 'La race humaine, c'est *moi*' [L II 301]. Man lives in a world of appearances, but has his being in the darkness at the centre of himself where he moves in response to unknown pressures emanating from the Great Outer Darkness which is God:

> Queer little breaks of consciousness seemed to rise and burst like bubbles out of the depths of his stillness.
> 'It's got to be done,' he said as he stooped to take the shirt out of the fender, 'it's got to be done, so why balk it?' . . .
> He did not think of anything, only knew that the wind was blowing.
>   [R 76–7]

It is not Tom Brangwen who makes this decision to propose marriage to Lydia Lensky, it is the wind that blows through him, bringing his inner darkness into creative contact with the 'starry multiplicity of the night', 'the greater ordering'.

The Brangwens move, in their crises, to rhythms which come to them out of the darkness. As his wife suffers her labour pains, Tom cannot watch, 'but his heart in torture was at peace, his bowels were glad'. When Anna becomes distraught, Tom takes her out to the barn:

> They were in another world now. The light shed softly on the timbered barn, on the white-washed walls, and the great heap of hay; instruments cast their shadows largely, a ladder rose to the dark arch of a loft. Outside there was the driving rain, inside, the softly illuminated stillness and calmness of the barn. [115]

As Tom fills the pan and 'carefully balancing the child on one arm, the pan in the other hand', feeds the beasts, making the journey several times, like a ritual, he soothes the child, and, at the same time, initiates her into this other, timeless world, with its assured fecundity and its permanent rhythms of husbandry: 'A new being was created in her for the new conditions'. This new being is created by Tom's love and care, but this is indistinguishable from the security and continuity which the physical conditions of the barn guarantee. The barn, just the place where a man would take his sobbing child on such a night, and invested with all the richness and immediacy of its colours and shadows, sounds and smells, simultaneously corresponds to and indicates the nature of the serenity at the heart of Tom's suffering, in which he is able to shelter Anna. The 'dark arch' of the loft corresponds to the rainbow arch of Tom's achieved marriage. A great weight of responsibility is lifted from Tom as he recognizes the shawl in which he has wrapped Anna as his mother's: 'He was back again in the old irresponsibility and security, a boy at home' [116]. Afterwards:

> He went downstairs, and to the door, outside, lifted his face to the rain, and felt the darkness striking unseen and steadily upon him.
> The swift, unseen threshing of the night upon him silenced him and he was overcome. He turned away indoors, humbly. There was the infinite world, eternal, unchanging, as well as the world of life. [118]

Even the rhythmic labour pains of his wife, and her moans like the sound of owls, are subsumed within this larger rhythm of birth, fruition and death, which is the Brangwen birthright.

Tom's marriage embodies some of the large achievements Lawrence claimed for marriage, yet at the same time there is a certain overripeness and bafflement. It begins by offering Tom a way forward into the unknown, but ends by providing him with a haven from the larger world beyond. His life is too full of energies which have nowhere to go, since his life is coterminous with his marriage. He fails to move outwards from his marriage towards expression and aspiration. His life lacks the vertical dimension. His body, finally, is taken back by the horizontal land in flood.

Tom and Lydia are, perhaps, the happiest couple in the novel, but Lawrence is not much interested in happiness. What he demands, on behalf of his characters, is self-effectuation, and that is a painful process. In the next generation Will and Anna reach for more, perhaps, at times, for too much. The pursuit of self-effectuation can easily degenerate into mere selfishness. They reach greater heights but cannot hold them; they plumb greater depths. What they gain in freedom and self-awareness, they lose in security and continuity. There is more conflict between them, but it is conflict, for the most part, out of which comes knowledge and development. We leave them, as the novel turns to Ursula, having achieved some real if limited fulfilment.

Lawrence makes Ursula just two years older than himself. She leaves school in 1900. We see her growing up, trying to discover how the life that is in her wants to be lived, in the complex, rapidly changing world of the twentieth century, continuity with the agricultural past gone for ever, more and more of life surrendering to the machine. In such a world emancipation is a burden, for it leaves one without bearings in a world whose values never engage with one's deepest needs. She begins to suspect that the world is conspiring to pass off on her as reality a mechanistic sham. Lawrence was deeply troubled by his own alienation. Shortly after finishing *The Rainbow* he wrote:

> But sometimes I am afraid of the terrible things that are real, in the darkness, and of the entire unreality of these things I see. It becomes like a madness at last, to know one is all the time walking in a pale assembly of an unreal world – this house, the furniture, the sky and the earth – whilst oneself is all the while a piece of darkness pulsating in shocks, and the shocks and the darkness are real. [L II 307]

An experience which, for the isolated individual, 'becomes like a madness', is transformed within the work of art into something representative, normative, largely, in this case, through a compelling image. Ursula comes to perceive that 'this world in which she lived was like a circle lighted by a lamp':

> Nevertheless the darkness wheeled round about, with grey shadow-shapes of wild beasts, and also with dark shadow-shapes of the angels, whom the light fenced out, as it fenced out the more familiar beasts of darkness. [R 487–8]

This seminal image, which provided Lawrence with a viable model of the relationship between human consciousness and the surrounding non-human world, derives, in part, from his reading, in 1913, of Bergson's *Creative Evolution*. He must have found particularly striking Bergson's claim that 'around our conceptual and logical thought' there is 'a vague nebulosity':

> Therein reside certain powers that are complementary to the understanding, powers of which we have only an indistinct feeling when we remain shut up in ourselves, but which will become clear and distinct when they perceive themselves at work, so to speak, in the evolution of nature.   [CE xiii]

The image is applicable not only to human knowledge in relation to the vast darkness of the unknown universe, but equally to the area of the human psyche which is illuminated by consciousness in relation to the fecund darkness of the unconscious. Fence out the beasts and you exclude the angels also. Or, in the last analysis, beast and angel might, for all we know, be one and the same.

Ursula's lover, Skrebensky, fails to give her access to any truer reality because 'his life lay in the established order of things':

> At the bottom of his heart his self, the soul that aspired and had true hope of self-effectuation lay as dead, still-born, a dead weight in his womb.   [R 374]

His child, in Ursula's womb, can only imprison her within 'the whole great social fabric'.

When Ursula becomes aware of her pregnancy she is strongly tempted to lapse from her struggle for self-effectuation and to take 'the life that was given'. She writes a moving letter to Skrebensky describing her former longings as crying for the moon, and asking him to take her back:

> This letter she wrote, sentence by sentence, as if from her deepest, sincerest heart. She felt that now, now, she was at the depths of herself. This was her true self, for ever. With this document she would appear before God at the Judgement Day.   [538]

If we had met this letter at the beginning of the book, we should have accepted Ursula's evaluation of it. It is true that her craving for self-satisfaction would have destroyed or driven off better men than Skrebensky, and that her attempts to create a life to fit herself are no more likely to be successful in the future than they have been in the past. It is clearly the crisis of Ursula's life, when an irrevocable decision must be made. And it seems that she has little alternative but to abandon her quest. But there is a crucial distinction to be made, as subtle and deep as that which defeats Peer Gynt – the distinction between being oneself and being oneself alone. Creating a life to fit yourself or accepting the given non-life are not the only alternatives.

In response to some deep prompting, Ursula feels impelled to go for a walk in a downpour to escape the suffocation of the house. Her overwrought, almost hysterical state, 'the seething rising to madness within her' [538], manifests itself as a hyperconsciousness of elemental life and primitive forces looming, incarnate, around her. Bushes become 'presences' . . . The great veil of rain swinging across the landscape causes it to swim and fluctuate before her eyes. 'It was very splendid, free and chaotic'. But only the chaos corresponds with her own inner experience, and so her response is fear: 'She must beat her way back through all this fluctuation, back to stability and security' [539].

Suddenly 'she knew there was something else'. At the narrative level it is a group of horses; but Lawrence makes it very clear that they are also, and primarily, externalizations of her own inner pressures and intimations:

> She did not want to know they were there . . . What was it that was drawing near her, what weight oppressing her heart? . . . In a sort of lightning of knowledge their movement travelled through her, the quiver and strain and thrust of their powerful flanks, as they burst before her and drew on, beyond . . . She went on, knowing things about them. She was aware of their breasts gripped, clenched narrow in a hold that never relaxed, she was aware of their red nostrils flaming with long endurance, and of their haunches, so rounded, so massive, pressing, pressing, pressing to burst the grip upon their breasts, pressing for ever till they went mad, running against the walls of time, and never bursting free. Their great haunches were smoothed and darkened with rain. But the darkness and wetness of rain could not put out the hard, urgent, massive fire that was locked within these flanks, never, never. [539–40]

In these horses repressed energies have turned violent and threatening – 'clenched', 'bursting', 'mad', like Ursula's inner life. The rhythms of the prose mime those of the horses, which in turn, as they approach, sheer off, circle, regroup, approach again, mime the rhythms of a mind struggling with its deepest problems and promptings, and moving, unconsciously, towards a resolution:

> The mind makes curious swoops and circles. It touches the point of pain or interest, then sweeps away again in a cycle, coils round and approaches again the point of pain or interest. There is a curious spiral rhythm, and the mind approaches again and again the point of concern, repeats itself, goes back, destroys the time-sequence entirely, so that time ceases to exist, as the mind stoops to the quarry, then leaves it without striking, soars, hovers, turns, swoops, stoops again, still does not strike, yet is nearer, nearer, reels away again, wheels off into air, even forgets, quite forgets, yet again turns, bends, circles slowly, swoops and stoops

again, until at last there is the closing-in, and the clutch of a decision or a resolve.   [P 249–50]

We hardly need the gloss provided by *Fantasia of the Unconscious* to realize that the horses represent 'the great sensual male activity':

A man has a persistent passionate fear-dream about horses. He suddenly finds himself among great, physical horses, which may suddenly go wild. Their great bodies surge madly round him, they rear above him, threatening to destroy him. At any minute he may be trampled down . . . Examining the emotional reference we find that the feeling is sensual, there is a great impression of the powerful, almost beautiful physical bodies of the horses, the nearness, the rounded haunches, the rearing.   [F 170–71]

This activity is normally repressed and seen as a menace to the soul's automatism, 'Whereas the greatest desire of the living spontaneous soul is that this very male sensual nature, represented as a menace, shall be actually accomplished in life'.

Ursula's experience with the horses stands in direct contrast to her earlier dance of death with Skrebensky under a great white moon. That moon corresponds to 'the fierce, white, cold passion in her heart':

She was cold and hard and compact of brilliance as the moon itself, and beyond him as the moonlight was beyond him, never to be grasped or known.   [R 366]

It is a denial of relationship, blanching, sterile and reductive, confirming her in her solipsism and licence, her 'cold liberty to be herself, to do entirely as she liked' [365]. In the horses she must recognize what was not in Skrebensky to be recognized, 'the triumphant, flaming, overweening heart of the intrinsic male' [369], the potency of life beyond her own will and self, to which she must submit if she is ever to come into being.

The novel has come full circle. Ursula, in her striving for expression, has quite lost the unselfconscious harmony with those energies which had characterized her ancestors:

They mounted their horses, and held life between the grip of their knees, they harnessed their horses at the wagon, and, with hand on the bridle-rings, drew the heaving of the horses after their will.   [42]

The horse symbolizes not only the 'male sensual nature', but all potency which is god-given:

Far back, far back in our dark soul the horse prances. He is a dominant symbol: he gives us lordship: he links us, the first palpable and throbbing link with the ruddy-glowing Almighty of potency: he is the beginning even of our godhead in the flesh. And as a symbol he roams the dark underworld meadows of the soul. He stamps and threshes in the dark fields of your soul and of mine. [A 101]

Ursula cannot escape the extinction of her ego. Her fall from the oak tree is the breaking of all her connections with 'the old, hard barren form of bygone living', which must precede the issuing of the 'naked, clear kernel' of herself, like an acorn bursting from its shell [R 547]. It is a leap taken into the beyond, blindly, with no assurances. She is terribly ill, and loses her child. But the experience enables that which she is to come forth. Ursula glimpses something of the eternal and unchangeable that she is, that life is, that others may be:

Who was she to have a man according to her own desire? It was not for her to create, but to recognize a man created by God. The man should come from the Infinite and she should hail him. She was glad she could not create her man. She was glad she had nothing to do with his creation. She was glad that this lay within the scope of that vaster power in which she rested at last. The man would come out of Eternity to which she herself belonged. [547]

There is a symbolic logic in the sequence horses–acorn–rainbow. There is fruitless conflict, leading to eruptions of violence, between the urgent massive fire locked within the flanks of the horses and the pouring rain which seeks to extinguish it. But that fire which, being denied, can only escape as lightning, is, nevertheless, a link of divine power between heaven and earth. 'The bluish, incandescent flash of the hoof-iron, large as a halo of lightning round the knotted darkness of the flanks' [541] is but a larger, more dynamic manifestation of the flash of eyes and fangs and swords of angels Ursula had earlier glimpsed in the darkness, 'lordly and terrible and not to be denied' [488]. The bursting of the hard shell which denies or makes impossible the link between innermost and outermost makes it possible for the warring opposites of fire and water to flow together as an arched and gleaming rainbow, linking a new heaven and new earth.

Nevertheless, we cannot but feel some forcing in the concluding pages. Intimations of rebirth are appropriate, and a sense that Ursula is now ready to meet her Mr Birkin. But the psychological realism and power of the horses episode hardly prepares us for a message direct from God (otherwise known as Eternity, Infinity and Truth), as in the days of Noah, that all shall be well, and that she, Ursula Brangwen, shall be sent one of the Sons of God, created uniquely for her. At the beginning of *Women in Love* a man does descend upon Ursula somewhat like a deus ex machina, his face 'gleaming like fire'. But it is only Rupert Birkin, Ministry Inspector: we expected at least a centaur.

Here, at last, we come up against the one aspect of Lawrence's metaphysic which is not subject to criticism within the work, his belief that the Holy Spirit or Reconciler is a benevolent external power with some of the characteristics of the Christian God. What had been hinted at earlier in the novel in phrases such as 'submissive to the greater ordering' [75], is now insisted on: 'a man created by God', 'The man should come from the Infinite', 'that vaster power in which she rested at last', 'the creation of the living God' [547]. There is a note of desperation in Lawrence's assertiveness. He is not putting his thumb in the balance; he is throwing his whole weight behind the insistence 'that all souls of all things do but compose the body of God, and that God indeed Shall *Be*' [L II 273]. The capitalization and underlining here betray a desperation which stems from Lawrence's fear that if this faith were ever lost, the powers of darkness would triumph.

Hardy, too, believed in a greater ordering, but not that it was good. And that, according to Lawrence, made his art 'execrable in the extreme' [STH 93], 'for nothing in his work is so pitiable as his clumsy efforts to push events into line with his theory of being'. Hardy's protagonists, he says, 'have not the necessary strength: the question of their unfortunate end is begged in the beginning' [50]. But is not a decision to give your characters the necessary strength equally question-begging?

Lawrence would argue that he had *proved* that life can be great. He had known suffering and frustration, but in his moment of greatest need fate had given him Frieda, and everything which had gone before had fallen into place as a necessary prelude and preparation. From this he generalized that life actively concerns itself with the fulfilment of those who have the courage to submit wholly to it. But Hardy was not pessimistic out of sheer perversity. The prevalence in his work of betrayal and frustration, the succession of wasted lives, the close correlation of misery and marriage, testify to a life which enforced such generalizations. This was life as he had experienced it, seen it in his friends, heard of it in village gossip and read about it in the newspapers.

Hardy, Bennett, Chehov, Mann, Tolstoy, and many other great writers who made Lawrence impatient, insisted on writing about men and women who did not despise life and yet were denied it. There is in Lawrence remarkably little undeserved suffering, loneliness, breakdown, loss, which is not a prelude to a resurrection. His metaphysic therefore excludes a large part of what has traditionally been regarded as tragic experience.

For criticism of Ursula's forced epiphany and a counterweight to Lawrence's optimistic metaphysic, we must wait for the sequel, *Women in Love*.

*

The Rainbow was published on 30 September 1915. The first important review appeared the following day in the *Standard*. Lawrence could hardly have wished for anything better:

> [The Brangwens] are strong as they rise from the soil on which for generations they have been settled, but there are influences of unrest which twist their passions this way and that. Education, the spread of a colliery town, the marriage of one of them with a Polish woman, religion, yet more education, have their necessary effect on the old stock. Something comes into them which may be called degeneracy, but is more likely a painful and tortuous development. It is not a comfortable book. Its very foundation is an agonizing struggle between bodies and minds. [CH 89]

This anonymous reviewer thought that Lawrence had enough genius to excuse his defiance of all conventions, but his fear that the novel might 'cause offence and be condemned' proved only too true. On 5 October Robert Lynd called it 'a monotonous wilderness of phallicism' [92]. On 22 James Douglas described the characters as 'immeasurably lower than the lowest animal in the Zoo' [93]. He accused Lawrence of gloating over 'unfathomable corruption'. That Douglas should relate the novel to the war was particularly significant in view of what was to follow:

> A thing like *The Rainbow* has no right to exist in the wind of war. It is a greater menace to our public health than any of the epidemic diseases which we pay our medical officers to fight . . . The young men who are dying for liberty are moral beings. They are the living repudiation of such impious denials of life as *The Rainbow*. The life they lay down is a lofty thing. It is not the thing that creeps and crawls in this novel. [94–5]

The following day Clement Shorter, while claiming to be in favour of 'frankness and freedom in literature', blamed the publishers for perpetrating such a book: 'There is no form of viciousness, of suggestiveness, that is not reflected in these pages' [96–7].

The novel had clearly triggered an outburst of insanity in these reviewers. James Douglas's own psychological problems are transparent in his review: 'Why open all the doors that the wisdom of man has shut and bolted and double-locked?' [94]. But unfortunately for Lawrence, that kind of incipient insanity passed for normality in England in 1915.

Even Murry, who was posing at the time as Lawrence's 'lieutenant', sided with these critics:

I could not understand it at all. I disliked it on instinct. There was a warm, close, heavy promiscuity of flesh about it which repelled me, and I could not understand the compulsion which was upon Lawrence to write in that fashion and of those themes; neither could I understand his surprise and dismay that the critics were out for his blood. As far as mere feeling went, I felt with them. I happened to be friends with Lawrence, and Robert Lynd didn't: that was about the only difference.   [BTW 351]

With friends like that, Lawrence needed no enemies.

On 3 November the Director of Public Prosecutions initiated proceedings against Methuen, requiring them to show why the 1,011 copies of *The Rainbow* which remained in their hands (of the 2,500 printed) should not be destroyed. Perhaps, as Lawrence believed, the National Council of Public Morals instigated the prosecution. But when Philip Morrell raised the matter in the House of Commons, the Home Secretary's brief had on it a mysterious note in red ink: 'As to a Mrs Weekley living at address of D. H. Lawrence, see 352857' [MW 241], indicating some Home Office involvement in the case. The government was anxious to discredit writers known to be against the war. Lawrence's dedication of *The Rainbow* to Frieda's sister Else cannot have helped. The magistrate, Sir John Dickinson, had lost his son at the front only six weeks earlier.

At the hearing on 13 November, Herbert Muskett, prosecuting, quoted Douglas and Shorter, and described the novel as 'a mass of obscenity . . . wrapped up in language which he supposed would be regarded in some quarters as an artistic and intellectual effort'. Methuen's representative regretted publishing the book, and blamed Lawrence (who had not even been informed of the proceedings) for not carrying out the required alterations. Thus Methuen diverted all the obloquy onto the absent Lawrence and avoided a fine. Legend has it that the 1,011 copies were burned by the public hangman outside the Royal Exchange.

A few friends rallied round, proposing various courses of action, but Lawrence lacked the energy for a fight:

As for the novel, I am not surprised. Only the most horrible feeling of hopelessness has come over me lately – I feel as if the whole thing were coming to an end – the whole of England, of the Christian era: as if ours was the age only of Decline and Fall. It almost makes one die. I cannot bear it – this England, this past . . . I wonder if ever I shall have strength to drag my feet over the next length of journey.   [L II 433]

FIVE

'BLASPHEMOUS LIVING': THE GENESIS OF *WOMEN IN LOVE*

More has been written about *Women in Love* than any other work of Lawrence's, but radical differences of interpretation are still possible. It may be that Lawrence failed to impose artistic coherence on so much diverse material; or it may be that the novel contains more than any one reader can digest. I believe that our sense of the novel's richness and coherence, our recognition of its 'characteristics', can be enhanced by tracing the stages of its composition in relation to the stages of Lawrence's life out of which it grew.

The major novel is a unique form in the world of art in that it can occupy the writer for several years in the course of which not only his concept of the novel in progress but his whole mood and metaphysic can undergo radical change. A long novel which has passed through several drafts contains and sometimes exposes several layers of its author's development, like geological strata. The finished novel is often quite different from anything the author had in mind at the outset. Later preoccupations and insights pull against the original ones, giving the novel much of its energy, complexity and capacity for growth.

Nowhere is this process more evident than in *Women in Love*. When he conceived the novel, as *The Sisters*, in the spring of 1913, the world was at Lawrence's feet. It was to be an epithalamium expressing his joy in his own marriage, his sense that 'this is the best I have known, or ever shall know' [L I 553], and his confidence that he had the cure for England's atrophy – 'a readjustment between men and women, and a making free and healthy of the sex' [544]. The war came as a great blow to Lawrence, but the early months of it were not enough to extinguish his tender and fragile hopes for the future. He was able to finish *The Rainbow* in March 1915 on a surge of buoyant optimism, and to launch it with the highest expectations: 'Now off and away to find the pots of gold at its feet' [L II 299].

But the year between completing *The Rainbow* and taking up *Women in Love* was to be the year of Lawrence's 'nightmare', a year of disappointments, frustrations, humiliations. *The Rainbow* was suppressed; the Lawrences began to suffer seriously from poverty; no new imaginative work engaged Lawrence's attention; there was carnage at the front, and he saw moral disintegration at home. It was Lawrence's thirtieth year, the end of his youth, and the end of his faith in European civilization. In November 1915 he wrote:

I think there is no future for England: only a decline and fall. That is the dreadful and unbearable part of it: to have been born into a decadent era, a decline of life, a collapsing civilisation. [441]

By January 1916 he felt spiritually nauseated by 'this banquet of vomit, this life, this England, this Europe' [500]. In 'The Crown' Lawrence had been able to welcome the destructive process as a necessary preliminary to any new phase of creation: 'Corruption will at last break down for us the deadened forms, and release us into the infinity' [P II 403]. Now he had difficulty holding on to any such consolation: 'it is rather terrible this being confronted with the end, only with the end' [L II 501].

So, in April 1916, Lawrence embarked on his apocalyptic novel which would 'contain the results in one's soul of the war'. It is difficult to imagine how he could have contemplated doing this in the form of a rewriting of the original *Sisters*, with its opposite, affirmative thrust, and its cast of characters drawn from those now-so-far-off Eastwood days. We do not know exactly how much of the old material Lawrence used. We know that *The Sisters* probably began with the meeting of Birkin and Ursula (then called Ella) when, in his capacity as Ministry Inspector, he visits her in her classroom. Later in the story they were to marry. Birkin was, of course, Lawrence himself. Ella was based partly on Frieda and partly on Louie Burrows (a 'graft' which had already caused difficulties). In contrast with their successful marriage was to be the failed relationship (though possibly also ending in marriage) between Gudrun and Gerald. Gudrun was modelled partly on Ethelreda Burrows and partly on Frieda's sisters. There was the impact of these 'remarkable females' on Beldover. Gerald Crich was a very detailed and accurate portait of Major Thomas Philip Barber, the Eastwood coal-owner. The relationship of Gerald to his parents, the accidental shooting of his brother in childhood, and the dual fatality at the water-party were all part of the Barber family history, well-known to everyone in Eastwood. Hermione was probably already there, called Ethel, and modelled on Jessie Chambers. At the end the two couples went to Switzerland (or at least Gerald and Gudrun did), where Gudrun apparently met Herr Loerke.[1]

What must be new is everything which derives from Lawrence's post-1913 relationships, experiences and reading. Gerald and Gudrun acquire aspects of John Middleton Murry and Katherine Mansfield; Hermione acquires all the external features of Lady Ottoline Morrell; Loerke acquires aspects of Mark Gertler; and a new set of characters, Halliday (Philip Heseltine) and the Soho crowd, appear. Though the 'grafting' of several real people onto one fictional character was by now Lawrence's well-established procedure, he had not previously attempted to graft two such different characters as Major Thomas Philip Barber and John Middleton Murry.

The complexity of characterization is matched by a complexity of structure, symbolism and language. Lawrence told his agent Pinker to tell Arnold Bennett that 'all rules of construction hold good only for novels which are copies of other novels' [L II 479]. What Bennett called 'faults' Lawrence called 'characteristics'; and *Women in Love* is rich in such formal and stylistic experiments. Within the novel is Birkin's complex metaphysic (deriving largely from 'The Crown' and the lost 'Goats and Compasses'), which he can express only in such symbolic jargon as 'star-equilibrium' and 'river of dissolution'; but the novel as a whole constitutes a running critique of that metaphysic, and Birkin continually modifies it under the pressure of his experiences.

As if the novel did not confront the reader with enough genuine difficulties, all trade editions of the novel have had extremely corrupt texts until the publication of the Penguin English Library edition in 1982. In the first English printing of the novel, Heseltine and his mistress (known generally as Puma) were very recognizably portrayed. Heseltine threatened libel action, and Secker asked Lawrence to make changes for the second impression. In April 1916 Heseltine had moved into a flat where he had several African carvings. One of these is described in detail and carries great symbolic weight in the 'Totem' chapter. The revised text changes its provenance from West Africa to the West Pacific in that chapter. But Lawrence apparently forgot that the carving is discussed again in 'Moony', where it remained African. This confusion was perpetuated in all English editions for sixty years.

In May 1913 Lawrence spoke of the relatively uncomplicated original *Sisters* as 'like a novel in a foreign language I don't know very well – I can only just make out what it is about' [L I 544]. It is hardly surprising that *Women in Love* should have been almost incomprehensible to many of its original readers. The reviewer in the *Westminster Gazette* found the two heroines 'almost as indistinguishable in character and conversation as they are in their amours and their clothing' [CH 167]. Even Birkin and Gerald became for him towards the end 'one and the same young man'. Murry, who had actually lived with the Lawrences during the writing of the novel, boasted in his review of having given three whole days to it, in spite of his repulsion and weariness:

we have striven with all our power to understand what he means by the experience x; we have compared it with the experience y, which takes place between the other pair of lovers, Gudrun and Gerald; we can see no difference between them . . . we can discern no individuality whatever in the denizens of Mr Lawrence's world. We should have thought that we should be able to distinguish between male and female, at least. But no! Remove the names, remove the sedulous catalogues of unnecessary clothing . . . and man and woman are indistinguishable as octopods in an aquarium tank. [170]

To many of the reviewers it seemed that most of the characters were mad. Lawrence had defended Hardy's characters against the similar charge that they do 'quite unreasonable things'. They 'explode out of the convention . . . into something quite madly personal':

They are people each with a real, vital, potential self, even the apparently wishy-washy heroines of the earlier books, and this self suddenly bursts the shell of manner and convention and commonplace opinion, and acts independently, absurdly, without mental knowledge or acquiescence.
[STH 20]

We are horrified by the Soviet policy of consigning dissidents to lunatic asylums, but this is only an extreme manifestation of our own society's tendency to define madness as inability to live within that society's norms. This makes society a closed, self-validating system. But Lawrence's conviction was that society itself, England, Europe, was mad, and that the primary function of the artist was to throw bombs into it to break the closed system and offer an escape route to sanity in the superior reality of the world of the imagination:

Only I feel, that even if we are all going to be rushed down to extinction, one must hold up the other, living truth, of Right, and pure reality, the reality of the clear, eternal spirit. One must speak for life and growth, amid all this mass of destruction and disintegration. [L II 394]

There is a dilemma here, several dilemmas inside each other. For perhaps the madness is not just a local and temporary aberration, but the death-throes of a doomed civilization, the final stages of a long process of dissolution which must be gone through, which cannot be averted, which, in the long term, is a desirable purging of the world prior to the advent of some new cycle of evolution. In that case, better to hasten it than resist.

Even if this were not so, if our world could still be saved, what claim has the artist to be its saviour, since he is himself a product of its madness? Can a man stand outside his society? 'We roam in the belly of our era' [P II 367]. The fish is in the water and the water is in the fish. To work in the medium of the novel is to put one's work into the hands of that society in the form of agents, publishers, libraries, reviewers, censors, societies for the protection of public morals, and, of course, the law. Lawrence hoped to bypass all this by founding, with Philip Heseltine, a publishing company, Rainbow Books and Music. The preliminary pamphlet stated:

It is proposed to attempt to issue privately such books and musical works as are found living and clear in truth; such books as would either be rejected by the publisher, or else overlooked when flung into the trough before the public. This method of private printing and circulation would also unseal those sources of truth and beauty which are now sterile in the heart, and real works would again be produced.   [NI 349]

Heseltine described it as a 'despairing project'. The circular elicited only thirty replies.

But even if such books could be freely published and distributed and find a readership, could those readers then walk after the author into freedom? 'If I know that humanity is chained to a rock, I cannot set forth to find it new lands to enter upon' [L II 284]. All these doubts and contradictions are built into the structure of the novel.

*

In the same letter to Viola Meynell in which he announced that he had finished *The Rainbow*, Lawrence looked forward with equal enthusiasm to his next project:

I am going to begin a book about Life – more rainbows, but in different skies – which I want to publish in pamphlet form week by week – my initiation of the great and happy revolution.   [299]

His partners in this enterprise were to be John Middleton Murry and Bertrand Russell. A few days later was to come the 'momentous' visit to Cambridge, where he hoped to recruit to the cause some of the foremost minds in the country. In the event he hated Cambridge 'beyond expression':

It was one of the crises of my life. It sent me mad with misery and hostility and rage.   [321]

For weeks he struggled with the Powers of Darkness. He even wrote describing his symptoms to the psychiatrist David Eder – 'he must cure me' [317].

Out of this sickness came some of the first of the images which were to reappear in *Women in Love*. There Loerke is to be described as 'like a rat, in the river of corruption, just where it falls over into the bottomless pit' [WL 522–3]. On 24 March 1915 Lawrence wrote to Lady Ottoline Morrell:

> I can imagine the mind of a rat, as it slithers along in the dark, pointing its sharp nose . . . It contains a principle of evil . . . I saw it so plainly in Keynes at Cambridge, it made me sick.   [L II 311]

What had sent Lawrence mad in Cambridge had not been any general disappointment in the people he met there as potential revolutionaries, but a specific and instantaneous vision of evil at the moment when Keynes emerged from his bedroom and Lawrence sensed his homosexuality:

> And as he stood there gradually a knowledge passed into me, which has been like a little madness to me ever since. And it was carried along with the most dreadful sense of repulsiveness – something like carrion – a vulture gives me the same feeling. I begin to feel mad as I think of it – insane.   [321]

In this remarkable letter to David Garnett Lawrence described 'men loving men' as 'triumphant decay' and 'this blasphemy against love', advising Garnett to 'love a woman, and marry her, and make life good, and be happy'. He claimed that his objection to homosexuality was not a matter of 'moral disapprobation':

> Why is there this horrible sense of frowstiness, so repulsive, as if it came from deep inward dirt – a sort of sewer – deep in men like K[eynes] and B[irrell] and D[uncan] G[rant].   [320]

And to Koteliansky he wrote:

> These horrible little frowsty people, men lovers of men, they give me such a sense of corruption, almost putrescence, that I dream of beetles.   [323]

In the past Lawrence had taken a very calm and rational attitude to homosexuality. In 1913 he had written to Henry Savage:

> I should like to know why nearly every man that approaches greatness tends to homosexuality, whether he admits it or not: so that he loves the *body* of a man better than the body of a woman – as I believe the Greeks did, sculptors and all, by far. I believe a man projects his own image on another man, like on a mirror. But from a woman he wants himself re-born, re-constructed. So he can always get satisfaction from a man, but it

is the hardest thing in life to get ones soul and body satisfied from a woman, so that one is free from oneself. And one is kept by all tradition and instinct from loving men, or a man – for it means just extinction of all the purposive influences. [115]

Though Lawrence is here tacitly admitting his own tendency to homosexuality, he does not fear it because he feels that the taboos against it and his own positive commitment to his marriage are strong enough to protect him:

Because the source of all life and knowledge is in man and woman, and the source of all living is in the interchange and the meeting and mingling of these two: man-life and woman-life, man knowledge and woman-knowledge, man-being and woman-being. [181]

Lawrence was so firmly committed to this encounter with the other that he condemned not only homosexuality but also masturbation and promiscuity under the term Sodomy: 'Sodomy only means that a man knows he is chained to the rock, so he will try to get the finest possible sensation out of himself' [285]. The occasion of this letter was a recent visit to Greatham by E. M. Forster, who had seemed to Lawrence just such a chained man, 'bound hand and foot bodily':

But why can't he act? Why can't he take a woman and fight clear to his own basic, primal being? [283]

Lawrence saw homosexuality, the 'blasphemy against love', as only a symptom of a larger blasphemy against life itself: 'he does not believe that any beauty or any divine utterance is any good any more'.

Lawrence's own faith in both marriage and 'divine utterance' was, however, under severe strain at that time. Lawrence and Frieda were quarrelling incessantly. Four months later they decided to live apart for a while. During their separation Lawrence read Burnet's *Early Greek Philosophy*, which made him decide to be rid of all his 'christian religiosity' and 'drop all about God' [364–5]. The only mention of God in *Women in Love* was to be Birkin's casual phrase ' – seeing there's no God' [WL 110].

A week after Forster's visit to Greatham came a visit from Murry. Lawrence nursed Murry through an attack of flu. Then they quarrelled over Murry's friendship with Gordon Campbell, which had just ended. Murry later recalled:

And, it seems to me now as I look back, that from that time onwards whatever capacity I possessed for affection towards a man was turned towards Lawrence himself. That, I suppose, was what he wanted. [RL 55]

153

Lawrence was apparently troubled by his feelings for Murry:

All I wanted from Lawrence was the warmth and security of personal affection. Up to a certain point he also wanted that between us; but his consciousness resented it. What his consciousness required was an impersonal bond between us: that we should be servants of the same purpose, disciples of the same idea. [NI 276]

The revelation of evil Lawrence had in Keynes's rooms a fortnight later was not simply a revelation of corruption in Keynes, or in Cambridge, or even in England, but the sudden recognition that it was everywhere: a 'massive creeping hell' had somehow been let loose upon the world, transforming men into insects. And he is no longer sure that he has anything to set against it. He can feel it working in himself as a desire to kill [315], or to 'walk over the edge of the cliff' [335], or, perhaps, to abandon his faith in marriage in favour of a relationship with a man, which must, by his lights, be ultimately deadly.

He began to have portentous nightmares. As early as May 1915 Lawrence begins to develop the image of London as 'some hoary massive underworld, a hoary ponderous inferno'. He is clearly thinking of Dante:

The traffic flows through the rigid grey streets like the rivers of Hell through their banks of dry, rocky ash. [339]

Anticipating Eliot's *Waste Land*, Lawrence drew on Dante in the same way. It is not known when he read Dante's *Inferno*, but certainly its structure and imagery provided him at this time with a way of looking at the world, and, a year later, with a way of structuring his novel. All the other characters in *Women in Love* are fully related to their past, their class, their environment; Birkin has no past, no class and no home. He seems to have a passe-partout, moving freely through all the book's milieux, but always as outsider, visitor, almost voyeur. And those milieux are the levels of hell. A hell is any way of life which is so encased, fixed in falsity, that it is cut off from the creative sources, disintegrates from the centre until it becomes an unreal ghost life.

At first it seemed to Lawrence that London was the locus of evil, the very lowest level of hell. On his train journey to London with Gerald, Birkin quotes 'Love Among the Ruins', where Browning imagines that 'a city great and gay . . . our country's very capital' is obliterated after 'whole centuries of folly, noise and sin', leaving only a 'plenty and perfection of grass'. As they pass through the 'huge arch of the station' and enter 'the tremendous shadow of the town', Birkin asks Gerald: 'Don't you feel like one of the damned?'

[WL 113]. When, years later, Lawrence recalled his 'nightmare' in *Kangaroo*, it was in terms of something which had originated in London:

It was in 1915 the old world ended. In the winter 1915–1916 the spirit of the old London collapsed; the city, in some way, perished, perished from being a heart of the world, and became a vortex of broken passions, lusts, hopes, fears, and horrors. The integrity of London collapsed, and the genuine debasement began, the unspeakable baseness of the press and the public voice, the reign of that bloated ignominy, *John Bull*.   [K 240]

It is as though the collapse of London created an opening and breeding ground for evil, let loose a 'massive creeping hell' to spread over all England, all Europe: 'But hell is slow and creeping and viscous, and insect-teeming: as is this Europe now – this England' [L II 331]. It seemed to Lawrence that Rupert Brooke, 'a Greek God under a Japanese Sunshade, reading poetry in his pyjamas, at Grantchester, at Grantchester, upon the lawns where the river goes' [330–31], was an extreme manifestation of the pose, the glamorous falsity of the past, the endless Edwardian garden-party. Brooke's death filled Lawrence with 'the sense of the fatuity of it all . . . O God Oh God, it is all too much of a piece: It is like madness' [330–31]. Lawrence's own near-madness arose from his sense that there was no alternative, no new world; that Brooke was but the forerunner, the soldiers dying at the front were but the first victims of a coming universal death:

I cannot tell you how icy cold my heart is with fear. It is as if we were all going to die.   [343]

The story Lawrence wrote that June, 'England, My England', expresses this fear of the cold touch of death. He described it as 'a story about the Lucases . . . the story of most men and women who are married today – of most men at the war, and wives at home' [386]. It begins by taking an ironic tone towards such families, essentially English in their niceness and ineffectuality. But in the last few pages, after the outbreak of war, the irony disappears as Lawrence finds himself more and more closely identified with the hero, Egbert. Egbert's last thoughts, as he lies dying in No Man's Land, are exactly Lawrence's in many of his letters of that period:

Better the terrible work should go forward, the dissolving into the black sea of death, in the extremity of dissolution, than that there should be any reaching back towards life.   [SSS 258]

The words of Genesis took on a new immediacy for him:

And GOD saw that the wickedness of man was great in the earth, and that every imagination of the thoughts of his heart was only evil continually.

And God looked upon the earth, and, behold, it was corrupt; for all flesh had corrupted his way upon the earth.

And God said unto Noah, The end of all flesh is come before me; for the earth is filled with violence through them; and, behold, I will destroy them with the earth.

In the same letter as the Dante reference, Lawrence wrote:

It would be nice if the Lord sent another Flood and drowned the world. Probably I should want to be Noah. [L II 339]

One of the titles Lawrence was later to consider for *Women in Love* was *Noah's Ark*. In April 1915 he wrote:

How dark my soul is! I stumble and grope about and don't get much further. I suppose it must be so. All the beauty and light of the days seems like an iridescence on a very black flood. Mostly one is underneath: sometimes one rises like the dove from the ark: but there is no olive branch. [330]

Unlike Dante, Lawrence often mistook hell for paradise. Unlike Lot, he could not resist looking back hopefully, and was turned to salt by his slow and painful and humiliating disillusion.

For example, Lady Ottoline's new home, Garsington Manor, which he visited in June, seemed to him at first a haven, a perfect retreat from the hellish world. It rekindled his hopes of Rananim:

That wonderful lawn, under the ilex trees, with the old house and its exquisite old front – it is *so* remote, so perfectly a small world to itself, where one *can* get away from the temporal things to consider the big things. We must draw together. Russell and I have really got somewhere. We must bring the Murrys in. [359]

The fly in the ointment was Frieda. Lawrence assured Lady Ottoline that Frieda would 'come round'. But Frieda was not so easily seduced by Lawrence's rhetoric and enthusiasm as Russell, Murry and Aldous Huxley. She knew that it was a product of desperation. She knew also that Lawrence's desperate need for allies would lead him into extraordinary blindness where his judgement of their suitability was concerned. Ottoline herself was much more realistic:

I should like to make this place into a harbour, a refuge in the storm, where those who haven't been swept away could come and renew themselves and go forth strengthened. But people are very difficult to manage. The young Cambridge men are so critical and superior and disdainful, and lift up their hands in horror at men like D. H. Lawrence who have fire and genius. They tolerate Bertie because he was at

Cambridge and is of course intensely intellectual. I feel despondent about it all. People are so rigid, and only like to move in little circles on little toy railway lines surrounded by their admirers, they don't want to venture forth, and are afraid of possible persecution. [O 280]

Later, when Lawrence took Philip Heseltine and Dikran Kouyo-umdjian to Garsington, Lady Ottoline reacted to them as we might have expected Lawrence to react had he not been blinded by his delusion that they were perfect candidates for Rananim. They seemed to her to 'pollute the atmosphere'; Heseltine in particular she found 'so degenerate that he seems somehow corrupt' [OG 77]. But the greatest problem was Frieda's suspicion of Lawrence's relationship with Ottoline herself:

These visits to Garsington seemed like a lull before the most stormy time in Lawrence's life. Frieda had begun to growl and paw the ground. She was very much annoyed that he and I had so much in common – politics, love of England, poetry – and she became violently jealous of what she thought was my influence over him. In a letter to me she said: 'I would not mind if you and he had an ordinary love-affair – what I hate is this "soul-mush" '. [78]

In July Lawrence claimed that he and Russell had 'almost sworn Blutbruderschaft' [L II 363], but by September their plans for a joint lecture tour were in ruins. Lawrence accused Russell of being 'too full of devilish repressions to be anything but lustful and cruel . . . It is a perverted, mental blood-lust' [392], and proposed that they should become strangers again. Murry now became his main hope. In October they published their new periodical *The Signature* in an attempt 'to rally together just a few passionate, vital, constructive people' [411]. Not enough such people sub-scribed to enable the magazine to get beyond three numbers.

Lawrence's contribution to *The Signature* was the first three parts of his six-part essay 'The Crown'. It is, as he himself described it, 'purely philosophic and metaphysical' [397], and hardly likely to inspire a revolution or even to start 'a new religious era' [399]. It is Lawrence's attempt to formulate his new insights as a meta-physic. It contains some wonderful passages, but also many pages of incomprehensible jargon. Lady Cynthia Asquith apparently made little of Lawrence's interpretation of the Lion and the Unicorn fable. Lawrence defended it as a way of avoiding abstrac-tion: 'the Lion and the Unicorn are at any rate better than "the universe consists in a duality, but there is an initial element called polarity etc etc" ' [411]. Indeed they are, but they quickly disap-pear, and what follows is often just as abstract as this.

Lawrence's argument is that each of the polar opposites, darkness and light, the senses and the spirit, is kept in stable equilibrium by the opposition of the other. Neither must ever triumph or both would cease. Seeking his 'consummation in utter darkness' man comes to woman; 'taking the road down the senses' back to the source, he enters the womb of creation. There he is broken down, melted out, new-created, and 'thrown back again on the shore of creation'. He opens his eyes to the light and knows the goal, 'the consummation in the Spirit' [P II 377–8]. Destruction is thus as necessary to life as creation. They must forever alternate, like the ebb and flow of the sea. It is in the third essay, 'The Flux of Corruption', that Lawrence loses control of his argument. Here he equates the direction towards darkness with death, decay and corruption, but apparently without intending the word 'corruption' to carry any sense of disapprobation, though he is shortly to use it, together with 'rottenness', to signify something evil, the assertion of the permanence of the ego, the attempt to triumph in the ego over the flux of time. This is not-being, a refusal to come into being, and is the condition, he claims, of the great majority. Those energies which should bring us to flowering, trapped within the hard shell of the ego, thresh us hollow:

This also we enjoy, this being threshed rotten inside. This is sensationalism, reduction of the complex tissue back through rottenness to its elements. And this sensationalism, this reduction back, has become our very life, our only form of life at all. We enjoy it, it is our lust.

It became at last a collective activity, a war, when, within the great rind of virtue we thresh destruction further and further, till our whole civilization is like a great rind full of corruption, of breaking down, a mere shell threatened with collapse upon itself . . .

And then, when a man seeks a woman, he seeks not a consummation in union, but a frictional reduction. He seeks to plunge his compound flesh into the cold acid that will reduce him, in supreme sensual experience, down to his parts.   [388, 394]

This state is vile, evil. But Lawrence goes on to elaborate it in terms hardly to be distinguished from those he had used to describe the disintegrative process as a necessary phase of life. The distinction he strains towards is that the process is evil when it takes place within the hard shell of the ego, whereas

The spirit of destruction is divine, when it breaks the ego and opens the soul to the wide heavens . . . And corruption, like growth, is only divine when it is pure, when all is given up to it. If it be experienced as a controlled activity within an intact whole, this is vile.   [402–3]

Elsewhere in the essay, however, he suggests that evil can be avoided only by involvement in both processes simultaneously. The same confusion is evident in Birkin's thinking in *Women in Love*, but in the novel the confusion is Birkin's, not Lawrence's; and it is there to be superseded.

Perhaps the most important contribution of 'The Crown' to *Women in Love* was the image of the envelope. We have reached a point, he claims, where we can no longer relate to or admit the reality of anything outside the human ego:

> The supreme little ego in man hates an unconquered universe . . . The back of creation is broken. We have killed the mysteries and devoured the secrets. It all lies now within our skin, within the ego of humanity.
>
> [391–2]

All our activity, when it is not overtly destructive, is analytical and introspective in further phases of separation and breaking down:

> All this goes on within the glassy, insentient envelope of nullity. And within this envelope, like the glassy insects within their rind, we imagine we fill the whole cosmos, that we contain within ourselves the whole of time, which shall tick forth from us as from a clock, now everlastingly.
>
> We are capable of nothing but reduction within the envelope. Our every activity is the activity of disintegration, of corruption, of dissolution, whether it be our scientific research, our social activity . . . our art, or our anti-social activity, sensuality, sensationalism, crime, war. Everything alike contributes to the flux of death, to corruption, and liberates the static data of the consciousness . . .
>
> It is like the decay of our flesh, and every new step in decay liberates a sensation, keen, momentarily gratifying, or a conscious knowledge of the parts that made a whole; knowledge equally gratifying.   [392]

This provides not only the thematic core of *Women in Love*, but also another dimension of its structure:

> How to get away from this process of reduction, how escape this phosphorescent passage into the tomb, which was universal though unacknowledged, this was the unconscious problem which tortured Birkin day and night.   [P II 98]

It also provides the unique double perspective of the novel, its extraordinary fusion of realism and phantasm. How to escape from something which is 'universal'. That which is universal must be 'reality', and 'reality' must be accepted. But in 'The Crown' Lawrence argues that to accept such an imperative is to accept as real a mere dream world of appearances, seductive surfaces which merely reflect our egotism and mask the corruption within.

The novel is simultaneously realistic, mythic and symbolic. Realistic in that it aims to give us 'the whole pulse of social

England' [WL 511] at a specific historical moment; mythic in that Lawrence concentrates in that moment the whole history of the race from its emergence from the slime to its ultimate extinction; symbolic in that the people, incidents, settings and language of the thinly realistic surface are but a deceptive envelope disguising the mythic inner significance. When she read the manuscript in 1916, Catherine Carswell, assuming the novel to be an attempt at social realism, asked Lawrence 'why he must write of people who were so far removed from the general run, people so sophisticated and "artistic" and spoiled, that it could hardly matter what they did or said?' Lawrence replied that 'it was only through such people that one could discover whither the general run of mankind, the great unconscious mass, was tending':

There, at the uttermost tips of the flower of an epoch's achievement, one could already see the beginning of the flower of putrefaction which must take place before the seed of the new was ready to fall clear. I gathered too that in the nature of the putrefaction the peculiar nature of an epoch was revealed.   [SP 38]

Hermione gathers about her at Breadalby what she takes to be the flower of that epoch's achievement. Birkin, after being taken in for a while, comes to see that the culture they represent, 'their England', has no more substance than a bubble. To Ursula they seem like witches:

There was an elation and a satisfaction in it all, but it was cruelly exhausting for the new-comers, this ruthless mental pressure, this power-ful, consuming, destructive mentality that emanated from Joshua and Hermione and Birkin and dominated the rest.   [WL 147]

It is all part of Hermione's 'dead show', and Hermione herself is 'the real devil who won't let life exist' [93]. Her 'loathsome little skull', Birkin tells her, should be 'cracked, like an insect in its skin' [92]. Birkin's skull really is cracked to release him both from her world and from his own 'destructive mentality'.

Colours carry great symbolic weight in *Women in Love*, and these derive largely from the imagery of 'The Crown'. The envelope frequently has the colours of a false rainbow, the lurid colours of witches' oils, the iridescent colours of the surface of a marsh, or of the wings and carapaces of insects. Metallic blues and greens are prominent, particularly in the clothing of Gudrun and Hermione. Hermione 'had put on a dress of stiff, old greenish brocade, that fitted tight and made her look tall and rather terrible, ghastly' [145]. Gudrun 'was fashionably dressed in blackish-green and silver, her hat was brilliant green, like the sheen on an insect, but the brim was soft dark green, brilliantly glossy, with a high collar of grey fur, and great fur cuffs, the edge of her dress showed silver and black velvet, her stockings and shoes were silver grey' [476]. This immediately after she has been unable to go on listening to Birkin's words about 'a return along the Flux of Corruption, to the original rudimentary conditions of being . . . the phosphorescent ecstasy of acute sensation', and 'flowers of mud', and burning with destructive fires.

While writing 'The Crown', Lawrence was also working on the final version of *Twilight in Italy*. He could not resist adding some twenty pages of 'philosophy' to 'The Lemon Gardens', though it has little relevance to the earlier material. He is obsessively reworking the same ideas and images as if they could provide a universal key, as here to 'the soul of the Italian since the Renaissance':

> Aphrodite, the queen of the senses, she, born of the sea-foam, is the luminousness of the gleaming senses, the phosphorescence of the sea, the senses become a conscious aim unto themselves; she is the gleaming darkness, she is the luminous night, she is goddess of destruction, her white, cold fire consumes and does not create . . . The flesh, the senses, are now self-conscious. They know their aim. Their aim is supreme sensation. They seek the maximum of sensation. They seek the reduction of the flesh, the flesh reacting upon itself, to a crisis, an ecstasy, a phosphorescent transfiguration in ecstasy.   [TI 42]

These images obstinately refuse to cohere into a philosophy. In discursive prose, cut off from the author's total experience and imaginative vision, they are merely wild assertions, obfuscations, spurious rhetoric, jargon. Cut off from the world, from the experience of writer or reader, the images go dead. Much more pregnant is the imagery which remains anchored in a direct response to experience, which expresses, for example, Lawrence's sense of the spirit of place. In 'The Return Journey' he tries to account for his feeling that the Alpine mountain-tops 'bright with transcendent snow, seemed like death, eternal death':

> The very pure source of breaking-down, decomposition, the very quick of cold death, is the snowy mountain-peak above. There, eternally, goes on the white foregathering of the crystals, out of the deathly cold of the heavens; this is the static nucleus where death meets life in its elementality. And thence, from their white, radiant nucleus of death in life, flows the great flux downwards, towards life and warmth. And we below, we cannot think of the flux upwards, that flows from the needle-point of snow to the unutterable cold and death.   [159]

This passage is part of the process by which Lawrence's imagination is making this Alpine landscape available to him as an appropriate symbolic setting for the ending of *Women in Love*, where ice, cold and whiteness are to carry exactly the opposite symbolic charge to the rainbow, symbol of relatedness, creative interchange, fertility, the whole spectrum of life's potentialities. The prose is difficult, but not entirely beyond our grasp. Snow and ice, white and cold, are archetypal images of death.

There is also a scientific basis for such imagery, as Lawrence was well aware, in Clausius' theory of entropic decay, leading, ultimately, to the world's 'death by perfect cold' as depicted by Wells in 'The Time Machine'.[2] *Women in Love* comes closest to this in Loerke's 'dream of fear' in which 'the world went cold, and snow fell everywhere, and only white creatures, polar-bears, white foxes, and men like awful white snow-birds, persisted in ice-cruelty' [WL 552]. It is important to note, however, that this is Loerke's vision, not Birkin's, for to Lawrence, and to Birkin by the end of the novel, the theory of entropic decay would seem typical of the kind of science which goes on inside the envelope of the disintegrating ego.

*

In a letter to Lady Cynthia Asquith about the death of her brother at the front, Lawrence wrote:

> In this war, in the whole spirit which we now maintain, I do *not* believe . . . And I am English, and my Englishness is my very vision. But now I must go away, if my soul is sightless for ever. Let it then be blind, rather than commit the vast wickedness of acquiescence.   [L II 414]

He would go to America, where he hoped to find a more responsive public for his work, perhaps to Florida with 'several young people very anxious to come' [490] – the Murrys, Aldous Huxley, Heseltine and Suhrawardy (a 'lineal descendent of the Prophet' [466]). He even invited Russell to 'come and be president of us' [490]. In the heart-sickness of hope long deferred, Lawrence's imagination seized on America as a New World, the Promised Land. His expectations of it were hardly realistic. To the Murrys he wrote:

> If only it will all end up happily, like a song or a poem, and we live blythely by a big river, where there are fish, and in the forest behind wild turkeys and quails: there we make songs and poems and stories and dramas, in a vale of Avalon, in the Hesperides, among the Loves.   [452]

But on the very day he got his passport, Lawrence heard that the magistrates had issued a warrant for all copies of *The Rainbow* to be seized. In a vain attempt to organize some defence of the novel, Lawrence delayed his departure. A few days later he visited

Garsington again. Far from providing a possible location for Rananim, it now seemed to him a perfect symbol of the decline and fall of England:

So much beauty and pathos of old things passing away and no new things coming: this house of the Ottolines – It is England – my God, it breaks my soul – this England, these shafted windows, the elm-trees, the blue distance – the past, the great past, crumbling down, breaking down, not under the force of the coming buds, but under the weight of many exhausted, lovely yellow leaves, that drift over the lawn and over the pond, like the soldiers, passing away, into winter and the darkness of winter – no, I can't bear it. For the winter stretches ahead, where all vision is lost and all memory dies out.

It has been 2000 years, the spring and summer of our era. What then will the winter be?   [431–2]

Thus Garsington became available to Lawrence as Breadalby in *Women in Love*:

He was thinking how lovely, how sure, how formed, how final all the things of the past were – the lovely accomplished past – this house, so still and golden, the park slumbering its centuries of peace. And then, what a snare and a delusion, this beauty of static things – what a horrible, dead prison Breadalby really was, what an intolerable confinement, the peace!

[WL 54]

The attitude of the people Lawrence talked to at Garsington is described in the novel as 'mental and very wearying' [139]. In reaction he embarked on a programme of intensive reading about primitive beliefs and customs, beginning with Frazer's *Golden Bough* and *Totemism and Exogamy*. The tragedy of Russell's life was, Lawrence wrote to him, 'that the mental and nerve consciousness exerts a tyranny over the blood-consciousness'. He explained the origin of totem to Russell as the transmitting of a 'blood-image' from the mother to the embryo [L II 470]. He was shortly to ask Lady Ottoline to lend him some books: 'Anglo-Saxon Ballads – like the Seaman, translated – or interesting Norse literature, or early Celtic, something about Druids (though I believe it's all spurious) or the Orphic Religions, or *Egypt*, or on anything really African, Fetish Worship or the customs of primitive tribes' [511]. The primary symbol of 'blood-consciousness' in the novel was to be an African totem of a pregnant woman.

In December Lawrence discovered, only a fortnight before his planned sailing on the *Crown de Leon* (the mental unicorn defeated?), that he would not be allowed to go without exemption from military service. He queued for two hours at Battersea recruiting station, then fled 'from all the underworld of this spectral submission' [474]. Perhaps, subconsciously, he feared to put America and Rananim to the test. Instead he would go to Cornwall, 'ready to leap off' [492].

But first there was Christmas to be spent with his relatives in Ripley. As a Christmas present, Lawrence and Russell had combined to buy Lady Ottoline a copy of *The Ajanta Frescoes*. Lawrence had loved them as expressing 'the complete, almost perfect relations between the men and the women'. He thought them 'the zenith of a very lovely civilisation, the crest of a very perfect wave of human development' [489]. But in the English midlands he found only 'the reduction to the lowest':

The strange, dark, sensual life, so violent, and hopeless at the bottom, combined with this horrible paucity and materialism of mental consciousness, makes me so sad, I could scream.   [489]

Beldover and the mining country become another of the novel's hells, 'a pit-head surrounding the bottomless pit' [P II 385]. Here is a literal underworld, a pervasive smell of sulphur. Gangs of men bring up some of its darkness on their demonic faces. To the sisters in the first chapter it is 'like a country in an underworld':

The people are all ghouls, and everything is ghostly. Everything is a ghoulish replica of the real world, a replica, a ghoul, all soiled, everything sordid. It's like being mad . . .   [WL 58]

It is also like the scene in the vestibule of hell where Dante sees the ghosts of those who had never lived, who had 'made the great refusal' [DCH 35]. Hell, for Lawrence, is a condition of fixity or of purely mechanical motion. Any man who gives up his individuality, his capacity for free choice, to become a slave of the great machine is a lost soul:

These men, whom I love so much – and the life has such a power over me – they *understand* mentally so horribly: only industrialism, only wages and money and machinery. They can't *think* anything else. All their collective thinking is in these terms only. They are utterly unable to appreciate any pure, ulterior truth: only this industrial – mechanical – wage idea. This they will act from – nothing else.   [L II 489]

It is not just the miners, of course. They are but one extreme manifestation of the almost universal refusal to make the 'effort at serious living' which seems to Lawrence to be man's only justification for living at all – the effort to make one's own soul and thereby 'come into being':

Very few men have being at all. They perish utterly, as individuals . . . Whether they live or die does not matter: except in so far as every failure in the part is a failure in the whole. Their death is of no more matter than the cutting of a cabbage in the garden, an act utterly apart from grace.

[P II 384]

Hence the horror of the sisters to have to witness 'these ugly, meaningless people, this defaced countryside':

They turned off the main road, past a black patch of common-garden, where sooty cabbage stumps stood shameless. No one thought to be ashamed. No one was ashamed of it at all. [WL 57]

What there is to be ashamed of is, in Birkin's terms, that 'the goodness, the holiness, the desire for creation and productive happiness' [330] has been allowed to lapse, as it has in all the other hells. That creative potential, denied, festers within, and sooner or later erupts as destructive violence, as in the war: 'there will be a big row after the war, with these working men' [L II 490]; 'they have the last stages of death to go through yet: and it will not be a lovely process' [L III 116].

Yet this 'amorphous squalor' attracts Gudrun even while it repels her. It has a 'foul kind of beauty' which fascinates her, a 'thick, hot attraction' which stupefies her like a narcotic [WL 173–4]. The word 'nostalgia' occurs several times in this passage, echoing its use in the passage where Gudrun first sees and feels drawn to Gerald (the presiding devil over the Beldover hell). There the word attaches itself to the cluster of Nordic images around Gerald, northern, glistening, arctic, icy (in Nordic mythology hell is icy, as is the lowest level of Dante's hell). In 'Sketch-Book', Gudrun is equally fascinated by the lurid colours of the water-plants 'that rose succulently from the mud' [178]. Birkin's later reference to marsh-flowers, 'flowers of dissolution – fleurs du mal' completes the circuit of meaning. Gudrun and Gerald, he tells Ursula, were 'born in the process of destructive creation . . . part of the inverse process' [238–9]. Gudrun's *nostalgie de la boue* is a desire to reverse the normal processes of human development, both in the species and the individual, towards integrity, responsible consciousness and 'productive happiness', and to break herself down with many spasms of extreme sensation, towards man's first slime. The obscene is what she thrills to. The contents of her unconscious are projected into the novel as images of primitive submerged life-forms from the bottom of the sea – crabs, cuttlefish, eels, octopuses, polyps.

On 6 January 1916 Lawrence received from Kot an account of a 'sordid brawl' at the Café Royal involving, it appears, some of his candidates for Rananim. He expressed his willingness to 'give up people altogether':

> As for their world, it is like artificial lights that are blown out . . . it must be all blown out to extinction. [L II 498]

On his way to London, early in *Women in Love*, Birkin tells Gerald about his friends in London Bohemia. He is already tired of them, but has not yet brought himself to repudiate what they stand for:

> There are a few decent people, decent in some respects. They are really very thorough rejecters of the world – perhaps they live only in the gesture of rejection and negation – but negatively something, at any rate.
> [WL 111]

That evening Birkin takes Gerald to the Café Royal. It is not named, but easily recognized by the 'great mirrors on the walls' and the 'red plush of the seats to give substance within the bubble of pleasure'. Gerald, with no illusions, sees the place and its denizens much more clearly than Birkin:

> He seemed to be entering into some strange element, passing into an illuminated new region, among a host of licentious souls . . . He looked over all the dim, evanescent, strangely illuminated faces that bent across the tables. [114]

These faces are repeated *ad infinitum* in the mirrors, so that the effect is the same as when Gerald, coming up from the bottom of the lake, reports: 'it's curious how much room there seems, a whole universe under there; and as cold as hell . . . There's room under that water there for thousands' [251]. The fictional name of the café is the Pompadour. Madame de Pompadour's famous words, though unspoken here, provide a ghostly commentary: 'Après nous le déluge'. Beneath its decadent gilt and plush splendour, the Pompadour is a 'small, slow, central whirlpool of disintegration and dissolution' [471]. Birkin resists its pull, but Gudrun cannot: 'she *had* to return'.

For weeks Lawrence's letters had been full of imagery of winter – 'It is winter with me, my heart is frost-bound' [L II 479]. On the last day of 1915 he wrote to Catherine Carswell that he would soon begin to write a story – 'a mid-winter story of oblivion' [493]. By 9 January he had written the first part, but didn't know 'how to go on' [501]. In the same letter, and in another of the same date, Lawrence avows his belief in 'the miracle'. When he finally finished the story a year later, it was called 'The Miracle' (though for publication the title was changed to 'The Horse Dealer's Daughter'). The heroine walks into a muddy pond in winter, seeking oblivion by drowning. She is rescued and miraculously restored to life by a young doctor. As he searches for her submerged body, the imagery of cold and mud gives us an intimation of Gerald's attempts to rescue his drowned sister:

> The bottom was deep, soft clay, he sank in, and the water clasped dead cold round his legs. As he stirred he could smell the cold, rotten clay that fouled up into the water. [SSS 267]

Finding he could not yet 'break into a new world' in his story, Lawrence turned again to philosophy. By 25 February he had finished 'the first, the destructive half' [L II 557], which he called *Goats and Compasses*. It has not survived. Lady Ottoline described it as 'a gospel of hate and violent individualism. He attacks the will, love and sympathy. Indeed, the only thing that he doesn't revile and condemn is love between men and women' [OG 93]. Cecil Gray described it as 'a bombastic, pseudo-mystical, psycho-philosophical treatise dealing largely with homosexuality' [CB I 582]. There is no contradiction in these two accounts. In a letter to Heseltine advising him to 'love a woman – not men', Lawrence explained how heterosexuality and homosexuality related to his larger 'gospel':

> One must fight every minute – at least I must – to overcome this great flux of disintegration, further analysis, self analysis. If it continues, this flux, then our phase, our era, passes swiftly into oblivion. – In physical life, it is homosexuality, the reduction process. When man and woman come together in love, that is the great *immediate* synthesis. When men come together, that is immediate reduction: those complex states, the finest product of generations of synthetic living, are *reduced* in homosexual love, liberating a conscious knowledge of the component parts. [L II 448]

To the Murrys he wrote: 'That is the right way to be happy – a nucleus of love between a man and a woman, and let the world look after itself' [507]. Yet Lawrence could not deny his own need to 'fight every minute' to try to save the world, nor his inability to find complete satisfaction in the synthesis of his marriage – 'Except that if there are friends who will help the happiness on, tant mieux'. Only three weeks later, in answer to Lady Cynthia Asquith's question 'about the message of the *Rainbow*', Lawrence replied:

> I don't know myself what it is: except that the old order is done for, toppling on top of us: and that it's no use the men looking to the women for salvation, nor the women looking to sensuous satisfaction for their fulfilment. There must be a new Word. [526]

This has little to do with *The Rainbow*, but the ambivalence is at the heart of *Women in Love*. Lawrence is following his usual habit of describing his next novel rather than his last. On the very same day he wrote in another letter:

> As far as I possibly can, I will stand outside this time, I will live my life, and, if possible, be happy, though the whole world slides in horror down into the bottomless pit. [528]

'As far as I possibly can', 'if possible', these phrases reveal his awareness of the difficulty, if not impossibility (given his Salvator Mundi temperament), of any such abdication of responsibility. This is to be Rupert Birkin's dilemma: whether, as Ursula urges him, to leave the world to its fate and seek his personal fulfilment in his marriage; or to become an outlaw, throwing bombs at the hated world to hasten its destruction; or to combine with such other men as he can find in more creative activity, teaching and preaching the new Word, sowing the seed of a new future.

Through the early months of 1916 Lawrence pressurized the Murrys to come and live in the adjacent cottage at Higher Tregerthen. He wanted 'a Blutbruderschaft between us all' [570]. At the beginning of April, against their better judgement, they came.

What drew Murry to Lawrence

> wasn't what the man said, so much as the warm and irresistible intimacy with which he surrounded one, an atmosphere established as it were by a kindly gardener who had, very precisely, decided that you were to grow, and who, by that act, awakened in you the feeling that there was something in you which could grow. [C B I 373]

Unfortunately, Murry could conceive of a close relationship with Lawrence only as an alternative to his relationship with Katherine. Nor did he know what, exactly, he was being required to believe in and commit himself to:

> He talked of the blood-brotherhood between us and hinted at the need of some inviolable sacrament between us – some pre-Christian blood-rite in keeping with the primeval rocks about us. Timidly, I withdrew only the more. And his exasperation increased. [375]

Katherine naturally regarded Lawrence as a disapproving rival, and could not bear the frequent violent clashes between him and Frieda:

> Lawrence isn't healthy any more; he has gone a little bit out of his mind. If he is contradicted about *anything*, he gets into a frenzy, quite beside himself and it goes on until he is so exhausted that he cannot stand and has to go to bed and stay there until he has recovered. And whatever your

disagreement is about he says it is because you have gone wrong in your
sex and belong to an obscene spirit.   [KM 78]

Within a week of the Murrys moving into their cottage, Lawrence
began *Women in Love* (though he did not think of that title until
July). The Murrys provided him with several new aspects of Gerald
and Gudrun. Gudrun shares Katherine's cynical detachment: 'This
finality of Gudrun's, this dispatching of people and things in a
sentence, it was such a lie' [WL 342]. Gudrun's art, like Katherine's,
is an art of the miniature, the wholly contained. Murry seemed to
Lawrence to lack a 'quick sufficiency in life', to be altogether too
parasitically dependent upon Katherine. Murry himself was well
aware that 'my certainty was real and present only in the self-
obliteration of the love between Katherine and me. Let that be
taken from me and I relapsed into a deathly self-consciousness'
[CB I 375]. In the novel Gerald says: 'I care for nothing on earth, or
in heaven, outside this spot where we are' [WL 414]. Without her,
thrown back on himself, he caves in: 'He felt like a pair of scales,
the half of which tips down and down into an infinite void' [412].

Lawrence had witnessed an incident at a Christmas party in
1914. In an improvised play Murry had been the husband whose
wife (Katherine) was supposed to be seduced by a lover played by
the artist Mark Gertler, then reconciled to her husband. But
Katherine embarrassed Lawrence by making love to Gertler very
realistically and refusing to act the reconciliation. While Lawrence
consoled Murry, Frieda took Gertler aside to warn him against
Katherine. Thus the Murrys and Gertler seemed to be casting
themselves in the roles Lawrence had already created for Gerald,
Gudrun and Loerke.

Amazingly, the Murrys did not recognize themselves when they
subsequently read the novel. When Frieda told Murry, he was
astonished, but saw that 'those two characters are, so to speak, our
counterparts in the pre-mental realm of which we had no cogni-
zance and in which Lawrence's imagination liked to dwell'
[CB I 377].

With the help of the novel, Murry was eventually able to
understand much of what, at the time, had baffled him:

Lawrence believed, or tried to believe, that the relation between
Katherine and me was false and deadly; and that the relation between
Frieda and himself was real and life-giving: but that his relation with
Frieda needed to be completed by a new relation between himself and me,
which I evaded . . . The foundation of it all is the relation between
Lawrence and Frieda. That is, as it were, the ultimate reality. That
foundation secure, Lawrence needs or desires a further relation with me,

in which Katherine is temporarily but totally ignored. By virtue of this 'mystical' relation with Lawrence, I participate in this pre-mental reality, the 'dark sources' of my being come alive. From this changed personality, I, in turn, enter a new relation with Katherine.   [378–9]

Murry recognized this as a 'half-truth', but felt that there was some self-deception on Lawrence's part: 'I felt that his demand for a more intimate relation with me sprang from the fact that some element in his nature was left profoundly unsatisfied by his marriage' [379].

*

After finishing *Goats and Compasses* in mid-February, Lawrence wrote nothing at all for over two months. On 16 April he wrote to Catherine Carswell:

> I begin really to feel better, strong again. Soon I shall begin to work. I am waiting for a novel manuscript to come from Germany. But after this last lapse, one is slow and reluctant.   [L II 595]

The manuscript was *The Insurrection of Miss Houghton*, which, in the event, Lawrence was not able to recover until after the war. The decision to rewrite instead another pre-war manuscript, *The Sisters*, must have been made very suddenly, for there is no mention of it in the letters until he announces it to Lady Cynthia Asquith on 26 April as already begun:

> I am doing another novel – that really occupies me. The world crackles and busts, but that is another matter, external, in chaos. One has a certain order inviolable in one's soul. There one sits, as in a crows nest, out of it all.   [601]

What caused him to take up so suddenly, and with such enthusiasm, the long-dormant *Sisters*? It must have been the convergence of several things: the realization of how his recent relationships could be incorporated into the existing characters, of how the story might accommodate his latest philosophical ideas and be shaped by a matrix of symbols drawn from both his dreams and his reading. The fallow months had allowed time for some fertile reading. He had read Frazer and Tylor on primitive culture, Petrie and Maspero on the ancient Egyptians, Jane Harrison and Gilbert Murray on the Greeks, Petronius' satire on a corrupt and collapsing civilization, Dostoevsky's fictional embodiments of spiritual and sensual and perverse extremes.

On 1 April he had written to Kot that he had nothing in his head but 'Greek Translations and Ethnology' [591]. The Greek translation which most impressed him and matched his mood was

Thucydides' *History of the Peloponnesian War*, which he continued to read through the writing of the first two drafts of *Women in Love*:

I read Thucydides too, when I have courage to face the facts of these wars of a collapsing era, of a dying idea. He is very good, and very present to one's soul . . .
The Peloponnesian war was the death agony of Greece, really, not her life struggle . . . It is too horrible to see a people, adhering to traditions, fling itself down the abyss of the past, and disappear. [614, 634]

In both Tylor and Harrison Lawrence read of living men visiting the land of the dead, suggesting a controlling motif for the new novel. Melville perhaps furnished him with a vision of its ending:

To the native Indian of Peru, the continual sight of the snow-howdahed Andes conveys naught of dread, except, perhaps, in the mere fancy of the eternal frosted desolateness reigning at such vast altitudes, and the natural conceit of what a fearfulness it would be to lose oneself in such inhuman solitudes. Much the same is it with the backwoodsman of the West, who with comparative indifference views an unbounded prairie sheeted with driven snow, no shadow of tree or twig to break the fixed trance of whiteness. Not so the sailor, beholding the scenery of the Antarctic seas; where at times, by some infernal trick of legerdemain in the powers of frost and air, he, shivering and half shipwrecked, instead of rainbows speaking hope and solace to his misery, views what seems a boundless churchyard grinning upon him with its lean ice monuments and splintered crosses. [MD 294]

And in Rolland's *Life of Michael Angelo*, he read and deeply registered Michelangelo's saying that 'a work of art is an act of faith', and this helped him, in spite of his feeling that he could not possibly offer serious work to 'a putrescent mankind like ours', to go on writing 'to the unseen witnesses' [L II 602].

*

Lawrence began 'the second half of the *Rainbow*' [L II 602], it seems, with a chapter called 'Prologue' which he later rejected. Birkin and Gerald Crich, we are told, had been first brought together by a common friend for a mountain-climbing holiday in the Tyrol. Thus, if Lawrence had already conceived his ending, this opening would have balanced it, hinting already at the negative symbolism of high mountains in phrases such as 'abstract isolation': 'they had trespassed into the upper silence and loneliness . . . the senses all raised . . . to one enkindled, transcendent fire, in the upper world' [P II 92]. Though nothing had been said or done, and they had parted casually and not met again in four

171

years, 'they knew they loved each other, that each would die for the other' [93].

Birkin is having an affair with Hermione Roddice. Lawrence's first thought for her first name was Ethel. She is clearly yet another version of the 'spiritual woman' [95] deriving from Jessie Chambers. Much in the description of her would be interchangeable with passages from *Sons and Lovers*:

He wrote also harsh, jarring poetry, very real and painful, under which she suffered; and sometimes, shallower, gentle lyrics, which she treasured as drops of manna . . . She had given him all her trembling, naked soul . . . She prepared herself like a perfect sacrifice to him . . . He had no pleasure of her, only some mortification . . . And it was this failure which broke the love between them. He hated her, for her incapacity in love, for her lack of desire for him . . . Still, for his spiritual delight, for a companion in his conscious life, for someone to share and heighten his joy in thinking, or in reading, or in feeling beautiful things, or in knowing landscape intimately and poignantly, he turned to her.   [94–101]

All this was probably carried over from *The Sisters*. One reason for the dropping of this chapter may have been Lawrence's realization that it was old hat, and that Birkin would have to be torn between Gerald and Ursula, not Gerald and Hermione.

Birkin is described as being in exactly Lawrence's own dilemma:

What should a man add himself on to? – to science, to social reform, to aestheticism, to sensationalism? The whole world's constructive activity was a fiction, a lie, to hide the great process of decomposition, which had set in. What then to adhere to? He ran about from death to death. [98–9]

The one thing Lawrence had himself found to adhere to is, at this stage, denied to Birkin, who believes himself to be incapable of loving any woman. Part of him wishes to be a 'saviour of mankind' and 'pour out his soul for the world', while another part wishes 'to jeer at all his own righteousness and spirituality, justly and sincerely to make a mock of it all . . . He knew that he was not very far from dissolution' [103].

That sentence: 'He ran about from death to death' gives us the clue to what was probably at this stage Lawrence's central idea for the structure of the novel. Much of this remains in the novel as we know it. Birkin makes a series of almost deadly mistakes, gives his allegiance to the wrong people and the wrong ideas. But the 'Prologue' chapter suggests that it may have been the original intention to take this a good deal further. It might, for example, have been Birkin, not Gerald, who was to have an affair with the Pussum:

To be spiritual, he must have a Hermione, completely without desire: to be sensual, he must have a slightly bestial woman, the very scent of whose skin soon disgusted him, whose manners nauseated him beyond bearing . . .   [102]

The concluding pages of 'Prologue' have commonly been interpreted as Lawrence's confession of his own homosexuality which fear of censorship or failure of nerve later caused him to retract. But the novel is not an autobiography, and Birkin is not Lawrence. Birkin is totally without bearings at the outset, drawn towards several people and life-modes which turn out to be false or perverse. He learns, painfully, from his mistakes. In him, Lawrence recapitulates his recent past, but deliberately exaggerates some errors and invents others, errors which he made, or came near to making, or might easily have made. Birkin, we are told, was attracted only by 'the soul of a woman and the physique of a man': 'He thought women beautiful purely because of their expression' [104]. It would be absurd to suggest that this could be true of the Lawrence who had written *Look! We Have Come Through!* Lawrence had certainly known homoerotic feelings in his youth, and had recorded them in *The White Peacock*. He was disturbed to find that such feelings were not dead when he found himself responding warmly to his Cornish neighbour William Henry Hocking. In 'Prologue' Birkin is made to recoil from deadly relationships with women with a much stronger physical attraction to men than Lawrence had ever felt, though he had observed it in several of his friends. It seems that his original intention had been to involve Birkin in a homosexual relationship with Gerald just as deadly as his heterosexual relationship with Hermione had been.

Birkin is particularly attracted to two types of men:

these white-skinned, keen-limbed men with eyes like blue-flashing ice and hair like crystals of winter sunshine, the northmen, inhuman as sharp-flying gulls, distinct like splinters of ice, like crystals, isolated, individual; and then the men with dark eyes that one can enter and plunge into, bathe in, as in a liquid darkness, dark-skinned, supple, night-smelling men, who are the living substance of the viscous, universal heavy darkness.   [105]

It is not immediately obvious what we are to make of this imagery, though, as Lawrence persists with it, both groups of images, 'eternal snow, and the flux of heavy, rank-smelling darkness', come to seem equally deadly. In the finished novel, the first group remains associated with Gerald, while the second group is transferred to the African statuette:

The white races, having the arctic north behind them, the vast abstraction of ice and snow, would fulfil a mystery of ice-destructive knowledge, snow-abstract annihilation. Whereas the West Africans, controlled by the burning death-abstraction of the Sahara, had been fulfilled in sun-destruction, the putrescent mystery of sun-rays.   [WL 331]

The end of 'Prologue' makes clear enough that if Birkin turns from Hermione to seek his satisfaction in Gerald, or any other man, he will be 'breaking away from her, his one rock, to fall into a bottomless sea' [P II 108].

Lawrence was perfectly explicit about his attitude to homosexuality in later subsequently cancelled passages in his penultimate draft:

Gerald and he had a curious love for each other. It was a love that was perhaps death, a love which was complemented by the hatred for woman . . . It tore man from woman, and woman from man. The two halves divided and separated, each drawing away to itself. And the great chasm that came between the two sundered halves was death, universal death.   [ML 175]

I believe Lawrence dropped 'Prologue', and such passages as this, and the whole theme of deadly homosexuality, primarily because he came to see that the position to which he had committed himself was not quite honest. He had lacked the courage to accept the implications of the most honest passage in 'Prologue':

His a priori were: 'I *should not* feel like this,' and 'It is the ultimate mark of my own deficiency, that I feel like this.' Therefore, though he admitted everything, he never really faced the question. He never accepted the desire, and received it as part of himself.   [P II 107]

He had allowed his horror of sodomy and of such degeneracy as he had seen in Cambridge to blind him to the possibility that other, more creative, forms of contact, even physical contact, might be possible, even desirable, between men. And he had invested so much in his marriage that he was loath to admit to himself that it was not enough.

*

The first draft came very quickly. Within a month Lawrence wrote:

I have got a long way with my novel. It comes rapidly, and is very good. When one is shaken to the very depths, one finds reality in the unreal world. At present my real world is the world of my inner soul, which reflects on to the novel I write. The outer world is there to be endured, it is not real – neither the outer life.   [L II 610]

This is the beginning of a long process by which Lawrence sought

to free himself from the great lie that the real is that which is
demonstrably out there, things palpably existing, events evidently
happening in the outer world. Though Lawrence showed little
interest in Blake, this is Blake's 'single vision and Newton's sleep'.
There is another, truer, world, the world of a man's 'inner soul'
where being is rooted in the darkness at the centre of the self:
'Nothing matters, in the end, but the little hard flame of truth one
has inside oneself, and which does not blow about in the draught
of blasphemous living' [657]. 'Blasphemous living' is what the
existentialists would call 'living in bad faith', acquiescence to the
values of the outer world which is 'one colossal madness, falsity,
a stupendous assertion of not-being' [593]. The alternative is to
say, as Rawdon Lilly says of the war in *Aaron's Rod*, that it was

not as real as a bad dream . . . The war was a lie . . . It never happened . . .
Not to me or to any man, in his own self. It took place in the automatic
sphere, like dreams do. But the *actual man* in every man was just absent –
asleep – or drugged – inert – dream-logged.   [AR 143–4]

When the 'actual man' comes awake, he speaks with the voice of
imagination, of art, which is why 'A book is a holy thing, and must
be made so again' [L II 534].

By the time he wrote his Foreword to *Women in Love* in September
1919, Lawrence had come to see the novel as a record of his own
existential 'struggle into conscious being' [P II 276]:

The creative, spontaneous soul sends forth its promptings of desire and
aspiration in us. These promptings are our true fate, which is our business
to fulfil. A fate dictated from outside, from theory or from circumstance,
is a false fate.   [275]

Birkin's role in the novel is to undergo this passionate struggle
against the several false fates his society seems to offer him; his
struggle to identify and clarify those inner promptings which are
the voice of his true fate.

On 29 May 1916 Lawrence reached the wedding of Birkin and
Ursula:

Two thirds of the novel are written. It goes on pretty fast, and very easy.
I have not travailed over it. It is the book of my free soul.   [L II 614]

The marriage takes place in Chapter XXVII of *Women in Love*, about
three-quarters of the way through the novel as we know it. Apart
from the first two chapters, 'Prologue' and 'The Wedding'
[B E44lb], which may, in any case, have been a false start, nothing
of this draft has survived. It may have been a good deal shorter
than the final version, and cannot have been much like it if Frieda

was anywhere near the mark in describing it as 'much jollier' than *The Rainbow*, and unlikely to 'shock the good people so much' [FL 212]. Although Lawrence took time to read Dana and *The Pickwick Papers*, this version was finished 'in effect' by the end of June: 'There is a last chapter to write, some time, when one's heart is not so contracted' [L II 627]. We do not know whether this 'last chapter' was 'Exeunt' or something corresponding to the never-to-be written 'Epilogue'.

What had made Lawrence's heart too contracted to finish the novel was the 'ignominy', 'humiliation' and 'degradation' of his medical examination at Bodmin on 28 June [618]: 'It was the underlying sense of disaster that overwhelmed me' [625]. This on top of the recent defection of the Murrys – 'it wearies me in my soul, this constant breaking with people' [623] – and his growing conviction that the novel could never be published. At the beginning of July Lawrence had only £6 in the world, and could not afford to pay for the typing of the novel. He tried to do it himself, estimating that it would take him three months, but had to give up within a fortnight: 'it got on my nerves and knocked me up' [637]. On 21 July Lawrence was 'scribbling out' the rest in pencil, and had revised about four-fifths. As he had only begun this 'fourth and final draft'[3] between 9 and 12 July, it can hardly have involved a great deal of new creation. There is evidence that some of the pencilled part was carried over to the next draft.[4] Otherwise this version has not survived.

The fact that Lawrence resumed work on the novel at all in July is indicative of a rise in spirits. He had spent the first week of July happily haymaking and working in his own garden – 'the things are growing splendidly' [621]. On 4 July he wrote to Kot:

> I am pretty well, because, for some reason, I feel I have conquered. I felt I conquered, in the barracks experience – my spirit held its own and even won, over their great collective spirit. I always feel ill when I feel beaten. [622]

In the same letter, he expresses his belief that the real terror will come after the end of the war. But there is no longer the helpless acceptance or even gloating anticipation we have seen in the first half of 1916: 'We must keep our heads, and see what we can do'. In February he had claimed that the 'crashing down of nations and empires' did not matter; nor did death in the individual [529]. If the only positive in Lawrence's first concept of the novel had been the marriage of Birkin and Ursula, they would have been Noah and his wife, watching, with some satisfaction, as the world slid beneath the rising waters. An achieved marriage, on the contrary, should release energies for constructive, collaborative work in the world, and that implies a society, a nation. In April Lawrence would have scorned such an idea; but in July, in the same letter in which he tells Thomas Dunlop that he has resumed work on the novel, he gives his definition of a nation as 'a number of people united to secure the maximum amount of liberty for each member of that nation, and to fulfil collectively the highest truth known to them' [629]. The crashing down of empires does matter to him now: '*All* Greece died. It must not be so again, we must have more sense' [635].

Though in the novel it is Birkin who insists that a self-contained marriage is merely 'egoism à deux', in real life it seems to have been Frieda who insisted that 'for perfect love you don't only have two people, it must include a bigger, universal connection' [FL 211–12]. Apparently the novel's bearings were being discovered in perpetual discussion between Lawrence and Frieda:

> Frieda's letter is quite right, about the *difference* between us being the adventure, and the true relationship established between different things, different spirits, this is creative life. And the reacting of a thing against its different, is death in life. So that act of love, which is a pure thrill, is a kind of friction between opposites, interdestructive, an act of death.
>
> [L II 636]

No doubt when Lawrence was in his most nihilistic moods, Frieda fought him much as Ursula fights Birkin: 'You want to destroy our hope. You *want* us to be deathly' [WL 240]. Ideas passionately held by Lawrence only a few months earlier take their place in the novel among the several deaths Birkin has to experience and repudiate.

*

The first indication that Lawrence has begun the novel yet again comes in a letter to Amy Lowell on 23 August:

> I am busy typing out a new novel, to be called *Women in Love*. Every day I bless you for the gift of the type-writer. It runs so glibly, and has at last become a true confrère. [L II 645]

It needed to be, for Lawrence typed the first twenty-two chapters solidly for the next five weeks, recomposing as he went. It was 'one of the labours of Hercules' [665], and at the beginning of October his health broke down. When he recovered he could not face the typewriter again, and wrote out the last nine chapters in ten notebooks in the second half of October. According to Charles Ross, four of these show signs of having been part of the previous draft [CR 112]; and Lawrence wrote, of this last third of the novel: 'there was a lot of the original draft that I *couldn't* have bettered' [L III 25].

This draft was by no means a mere revision of the earlier one. It contains a great deal which could not have existed before, and, though it was to be extensively revised several more times before its publication in 1920,[5] it is the first version we can properly call *Women in Love*.

The letter in which Lawrence makes his first mention of this draft also contains a remarkable passage about militarism and homosexuality, where these are attacked not, as before, because they threaten marriage and creativity, but because they destroy 'the individual and the constructive social being' [L II 644]. The 'constructive or social-creative' emerges as a new positive in terms of which Birkin's early nihilism is to be superseded later in the novel.

A letter of 4 September to Kot illustrates Lawrence's tendency now to interpret events in his personal life in terms of the fall of nations and empires, and to associate London Bohemia with Sodom. Kot had described how Katherine Mansfield, hearing Heseltine at another table at the Café Royal reading aloud to his cronies from *Amores* with malicious mockery, had snatched the book from him and stalked out with it. Kot called it a 'Dostoevski evening'. His account gave Lawrence 'a real feeling of horror':

I dare not come to London, for my life. It is like walking into some horrible gas, which tears one's lungs. Really – Delenda est Carthago . . .
I think truly the only righteousness is the destruction of mankind, as in Sodom. Fire and brimstone should fall down . . .
If only there were not more than one hundred people in Great Britain! – all the rest clear space, grass and trees and stone! [650]

Perhaps those exclamation marks indicate the first signs of self-consciousness, even self-parody about such sweeping misanthropy, which is mocked in the novel by Ursula:

'And if you don't believe in love, what *do* you believe in?' she asked mockingly. 'Simply in the end of the world, and grass?' [WL 190]

The incident at the Café Royal went straight into the novel, where London figures as a centre of 'blasphemous living' [L II 657], of a foul world which Lawrence would not 'accept or acknowledge or even enter' [659].

But even in his Cornwall fastness, Lawrence continued to receive messages and tokens from that world. On 9 October he received a photograph of Mark Gertler's latest painting, *The Merry-Go-Round*.[6] Lawrence told Gertler it was the best modern picture he had seen, but that he would probably be 'too frightened to come and look at the original':

> But I *do* think that in this combination of blaze, and violent mechanical rotation and complex involution, and ghastly, utterly mindless human intensity of sensational extremity, you have made a real and ultimate revelation . . . You are all absorbed in the violent and lurid processes of inner decomposition: the same thing that makes leaves go scarlet and copper-green at this time of year. It is a terrifying coloured flame of decomposition, your inner flame. – But dear God, it is a real flame enough, undeniable in heaven and earth. [660]

Here is another of Birkin's dilemmas. If the artist is the truth-teller; if it is his function to live out and give expression to the reality of his time, 'then, since obscenity is the truth of our passion today, it is the only stuff of art – or almost the only stuff' [660]. In the novel Birkin claims that the 'dark river of dissolution' is 'all our reality, nowadays . . . If it is the end, then we are of the end – fleurs du mal if you like' [WL 238–9]. But Lawrence/Birkin is not totally committed to the idea that we will find our only satisfaction in going through with the death-process; or, as an artist, in depicting it and prophesying the end of the world. That is Loerke's role, and Loerke's factory frieze, which had previously been a scene of wolves and peasants, Lawrence now changed to 'a representation of a fair, with peasants and artisans in an orgy of enjoyment, drunk and absurd in their modern dress, whirling ridiculously in round-abouts, gaping at shows, kissing and staggering and rolling in knots, swinging in swing-boats, and firing down shooting galleries, a frenzy of chaotic motion' [517]. Lawrence's afterthought '– or almost the only stuff' – is equivalent to Birkin's concession to Ursula that he does not feel they are *'altogether'* fleurs du mal.

Unlike the Murrys, Catherine Carswell saw how creative was the quarrelling of the Lawrences, that Frieda compelled Lawrence to admire her 'magnificent female probity of being' [C B I 394]. When she visited them at the end of September, they told her of a recent quarrel in which Frieda had brought a stone dinner plate down on Lawrence's head from behind, an incident which no doubt suggested to him Hermione's blow with the paperweight. But they felt that they had come through the worst of their conflict:

> Frieda and I have finished the long and bloody fight at last, and are at one. It is a fight one has to fight – the old Adam to be killed in me, the old Eve in her – then a new Adam and a new Eve. Till the fight is finished, it is only honorable to fight. But oh dear, it is very horrible and agonising.[7]
> [L II 662]

In a poem, 'Elysium', written at this time in one of the *Women in Love* notebooks, Lawrence gives Frieda ('Eve') the credit for having delivered him from the 'monstrous womb/Of time', having found the source of his 'subjection/To the All, and severed the connection' [CP 262]. It is a difficult poem made easier if one knows that an earlier title was 'Blind', and that it was originally dedicated to 'the Soldiers and Sailors who are made blind'.[8] What she has destroyed, in the poem's imagery, is the tyranny of sight, binding the man to the world of appearances. Similarly, Birkin is grateful to Hermione for the blow which releases him from all his ties to the 'extraneous' world, into his own Eden: 'Here was his world, he wanted nobody and nothing but the lovely, subtle, responsive vegetation, and himself, his own living self . . . This was his place, his marriage place' [WL 166]. It is a rite of passage for Birkin, but not a true Eden. It frees him to grope his way towards his true marriage.

*

The version of *Women in Love* which Lawrence finished at the end of October 1916 and lightly revised in November was not regarded by him as yet another draft. It was the finished novel, which he would gladly have published in that form had he been able to find a publisher. In that event, we should have had a very different *Women in Love*. The three-year delay in finding a publisher gave Lawrence the opportunity to do a great deal more work on it. It was, in his own words, 'altogether re-written' [P II 275] between August and November 1917. There was further significant revision in August and September 1919, and again on the proofs in November 1920.

In July 1917 Lawrence described the novel to Waldo Frank as 'purely destructive, not like the *Rainbow*, destructive-consummating . . . But, alas, in the world of Europe I see no Rainbow. I believe the deluge of iron rain will destroy the world here, utterly: no Ararat will rise above the subsiding iron waters' [L III 142–3]. This may seem to us a somewhat distorted view of *Women in Love*, until we remember that it describes the 1916 version, appropriately subtitled *Dies Irae*.[9] By mid-November 1917, when Lawrence must have done most of his rewriting, he was proposing to change the title to *Noah's Ark*, a much more 'destructive-consummating' title.

The spirit of the 1916 version is expressed in the letter to Forster in which Lawrence announces that he has finished his 'rather wonderful and terrible novel':

The process of violent death will possess humanity for many a generation yet, till there are only a few remaining of all these hordes: a slow, slow flood of death will drown them all. I am glad, for they are too corrupt and cowardly . . . I am weary to death of my fellow men. I think it would be good to die, because death would be a clean land with no people in it: not even the people of myself. Where to go, where to go away from them! [L III 21]

Birkin's position is clearer in this version, partly because it is expounded at greater length, with large chunks of essay material which would look equally at home in 'The Crown', partly because it changes less in the course of the novel. In the 'Classroom' chapter, for example, we get this from Birkin:

Let us be consciously sensuous till we are satisfied, till we reach a point of death . . . We've got to finish the great analytic adventure, the quest for knowledge. And if we have to push on into the darkest jungle of our own physical sensations, and discover the elements of sensuality in ourselves, we need not pretend we are being simple animals. We are the last products of the decadent movement, the analytic, lyrical, emotional, scientific movement which has had full sway since the Renaissance, and which we've been so proud of . . . The adventure of knowledge is not finished for us till we have got back to the very sources, discovered satisfactorily to ourselves our own sources, in sensation, as one traces back a river . . . It is a form of immediate anthropology, we study the origins of man in our own immediate experience, we push right back to the first, and last, sensations of procreation and death. [B E441d]

Clearly, on artistic grounds, Lawrence was right to reduce the amount of this sort of thing. It does, however, make much clearer the nature of Birkin's relationship with Hermione, the sort of contributions he makes to the sterile intellectualism of Breadalby, his willingness to associate with, and to some extent approve of, the Soho Bohemians, the attraction Halliday's African carving has for him (there is here no subsequent repudiation of it), and Ursula's reasons for her initial reluctance to begin a relationship with Birkin, and her subsequent hostility towards his metaphysic.

There are other good reasons for that hostility. Far from proposing a relationship based on 'star-equilibrium', Birkin 'wanted an absolute surrender, unconditional, only purely voluntary . . . He wanted, like Mohammed, a wife who believed utterly' [244]. He sets himself up in opposition not only to woman as white moon-goddess, man-eater, but also to woman as Magna Mater:

The woman, the great producer of life, she stood against the unknown, and to the unknown she owed her allegiance. She proceeded from the supreme unknown, and from her proceeded life, man and all his words and deeds. Now Birkin, in his very body, would reverse this. He would put her down, claim her vassalage. She must serve *him*, or his truth. As if she were not more than him and his truth and all the male host!   [245]

This conflict is never fully resolved. Nor is Ursula developed as an effective counterweight to Birkin, either in terms of the satirical thrust of her arguments, or in terms of the imagery of flame and lambency which is in later revision to be associated with her.

Birkin insists that 'Flux is just as *good* as Flame' [211]. It follows from this refusal to condemn the flux that he cannot logically condemn those individuals who are given over to it. The novel's disapprobation of the 'blasphemous living' of Gerald, Gudrun and Loerke is to be much intensified in the revisions.

Birkin's love for Gerald, as in the rejected 'Prologue', is regarded as another death to which Birkin runs in reaction after his failure with Ursula:

Gerald and he had a curious love for each other. It was a love that was perhaps death, a love which was complemented by the hatred for woman. It was a love that tore apart the two halves, and brought universal death . . . It needs a man and a woman. And if the woman refuse, then the life is uncreated and death triumphs.   [MWL 175–6]

In the end, Ursula does not refuse Birkin. Nevertheless, he remains preoccupied with death. He says of the dead Gerald:

He had kept death at bay, during his lifetime, instead of accepting, submitting, and rising again in living indestructibility.   [664]

But there is nothing in the novel to indicate what 'living indes-tructibility' might mean. Birkin has not arrived at a viable meta-physic. He has not 'come through' with Ursula to anything final. At the end there is no forward looking, no affirmation of faith in anything. We leave Birkin mourning over the corpse of his friend, wondering if Gerald's 'very failure' might be a fulfilment that he is wrong to oppose:

The tears ran out of Birkin's heart, and it was hard to keep that inner peace, which is the reality of faith.

*

Despite Frieda's suggestion that the novel should be called *Dies Irae*, it was no doubt largely as a result of her 'long and bloody fight' with Lawrence that *Women in Love* is not more destructive and apocalyptic than it is. While waiting for the typescript to come from his agent Pinker, Lawrence wrote: 'The book frightens me: it is so end-of-the-world. But it is, it must be, the beginning of a new world too' [LIII25]. A few days later he affirmed: 'A man who has a living connection with a woman, is, *ipso facto*, . . . an essential creator' [27]. That creativity must find expression, if not through membership of a nation, then in 'a little community, a monastery, a school – a little Hesperides of the soul and body' [70].

The end of winter brought, as usual, a renewal of hope in the world. Lawrence craved for spring to 'Come quickly, and vindicate us / against too much death' [CP 273]. In 'Whistling of Birds' he asserts that 'the dead must bury their dead':

> We may remain wintry and destructive for a little longer, if we wish it, but the winter is gone out of us, and willy-nilly our hearts sing a little at sunset.   [P 4]

'The Reality of Peace' looks forward to the inevitable coming of spring:

> If we will have a new creation on earth, if our souls are chafing to make a beginning, if our fingers are itching to start the new work of building up a new world, a whole new world with a new open sky above us, then we are transported across the unthinkable chasm, from the old dead way to the beginning of all that is to be.   [675]

When spring actually came, however, it brought no new work for Lawrence in terms of either art or life: 'I wish one could *do* something: I wish one could see where to lay hold, to effect something fresh and clear, just to begin a new state' [L III 110]. Rather he turned away from art, which he identified with 'emotions and squirmings and sensations' towards 'pure abstract thought'. When he had finished the seven short essays called 'The Reality of Peace',[10] he embarked on a more ambitious philosophical work, the lost 'At the Gates', which in turn became the philosophical springboard for the first version of *Studies in Classic American Literature*, begun in August 1917. Utterly deprived of a readership for his work (Pinker had not even bothered to send *Women in Love* to any publishers), Lawrence tried to make a virtue of necessity by arguing that 'there should be again a body of esoteric doctrine, defended from the herd' [143]. But as soon as publishers began to show an interest, first Huebsch in America, then Maunsel in Dublin, he took up *Women in Love* again and revised it so radically that he was hardly exaggerating when he later described it as having been 're-written' at this time.

The 1917 revision brought the novel very close to the *Women in Love* we know. The role of Birkin becomes much more clearly progressive. At the beginning he is, for all his protestations, a participant in the death process. In the 'Classroom' chapter his ideas are presented less sympathetically. 'He sounded as if he were addressing a meeting' [WL 94]. He is a phrase-maker. He is, as Hermione says, a satanist. He stands convicted of what he charges Hermione with, sensuality in the head. He says to her: 'You want it all in that loathsome little skull of yours, that ought to be cracked like a nut. For you'll be the same till it *is* cracked, like an insect in its skin' [92]. But it is Birkin's own skull which must be cracked before he can get clear of all his false attachments. He recovers, but remains, henceforth, an outsider, like the one living man in the underworld, the 'ghost life', unable to find his way to the land of living, convinced that hell is other people, and that every relationship which offers is but another death. He has an idea of 'perfect union with a woman – sort of ultimate marriage' [110], but this is subsumed within his larger hope that humanity should 'disappear as quick as possible' [111].

In September 1917 Lawrence wrote to Waldo Frank:

> What I should like would be another Deluge, so long as I could sit in the ark and float to the subsidence. – To me, the thought of the earth all *grass* and trees – grass, and no works-of-man *at all* – just a hare listening to the inaudible – that is Paradise. [L III 160]

A week later he wrote to Kot:

> God above, leave me single and separate and unthinkably distinguished from all the rest: let me be a paradisal being, but *never* a human being: let it be true when I say '*homo sum, humani omnis a me alienum puto.*' Henceforth I deal in single, sheer beings – nothing human, only the star-singleness of paradisal souls. This is the latest sort of swank: also true. [162]

These ideas and images went into the novel, but not, as would have been the case a year earlier, at face value. The ironic distance Lawrence had now put between himself and Birkin enabled him to take himself, even outside the novel, less seriously. Ursula's irony now deflates such swank in the novel, but without destroying the element of truth. She rightly distrusts Birkin when he drags the stars in; but she respects his courage and pride and purity of spirit.

In the earlier part of the novel Ursula has the better of the arguments. She refuses to allow Birkin to repudiate his humanity and his obligation to make the best of the given world. She fights against his facile generalizations about 'all our reality, nowadays', insisting that she, for one, is no fleur du mal. Birkin is won over, finally, not by the strength of Ursula's arguments but by falling in love with her, not simply as an attractive woman, but as a woman who is herself, in her very womanhood, a living disproof of his theories:

He saw her face strangely enkindled, as if suffused from within by a powerful sweet fire. His soul was arrested in wonder. She was enkindled in her own living fire. Arrested in wonder and in pure, perfect attraction, he moved towards her. She sat like a strange queen, almost supernatural in her glowing smiling richness.   [WL 190]

Progressively, Ursula comes to see the justice of some of Birkin's beliefs. She accepts the need to cut their ties of family, work and culture. She even accepts that 'love' is not a universal panacea, and may even, in its possessive, exclusive form, be a form of death. Simultaneously, Birkin moves through increasing trust in and admiration for Ursula, away from his exaggerated fear of woman as possessive mother or triumphant, man-eating siren. Ursula frees Birkin from the tyranny of his own intellectualism, teaches him to lapse from his self-imposed role as Salvator Mundi, to find the peace and richness of his own singleness, to live in the simple here and now, in the mutual appreciation of a flower or the sharing of good food.

At the beginning Birkin holds in an exaggerated form Lawrence's own former belief in blood-consciousness. He believes that only through sensual, particularly phallic experience can he gain real knowledge, penetrate to the dark heart of life's mysteries: 'he knew he did want a further sensual experience – something deeper, darker, than ordinary life could give' [330].[11] It is not until the new pages Lawrence now inserted into 'Moony', at the heart of the novel, that Birkin connects this idea with his most fundamental and tenaciously-held complex of ideas deriving from 'The Crown' and centring on the flux of corruption. It is the African carving which enables him to make the essential connection. His earlier admiration for it had been tempered by the admission: 'this isn't everything'; but he had not, until now, become fully conscious of what it excluded. The carving is the end-product, thousands of years ahead of him, of 'the process of purely sensual understanding' [331]. It 'was one of his soul's intimates', but he had never before recognized its reductiveness, sub-human, insect-like, obscene. He realizes that to separate the senses from the mind is to untie what Donne called 'that subtle knot, which makes us man', and that, whichever form of knowledge is chosen can only lead to corruption and dissolution, a loss of the creative potential which makes man superior to the insects:

Thousands of years ago, that which was imminent in himself must have taken place in these Africans; the goodness, the holiness, the desire for creation and productive happiness must have lapsed, leaving the single impulse for knowledge in one sort, mindless, progressive knowledge through the senses, knowledge arrested and ending in the senses, mystic knowledge in disintegration and dissolution, knowledge such as the beetles have, which live purely within the world of corruption and cold dissolution.   [330]

This recognition regenerates Birkin's own 'desire for creation and productive happiness' and enables him to see that 'there was another way, the way of freedom':

There was the paradisal entry into pure, single being, the individual soul taking precedence over love and desire for union, stronger than any pangs of emotion, a lovely state of free-proud singleness, which accepted the obligation of the permanent connection with others, and with the others, submits to the yoke and leash of love, but never forfeits its own proud individual singleness, even while it loves and yields.   [332]

However, it is easier to conceive this than to achieve it, this side of Paradise, and Birkin's struggle is by no means over.

From time to time he lapses from the struggle into a fatalism, a belief that people 'acted and reacted involuntarily according to a few great laws, and once the laws, the great principles, were known, people were no longer mystically interesting' [386]. These principles are basically two, creation and destruction. When Birkin is in the toils of his apocalyptic vision it seems to him that an era of evolution and creation will necessarily be followed by an era of disintegration, reduction back to chaos, the original elements. Man has no right to pass judgement on this process, to claim that one phase of it is any better than another. During a destructive era, we shall find our only satisfaction in going through with our fate, giving ourselves over wholly to the destructive process, as Loerke does. If humanity is doomed, what can the individual do but accept his fate. 'If it is the end, then we are of the end'. There will be a new world, but 'after us'. When Birkin extricates himself from the toils of this vision, he sees rather that it is civilization, not the whole world, which is dying; that it can be abandoned like a sinking ship. The new world will begin as a handful of seeds among the ruins of the old, and his own marriage can be such a seed.

At the end of 'The Reality of Peace' Lawrence had affirmed that reintegration was possible, between the mind and the senses, and between the creative and destructive principles within us:

I extricate myself into singleness, the slow-developed singleness of manhood. And then I set out to meet the other, the unknown of womanhood. I give myself to the love that makes me join and fuse towards a universal oneness; I give myself to the hate that makes me detach myself, extricate myself vividly from the other in sharp passion; I am given up into universality of fellowship and communion, I am distinguished in keen resistance and isolation, both so utterly, so exquisitely, that I am and I am not at once; suddenly I lapse out of the duality into a sheer beauty of fulfilment. I am a rose of perfect peace.   [P 694]

But this fulfilment can be achieved only by coming clear of death and everything else in ourselves which we turn away from and refuse to acknowledge ours. To try to turn away is to 'fall into the cesspool of our own abhorrence':

If there is a loathsome thought or suggestion, let us not dispatch it instantly with impertinent righteousness; let us admit it with simplicity, let us accept it, be responsible for it . . . It is necessary to balance the dark against the light if we are ever going to be free. We must know that we, ourselves, are the living stream of seething corruption, this also, all the while, as well as the bright river of life. We must recover our balance to be free.   [676–7]

Just before the 1917 rewriting of Women in Love Lawrence had written to Eunice Tietjens explaining the implications of this in relation to sex:

There is all the difference in the world between *understanding* the extreme and awful workings of sex, or even fulfilling them, responsibly; and abnormal sex. Abnormal sex comes from the fulfilling of violent and extreme desires, *against the will* . . . It is the labouring under the burden of self-repudiation and shame which makes abnormality. And the repudiation and shame come from the false doctrines we hold. Desire is from the unknown which is the Creator and Destroyer, beyond us, that which precedes us and brings us into being. Therefore Desire is holy, belonging to the mystic unknown, no matter *what* the desire. – Abnormality and insanity comes from the split in the self, the repudiation and the condemning of the desire, and the furtive fulfilment at the same time. This makes madness.   [L III 140–41]

The episode in 'Continental' where Birkin and Ursula make love in a way which seemed to her at first 'so bestial . . . so degraded!' was already there. But now Lawrence expanded it:

Why not be bestial, and go the whole round of experience? She exulted in it. She was bestial. How good it was to be really shameful! There would be no shameful thing she had not experienced. – Yet she was unabashed, she was herself. Why not? – She was free, when she knew everything, and no dark shameful things were denied her.   [WL 506]

Some readers have found it difficult to distinguish between the licentiousness of Gerald and Gudrun, or even Gudrun and Loerke, and that of Birkin and Ursula here. Lawrence refuses to oversimplify. The rejection of sensuality as an end does not in the least prevent him from advocating it as a means – to the burning out of false shames and the recovery of wholeness. A sexual relationship which is always and only licentious is obviously very different from one which occasionally loses itself in licence, but most of the time expresses itself in other modes.

The 1917 revision also brought a major change in the relationship between Birkin and Gerald. In the first draft, the impetus towards a closer relationship had come mainly from Gerald. Now it is Birkin who takes the initiative, overcoming the false shame which normally attaches to any declaration of 'love' between men:

'We will swear to each other, one day, shall we?' pleaded Birkin. 'We will swear to stand by each other – be true to each other – ultimately – infallibly – given to each other, organically – without possibility of taking back.'

Birkin sought hard to express himself. But Gerald hardly listened. His face shone with a certain luminous pleasure. He was pleased. But he kept his reserve. He held himself back.

'Shall we swear to each other, one day?' said Birkin, putting out his hand towards Gerald.

Gerald just touched the extended fine, living hand, as if withheld and afraid.

'We'll leave it till I understand it better,' he said, in a voice of excuse.

Birkin watched him. A little sharp disappointment, perhaps a touch of contempt, came into his heart.   [278]

Rather than a threat of death to Birkin, the relationship becomes a source of possible salvation for Gerald.

As recently as August 1916 Lawrence had written of 'the kind of love that was between Achilles and Patroclus . . . if once that lays hold of a man, then farewell to that man forever, as an independent or constructive soul' [L II 644]. The 1919 revision of *Women in Love* is largely devoted to affirming exactly the opposite, that only through such relationships can men become independent and constructive souls. Since those three years had brought Lawrence no such relationships, rather a series of what seemed to him betrayals, I can explain his volte face only as a response to his reading of Whitman. Particularly in the 'Calamus' poems Whitman had shown the courage of his own true feelings which must have made Lawrence ashamed of the extent to which he had allowed himself to be cowed by his conditioned reflex that he *should* not have such feelings. Of course, it was not only a matter of Lawrence's respect for (or fear of) 'tradition'. There was also his horror of pederasty, and his hostility to any relationship which might supplant marriage. But now, taking strength from Whitman, he was prepared to express what he felt to be vital in male friendships beyond marriage.

The second version of Lawrence's essay on Whitman, unlike the first and third, concentrates on this theme, 'the mystery of manly love, the love of comrades':

> Continually he tells us the same truth: the new world will be built upon the love of comrades, the new great dynamic of life will be manly love. Out of this inspiration the creation of the future . . .
>
> *True* marriage is eternal; in it we have our consummation and being. But the final consummation lies in that which is beyond marriage. And when the bond, or direct circuit of perfect comrades is established, what then, when we are on the brink of death, fulfilled in the vastness of life? Then, at last, we shall know a starry maturity. [SM 261, 264]

When Lawrence sent his *Classic American* essays to Huebsch, he wrote: 'The essay on Whitman you may find it politic not to publish – if so leave it out altogether – don't alter it' [L III 400]. The essay was written in the same month, September 1919, in which Lawrence probably did his final revision of *Women in Love*. Near the end of 'Marriage or Not' he added this dialogue between Birkin and Gerald:

> 'You've got to take down the love-and-marriage ideal from its pedestal. We want something broader. – I believe in the *additional* perfect relationship between man and man – additional to marriage.'
>
> 'I can never see how they can be the same,' said Gerald.
>
> 'Not the same – but equally important, equally creative, equally sacred, if you like.'
>
> Gerald moved uneasily. – 'You know, I can't feel that,' said he. 'Surely there can never be anything as strong between man and man as sex love is between man and woman. Nature doesn't provide the basis.'
>
> 'Well, of course, I think she does. And I don't think we shall ever be happy till we establish ourselves on this basis. You've got to get rid of the *exclusiveness* of married love. And you've got to admit the unadmitted love of man for man. It makes for a greater freedom for everybody, a greater power of individuality both in men and women.' [WL 439–40]

At the end of the next chapter Lawrence added the passage in which Birkin tells Ursula that he wants other people with them: ' "I always imagine our being really happy with some few other people – a little freedom with people" ' [452]. While correcting the proofs in November 1920, Lawrence added another passage, in answer to Ursula's assertion that there is no other world than the given world:

> 'Yes there is,' he said. 'There's somewhere where we can be free –

somewhere where one needn't wear much clothes – none even – where one meets a few people who have gone through enough, and can take things for granted – where you be yourself, without bothering. There is somewhere – there are one or two people –'

'But where?' she sighed.

'Somewhere – anywhere. Let's wander off. That's the thing to do – let's wander off.'

'Yes,' she said, thrilled at the thought of travel. But to her it was only travel.

'To be free,' he said. 'To be free, in a free place, with a few other people!'

'Yes,' she said wistfully. Those 'few other people' depressed her. [398]

Raymond Williams has accused Lawrence in *Women in Love* of contributing to what Williams regards as a disabling split between the personal and the social which is characteristic of much twentieth-century literature. He claims that the novel seeks to vindicate Birkin's principle of 'free, proud singleness', ends with simply 'a separation from society . . . in the action of resignation and flight' [MT 135], and therefore fails to give any substance to such phrases as 'the desire for creation and productive happiness' and 'the obligation of the permanent connection with others'. This might have been a fair reading of the 1917 version of the novel, but it completely ignores the 1919 revision. It ignores the progressive nature of the finished novel, where 'free, proud singleness' expresses a point reached by Birkin half-way through the novel, to be later superseded by the 'star-polarity' of his relationship with Ursula, which in turn, by the end, he has ceased to find adequate to his 'desire for creation and productive happiness'. The novel ends, in fact, with Birkin's growing realization that he cannot cut himself off from a dead society merely by 'resignation and flight', by 'travel'; that the road leading south to Italy is 'only a way in again' [WL 579–80]; that what he has gained in 'free, proud singleness' and the 'star-polarity' of his marriage is wasted without a wider human context in which the freedom and creativity achieved can be used to create 'a new colony of morality' [P 420]. The relationship with another man in comradeship and brotherly love is finally subsumed within a tentative resurgence of a faith in community.

Nevertheless, the flight was necessary. One cannot, as Williams does, speak of the loss of the rootedness of the characters in *The Rainbow* as impoverishment. The rootedness of the early Brangwens was inseparable from the narrowness of their horizons. By the end of that novel it had become impossible to distinguish between roots and bonds. *Women in Love* attempts a much more wide-ranging judgement upon society, and in a much less realistic mode. In Birkin's case, for example, it is not that his roots are tenuous – they are non-existent. He has no family and no past. He might have dropped from another planet. And this is a deliberate artistic strategy. Birkin moves freely through all the levels of hell, but is not himself one of the damned. He is in perpetual danger of being sucked into the whirlpool, but struggles to hang onto a vision so large that it contains the whirlpool. The attempt to evaluate a whole society involves finding a standpoint outside it from which it can be seen whole. Travel is both an aid to this and a metaphor for it. Birkin's dilemma is that the choice before him seems to be either to try to bully other people to join with him, or to 'take no steps at all . . . just go on as if one were alone in the world – the only creature in the world' [WL 452], when he knows that neither course will yield what he needs – 'a sort of further fellowship', 'a little freedom with people'.

Williams concludes that the novel leaves us with the conviction that 'only death is possible' [MT 138]; that its distinction is in the intensity with which it 'shows us the disintegration in progress'; and that its separation of the individual from society involves 'a loss of belief in both'. I believe on the contrary that though the novel is much more tentative than the essay and aware of practical difficulties, it contains just such a 'hushed, deep responsibility' as Lawrence expresses in the Whitman essay:

First, the great sexless normal relation between individuals, simple sexless friendships, unison of family, and clan, and nation, and group. Next, the powerful sex relation between man and woman, culminating in the eternal orbit of marriage. And, finally, the sheer friendship, the love between comrades, the manly love which alone can create a new era of life. [SM 263]

*

Emile Delavenay speaks for several critics when he claims that Lawrence does not achieve, in Women in Love, a synthesis of the many component elements which went into it, that 'there does not emerge a fully independent work of art, a universe fully intelligible and readily accessible to the reader' [MW 393]. But behind these apparently reasonable terms, 'independent', 'intelligible', 'accessible', lie several basic assumptions about Lawrence's art and art in general which are completely at odds with the novel's purposes and nature. Delavenay opens his account of the novel with several perfectly true statements – that it 'does not clearly and decisively proclaim a doctrine or new-world vision', that it 'ends on a note of doubt and dissatisfaction', and that it 'raises more problems than it solves'. All these are indeed part of the novel's nature and of Lawrence's intention, yet Delavenay seems to regard them as disabling faults. He requires of the novel that it should be homogeneous and clear and conclusive, that it should 'illustrate unequivocally the novelist's ideas' [428]. When Lawrence wanted to do that he wrote his philosophical essays, which may produce theoretical answers, but answers which, unless they have already been validated by the 'pure passionate experience' [F 15] of the art, are unlikely to carry much weight with those readers who go to imaginative art for something much more complex and rewarding than illustrations of the writer's 'ideas'.

Art resists, tests and modifies metaphysic. In Lawrence's case the several drafts of each novel and the time-span covered by the composition are a great benefit. As we saw, *Sons and Lovers* began as a eulogy of the mother, but came to incorporate radical criticism of her in a much more open and flexible attitude to the paradox of all mother-son relationships. *The Rainbow* began as an epithalamium, but ended as, among other things, a wide-eyed examination of the potentialities and limitations of sex and marriage. *Women in Love* began (the 1916 version) as a misanthropic, apocalyptic novel, with marriage as its only positive, and a corresponding horror of man-to-man relationships, developed into an even more 'purely destructive' vision, but ended reopening the possibility of a constructive human future through male comradeship beyond marriage. In each case the tale goes in a direction quite unforeseen at the outset. It refuses to be nailed down.

In *Women in Love* Lawrence is concerned to show that experience is equivocal, ambivalent, that there are no clear answers or wholly adequate resolutions. As John Worthen says, the novel is 'designed to elicit paradox rather than fall helplessly into it' [IN 95]. Or in Richard Drain's words:

> The stresses he treats are those of our time; and of problems that no doctrine can bring to a final resolution . . . The purpose of the novel is to reveal to us an emotional underlife we had ignored that stirs with just such ambiguities; and to trace within it patterns that serve to anatomize a whole society. [CS 91, 70]

Delavenay makes the common assumption that Birkin is in the novel merely as a mouthpiece for Lawrence; that he is supposed to articulate the novel's doctrine or message – a coherent set of positive values, what Lawrence 'stands for'. Not much coherence could be found in the novel if that were so. Delavenay is, of course, well aware of the symbolism with which the books abounds, but regards this as unintegrated with plot and character, dragged in from Lawrence's reading or real-life experiences simply because it happened to come into his mind at the time of writing the novel. I hope I have demonstrated what has already been shown by Leavis, Ford, Drain, Worthen, and others, that the whole style and vision of the novel, not just its more overtly symbolic passages, is all of a piece, all contributing to the alienation of those readers who want life and art to be 'intelligible' and meanings 'accessible'. For the novel is about a world in which all the characters are in some sense alienated – from reality, from their own natures and needs, and from the holiness and larger purposes of nature itself. The unique style, unique even in Lawrence, is a way of forcing the reader to experience that alienation himself, or rather, since we all experience it, and evade the knowledge of it in real life, to confront it in its most extreme and lurid forms.

Women in Love is an incredibly detached, objective and controlled account of a particularly difficult and painful and unsatisfactory phase of Lawrence's life-adventure, as he struggles to see modern life as it is, to adopt a world-view uncontaminated by human arrogance, and yet to retain some spark of faith in 'humanity and the human potential to evolve something magnificent out of a renewed chaos' [F 14].

SIX

'LITTLE LIVING MYTHS':
BIRDS, BEASTS AND FLOWERS

After the burning of *The Rainbow* in 1915 and the interminable delay in finding a publisher for *Women in Love*, Lawrence was understandably reluctant to invest as much of himself in his next novel. It was just possible to write a visionary, apocalyptic novel such as *Women in Love* to the 'unseen witnesses', but a more ordinary story-novel such as *Aaron's Rod* required some confidence in the existence of a body of real live readers out there, with a modicum of sympathy and understanding, a confidence Lawrence could no longer muster: 'It makes me swear – such a damned mean, narrow-gutted, pitiful, crawling, mongrel world, that daren't have a man's work and won't even allow him to live' [L III 209]. His references to *Aaron's Rod* in the letters conspicuously lack the enthusiasm with which he had formerly discussed his novel-in-progress: 'I am doing . . . very spasmodically, another daft novel. It goes slowly – very slowly and fitfully. But I don't care' [216]. That was February 1918. Several months later it was still the same story: 'I am slowly working at another novel: though I feel it's not much use. No publisher will risk my last, and none will risk this, I expect. I can't do anything in the world today – am just choked' [280]. No longer can Lawrence produce those amazing bursts of creativity which had characterized his work on *The Rainbow* and *Women in Love*. By the end of 1919 *Aaron's Rod* had ground to a halt, and Lawrence set it aside in favour of *The Insurrection of Miss Houghton*, the manuscript of which he was at last, in February 1920, able to obtain from Germany.

Although he did not actually incorporate the 200-page manuscript of *The Insurrection of Miss Houghton* into *The Lost Girl*, it gave him the impetus to be able to finish the novel in about three months. But the letters betray an uncertainty of tone which carried over into the novel itself. Since he can no longer write with the expectation of being taken seriously, he adopts, for self-protection, a would-be 'amusing' tone. The word 'amusing' occurs in almost all his descriptions of the novel to his correspondents, and he has hardly

194

anything more to say about it. Yet despite the self-deprecation – 'a novel which amuses me but perhaps won't amuse anybody else' [498] – Lawrence did care deeply about the reception of his first novel to be published for five years. The reviews of *The Lost Girl* in December 1920 confirmed his worst fears. He wrote to Martin Secker:

> I have seen the *Observer* and the *Times Lit. Sup.* – and snap my fingers at them: the drivel of the impotent. – Therefore, if you choose to bring out *Women in Love*, publicly, and to advertise it as you do *The Lost Girl*, and merely refrain from sending out review copies, that, I think, is the best way. It will give reviewers a chance to say nothing, which is best. [638]

The review in the *Times Literary Supplement* was by Virginia Woolf, who had apparently been unable to get beyond the first few chapters. She complains that sex disappears from the novel with Alvina's return to Woodhouse at the end of the third chapter, and that the novel must be read as one would read Arnold Bennett. This must have been particularly galling to Lawrence, since *The Lost Girl* had been conceived in 1912 specifically as his answer to Bennett's resignation. If Virginia Woolf had got as far as Chapter VI she would have reached Lawrence's assurance to the reader that the novel was not going to continue in the Bennett vein: 'But we are not going to follow our song to its fatal and dreary conclusion', and that Alvina was to be no '*ordinary*' old-maid heroine' [LG 85]. But Virginia Woolf did not get as far as Ciccio, let alone Pescocalascio.

There was worse to come with Murry's review in *Athenaeum*. Murry missed the point of the Woodhouse section completely, regretting that 'there is no garment of magical beauty flung over it, like that which gleamed out of the opening pages of *Sons and Lovers*' [CH 148]. He liked the later part of the novel still less: 'Mr Lawrence would have us back to the slime from which we rose' [150].

The reviews arrived when Lawrence had just begun Part II of *Mr Noon*. Part I had been written in a flippant, embarrassingly arch tone, but at least the tone there is consistent. In Part II, however, Lawrence had undertaken to describe his most intimate experiences, deepest feelings, and most cherished beliefs, to readers who must, he felt, be continuously cajoled into not taking him seriously, since to do so would certainly lead to disgust and outright rejection. The reviews of *The Lost Girl*, which Lawrence actually discusses at the beginning of the second chapter of Part II, undoubtedly undermined what little faith he had in the whole enterprise. The excruciating uncertainty of tone is punctuated by coy flirtation with the supposed female 'dear reader' until, finally, Lawrence's disdain for such readers erupts on the final page of the abandoned manuscript:

> Do not imagine, ungentle reader, that by just chasing women you will ever get anywhere. Gilbert might have had a thousand Emmies, and even a thousand really nice women, and yet never have cracked the womb. It needed the incalculable fight such as he fought, unconscious and willy-nilly, with his German Johanna: and such as I fight with you, oh gentle but rather cowardly and imbecile reader: for such, really, I find you.
>
> [MN 291–2]

As early as May 1917, Lawrence had written to Murry: 'I find people ultimately boring: and you can't have fiction without people. So fiction does not, at the bottom, interest me any more' [L III 127]. Yet fiction seemed the only way to earn a living. Without that pressure, Lawrence might have turned even more wholeheartedly to poetry at this stage of his career. The audience for poetry could be assumed to be more judicious than that for fiction. The poet, in any case, does not have the same obligation to write for a specific audience. A poem is an act of awareness, a communion between the poet and the object or experience. It is naturally addressed to the 'unseen witnesses'. And it breaks the womb of the exclusively human, issuing forth into the fresh, sacred, and resonantly symbolic world of birds, beasts and flowers.

*

Lawrence's first poems were about flowers; the last words of his last poem are 'immortal bird'. Between, there are hundreds of poems about birds, beasts and flowers, not only in the volume of that name, and hundreds more containing references to them. We know that from earliest childhood Lawrence was fascinated by the natural world, and soon became very knowledgeable about it. 'There seemed no flower nor even weed whose name and qualities Lawrence did not know' [PR 34]. It was the wood and its flora which drew Lawrence as much as anything to Haggs Farm as a boy. May Chambers recalled:

> Bert had a wonderful knowledge of the wild flowers of the wood. It was a bluebell wood with violets and forget-me-nots but no yellow flowers except the celandine, and he seemed to love especially its bright, glossy petals.
>
> 'Do you know why the earliest spring flowers are mostly yellow?' he asked us. Some of us did not know, and he explained it was because of the scarcity of insects and therefore the need of bright colours to attract. In such informal manner our family learned much we would otherwise have missed. For we were not all students, but all liked the bits of information

Bert let fall because there was always the spice he imparted of its being a discovery.   [CB III 592–3]

Lawrence continued to do this all his life. Many of his friends have testified to his ability to make the natural world come alive for them as never before.

But, as we have seen, Lawrence's interest in nature comes across in the early poems too often as sentimental indulgence, and in the early fiction as a decorative backdrop. Lawrence's attempts to relate the lives of the characters to the natural background are usually anthropomorphic, or crude manifestations of the pathetic fallacy.

The next stage of Lawrence's development was to find in nature a rich store of analogues for human emotional and psychological states. It is one characteristic among many (including 'a joy of natural things' [P 305]) which made it perfectly appropriate, for a while, for Lawrence to align himself with the Georgians. In 'Snap-Dragon', his contribution to the first Georgian anthology, we find the description of the flower merging with his own repressed sexuality:

She laughed, she reached her hand out to the flower,
Closing its crimson throat. My own throat in her power
Strangled, my heart swelled up so full
As if it would burst its wine-skin in my throat,
Choke me in my own crimson. I watched her pull
The gorge of the gaping flower, till the blood did float

Over my eyes, and I was blind –   [CP 123]

It was a method which lent itself to development in the novel, from the simple flower analogues of *Sons and Lovers* to the full-blown charting of a psychic landscape through animal images in *The Rainbow*.

The review which Lawrence wrote in February 1913 of the first *Georgian Anthology* was characterized by an optimism which he did not finally abandon until after the completion of *The Rainbow*: the note of 'hope, and religious joy. Nothing is really wrong'; the 'faith in the vastness of life's wealth . . . There is no winter that we fear'; the faith in the self as the 'quick of all growth . . . This flesh and blood sitting here writing, the great impersonal flesh and blood, greater than me, which I am proud to belong to, contains all the future' [P 305–6]. Lawrence singled out for praise 'Mr Rupert Brooke's brightness'. But the collapse of 1915 contained the realization that the 'exultation' of the Georgians had been no more than naïveté which, given the new perspective of the war, came to look like madness:

The death of Rupert Brooke fills me more and more [. . .] with the sense of the fatuity of it all. He was slain by bright Phoebus shaft – it was in keeping with his general sunniness – it was the real climax of his pose. I first heard of him as a Greek God under a Japanese Sunshade, reading poetry in his pyjamas, at Grantchester, at Grantchester, upon the lawns where the river goes. Bright Phoebus smote him down. It is all in the saga.
O God Oh God, it is all too much of a piece: It is like madness.

[L II 330–31]

What saved Lawrence himself from madness or nihilism at that time was the fact that as his faith in humanity died, his faith in the non-human world as a source and standard of sanity grew to replace it. This same letter ends:

It isn't my disordered imagination. There is a wagtail sitting on the gatepost. I see how sweet and swift heaven is. But hell is slow and creeping and viscous, and insect-teeming: as is this Europe now – this England.

At the beginning of August 1915 the Lawrences lived for a few days on the sea-shore near Littlehampton. Lawrence loved it because there were 'no people, no people at all, no houses, no buildings':

It is a great thing to realise that the original world is still there – perfectly clean and pure, many white advancing foams, and only the gulls swinging between the sky and the shore: and in the wind the yellow sea-poppies fluttering very hard, like yellow gleams in the wind: and the windy flourish of the seed-horns. [375]

The natural world has ceased to be a source of analogues for the human world; it is now an alternative to it, with inherent, autonomous meanings, independent of any human observer:

The world of nature is wonderful in its revivifying spontaneity. But oh god, the world of man . . . At any rate, the cooing of the doves is very real, and the blithe impertinence of the lambs as they peep round their mothers. They affect me like the Rainbow, as a sign that life will never be destroyed, or turn bad altogether. [L III 97]

*

In September 1915 Lawrence had recalled the cyclamens of Lake Garda as 'little living myths that I cannot understand' [TI 88]. He felt that by assiduous reading and hard thinking he could refashion his metaphysic, first formulated in 'Le Gai Savaire', and refine it to the point where it would yield such understanding. There were still important lessons to be learned from Nietzsche. In *The Joyful Wisdom* Lawrence would have read:

I fear the animals regard man as a being like themselves, seriously endangered by the loss of sound animal understanding; – they regard him perhaps as the absurd animal, the laughing animal, the crying animal, the unfortunate animal.   [JW 224]

He would be reminded by that of one of his favourite passages in Whitman:

> I think I could turn and live with animals, they are so placid and self-
>   contain'd,
> I stand and look at them long and long.
>
> They do not sweat and whine about their condition,
> They do not lie awake in the dark and weep for their sins,
> They do not make me sick discussing their duty to God,
> Not one is dissatisfied, not one is demented with the mania of owning
>   things,
> Not one kneels to another, nor to his kind that lived thousands of
>   years ago,
> Not one is respectable or unhappy over the whole earth.
>
> So they show their relations to me and I accept them,
> They bring me tokens of myself, they evince them plainly in their
>   possession.   [WW 94]

The trouble, according to Nietzsche, lay in the very nature of human consciousness:

> the world of which we can become conscious is only a superficial and sym-
> bolic world, a generalised and vulgar world; . . . everything which becomes
> conscious *becomes* just thereby shallow, meagre, relatively stupid, – a
> generalisation, a symbol, a characteristic of the herd . . .   [JW 354]

Consciousness, he claims, would long ago have led to the break-down of mankind, had it not been for the 'conserving bond of the instincts'. But somewhere between mental consciousness and those preservative instincts there is another, largely untapped, reservoir of knowledge:

> I have *discovered* for myself that the old humanity and animality, yea, the
> collective primeval age, and the past of all sentient being, continues to
> meditate, love, hate, and reason in me . . .   [54]

This was the part of himself Lawrence wanted to discover. He tried, in his reading, to get back beyond the fall, the fall into our kind of blinkered consciousness, before Plato and Christianity.

In June 1915 he read Burnet's *Early Greek Philosophy*, and discovered, with joy, what amazing leaps the mind is capable of when it is not dissociated from the senses, not crippled by methodologies or burdened by accumulations of what is assumed to be already known. 'These early Greeks have clarified my soul' [L II 364], Law-

Life into Art

rence wrote to Russell. The next version of Lawrence's 'philosophy' was 'The Crown', which shows strongly the influence of Herakleitos and the other early Greeks. The essay ends on a high note:

Our universe is not much more than a mannerism with us now. If we break through, we shall find, that man is not man, as he seems to be, nor woman woman. The present seeming is a ridiculous travesty. And even the sun is not the sun as it appears to be. It is something tingling with magnificence. And then starts the one glorious activity of man: the getting himself into a new relationship with a new heaven and a new earth.
[P II 415]

But the Greeks could not take Lawrence very far along this road. Perhaps the anthropologists would help him to go further. In December 1915 he read Frazer's *Golden Bough* and *Totemism and Exogamy*, and wrote excitedly to Russell:

Now I am convinced of what I believed when I was about twenty – that there is another seat of consciousness than the brain and the nerve system: there is a blood-consciousness which exists in us independently of the ordinary mental consciousness . . .

Do you know what science says about these things? It is *very* important: the whole of our future life depends on it.   [L II 470–71]

Lawrence was already familiar with Jane Harrison's *Ancient Art and Ritual*, and was able to interpret Frazer's material in her less rationalistic, more psychological and religious manner.

In February 1916 Lawrence borrowed Gilbert Murray's *Four Stages of Greek Religion*. There Murray explained what the word *theos* meant to the Greek poets – any irreducible or absolute manifestation of being, physical or emotional, in the self or the other. Murray also argued that the 'development' of the Greek gods from the theriomorphic to the anthropomorphic represented a decline and a symptom of imaginative laziness. Christopher Pollnitz concludes his much fuller account of these influences:

By placing Harrison's subject, the religiously yearning savage, next to Murray's object, nature with its slippery *theoi*, Lawrence was able to ratify his own epistemological model, of deep calling to deep at the living moment, as being man's oldest and most abiding experience of his circumambient universe.   [DHLR 15 25]

*

Through 1916 Lawrence became more and more convinced that 'this world of ours has got to collapse', to slide in horror 'down into the bottomless pit':

It was a beautiful day here today, with bright, new, wide-opened sunshine, and lovely new scents in the fresh air, as if the new blood were rising. And the sea came in great long waves thundering splendidly from the unknown . . . What does it matter about that seething scrimmage of mankind in Europe. If that were indeed the only truth, one might indeed despair. [L II 528]

Seagulls swept in from the sea with sharp cries:

A very big seagull just flew up from the east, white like lime-stone, and hovered just in front of me, then turned back in the sky. It seemed like a messenger. [599]

There were other messengers, aristocrats of the natural world:

Yesterday I saw an adder sleeping on the grass. She was very slim and elegant, with her black markings. At last she was disturbed, she lifted her slender head and listened with great delicacy. Then, very fine and undulating, she moved away. I admired her intensely, and liked her very much. If she were a familiar spirit, she was a dainty and superb princess. [599]

She stayed with him like a vision. Months later he recalled:

I saw a most beautiful brindled adder, in the spring, coiled up asleep with her head on her shoulder. She did not hear me till I was very near. Then she must have felt my motion, for she lifted her head like a queen to look, then turned and moved slowly and with delicate pride into the bushes. She often comes into my mind again, and I think I see her asleep in the sun, like a Princess of the fairy world. It is queer, the intimation of other worlds, which one catches. [L III 40]

When writing 'The Reality of Peace' in February 1917, he remembered her again:

The brindled, slim adder, as she lifts her delicate head attentively in the spring sunshine – for they say she is deaf – suddenly throws open the world of unchanging, pure perfection to our startled breast. In our whole understanding, when sense and spirit and mind are consummated into pure unison, then we are free in a world of the absolute. [P 680]

It is very typical of Lawrence's prose of this period that he should move so quickly from the particular to the general, the concrete to the abstract, the perceptive to the assertive. It is full of strained arguments and loose connections. The habit of transforming encounters with the natural world into misty rhetoric is Wordsworthian, and Lawrence is in danger here of doing what he accuses Wordsworth of doing to the primrose, reducing the object to a mere token of himself. In asserting his understanding of the primrose, Wordsworth in effect plucks it, denies its 'communion with all things'.

> The sky is with me, and the dim
> Earth clasps my roots   [P II 448]

says the primrose, in Lawrence's parody of 'Peter Bell'. To assume
that a primrose can be assimilated by the poet's mind is an impertinence. Yet in 'The Reality of Peace' Lawrence goes much further,
asserting that life itself, death itself, can be understood and assimilated.

The unison he speaks of, in the passage I have quoted, is not
between the poet and the snake, but between sense, spirit and
mind. The 'world of pure perfection' is the 'whole understanding'
which has instantaneously incorporated the world revealed by the
adder. The adder provides him with an epiphany, a timeless
moment:

> The timeless quality of *being* is understanding; when I understand fully,
> flesh and blood and bone, and mind and soul and spirit one rose of unison,
> then I *am*. Then I am unrelated and perfect. In true understanding I am
> always perfect and timeless. In my utterance of that which I have under-
> stood I am timeless as a jewel.   [P 680]

This unison is entirely internal. And this unified, unrelated, perfect
'I' is 'free', 'transcending into absolution'. Free from what, transcending what, absolved from what? From time, of course. From
relatedness with all things. Ultimately, from 'flesh and blood and
bone'. For 'understanding', which here lays claim to be a faculty of
the whole man, gradually, in the ensuing paragraphs, repudiates
the body, becomes indistinguishable from 'mind':

> Understanding is not necessarily mental. It is of the senses and the spirit.
> But we live also in the mind. And the first great act of living is to encompass
> death in the understanding. Therefore the first great activity of the living
> mind is to understand death in the mind. Without this there is no freedom
> of the mind, there is no life of the mind, since creative life is the attaining
> a perfect consummation with death. When in my mind there rises the idea
> of life, then this idea must encompass the idea of death, and this encom-
> passing is the germination of a new epoch of the mind.   [682]

We are not far here from Wordsworth's worship of 'the Mind
of Man' as an all-encompassing absolute – the egotistical sublime.

It is clear that Lawrence could not yet have written 'Snake', or
any of the best poems in *Birds, Beasts and Flowers*, which are indeed
poems of flesh, blood and bone, mind, soul and spirit, and for that
reason are poems of time, and relatedness, and, ultimately, the
impossibility of understanding. And the 'utterance' in those poems
is not at all jewel-like. In 'Poetry of the Present' (1919) Lawrence

specifically rejects 'gem-like' poetry, the poetry of 'completeness', 'consummateness', 'finality' and 'perfection':

> Do not ask for the qualities of the unfading timeless gems . . . There must be the rapid momentaneous association of things which meet and pass on the for ever incalculable journey of creation: everything left in its own rapid, fluid relationship with the rest of things.   [220]

*

In January 1916 Lawrence had written:

> The essence of poetry with us in this age of stark and unlovely actualities is a stark directness, without a shadow of a lie, or a shadow of deflection anywhere. Everything can go, but this stark, bare, rocky directness of statement, this alone makes poetry, today.   [L II 503]

Pound (echoing Whitman) had been saying the same thing for years. Yeats, after years of writing poems about the necessity and impossibility of 'going naked', had at last broken through that block with 'Easter 1916'. Lawrence's poetry of that period certainly changed, shed a great deal, the last trappings of formal verse, the last wisps of Georgianism. His verse became, for the first time, totally free. As late as 1919 Lawrence was still saying:

> Whitman pruned away his clichés – perhaps his clichés of rhythm as well as of phrase. And that is about all we can do, deliberately, with free verse. We can get rid of the stereotyped movements and the old hackneyed associations of sound or sense. We can break down those artificial conduits and canals through which we do so love to force our utterance. We can break the stiff neck of habit.   [P 221]

The purpose of this negative, getting-rid and breaking-down stage is to transform verse from that which shapes to that which is shaped. Not a bottle or a canal, but an open landscape over which inspiration can flow in its natural course, like a river. The discipline is pushed back a stage, before utterance. It becomes a discipline of concentration, awareness, sensitivity: 'We can be in ourselves spontaneous and flexible as flame, we can see that utterance rushes out without artificial form or artificial smoothness'.

Even in the best poems of 1916–17, we feel that, though Lawrence has successfully done what he could do, deliberately, has cleared the channels, given himself total freedom, he has not yet clarified his vision and achieved that delicate adjustment of sensibility which was needed for a breakthrough into free verse poems which would have the shape and immediacy, the thereness, of living creatures. What he pours into the poems is a rather desperate generalized sweeping rhetoric which is hardly to be distinguished from the rhetoric of his contemporary prose essays. Here are two typical passages:

> There is another world. The winter is gone.
> There is a new world of spring.
> The voice of the turtle is heard in the land
> But the flesh shrinks from so sudden a transition.
> Surely the call is premature while the clods are still frozen,
> And the ground is littered with the remains of wings!
> Yet we have no choice.
> In the bottoms of impenetrable blackthorn,
> Each evening and morning now,
> Out flickers a whistling of birds.

> The gush of spring is strong enough to play with the globe of earth like a ball on a fountain; at the same time it opens the tiny hands of the hazel with such infinite patience. The power of the rising, golden, all-creative sap could take the earth and heave it off among the stars, into the invisible; the same sets the throstle at sunset on a bough singing against the black-bird; comes out in the hesitating tremor of the primrose, and betrays its candour in the round white strawberry flower, is dignified in the foxglove, like a Red-Indian brave.

Is it immediately obvious that I have printed the prose passage (from 'The Whistling of Birds') as verse, and the verse passage (from 'Craving for Spring') as prose?

*

One problem, as we have seen, was Lawrence's drift towards the abstract and transcendental. In April 1917 he wrote:

> The pure abstract thought interests me now at this juncture more than art. I am tired of emotions and squirmings of sensation. Let us have a little pure thought, a little perfect and detached understanding.   [L III 110]

Lawrence was well aware that there is no such thing as abstract art. You cannot create novels or poems out of 'detached' understanding. At the time when the great poems were being written, Lawrence was to say 'damn understanding more than anything' [CL 669]. In May he wrote:

> Philosophy interests me most now – not novels or stories. I find people ultimately boring: and you can't have fiction without people. So fiction does not, at the bottom, interest me any more. I am weary of humanity and human things. One is happy in the thoughts only that transcend humanity.   [127]

The attempt to transcend 'humanity and human things' is bound to lead to the weakening of one's sense of one's own humanity, which includes one's relationship, as a living creature, with the non-human world. This degree of detachment was bad for Lawrence's health, especially his mental health: 'Yesterday I began to type out the "Peace" articles . . . But suddenly I felt as if I was going dotty, straight out of my mind, so I left off' [125].

The transcendental drift of the 'Peace' articles led Lawrence directly into his next project, a set of essays to be called 'The Transcendental Element in Classic American Literature' or 'The Mystic Import of American Literature'. The first of these essays, on Crèvecœur, was written in September 1917. It begins in exactly the same vein as 'The Reality of Peace', discussing the duality of 'spirit and senses, soul and body, mind and matter':

> From this duality in first-consciousness, this duality in root-knowledge, arises the subsequent oneness and wholeness of full mental consciousness . . . one third pure state of wholeness, whole understanding . . . I draw all things into me . . . for my power and perfection . . . the single, rich splendour of the positive 'I', the self paramount, that moves undiminished in a contributed universe. . . . I encompass the unknown within the dominion of myself. [SM 55–60]

All these opening pages of 'philosophy' were later dropped, probably in the 1920 revision, for in the 1920 version of the Whitman essay (the only essay to have survived in this intermediate form) Lawrence castigates Whitman for doing what he had himself approved in 1917: 'All adds up to one in him . . . His One Identity is a prison of horror, once realized' [258–9].

When he conceived these essays, Lawrence's attitude towards transcendentalism was sympathetic, or at least neutral. For all their 'blood and thunder' and their 'soul-searching' (L III 156], they were to be, for Lawrence, relatively objective, suitable for delivering as lectures at the great American universities or publishing as articles in the *Yale Review* or *The New Republic*. By the time they reached their final form in 1923, they had been transformed into a savage attack on transcendentalism, which Lawrence hunts down with a fervour matching Captain Ahab's in the opposite cause. What happened between 1918 and 1920 to bring about this volte face?

I believe that the most important factor was Lawrence's rereading of Whitman. We know that *Leaves of Grass* was already one of Lawrence's 'great books' in the Eastwood days, but it is quite possible that he did not return to it until 1918. For all the reservations about Whitman which Lawrence developed in his later essays on him, his plunge into *Leaves of Grass* in 1918 was sheer release and joy. If any writer ever clarified Lawrence's soul, it was Whitman.

Lawrence may have begun his reading of Whitman before writing 'The Two Principles' early in 1918. Here is the first significant modification of the disabling dualism of 'The Reality of Peace' and the Crèvecœur essay, where Lawrence had gone so far as to claim that 'the creative mystery . . . is . . . beyond and before the whole material universe' [58]. In 'The Two Principles' he writes:

Surely the universe has arisen from some universal living self-conscious plasm, plasm which has no origin and no end, but is life eternal and identical, bringing forth the infinite creatures of being and existence, living creatures embodying inanimate substance. There is no utterly immaterial existence, no spirit. [180]

This plasm is composed of the fundamental elements of fire and water, whose opposition and interplay 'spontaneously brings forth the living forms we know' [181]. This opposition and interplay continues within each creature. Its primary manifestation in the higher forms is 'sexual polarity', 'the mystery of creative *otherness*' [185].

The whole essay reads like a commentary on the opening of Section 3 of 'Song of Myself':

I have heard what the talkers were talking, the talk of the beginning
    and the end,
But I do not talk of the beginning or the end.

There was never any more inception than there is now,
Nor any more youth or age than there is now,
And will never be any more perfection than there is now,
Nor any more heaven or hell than there is now.

Urge and urge and urge,
Always the procreant urge of the world.
Out of the dimness opposite equals advance, always substance and
    increase, always sex,
Always a knit of identity, always distinction, always a breed of
    life. [WW 65]

'The Two Principles' is still, as the title implies, dualistic, but it is a dualism like that of Whitman's 'opposite equals' with no transcendental term, no repudiation of the material world, no hubristic striving to comprehend the universe from beginning to end. It is a dualism of balance and wholeness and creativity.

The first version of the Whitman essay was written in June 1918. It has not yet been published. It concentrates, much more than the later versions, on Whitman's free-verse technique, in terms close to those of the essay 'Poetry of the Present' which Lawrence wrote in August 1919. Here Lawrence describes the kind of free verse he now wishes to write, 'the ungraspable poetry of the sheer present', which is the utterance of 'the instant, whole man':

Whitman's is the best poetry of this kind. Without beginning and without end, without any base and pediment, it sweeps past for ever, like a wind that is for ever in passage, and unchainable. Whitman truly looked before and after. But he did not sigh for what is not. The clue to all his utterance lies in the sheer appreciation of the instant moment, life surging itself into utterance at its very well-head . . . Because Whitman put this into his poetry, we fear him and respect him so profoundly . . . He is so near the quick . . . The quick of all the universe, of all creation, is the incarnate, carnal self. Poetry gave us the clue: free verse: Whitman. Now we know. [P 220–22]

The bulk of the essay is a definition of free verse. But since free verse is defined not as a verse form like blank verse, nor as a skill, but as the utterance of a spontaneous and flexible aliveness, relatedness, it is also a definition of a whole humanity. Insofar as it is a technique, it is a technique for by-passing the self-conscious ego, the mental 'understanding'. As Whitman himself wrote in the preface to the first edition of *Leaves of Grass*:

The great poet has less a marked style, and is more the channel of thoughts and things without increase or diminution, and is the free channel of himself. He swears to his art, I will not be meddlesome, I will not have in my writing any elegance, or effect, or originality, to hang in the way between me and the rest like curtains. I will have nothing hang in the way, not the richest curtains. What I tell I tell for precisely what it is. Let who may exalt or startle or fascinate or soothe, I will have purposes as health or heat or snow has and be as regardless of observation.

[WW 749–50]

*

As important as the influence of Whitman was Lawrence's escape to Italy in November 1919. 1918 had been an appalling year for him. Hounded out of the Cornwall cottage and unable to find a publisher for either *The Rainbow* or *Women in Love*, Lawrence was dependent on charity for a roof over his head. He described himself as feeling 'like a wild cat in a cage' [L III 226]; and on his thirty-third birthday, 11 September 1918, he wrote to Amy Lowell:

I don't know how on earth we shall get through another winter – how we shall ever find a future. Humanity as it stands, and myself as I stand, we just seem mutually impossible to one another. The ground dwindles under one's feet – what next, heaven knows. [280]

Through the winter, ill much of the time, he waited 'paralysed for some sort of release' [313]. That release, when it came, was almost a rebirth. We can measure the importance of it by comparing the dispirited prose of these 1918 letters with the vitality of his 1920 letters. From Capri in January he wrote to Lady Cynthia Asquith:

> To look down the Salernian Gulf, South-east, on a blue day, and to see the dim, sheer rocky coast, the clean rock mountains, is so beautiful, so like Ulysses, that one sheds ones avatars, and recovers a lost self, Mediterranean, anterior to us. [462]

That recovered self had all the courage of Ulysses, setting out to discover new worlds, embarking on the life-adventure:

> In early April I went with my wife to Syracuse for a few days: lovely, lovely days, with the purple anemones blowing in the Sicilian fields, and Adonis-blood red on the little ledges, and the corn rising strong and green in the magical, malarial places, and Etna flowing now to the northward, still with her crown of snow. The lovely, lovely journey from Catania to Syracuse, in spring, winding round the blueness of that sea, where the tall pink asphodel was dying, and the yellow asphodel like a lily showing her silk. Lovely, lovely Sicily, the dawn-place, Europe's dawn, with Odysseus pushing his ship out of the shadows into the blue. Whatever had died for me, Sicily had then not died: dawn-lovely Sicily, and the Ionian sea.
>
> We came back, and the world was lovely: our own house above the almond trees, and the sea in the cove below. Calabria glimmering like a changing opal away to the left, across the blue, bright straits and all the great blueness of the great dawn-sea in front, where the sun rose with a splendour like trumpets every morning, and me rejoicing like a madness in this dawn, day-dawn, life-dawn, the dawn which is Greece, which is me. [P II 328]

This was the recovered pristine self, the 'instant, whole man', whose newly clarified vision found its natural utterance in the poems of *Birds, Beasts and Flowers*.

*

As Sandra Gilbert has shown, *Birds, Beasts and Flowers* is much more than the sum of its parts, and there is much to gain from reading the poems in the order in which Lawrence carefully arranged them. It is, however, equally revealing to read them in the order in which they were written.

The earliest poems are probably a group of three short and untypical poems, 'Tropic', 'Peace' and 'Southern Night', written at the beginning of June, when Lawrence had been living in Sicily for nearly three months. In 'The Spirit of Place' (1918) Lawrence had formulated the law that 'every great locality expresses itself perfectly, in its own flowers, its own birds and beasts, lastly its own men, with their perfected works' [SM 30]. In 'The Two Principles' he tried to explain how the spirit of a place can express itself in men:

There certainly does exist a subtle and complex sympathy, correspondence between the plasm of the human body, which is identical with the primary psyche, and the material elements outside. The primary human psyche is a complex plasm, which quivers, sense-conscious, in contact with the circumambient cosmos.   [176]

Thus, whenever a man moves to a new part of the earth, there must take place in him incalculable and profound chemical and psychic changes. When the first Europeans settled in America:

They walked a new earth, were seized by a new electricity, and laid in line differently. Their bones, their nerves, their sinews took on a new molecular disposition in the new vibration . . . Their subtlest plasm was changed under the radiation of new skies, new influence of light, their first and rarest life-stuff transmuted.   [29]

When Lawrence moved to Sicily he realized the full truth of his intuition. He had, of course, lived in Italy before the war, but never further south than Lerici. Sicily was completely different, part Greek, part African, volcanic, hot. So hot that on 1 June Lawrence wrote to Amy Lowell: 'I shouldn't wonder if my skin went black and my eyes went yellow, like a negro's'. He felt he was undergoing a reconstitution of his blood and transformation of consciousness as his whole metabolism adjusted itself to the new geological and astronomical and climatic conditions of Sicily, its distinctive magnetism, the spirit of place. These three poems strive to express what this metamorphosis felt like and meant. In so doing they form a kind of overture to *Birds, Beasts and Flowers*, announcing many of its major themes.

In 'Tropic', Lawrence confronts the dark sun of Sicily:

Behold my hair twisting and going black.
Behold my eyes turn tawny yellow
Negroid;
See the milk of northern spume
Coagulating and going black in my veins
Aromatic as frankincense.   [CP 301]

'Negroid' evokes not merely certain physical characteristics, but a distinctive non-European consciousness, a capacity for 'naked communion' with his world. In August Lawrence borrowed from Jan Juta a collection of African Bushman folklore which strengthened Lawrence's belief in an older animistic consciousness. In 'Grapes', wondering who to ask about the vine, Lawrence replies 'The negro might know a little':

> Once God was all negroid, as now he is fair.
> But it's so long ago, the ancient Bushman has forgotten more utterly
>   than we, who have never known.   [286]

But if Nietzsche is right in his contention that 'the old human and animal world, indeed the entire prehistory and past of all sentient being, works on, loves on, hates on, thinks on in me', then Lawrence need not study the Bushman or seek the aid of anthropologists in travelling 'back, back down the old ways of time' [SS 131]. The dark gods are waiting for him in the depths of his own soul. They show themselves in dreams, and one method of releasing such dreams is intoxication:

> And if we sip the wine, we find dreams coming upon us
> Out of the imminent night.
> Nay, we find ourselves crossing the fern-scented frontiers
> Of the world before the floods, where man was dark and evasive
> And the tiny vine-flower rose of all roses, perfumed,
> And all in naked communion communicating as now our clothed
>   vision can never communicate.   [CP 286]

The sun of Sicily is hostile and black, more like the phallic heat of Dionysos than the mental light of Apollo. The flood of heat downwards from the sun at the beginning of 'Tropic', since above and below are the same, calls forth a corresponding upward flood from subterranean fires within the psyche:

> What is the horizontal rolling of water
> Compared to the flood of black heat that rolls upwards past my eyes?
>   [302]

All life, as we saw in 'The Two Principles', is a mixture of fire and water: 'In the sun and the material waters the two principles exist as independent elements' [SM 180]. Within humanity, the elements exist in their most independent form as man and woman, or the male and female, horizontal and vertical, divisions within the individual psyche. The eruption of this flood of heat puts out the light of our northern consciousness; but it is also phallic – 'columns dark and soft', 'soft shafts' – and therefore procreative. Darkness is 'horrific' to our normal consciousness; and the imagery echoes Yeats's 'The Second Coming' of the previous year: 'The blood-dimmed tide is loosed'. Lawrence hints at a second coming with 'aromatic as frankincense', but 'brimstone' suggests a devilish parentage and monstrous birth. The yellow eyes are the eyes of goats, and Lawrence later calls his he-goat 'old Satan' [CP 383]. As for the she-goat, 'She is brittle as brimstone' [386]. But *Birds, Beasts and Flowers* is Lawrence's *Marriage of Heaven and Hell*, where the true god is not the Nobodaddy of the Christians, but a 'king in exile' long confined 'in the burning bowels of the earth', 'now due to be crowned again' [351]. For 'the Christians, phase by phase, set out actually to *annihilate* the sensual being in man' [SM 255]. For Lawrence, the goat too has his distinctive divinity:

> And he-goat is anvil to he-goat, and hammer to he-goat
> In the business of beating the mettle of goats to a godhead.   [CP 381]

Nor is destructiveness to be equated with evil. At the end of 'The Crown' Lawrence had written:

> In truth, we proceed to die because the whole frame of our life is a falsity, and we know that, if we die sufficiently, the whole frame and form and edifice will collapse upon itself. But it were much better to pull it down and have a great clear space, than to have it collapse on top of us . . . We must burst out, and move under a greater heavens.   [P II 415]

Blind Samson is Lawrence's spokesman when he says:

> See if I don't move under a dark and nude, vast heaven
> When your world is in ruins, under your fallen skies.
> Caryatids, pale-faces.
> See if I am not Lord of the dark and moving hosts
> Before I die.   [CP 289]

In 'Southern Night', the moon, too, is given a reversed symbolic meaning, the cold, white, immaculate, virgin goddess of the north becomes a red thing, a maculate anathema, 'blood-dark', rupturing 'the night's membrane of tranquil stars' [302], and the soul's membrane which protects the soul from such forbidden knowledge.

Lawrence's new home, the Fontana Vecchia in Taormina, was within sight of Etna, which was always smoking, and might, at any moment, erupt. It was always a living presence in his consciousness, and provided apt symbolism in several poems. The threshold was made of lava, and some previous occupant had carved on it the word 'PACE'. The very substance of the lava seemed to Lawrence to give the lie to the word. It seemed wrong to Lawrence for the same reason that Herakleitos thought Homer wrong in saying 'Would that strife might pass away from among gods and men!':

> He did not see that he was praying for the destruction of the universe; for, if his prayer were heard, all things would pass away – for in the tension of opposites all things have their being – [1]   [348]

In the poem 'Peace', Lawrence claims that his heart will know no peace until a new eruption takes place:

> Forests, cities, bridges
> Gone again in the bright trail of lava.

> Naxos thousands of feet below the olive-roots,
> And now the olive leaves thousands of feet below the lava fire.

Naxos is famous as the place where Dionysos, god of resurgent life, and of the underworld (for 'Hades is the same as Dionysos', as Herakleitos said), married the Great Moon Goddess Ariadne. According to Kerenyi, 'Ariadne is the archetypal reality of the bestowal of soul, of what makes a living creature an individual':

> In the union of two archetypal images, the divine pair Dionysos and Ariadne represent the eternal passage of *zoë* [the life-force] into and through the genesis of living creatures. [D 124–5]

This is Ariadne the white goddess. But in her other aspect she is also the red goddess of orgiastic rites and human sacrifice. One of her victims was Orpheus.

The figure of Dionysos, whom Lawrence conflates with Orpheus and Osiris, Pluto and Dis, Hades and Satan, is a shadowy presence in several of these poems, not the more familiar Dionysos 'full of sap, milk and honey, and northern golden wine' [CSN 234], but, like Count Dionys in 'The Ladybird', a 'master of the underworld. Master of the life to come' [270], Dionysos of the Orphic mysteries, Zagreus, son and spouse of Persephone, torn apart by the jealous titans, but resurrected to be god of the underworld, and, like Persephone, a promise of the continual renewal of life:

> I say, wonderful are the hellish experiences,
> Orphic, delicate
> Dionysos of the Underworld. [CP 280]

Lawrence would also know the version of the birth of Dionysos in which Zeus fertilizes the virgin Persephone in the form of a snake ('the most naked form of *zoë* absolutely reduced to itself'):

> . . . through marriage with this heavenly dragon
> Persephone's womb became fruitful, prepared
> To give birth to Zagreus, the horned infant. [D 114]

But Zagreus *is* Zeus in his underworld aspect, continually giving birth to himself, as the snake was believed to do by shedding its skin. In the Orphic rites 'snakes were ritually torn to pieces, but *the* snake, the genus as a whole, was indestructibly present, bearing witness to the indestructibility of life in what was, in a manner of speaking, its lowest form' [115]. Lawrence would also know that the scene of this primal rape (this 'burst membrane', this 'integument . . . ruptured' [CP 278], from which came all birds, beasts and flowers, was 'in Sicily, on the meadows of Enna' [308].

In 'Peace' Lawrence imagines successive eras of fruitfulness,

peace and plenty, symbolized by the olive tree, as layers of culti-
vation and civilization each obliterated by a layer of lava, the
equally necessary eras of cataclysm or slow decomposition which
are also part of the process of change and renewal. The lava moves
down the mountain 'like a royal snake'. A god is just as divine in
his destructive or underworld aspect, and 'the hellish experiences'
are just as wonderful as the growing and blossoming of the upper
world. The slow disintegration into rottenness, decay, excrement
even, is celebrated in 'Medlars and Sorb Apples' as the 'Orphic
farewell':

> A kiss, and a spasm of farewell, a moment's orgasm of rupture,
> Then along the damp road alone, till the next turning.
> And there, a new partner, a new parting, a new unfusing into twain,
> A new gasp of further isolation,
> A new intoxication of loneliness, among decaying, frost-cold
>   leaves.   [280–81]

In 'David', written in October 1919, Lawrence had spoken of
Florence as marking the boundary between northern and southern
consciousness. The northern consciousness is the female, corresponding to 'the horizontal rolling of water' [302]:

> The level sweep of waters, waters overwhelming. Morality, chastity –
> another world drowned: equality, democracy, the masses, like drops of
> water in one sea, overwhelming all outstanding loveliness of the individual
> soul. Quenching of all flame in the great watery passivity which bears
> down at last so ponderous.   [P 63]

But, in yet another version of the birth of Dionysos (here identified
with Bacchus and with Michelangelo's statue of David), the vertical
flame of Zeus is too lovely to be overwhelmed, too hot to be
quenched:

> Semele, scarred with lightning, gave birth prematurely to her child . . .
> Too fierce a mating, too fiery and potent a sire . . . It was fire overwhelming,
> over-weening, briefly married to the dew, that begot this child. The South
> to the North. Married! The child, the fire-dew, Iacchus, David.   [62]

The north is the horizontal world of the ordinary, of history, of men
in masses with their exclusively human values. It is the world of
prose. But these poems register the almost overwhelming eruption
into Lawrence's consciousness of that other vertical dimension, the
divine fire, the miracle, the incarnation. These poems have no narrative or description, which belong to the temporal surface world.
They are pure, naked symbol. In the poems which follow, there is
plenty of narrative and description. But the symbols are always
moving just below the surface, producing tensions, tremors, and

sometimes cracks in that surface through which another reality gleams. The poems dramatize the continuing, permanent creative conflict between north and south, conscious and unconscious, male and female, human and non-human, secular and divine.

*

Another way of putting it would be to say that the best poems in the collection work on several levels at once, on all the levels at which it is possible for poems about living creatures to work. Beginning at the most superficial (and most traditional) level, they describe the beauty and distinctiveness of the creature; but with so much more real attention to the creature and respect for it, such determination to see the creature in its own terms, not only ours, that the poems become significant contributions to natural history. No line in poetry aroused more anger in Lawrence than Shelley's 'Bird thou never wert'. What interests Lawrence in a creature is precisely what makes it uniquely a skylark or a tortoise, and, ultimately, the incommensurability of its nature as skylark or tortoise with anything human. Every poem is also, therefore, an encounter between the poet, as representative of the human world, with the non-human world, a little drama of the meeting of aliens. The poet attempts to empathize with the creature, to get inside it and share its perception of the world and himself. He succeeds to a degree which seems to ordinary mortals, and in comparison with ordinary poets, occult. Yet, because he refuses to be sentimental or anthropomorphic, he must, in the last analysis, fail. Other creatures are all ultimately unknowable. Perhaps the very attempt to know them is impertinent, Faustian. Man is not the measure of creation.

Nevertheless, since each creature, as microcosm, contains the whole, it must be possible to draw certain parallels between aspects of human behaviour or being and that of other creatures. The poems are full of such analogues. Moreover, the non-human creation, being so much purer and closer to the source than we are, is a primary source of archetypal symbols. Animals invade our dreams. They carry the same charge and embody the same meanings in all times and places. They seem to be messengers or tokens from an unknown world which also exists deep within ourselves. They put us in touch with a buried animal self within us, a self we must be aware of and negotiate with, yet which we can communicate with only in its own language, the language of symbols. A drama acted out in this language is a myth. Every flower acts out the myth of Persephone, every snake that of Dionysos. Every creature its own unique yet similar myth. It is not a matter of searching for these myths in libraries and museums, for even when such myths have survived, their living meanings have not. The poets of every generation must renew the search for the sources of these myths within their own psyches and within the natural world if we are to rediscover their relevance to our most urgent problems, whether in 1920 or 1985.

*

'Tropic', 'Southern Night' and 'Peace' were untypical of *Birds, Beasts and Flowers* because they were not about individual creatures, but about *zoë*, life itself before it became differentiated. One of the passages in Crèvecœur which had particularly impressed Lawrence was about humming-birds:

> We have read various descriptions of humming birds. W. H. Hudson has a good one. But this one gives a curiously sharp, hard bit of realisation, something surely intrinsic, a jewel-sharpness and refraction inherent in the little soul of the creature . . . He sees their dark, primitive, weapon-like souls. He sees how they start and flash their wings darkly, in the spontaneous wonder of the retraction into isolation, or in a kind of vindictive self-arrogance. [SM 64]

Lawrence is here interpreting Crèvecœur's description in terms of his own metaphysic of creation as set out in 'The Two Principles':

> Dual all the time is the creative activity: first comes forth the living apparition of new being, the perfect and indescribable singleness; and this embodies the single beauty of a new substance . . . The gems of being were created simultaneously with the gems of matter, the latter inherent in the former. [179]

Lawrence saw the humming-bird as the first jewel-like entity thrown off by hitherto undifferentiated matter, the first isolated arrogant soul. In January 1919, he read about humming-birds again in H. W. Bates, *The Naturalist on the River Amazon*. It may have been in June 1920, while revising the Crèvecœur essay, that he wrote 'Humming-Bird':

> Before anything had a soul,
> While life was a heave of Matter, half inanimate,
> This little bit chipped off in brilliance
> And went whizzing through the slow, vast, succulent stems. [CP 372]

It is the only poem in the collection about a creature Lawrence had never seen. The actual encounter was Crèvecœur's, not his. And this seemed to worry Lawrence, for in *Birds, Beasts and Flowers* he signed the poem (certainly written in Italy) Española, a village

215

near Taos in New Mexico where he had seen plenty of humming-birds, but more than two years after writing the poem.

The earliest of Lawrence's actual encounters may have been the one recorded in 'The Mosquito', for the poem is signed Siracusa, where he had spent a night at the Grand Hotel in May:

> It is rather a drear hotel – and many bloodstains of squashed mosquitoes on the bedroom walls. Ah, vile mosquitoes! [P II 343]

But at the time of his visit to Syracuse, Lawrence had never been to Venice, and yet the poem has the lines:

> I heard a woman call you the Winged Victory
> In sluggish Venice. [CP 332]

Nor is there any record of Lawrence visiting Syracuse again after his visit to Venice in August 1920. Either the poem was written in May and revised after August, or written after August and signed Siracusa because the encounter had taken place there, though the killing of mosquitoes must have been a frequent occurrence.

The poem is in the mature *Birds, Beasts and Flowers* manner, confident, colloquial, witty, and in the form of a dialogue, the man garrulous, the spaces between the lines representing the silence of the mosquito, its invisibility, its 'evil little aura', or, later, its 'hateful little trump'. In the whole book, the poet kills only two creatures, the mosquito and a fish. Over the death of the fish there is much breast-beating; but there is no compunction over the killing of the mosquito. After all, the blood shed is more his own than the mosquito's. He hates the mosquito much more than any other creature, much more than the bat which invades his room. For the mosquito has invaded his very blood-being:

> Blood, red blood
> Super-magical
> Forbidden liquor.

> I behold you stand
> For a second enspasmed in oblivion,
> Obscenely ecstasied
> Sucking live blood,
> My blood. [333]

Lawrence makes no attempt to enter into the mosquito, or to take its otherness into himself. By violating his own separateness it has crossed a forbidden frontier, and that is obscene. The voice which says 'mosquitoes must be killed' is never questioned. Perhaps, of all the other creatures in the book, the one which arouses most hatred in the poet is his pup Bibbles, and, in a way, for the same reason. She came too close, lacked the reserve and respect there should always be between species. Too much loving is also an obscenity:

You miserable little bitch of love-tricks,
I know your game.
. . .
All humanity is jam to you.

Everybody so dear, and yourself so ultra-beloved
That you have to run out at last and eat filth,
Gobble up filth, you horror, swallow utter abomination and fresh-
       dropped dung.

You stinker.
You worse than a carrion-crow.
Reeking dung-mouth.
You love-bird.   [398]

*

At the beginning of 1920 a friend of Lawrence's, Rosalind Thorneycroft Popham, had settled in an ancient villa, the Villa Canovaia, at San Gervasio, Fiesole, and invited Lawrence to visit her there during the tour of northern Italy he proposed to make while Frieda was in Germany in August and September. But at the beginning of August, an explosion at a nearby ammunition dump blew out all the windows at the Villa Canovaia, forcing Mrs Popham to move into a villa in Fiesole until repairs could be done. Lawrence asked if he could stay in the abandoned villa for a while, and spent most of September there. The place was rich in flora and fauna. Rosalind Popham recalled:

While he was there he wrote 'The Evangelistic Beasts', the tortoise poems, 'The Pomegranate', 'The Peach', and 'The Figs' . . . It was here several other poems were suggested – 'Cypresses', for example. I remember very well meeting with the Turkey Cock, the swart grape, and the sorb apple, and how Lawrence spoke of these things as we were walking among the farms and country lanes above Fiesole.   [CB II 49–50]

Lawrence saw the cypresses as 'brooding, softly-swaying pillars of dark flame', 'Folded in like a dark thought / For which the language is lost' [CP 297]. Their scent was like 'an aroma of lost human life'. The secret of the dead Etruscans is 'inviolable' in them. The trees are tokens of the indestructibility of what the Romans tried to obliterate in the Etruscans, calling them vicious. The cypresses themselves seem almost vicious to us, in their subtly smiling phallicism, so impenetrable to our understanding. Were the Etruscans vicious, Lawrence asks: 'Or was their way only evasive and different, dark, like cypress-trees in a wind?'

'Cypresses' is made up almost entirely of questions, all of them unanswered. If the trees are messengers, their message is undecipherable, cannot be rendered into discursive language. But the very need to understand in the abstract, to translate into discursive language, is symptomatic of the life-denying consciousness of Rome, the mechanical consciousness of America, where the Aztecs perished like the Etruscans. Lawrence is here groping towards the theory he was to develop a year later in *Fantasia of the Unconscious*, that our era was preceded by 'the great pagan world which . . . had a vast and perhaps perfect science of its own, a science in terms of life', and that certain races, including the Etruscans and Amerindians, had refused to forget, 'but taught the old wisdom, only in its half-forgotten, symbolic forms', forms now wholly forgotten by Western man [F 12–13].

So the fact that Lawrence cannot interpret the cypresses does not mean that he has failed to communicate with them. In recognizing the cypresses as symbols and opening himself to them, he is taking something of their otherness into his blood-knowledge:

> In the sensual vision there is always the pause of fear, dark wonder, and glamour. The creature beheld is seen in its quality of *otherness*, a term of the vivid, imminent unknown. And the new knowledge enters in rich, dark thrills into the soul. [SM 60]

Lawrence is beginning to achieve the kind of art he praised in Crèvecœur: 'his art is in terms of the great sensual understanding, dark and rich and of that reserved, pagan tenderness to which we have lost the key'.

'Cypresses' is typical of the volume in that it is not the end-product of a struggle to convert experience into words and meanings; it is a running commentary on that struggle. Hostile critics have called Lawrence's poems 'sketches for poems'[2]; but a sketch is often superior, in terms of life, to the finished product. Each poem here revises itself as it goes along, yielding layer after layer of deeper meaning, yet never finished, for the meaning of any encounter with the natural world is inexhaustible. Lawrence is interested in making discoveries, not artifacts. What he hopes to discover cannot be fixed like a fly in amber. Each poem is exploratory. It does not seek to be gem-like, self-contained, finished, outside time. It exists in the dimension of time and process, and that is its life. A flower, taken out of time, an immortelle, has form

without meaning. A flower in time is part of the process of bloom-
ing, seeding, dying and being reborn.

Far from seeking to be self-contained, each poem seeks the maximum of relatedness to everything beyond itself, 'naked contact
with all influences at once'. It may be satisfying to see a well-
wrought urn, but how much more exciting to see a lump of clay
gradually taking shape, almost collapsing, always at risk of flying
off the wheel, but caught up again, finding its shape, though never
a perfect shape, for perfection is mechanical and sterile. The
Chinese master potters, if they found they had made too perfect
a pot, would gently nudge it out of perfect symmetry with the
heel of the hand before the wheel stopped. And Navaho weavers
always run the pattern out at the edge so that its soul shall not be
trapped.

Another feature of this kind of poetry is the spontaneity and
improvisation of an intelligence at play. By freeing his intelligence
to play with words, ideas, perceptions, by a flexibility of tone which
moves freely from earnestness to flippancy, from reverence to
mockery, from heightened vatic language to colloquial banter, by
toying with the expectations of the reader, Lawrence achieves a
distinctive wit hardly met with in English poetry since the Meta-
physicals (though part of Whitman's comic genius), wit which
makes possible leaps of imagination which could hardly have been
achieved by other means.[3]

This wit is particularly evident in the poems about fruits, written
by 15 September 1920, when Lawrence sent them to his American
agent with the warning not to be 'scared by them' [L III 596]. The
fruit poems are heavily and overtly sexual. The wit, the jocular
effrontery, helps Lawrence to get away with considerable outspokenness. It was hardly necessary for him to spell out this aspect
of the poems in the 'mystical note' with which he introduced
'Fruits' in the 1930 edition:

> For fruits are all of them female, in them lies the seed. And so when they
> break and show the seed, then we look into the womb and see its secrets.
> So it is that the pomegranate is the apple of love to the Arab, and the fig
> has been a catch-word for the female fissure for ages.   [CP 277]

'Figs' is just as explicit:

> The fig is a very secretive fruit.
> As you see it standing growing, you feel at once it is symbolic:
> And it seems male.
> But when you come to know it better, you agree with the Romans, it is
>   female.

> The Italians vulgarly say, it stands for the female part; the fig-fruit:
> The fissure, the yoni,
> The wonderful moist conductivity towards the centre.
>
> Involved,
> Inturned,
> The flowering all inward and womb-fibrilled;
> And but one orifice.
>
> The fig, the horse-shoe, the squash-blossom.
> Symbols.   [282]

But Lawrence makes the fig too explicitly symbolic for the good of
the poem. Since the symbolism is a known quantity from the outset,
the fig is deprived of its mystery. There is no need to give it the
kind of sensitive attention we find in the best poems. Lawrence is
too eager to turn away from the actual fig to what it symbolizes,
and the poem degenerates into a series of satirical assertions about
'women the world over'. Lawrence moves so far from the fig that
it ceases to be a symbol and becomes merely an emblem.

'Pomegranate' is a much better poem. The eye remains on the
object, and Lawrence forces the reader to keep his eye on the object
too, and recognize its implications:

> And, if you dare, the fissure!
>
> Do you mean to tell me you will see no fissure?
> Do you prefer to look on the plain side?
>
> For all that, the setting suns are open.
> The end cracks open with the beginning:
> Rosy, tender, glittering within the fissure.
>
> Do you mean to tell me there should be no fissure?
> No glittering, compact drops of dawn?
> Do you mean it is wrong, the gold-filmed skin, integument, shown
>   ruptured?
>
> For my part, I prefer my heart to be broken.
> It is so lovely, dawn-kaleidoscopic within the crack.   [278–9]

That sudden disconcerting shift from the ruptured pomegranate to
the broken heart is Lawrence's wit at its most serious. The womb
does not reveal its secrets and its radiance for nothing. The hard-
hearted, even the whole-hearted, are blind to it. Only the sore or
broken-hearted are initiated into the mystery. As Christopher Pollnitz has put it, 'the admission of otherness has to be wrung from
the heart' [DHLR 15 34].

'Pomegranate' contains no mythological references. But the

pomegranate figures prominently in just those myths in which Lawrence at the time was most interested. According to Robert Graves:

> The pomegranate which sprang from Dionysus's blood was also the tree of Tammuz-Adonis-Rimmon; its ripe fruit splits open like a wound and shows the red seeds inside. It symbolizes death and the promise of resurrection when held in the hand of the goddess Hera or Persephone.
> [WG 110]

It was the eating of pomegranate seeds, the food of the dead, which committed Persephone to return to Hades. According to Frazer, the virgin Nana conceived by putting a pomegranate in her bosom, and gave birth to Attis/Adonis. Any ripening and rotting fruit enacts this dual process, of breaking down and losing its identity, returning to the source, and, at the same time, nurturing the seed in darkness. The Persephone myth is one to which even Frazer responds with imaginative sympathy:

> Therefore we do no indignity to the myth of Demeter and Persephone – one of the few myths in which the sunshine and clarity of the Greek genius are crossed by the shadow and mystery of death – when we trace its origin to some of the most familiar, yet eternally affecting aspects of nature, to the melancholy gloom and decay of autumn and to the freshness, the brightness, and the verdure of spring.   [GB 525]

Persephone means 'bringer of destruction'. In 'The Crown' Lawrence had written:

> The spirit of destruction is divine, when it breaks the ego and opens the soul to the wide heavens. In corruption there is divinity. Aphrodite is, on one side, the great goddess of destruction in sex, Dionysus in the spirit . . . In the soft and shiny voluptuousness of decay, in the marshy chill heat of reptiles, there is the sign of the Godhead. It is the activity of departure. And departure is the opposite equivalent of coming together; decay, corruption, destruction, breaking down is the opposite equivalent of creation . . . And corruption, like growth, is only divine when it is pure, when all is given up to it.   [P II 402–3]

The 'fissure' is not just sexual; it is any point where divinity erupts through the surface of our normally desacralized world, the world which man attempts to remake 'round and finished like a billiard ball'; any point of access to the otherworld, the underworld, the reality beneath appearances. Orgasm is a means of access to that world, the little death, but so is any opening of the self to the other, any genuine perception of the non-human, and intoxication, Bacchic ecstasy, and, of course, death itself. In these poems Lawrence undertakes an imaginative journey into that other world on our behalf, from his own broken heart into the heart of the fruit, there to eat and become the seed:

And we must cross the frontiers, though we will not,
Of the lost, fern-scented world:
Take the fern-seed on our lips,
Close the eyes, and go
Down the tendrilled avenues of wine and the otherworld.   [CP 287]

The eating of fern-seed was supposed to bring invisibility, and the power to divine what was under the earth, particularly gold, the underworld equivalent of the sun's fire.

The myths are recycled through Lawrence, reduced back to their origins in primal human experience. By discovering what, in himself, responds to the 'rare, powerful, reminiscent flavour' of medlars and sorb-apples, he crosses that frontier, becomes the departing god, Dionysos of the Underworld, Orpheus going down 'the winding, leaf-clogged, silent lanes of hell' [280]. In the words of Sandra Gilbert, 'he himself has become a seed falling through the dead walls of the fruit into the labyrinthine ways of an underworld where he must re-create his own energies' [AA 83].

As early as January 1909, Lawrence had felt dissatisfied with Yeats: 'so much vapour of words, till we are blind with coloured wordiness' [L I 107]. When he read Yeats again at the end of 1912 he seemed 'awfully queer stuff to me now – as if he wouldn't bear touching' [488]. Yeats's 'Rose of all Roses, Rose of all the World' [WBY 37] is 'eternal beauty' as opposed to such 'common things' as

The weak worm hiding down in its small cave,
The field-mouse running by me in the grass,
And heavy mortal hopes that toil and pass.   [31]

'Grapes' is Lawrence's reversal of those values, his repudiation of the ideal, the 'explicit rose' in favour of 'creatures webbed and marshy':

And on the margin, men soft-footed and pristine,
Still, and sensitive, and active,
Audile, tactile sensitiveness as of a tendril which orientates and
    reaches out,
Reaching out and grasping by an instinct more delicate than the
    moon's as she feels for the tides.

Of which world, the vine was the invisible rose,
Before petals spread, before colour made its disturbance, before eyes
    saw too much.   [CP 285]

As Herakleitos said: 'Nature loves to hide'. Lawrence's 'rose of all roses' is the vine:

Look now even now, how it keeps its power of invisibility!
Look how black, how blue-black, how globed in Egyptian darkness
Dropping among his leaves, hangs the dark grape!   [286]

Lawrence groups 'The Revolutionary' with his 'Fruits'. It is a sequel to 'Grapes', where the desire to go back 'before eyes saw too much' to a world where men lived more by hearing and touch, leads to the determination to 'close the eyes' and cross the dangerous frontier. Blind Samson has just such developed senses:

To me, the earth rolls ponderously, superbly
Coming my way without forethought or afterthought.
To me, men's footfalls fall with a dull, soft rumble, ominous and
      lovely,
Coming my way.   [288]

Samson's prison is 'the dome of high ideal heaven', 'this ideal civilization', 'all your ponderous roofed-in erection of right and wrong'. But for all its rigidity, it is a fragile erection, impotent against such power as can be drawn from darkness:

See if I don't move under a dark and nude, vast heaven
When your world is in ruins, under your fallen skies.
Caryatids, pale-faces.
See if I am not Lord of the dark and moving hosts
Before I die.   [287–8]

'The Revolutionary' makes explicit the principle behind all the poems in 'Fruits', that it is only by overturning everything we have constructed upon a basis of false consciousness that the human world can be opened once more to the divine. The same principle is implicit in all the fruit poems, which, in the words of Gail Mandell, 'allude mythically to the rebellious act of tasting forbidden fruit and, as a consequence, of falling into a hellish order of existence', which is 'the natural order of life' as in Blake's *The Marriage of Heaven and Hell* [PP 108].

*

One day in the garden at San Gervasio Lawrence found a baby tortoise no bigger than his thumb-nail, 'a tiny, fragile, half-animate bean'. 'Baby Tortoise' has a very distinctive movement. The first seven lines are rhythmically inert, too short to generate any rhythmic impetus: 'Not yet awake', 'Not quite alive'. Slowly, the poem comes alive, miming the tortoise's own emergence from inertia:

223

To open your tiny beak-mouth, that looks as if it would never open,
Like some iron door;
To lift the upper hawk-beak from the lower base
And reach your skinny little neck
And take your first bite at some dim bit of herbage.   [CP 352]

Then the lines shorten again, the rhythm comes to a halt, as though the effort were too much:

Alone, small insect,
Tiny bright-eye,
Slow one.

The poem moves forward, step by step, tentative, through a series of apostrophes which begin as pure description, then range further and further in exploratory metaphor. They also recapitulate evolution, moving from bean to insect, to bird, to baby. The poet sheds all his habitual ways of seeing and responding to the creature, gives it his whole attention, as though it had just been created, and its nature had to be apprehended afresh, or as though it were the first creature in the universe, and all the laws of creation had to be inferred from it.

The garden is large and overgrown. In proportion to the baby tortoise it is a vast universe of chaos and inertia which he challenges with the briliance of his tiny eye, his 'eye of a dark disturbed night':

Are you able to wonder?
Or is it just your indomitable will and pride of the first life
Looking round
And slowly pitching itself against the inertia
Which had seemed invincible?   [353]

'In the origin', Lawrence had written in 'Le Gai Savaire', 'life must have been uniform, a great unmoved, utterly homogeneous infinity, a great not-being' [STH 42]. The baby tortoise both represents and re-enacts the fragile stirring of the first life, taking the first steps out of the non-life, the dark night, then moving forward with dogged persistence, on and on in arrogant affirmation of selfhood, the life-adventure. He represents that crucial breakthrough in evolution when the first creatures began to move freely over the earth about their own business, the first incarnation of active, free-ranging life on earth, the prototype of all higher forms. The apostrophes progressively identify the baby tortoise with the human challenger, pioneer, as he rows forward. The perfect image of rowing leads with perfect aptness to the first comparison with an individual human being, 'little Ulysses'. Another momentous breakthrough came when men stopped hugging the coasts in their ships and sailed for the horizon:

> Over the garden earth
> Small bird,
> Over the edge of all things. [354]

Lawrence sees both breakthroughs as manifestations of the same urge, the urge, the compulsion, to assert the self against the unknown. The child of Heaven and Earth ('little Titan, under your battle-shield') takes up arms against the primeval gods of chaos. He knows that the life in him is more vivid, and the life in his loins may be more vivid yet. The biochemical origins of life and the highest pitch of evolution, the human adventure, are both contained or adumbrated in this 'invincible fore-runner'.

The penultimate line of 'Baby Tortoise' – 'All life carried on your shoulder' – seems like a rather throwaway version of the ending of Lawrence's mystical note to 'Reptiles':

> The wise tortoise laid his earthy part around him, he cast it round him and found his feet. So he is the first of creatures to stand upon his toes, and the dome of his house is his heaven. Therefore it is charted out, and is the foundation of the world. [348]

But the next poem in the sequence, 'Tortoise Shell', is to be entirely an expansion of this idea. In 'The Two Principles' Lawrence had written:

> Thus all creation depends upon the fourfold activity. And on this root of four is all law and understanding established. Following the perception of these supreme truths, the Pythagoreans made their philosophy, asserting that all is number, and seeking to search out the mystery of the roots of three, four, five, seven, stable throughout all the universe, in a chain of developing phenomena. But our science of mathematics still waits for its fulfilment, its union with life itself. For the truths of mathematics are only the skeleton fabric of the living universe . . . And the Cross, the epitome of all this fourfold division, still stirs us to the depths with unaccountable emotions, emotions which go much deeper than personality and the Christ drama. [SM 184]

In 'Tortoise Shell' Lawrence attempts just such a union of mathematics and life itself as formed the primary objective of the alchemists:

> It needed Pythagoras to see life playing with counters on the living
>   back
> Of the baby tortoise;
> Life establishing the first eternal mathematical tablet,

225

> Not in stone, like the Judean Lord, or bronze, but in life-clouded, life-
> rosy tortoise shell.   [355]

The word 'rosy' hints at the mystery of the Rosy Cross (which Lawrence had discussed in 'The Two Principles'), symbol of that chemical wedding, the mysterious conjunction of body and soul:

> The Cross, the Cross
> Goes deeper in than we know,
> Deeper into life;
> Right into the marrow
> And through the bone.

The pattern of the tortoise-shell is, as Lawrence interprets it, basically fourfold, cruciform. His playful, witty, mathematical fantasia culminates with the wholly serious fancy:

> The Lord wrote it all down on the little slate
> Of the baby tortoise.
> Outward and visible indication of the plan within.

The whole poem would have delighted Sir Thomas Browne, who wrote:

> I hold there is a general beauty in the works of God, and therefore no deformity in any kind or species of creature whatsoever. I cannot tell by what logic we call a Toad, a Bear, or an Elephant ugly; they being created in those outward shapes and figures which best express the actions of their inward forms.   [*Religio Medici*]

The inward form of the baby tortoise, the 'plan within', is also cruciform, a 'cross-wise cloven psyche', which is the last thing we expected to find in so dignified and self-sufficient a creature. The image of the tortoise on his back, 'a sprottling insect', together with the insistence on five, strongly evokes the crucifixion, though we do not yet grasp its relevance. What is this 'long cleavage of division' in his nature, and what has it to do with Christ? For the answers we must turn to look at mother and father tortoise.

'Tortoise Family Connections' begins with two new apostrophes, 'bud of the universe' and 'brisk egg' [CP 356]. In *Fantasia of the Unconscious* (written a year later than *Tortoises*) Lawrence writes:

> The first great division in the egg remains always the same, the unchanging great division in the psychic and the physical structure; the unchanging great division in knowledge and function. It is a division into polarized duality, psychical and physical, of the human being. It is the great vertical division of the egg-cell, and of the nature of man.   [F 37]

The first consciousness, as we saw in 'Baby Tortoise', is that 'I am

I'. There remains through life the absolute need to define the self in terms of distinction from the rest of the universe.

When, in the daytime, our life is polarized upwards, towards the upward sun-wakened eyes and the mind which sees in vision, then the powerful dynamic centres of the lower body act in subservience, in their negative polarity. And then we flow upwards, we go forth seeking the universe, in vision, speech, and thought – we go forth to see all things, to hear all things, to know all things by acquaintance and by knowledge. One flood of dynamic flow are we, upwards polarized, in our tallness and our wide-eyed spirit seeking to bring all the universe into the range of our conscious individuality, and eager always to make new worlds, out of this old world, to bud new green tips on the tree of life. [179]

This daytime life-adventure, summoned by the sun, is distinctively male. The brisk male baby tortoise is blithely oblivious of his earthy mother:

It is no use my saying to him in an emotional voice:
'This is your Mother, she laid you when you were an egg.'

He does not even trouble to answer: 'Woman, what have I to do with
thee?' [CP 357]

Adolescence will put an end to his arrogance, when he will come 'under the spell of the moon, of sea-born Aphrodite, mother and bitter goddess':

For I am carried away from my sunny day-self into this other tremendous self, where knowledge will not save me, but where I must obey as the sea obeys the tides . . . This, then, is the duality of my day and my night being: a duality so bitter to an adolescent. For the adolescent thinks with shame and terror of his night. He would wish to have no night-self . . . Without the night-consummation we are trees without roots. [F 184–5]

This second consciousness is of the absolute need to be part of the living unity, to distinguish other beings from pebbles, bits of earth and old tins. Isolation is not his birthright. As long as Adam remains 'all to himself' life goes no further. It is the doom of every cell to split and split again, of every creature to submit to the duality of life – self and not-self, male and female, body and spirit, birth and death, of every human being to suffer 'the calvary of human consciousness' [217].

In 'Lui et Elle' and 'Tortoise Gallantry' the father tortoise, the 'dignified stalker through chaos', is transformed into a ridiculous fool pathetically scuffling after his large, apathetic spouse:

Alas, the spear is through the side of his isolation.
His adolescence saw him crucified into sex,

> Doomed, in the long crucifixion of desire, to seek his consummation
> > beyond himself.
> Divided into passionate duality,
> He, so finished and immune, now broken into desirous
> > fragmentariness,
> Doomed to make an intolerable fool of himself
> In his effort toward completion again. [CP 360]

Ulysses/Adam has now become the torn Osiris/Christ. But the comparison is surely far-fetched, a pretentious conceit? We learn in the final poem 'Tortoise Shout' how seriously we must take it.

The uncanny tortoise scream, in extremis, is heard as the type of all cries which are torn from us in extremity of pleasure or pain, cries of submission and abandonment to joy or passion or pain or death, when the very membrane of the soul, which keeps us integral and inviolable, is torn and we must call 'across the deeps'. The continuity of the tortoise poems from 'Fruits' is evident when Lawrence asks:

> Why were we crucified into sex?
> Why were we not left rounded off, and finished in ourselves,
> As we began.

Like billiard balls. The answer is that 'life cannot progress without these ruptures, severances, cataclysms; pain is a living reality, not merely a deathly' [F 220–21].

> The male tortoise screams
>
> Tiny from under the very edge of the farthest far-off horizon of life.

The cry goes straight to the 'primeval rudiments of life' in the poet's own body. It sounds 'on the plasm direct'. It opens Lawrence to the perception that the moment the ghost is given up is also the moment it is received:

> Torn, to become whole again, after long seeking for what is lost,
> The same cry from the tortoise as from Christ, the Osiris-cry of
> > abandonment,
> That which is whole, torn asunder,
> That which is in part, finding its whole again throughout the
> > universe. [CP 366]

The call across the deeps is always answered, the torn god or man always resurrected. The cry is 'consummatum est', which means both 'it is finished' and 'it is accomplished'. Sexuality, like mortality, is a tragic condition in that it involves the violation of the self. But only through such tragic experience can man find wholeness. For wholeness involves the opening of the self to God:

In the very darkest continent of the body, there is God. And from Him issues the first dark rays of our feeling, wordless, and utterly previous to words; the innermost rays, the first messengers, the primeval, honorable beasts of our being, whose voice echoes wordless and forever wordless down the darkest avenues of the soul, but full of potent speech. Our own inner meaning. [STH 205]

*

'The Evangelistic Beasts' are, as Sandra Gilbert has said, anti-Christian satires, like the works of a more mischievous Blake. 'St Matthew' is by far the best of them. Here Lawrence seems to stand back, to survey the poems written so far, the insights gained, then to try to sum them up by asking 'What, then, is a man?'

Matthew, as spokesman for man, argues that Christ, in seeking to draw all men unto him, is thereby denying their nature. Matthew, like Will Brangwen, responds passionately, with wildly beating heart, to the promise of being lifted up; but like Anna, he insists also on the life of the body and the horizontal land:

So I will be lifted up, Saviour,
But put me down again in time, Master,
Before my heart stops beating, and I become what I am not.
Put me down again on the earth, Jesus, on the brown soil
Where flowers sprout in the acrid humus, and fade into humus again.
Where beasts drop their unlicked young, and pasture, and drop their
        droppings among the turf.
Where the adder darts horizontal.
Down on the damp, unceasing ground, where my feet belong
And even my heart, Lord, forever, after all uplifting:
The crumbling, damp, fresh land, life horizontal and ceaseless.
[CP 321]

Man's being contains many beasts, and there is a time for each to receive expression; a time for lark-like exaltation on the wings of the spirit, but also for moving among the ordinary creatures of earth, and the mysterious creatures of under-earth and under-water, creatures of the darkness:

Matthew I am, the man.
And I take the wings of the morning, to Thee, Crucified, Glorified.
But while flowers club their petals at evening
And rabbits make pills among the short grass
And long snakes quickly glide into the dark hole in the wall, hearing
        man approach,
I must be put down, Lord, in the afternoon,
And at evening I must leave off my wings of the spirit
As I leave off my braces,

And I must resume my nakedness like a fish, sinking down the dark
      reversion of night.

Jesus himself, in denying his earthbound manhood and becoming
Dove of the Spirit, caused the dregs of his terrestrial manhood to
fall 'to the dark zenith of Thine antipodes', there to 'thread and
thrill and flicker' like bats. Matthew, though by nature 'a traveller
back and forth', finds his own 'bat-winged heart' more undeniable
than his heart which 'like a lark at heaven's gate singing, hovers
morning-bright to Thee'. He is obviously uncomfortable about an
experience which expresses itself in such clichés as 'at heaven's
gate' and such Moody and Sankey rhythms as 'hovers morning-
bright to Thee'. Such an experience is inadequate because it strives
to be exclusive and to deny its opposite:

But remember, Saviour,
That my heart . . .
Throws still the dark blood back and forth
In the avenues where the bat hangs sleeping, upside-down
And to me undeniable, Jesus.

The other Evangelistic Beasts are no longer living symbols. They
are examples of the disastrous process of transforming our symbolism of the gods from the theriomorphic to the anthropomorphic.
Thus the gods are incorporated into the dead mass of that which
is already known. Lawrence's effort is to restore to the animal world
its otherness and mystery and majesty. Blake strove to imagine a
God who made both the lamb and the tiger. If God made all creatures in his own image, it was no God of sweetness and light, no
God known or knowable to man, who made the snake, the bat and
the fish. This is to be the theme of some of the finest of the poems
which followed.

*

In October, back in Taormina, Lawrence wrote the first of the flower
poems, 'Sicilian Cyclamens', where these autumnal flowers seem
nevertheless to belong to 'the world's morning'. The delicate rosy
flowers, 'dawn-pink', 'dawn-pale', are like such swift creatures of
the morning as 'very-young greyhound bitches' or 'bunches of wild
hares', ecstatic. But they issue from among the 'squat toad-leaves',
leaves which are

Toad-filmy, earth-iridescent
Beautiful
Frost-filigreed

Spumed with mud
Snail-nacreous
Low down.   [310]

Leaves which seem to belong to a still earlier world-age, whose
dark secrets are known only to the cyclamen flowers 'whispering
witchcraft/Like women at a well'.

The theme of plants as dumb messengers ('Ah, if it could but
answer! or if we had tree-speech!' [SS 97]) is continued, but not
developed, in the next two poems, 'Bare Almond Trees' ('Do you
take in messages in some strange code?') and 'Bare Fig Trees' ('this
wicked tree,/That has kept so many secrets up its sleeve'). The next
major poem, 'Almond Blossom', was written in January 1921.

The poem begins with the recognition of miracle:

Seeing iron break and bud
Seeing rusty iron puff with clouds of blossom.   [CP 304]

They are not flakes of snow, nor is the miracle in any sense from
above:

Flying not down from heaven, but storming up,
Strange storming up from the dense under-earth
Along the iron, to the living steel
In rose-hot tips, and flakes of rose-pale snow
Setting supreme annunciation to the world.

The re-birth of the almond-tree announces the re-birth of all vegetation. The more scarred and wounded the tree, like the vine and fig,
the more unquenchable its 'heart of blossom', its 'heart of delicate
super-faith'. The annual miracle of the sprouting of the tree of life is,
for Lawrence, 'supreme', the true resurrection, which does not
degrade and destroy the body in order to release an immortal soul:

Sweating his drops of blood through the long-nighted Gethsemane
Into blossom, into pride, into honey-triumph, into most exquisite
        splendour.
Oh, give me the tree of life in blossom
And the Cross sprouting its superb and fearless flowers!   [305]

That, indeed, is a 'great and sacred forthcoming'.

It is not a matter of preferring body to spirit. Rather such a miracle
testifies to 'that subtle knot' of flesh and spirit which makes all
living things:

Knots of pink, fish-silvery
In heaven, in blue, blue heaven,
Soundless, bliss-full, wide-rayed, honey-bodied,

Red at the core,
Red at the core,
Knotted in heaven upon the fine light.   [307]

All such knots are red at the core 'with the last sore-heartedness' because resurrection can only follow a crucifixion. All living things which participate in the mystery are 'open' and 'given' and 'perfect', 'six times wide open', which is one more opening than the wounds of the crucified Christ, open, finally, to the bride who comes from 'the dense under-earth', Persephone, as well as the 'fine light' of heaven.

Persephone is not mentioned in 'Almond Blossom', but she surfaces in 'Purple Anemones'. Here Lawrence imagines, with high-spirited wit, that Pluto, or Dis, let Persephone up from the underworld in spring only for the sport of tracking her down with the aid of those hounds of hell, the flowers:

She thought she had left him;
But opened around her purple anemones,

Caverns,
Little hells of colour, caves of darkness,
Hell, risen in pursuit of her; royal, sumptuous
Pit-falls.   [308]

Purple anemones are 'Hell's husband-blossoms', 'Hell rearing its husband-splendid, serpent heads'. Persephone is lost.

It is spring.

Between 'Almond Blossom' and 'Purple Anemones' had come the very different 'Hibiscus and Salvia Flowers', Lawrence's protest at the misuse of these flowers as symbols of a false revolution in the name of such dead ideals as equality and democracy.

*

At the end of July 1920 Lawrence wrote: 'It has been hot blazing sun for week after week, day after day, and so hot lately it was too much. I have lived for weeks in a pair of pyjamas' [L III 581]. Since 'Snake' takes place 'on a hot, hot day, and I in pyjamas for the heat', a 'day of Sicilian July', and is signed Taormina, there seems to be no problem about dating it. But Christopher Heywood has recently argued that the poem was deeply influenced by an encounter with a snake described in *Specimens of Bushman Folklore* which Lawrence borrowed from Jan Juta in Anticoli at the beginning of August 1920. The attitude of the editor, Lucy Lloyd, is perhaps even closer to Lawrence's poem than the Bushman narrative itself:

On one occasion I saw a snake close to the coping of a burial place; and showed it to !Nanni, expecting him to destroy it. He merely looked at it in rather a strange way, and allowed it to depart uninjured; saying something about its being near a grave; which, at the time, I did not clearly understand. [DHLR 15 94]

In the actual narrative, the snake is in water in the hollow of a tree: 'We think that it will drink the water . . . We think that we will strike it, and it gives us its belly, we turn back, we go away . . .' Heywood sums up:

This foreshadowing of Lawrence's poem, the self-confessed original incomprehension of the editor and her eventual recognition of another level of apprehension about snakes, the water-drinking and the indecision of the narrator about whether to strike or not, the association of the animal with life and death, all point to the strength of the impression made by this work on Lawrence. Lawrence's repetitions, 'And truly I was afraid, I was most afraid' and 'I . . . must wait, must stand and wait', the 'hot, hot day', etc., catch the accent of San speech, as in !Nanni's 'and it lies, lies, lies . . .' and 'we approach it, approach it, approach it . . .'   [94–5]

The poem has other literary sources. Lawrence himself, within the poem, draws attention to the parallel with 'The Ancient Mariner'; and it is difficult to believe that he had not read W. H. Hudson's autobiography *Far Away and Long Ago*, published in 1918. We know of Lawrence's enthusiasm for some of Hudson's earlier works. In the chapters 'Serpent and Child' and 'A Serpent Mystery', Hudson recalls several encounters with snakes near his childhood home on the South American pampas. Like all other boys, he was educated to believe that a serpent was 'dangerous to human beings, therefore a creature to be destroyed at sight and pounded to a pulp' [FA 224]:

When my courage and strength were sufficient I naturally began to take an active part in the persecution of serpents; for was not I also of the seed of Eve? [219]

Later he witnesses the spontaneous saving of a snake from a man with a stick, by a woman, which leads him to 'consider whether it might not be better to spare than to kill; better not only for the animal spared, but for the soul' [220]. A further change takes place in his attitude to snakes when, on a hot day, on a small piece of waste ground at the far end of the plantation and on the edge of the moat, he encounters a large black snake of unknown species. Despite his sense of danger he is drawn back to the spot with fascination, by the 'desire to look again at that strange being' [227]. He sees it again:

About a yard from me there was a hole in the ground about the circum-
ference of a breakfast cup at the top, and into this hole the serpent put his
head and slowly, slowly drew himself in . . .   [228]

He refers to it now as 'majestical', and 'my wonderful creature'.
There is a third and last encounter, in which the great black snake
slowly draws its long coil across his instep:

That last encounter had left in me a sense of a mysterious being, dangerous
on occasion as when attacked or insulted, and able in some cases to inflict
death with a sudden blow, but harmless and even friendly or beneficent
towards those who regarded it with kindly and reverent feelings in place
of hatred.   [231]

He is left also with a 'sense of something supernatural in the serpent' [224].

Whether or not Lawrence had read this, 'Snake' seems to be not
so much a record of a specific encounter as, like 'The Ancient Mariner' itself, an amalgamation of several experiences with his reading from several sources in a new imaginative whole.

There is further evidence to suggest that the poem was not written in July 1920. It is conspicuously absent from the notebook
[B E47a] in which Lawrence wrote what are apparently the first
drafts of almost all the poems written in Taormina in 1920. The
first mention of 'Snake' in the letters is on 28 January 1921, when
Lawrence sent it to Mountsier, his American agent, together with
three other freshly written poems: 'Almond Blossom', 'Bare
Almond-Trees' and 'Bare Fig Trees'. If it had been written when
he sent the first *Birds, Beasts and Flowers* manuscript to Mountsier
in December he would presumably have sent it then.

In any case, I do not believe the poem is an accurate record of an
actual encounter. Though Lawrence may well have found a poisonous snake before him at his water-trough at the Fontana Vecchia
in July, I do not believe he would have thrown a log at it. Nothing
of that kind had entered his head when he encountered the brindled adder in Cornwall. And Lawrence had a much greater awareness of the psychological significance of such behaviour than the
narrator in the poem. He had already written his Blake-like
response to Freud:

With dilated hearts we watched Freud disappearing into the cavern of
darkness, which is sleep and unconsciousness to us, darkness which issues
in the foam of all our day's consciousness. He was making for the origins . . . What was there in the cave? Alas that we ever looked! Nothing
but a huge slimy serpent of sex, and heaps of excrement, and a myriad
repulsive little horrors spawned between sex and excrement. Is it true?

Does the great unknown of sleep contain nothing else? No lovely spirits in the anterior regions of our being? [F 203]

Still earlier, in 'The Reality of Peace', Lawrence had given detailed instructions on how to respond to that serpent:

> If there is a serpent of secret and shameful desire in my soul, let me not beat it out of my consciousness with sticks. It will lie beyond, in the marsh of the so-called subconsciousness, where I cannot follow it with my sticks. Let me bring it to the fire to see what it is. For a serpent is a thing created. It has its own *raison d'être*. In its own being it has beauty and reality. Even my horror is a tribute to its reality. And I must admit the genuineness of my horror, accept it, and not exclude it from my understanding . . . There is a natural marsh in my belly, and there the snake is naturally at home. Shall he not crawl into my consciousness? Shall I kill him with sticks the moment he lifts his flattened head on my sight? Shall I kill him or pluck out the eye which sees him? None the less, he will swarm within the marsh. Then let the serpent of living corruption take his place among us honourably . . . For the Lord is the lord of all things, not of some only. And everything shall in its proportion drink its own draught of life.
> [P 677–9]

The poem, then, is a parable, beautifully grounded in immediate dramatic experience, and working on several levels. The first section of the poem is all heat and stillness and languor. There is no hint of danger or fear or any sort of conflict. The smoke from Etna testifies to the powers of the inner earth, but they are sleeping. The snake is

> earth-brown, earth-golden from the burning bowels of the earth
> On the day of Sicilian July, with Etna smoking. [CP 349]

These lines give such a strong sense of harmony embracing the whole scene that it seems a primal scene from before the fall, not only before the fall of man, but, as we shall see, before the fall of Lucifer.

The harmony is spoiled by one incongruous element, one intruder, the man who is not at home in the noonday sun, who would have stayed in his house but for the need for water, the fundamental life-element. The water-trough is the essential female complement to the otherwise too fiery maleness of the scene. The snake, drawn by the same basic need, comes to the frontier of its world, and there they meet. They have come from opposite directions, he from the human, civilized world, the snake from the wild, the natural world. They are opposites not only on the horizontal plane, but on the vertical too, the man more upright and overreaching than any other creature of earth, and the snake 'who must go

235

with his belly on the ground' [348]; the man from the world of daylight, the snake from 'the burning bowels of the earth'. The man is not 'earth-golden' but pale-face, not naked, but wearing those ridiculous pyjamas, no doubt striped. The snake belongs, the man is alien, both as Englishman in Sicily and as trespasser into the wilderness the end of his neglected garden has become. The snake assumes a natural priority, altogether unself-conscious and unconscious of the man, while he is acutely conscious of the snake, and self-conscious about the need to choose between opposite responses to it.

Why 'must' he stand and wait? It isn't just the Englishman's compulsion to start a queue. He instinctively yields priority to the snake as first comer, not only to the water-trough, but to Sicily and to the world. Perhaps he even yields it priority of being: the snake is more a snake than he is a man. Its message is: I exist. I am not only swift and sure in my own snakehood, I am also continuous with the whole environment, flora, landscape, climate, geology, a distinctive golden strand in the total pattern. I pass freely through the dark door which separates this world apprehended by man from the underworld he can never enter, even in imagination.

Both Etna and the snake's hole are 'dark doors of the secret earth'. The snake's black tongue flickers 'like a forked night on the air', a flash of black lightning plunging the noonday scene into momentary night. Powers of darkness inhabit that underworld. Etna might erupt, the snake might strike. Drive it back. Block the doors. So conflict enters the poem with the second and opposite imperative, 'He must be killed'. Suddenly the tone of the poem becomes harsh and ugly. The man's spontaneous reaction had been to honour the snake as a god, a lord of life. Now the voice of his education tells him that the snake is dangerous, that everything it stands for must be denied and repressed. His new reaction is the conditioned reflex of a puritanical and rationalistic culture.

Perhaps the nearest man can come, before death, to entering that 'dark hole', that 'fissure', is in sexual intercourse. The elaboration of 'fissure' in the fruit poems has ensured that even the most naive reader must make this connection. Every such return to the 'burning bowels' of the earth-mother reverses two thousand years of Christianity. Hence the fears and taboos surrounding the act, its close association with ideas of sin and evil. It is a short step for the diseased puritan imagination to equate the vagina with hell:

But to the girdle do the Gods inherit,
Beneath is all the fiend's: there's hell, there's darkness,

> There is the sulphurous pit – burning, scalding,
> Stench, consumption; fie, fie, fie! pah, pah!   [*King Lear*, IV.6.128–31]

Similarly, Lawrence's narrator becomes incoherent. His disgust expresses itself in the schoolgirl hysteria of such words as 'dreadful' and 'horrid'. It is not the snake itself, nor even the hole, but the act of entering the hole, the 'earth-lipped fissure', that finally drives him in horror to his cowardly attack. The snake, once denied, loses its dignity, and becomes the obscene writhing thing the voice of his education tells him it is, a reptile of the mind.

Afterwards, he thinks of the albatross. That is, he associates himself with the Ancient Mariner who, by shooting 'the bird that made the breeze to blow', cut himself off from sustaining nature and brought the curse of drought. At first the mariner looks on the creatures of the calm with disgust, as mere 'slimy things'. Later, when a spring of love spontaneously breaks from his heart, he blesses the water-snakes. The spell breaks and it begins to rain. Natural fertilizing interchange resumes.

Lawrence's narrator also repents, seeing the snake to be

> Like a king in exile, uncrowned in the underworld,
> Now due to be crowned again.   [CP 351]

We cannot but think of Lucifer, once brightest of angels, and of what Frederick Carter calls 'the mysterious triple communion in the garden between woman and snake and man from which it would seem came the discovery of seed and its purpose' [BM 29]. According to Jung, when God cast Lucifer out of heaven, he cut off a vital part of himself, his procreative ability, his potency, his link with the world of the flesh. He repudiated nature itself. The Great God Pan became Satan. Lawrence summons him back to take his place, not as the exclusive lord of life, but as 'one of the lords of life' needed to balance the other lordships of mind and spirit.

*

Though the ass, bat and goat poems are excellent, the only other European poem to break new ground is 'Fish', written at Zell-am-See in August 1921. I cannot improve on Pollnitz's account of how the early part of the poem works:

> The first movement of 'Fish' is in many ways a remarkable performance. Weighty matters are handled with a lightness of touch, an *esprit* that refuses to be portentous about creation or identity. Parallelism is an almost infinitely flexible device. Here we should pay homage to the sheer intellectual power it makes possible, in conjunction with a conversational unhurriedness, the sense of a mature poet choosing to stay or pass on as he pleases,

confident of his resources and his theme's coherence. 'Performance' is not an unapt term for Lawrence's free verse. We have read stalled, didactic passages in Lawrence often enough to know that they do not always surface, as here, with the brilliant, unexpected image. When he is in full career, though, pivoting on one association and surging forward to the next, the end unforeseen and 'the strands . . . all flying, quivering, intermingling into the web', his verse gives the pleasure a dancer's extempore improvisations give, of risk and difficulty suddenly overcome.   [DHLR 15 30]

But it is not a performance in the sense of drawing attention to itself and seeking applause. All this technical skill is entirely at the service of Lawrence's imagination, and his imagination is wholly concentrated on the task of 'understanding' fish. The poem goes straight to the heart of the matter, which must be the relationship, the uniquely close relationship, between fishes and their element, water:

> As the waters roll
> Roll you.
> The waters wash,
> You wash in oneness
> And never emerge.   [CP 335]

No English poet has ever got closer to this strange life-mode:

> Your life a sluice of sensation along your sides,
> A flush at the flails of your fins, down the whorl of your tail,
> And water wetly on fire in the grates of your gills;
> Fixed water-eyes.

He breaks down the fish's motivation into 'food, and fear, and joie de vivre', and each is so convincingly mimed that we think we know what it is 'to be a fish / In the waters'. But there is one remaining obstacle to empathy; the life of a fish is 'all without love'.

Lawrence's imagination balks at this obstacle. He had found it easy to identify with the ass, 'the first of all animals to fall finally into love' [378], or with the tortoise, crucified, at adolescence, into sex. But fishes were 'born before God was love, /Or life knew loving'. Even a water-serpent he can recognize as belonging to the same world and the same God as himself – 'He's a rare one, but he belongs . . .' But fish do not belong, are, finally, inaccessible, even to the poetic imagination at its most penetrating:

> I said to my heart, *who are these?*
> And my heart couldn't own them . . .

The word 'own' is perfectly judged. It means, of course, 'recognize', but that is hardly enough to explain what follows. For that we need the stronger meanings of 'possess' and 'countenance'. What the human heart cannot own, in these senses, it is strongly tempted to deny and destroy.

Suddenly, the poem changes course. It makes a last desperate effort to bully the creature, by anthropomorphic metaphor, into yielding its being to the understanding, but the effort fails:

> A slim young pike, with smart fins
> And grey-striped suit, a young cub of a pike
> Slouching along away below, half out of sight,
> Like a lout on an obscure pavement . . .
>
> Aha, there's somebody in the know!
>
> But watching closer
> That motionless deadly motion,
> That unnatural barrel body, that long ghoul nose, . . .
> I left off hailing him.
>
> I had made a mistake, I didn't know him,
> This grey, monotonous soul in the water,
> This intense individual in shadow,
> Fish-alive.
>
> I didn't know his God.
> I didn't know his God.   [338]

There may be a pun on 'hailing'. The failure of the attempt to bully the fish verbally leads on to a more violent and destructive 'haling', the violation of wrenching the fish from its element into ours:

> And the gold-and-green pure lacquer-mucus comes off in my hand,
> And the red-gold mirror-eye stares and dies,
> And the water-suave contour dims.
>
> But not before I have had to know
> He was born in front of my sunrise,
> Before my day.   [339]

The lovelessness and loneliness of fishes, he concludes, and their strange white meat so attractive to hot-blooded creatures, 'sun-beasts', can only be accounted for by the theory that, unlike all the creatures of the upper world, they are 'things of one element' which cannot long survive exposure to the 'horror of daylight', our world where everything is mixed, generated by a mixture of the first element of water with the second of fire.

The reference to Jesus in the poem's final lines is obscure. It has been explained at length by Pollnitz, and by Lawrence himself in his 1923 essay 'The Proper Study', but these explanations take us

239

outside the terms of reference of this poem, even of *Birds, Beasts and Flowers* as a whole. Within those terms, I can only suggest this meaning. What followed from our 'sunrise' was a world of individuals, and of duality within and without. The world of the beginning and the end, before and after, is a world of oneness, single creatures merging with their single element, the waters under the earth. If we call that oneness Love, then it is Love which excludes love, for love is characteristic only of mixed and divided individuals. Christ belongs to the element of pure oneness, of Love. He was wrenched from that element and forced to attempt to live the life of a man on earth. It was a crucifixion. Pure Love is not an element man can breathe any more than Christ could breathe in the world of impure love. Man belongs to the incarnate world, as Christ did not; therefore 'His God stands outside my God'.

*

Lawrence wrote only one poem in Ceylon, 'Elephant' (March 1922), and one in Australia, 'Kangaroo' (July 1922). Each is a remarkable evocation of the spirit of place; but it needed New Mexico to stimulate new developments in Lawrence's vision. His journey to Ceylon and Australia had been a way of deferring his longed-for and feared confrontation with America: 'I will go east, intending ultimately to go west' [RC 27]. That intention he had firmly held for several years. Two of the poems written in Europe had been about it. In 'Turkey Cock' (September 1920) he had asked if he should:

> Take up the trail of the vanished American
> Where it disappeared at the foot of the crucifix.
> Take up the primordial Indian obstinacy,
> The more than human, dense insistence of will,
> And disdain, and blankness, and onrush, and prise open the new day
> with them?   [CP 371]

In 'The Evening Land' (May 1921), Lawrence explains one reason for his fear of America, for believing that it might be 'the grave of our day' [289]. He sees in modern America a 'more-than-European idealism', 'boundless love/Like a poison gas'. He is clearly thinking of Whitman, whom he mentions in the last lines. Whitman saw as clearly as it has ever been seen that the quality of human life depends on a right, that is a sacramental, relationship with the non-human world. But Whitman was also an idealist, whose democratic ideals and 'goal of Allness' caused Lawrence to associate him closely with Christ: 'His One Identity is a prison of horror, once realized' [SM 259]. Whitman had a strong faith that a modern industrial democracy could be built on these principles. By Lawrence's time it had become clear that, on the contrary, such a society inevitably accelerated the process of dehumanizing men and degrading and possibly destroying the natural world.

But there was something else in America, 'something in you which carries me beyond . . . what we call human. Carries me where I want to be carried . . .' [CP 291]. There was also 'a dark, unfathomed will', a 'demonish New World nature' that Lawrence was in love with, though he feared to seek it, lest it should prove to be no more than his own 'imaginings'. He could not bear it if America turned out to be only the evening land, and not also the land of the new dawn.

The first poem Lawrence wrote in New Mexico was probably 'Autumn at Taos'. Here he testifies that the landscape at least had not disappointed him. The sides of the Rockies, brindled with aspen, are 'Jaguar-splashed, puma-yellow, leopard-livid slopes of America', and the mesa is like 'a wolf's wild pelt'. This yellow autumn landscape seemed to be the very body of a savage sun-god:

When I trot my little pony through the aspen-trees of the canyon,
Behold me trotting at ease betwixt the slopes of the golden
Great and glistening-feathered legs of the hawk of Horus;
The golden hawk of Horus
Astride above me.   [409]

The American equivalent of Horus was the 'Eagle, with Egyptian darkness jutting in front of your face':

The God-thrust thrusting you silent and dark from beneath.
From where?
From the red-fibred bough of the cedar, from the cedar-roots, from the
    earth,
From the dark earth over the rock, from the dark rock over the fire,
    from the fire that boils in the molten heart of the world.   [782]

The eagle is the opposite of the fish, a creature of pure fire: 'You who came before rock was smitten into weeping'. Lawrence imagines that 'the old Father of life at the heart of the world, life-fire at the middle of the earth' had sent out the sun to 'flutter in heaven' and the eagle to 'keep an eye on him', constantly threatening to 'strike the sun's heart out again'. This opposition between eagle and sun seems to stem from the observed fact that the eagle seems always to be staring into the sun 'with a dagger of dark, live iron/That's been whetted and whetted in blood'; but it goes against the role of the eagle or hawk in both Egyptian and Mexican mythology, and this is perhaps why Lawrence recast the poem for *Birds, Beasts and Flowers*, making the eagle rather the sun's priest:

> When you pick the red smoky heart from a rabbit or a light-blooded
> bird
> Do you lift it to the sun, as the Aztec priests used to lift red hearts of
> men?   [374]

The spirit of place in New Mexico was so much more savage and inhuman than anything Lawrence had met with before that he must conceive new gods and new myths. The myths of the Mediterranean, even of Egypt, were too gentle for this place. If the myths of Persephone and Dionysos and Osiris were appropriate to the almond blossom and purple anemones and handsome golden snakes of Sicily, they were not so to the pine trees and cactus flowers and coiled and fanged rattlesnakes of New Mexico. The gods of this place were larger, but lower, gods not of resurrection but of blood-sacrifice. Power can still be won from them, but by different means:

> It is a battle, a wrestling all the time. The Sun, the nameless Sun, source of all things, which we call sun because the other name is too fearful, this, this vast dark protoplasmic sun from which issues all that feeds our life, this original One is all the time willing and unwilling. Systole, diastole, it pulses its willingness and its unwillingness that we should live and move on, from being to being, manhood to further manhood. Man, small, vulnerable man, the farthest adventurer from the dark heart of the first of suns, into the cosmos of creation. Man, the last god won into existence. And all the time, he is sustained and threatened, menaced and sustained from the Source, the innermost sun-dragon. And all the time, he must submit and he must conquer. Submit to the strange beneficence from the Source, whose ways are past finding out. And conquer the strange malevolence of the Source, which is past comprehension also.   [MM 86–7]

The eagle is the sun-dragon in its malevolent aspect, but

> Even the sun in heaven can be curbed and chastened at last
> By the life in the hearts of men.
> And you, great bird, sun-starer, heavy black beak
> Can be put out of office as sacrifice bringer.

In 'The Red Wolf', probably written in November 1922, Lawrence imagines himself actually meeting and conversing with one of these gods, or demons, the 'old Father of life'. It is nightfall; day has gone 'like a white Christus fallen to dust from a cross':

> And a black crucifix like a dead tree spreading wings;
> Maybe a black eagle with its wings out

> Left lonely in the night
> In a sort of worship.   [CP 403]

It is the scene for a black mass. The demon who comes claims to be
Old Nick himself, here god of the upper world as much as the lower.
Lawrence, the interloper of 'Snake', the man at the pale of his being,
looking outwards with pure incomprehension in 'Fish', is now in
a situation where he might be expected to feel even more alien and
out of his depth, especially when the demon tells him to go home,
and threatens to set the pueblo dogs on him: 'We take no hungry
stray from the pale-face . . .' The poem develops from the first essay
Lawrence had written in New Mexico, recording his first unsatisfactory encounter with the Indians:

> I was born of no virgin, of no Holy Ghost. Ah, no, these old men telling
> the tribal tale were my fathers. I have a dark-faced, bronze-voiced father
> far back in the resinous ages . . . But he, like many an old father with a
> changeling son, he would like to deny me. But I stand on the far edge of
> their firelight, and am neither denied nor accepted. My way is my own,
> old red father; I can't cluster at the drum any more.   [P 99]

In the poem Lawrence denies that he is a lost white dog, homeless
in the universe. He stands up for his right to go his own way. For
the only time in these poems he is confronting the god himself, not
his dumb messengers, but he does not panic and is not blasted. In
'Song of Myself', Whitman beholds the day-break:

> Dazzling and tremendous how quick the sun-rise would kill me,
> If I could not now and always send sun-rise out of me.   [Section 25]

Similarly, Lawrence asks what, in himself, can answer to the power
of this demon. What he finds is his redness:

> Touch me carefully, old father,
> My beard is red.   [CP 405]

To be red is no more nor less than to be alive:

> But blood is red, and blood is life. Red was the colour of kings. Kings,
> far-off kings, painted their faces vermilion, and were almost gods.   [303]

His long discipline of communion with birds, beasts and flowers
has taught Lawrence how to commune with and draw power from
the God at the centre of himself:

> Listening inwards, inwards, not for words nor for inspiration, but to the
> lowing of the innermost beasts, the feelings, that roam in the forest of the
> blood, from the feet of God within the red, dark heart.   [P 759]

The demon is forced by his effrontery to recognize the god in him
and accord him the grudging title of 'thin red wolf'. It is enough:

I'm the red wolf, says the dark old father.
All right, the red-dawn-wolf I am.   [CP 405]

*

The last two months of 1922 were spent largely on the final revision of *Studies in Classic American Literature* ('It is the American Demon indeed' [TS 48]). In the essay on Benjamin Franklin Lawrence attacks the mechanical, moralistic rationalism of Franklin's creed, and offers his own alternative. It is, perhaps, the best possible summary of the qualities which have informed *Birds, Beasts and Flowers*:

> This is what I believe:
>
> *'That I am I.'*
> *'That my soul is a dark forest.'*
> *'That my known self will never be more than a little clearing in the forest.'*
> *'That gods, strange gods, come forth from the forest into the clearing of my
> known self, and then go back.'*
> *'That I must have the courage to let them come and go.'*
> *'That I will never let mankind put anything over me, but that I will try
> always to recognize and submit to the gods in me and the gods in
> other men and women.'*   [S 22]

In January 1923 Lawrence wrote 'Mountain Lion'. It is a beautiful poem, but it ends:

> And I think in this empty world there was room for me and a
> mountain lion.
> And I think in the world beyond, how easily we might spare a million
> or two of humans
> And never miss them.
> Yet what a gap in the world, the missing white frost-face of that slim
> yellow mountain lion!   [CP 402]

We can understand Lawrence's outrage at the mindless slaughter of a godly creature; but are we to assume that some humans, many humans, have no gods in them?

In February, Lawrence sent off the manuscript of *Birds, Beasts and Flowers* to his American publisher Thomas Seltzer. A month later, however, a few days before setting off for Mexico to begin his new novel, he sent on one last poem, 'The American Eagle'. It is the worst poem in the volume. It is not about a real eagle, or any other bird, beast or flower. There is no visitation from any god. It is Lawrence at his most sarcastically didactic. The early part is a mildly amusing account of the American Eagle, a purely emblematic bird, trying to be the dove of Liberty or the pelican of prosperity. At the end, however, the satirical tone is dropped, and we are told what the American Eagle should really stand for:

The new Proud Republic
Based on the mystery of pride.
Overweening men, full of power of life, commanding a teeming
    obedience.
Eagle of the Rockies, bird of men that are masters,
Lifting the rabbit-blood of the myriads up into something splendid,
Leaving a few bones;
Opening great wings in the face of the sheep-faced ewe
Who is losing her lamb,
Drinking a little blood, and loosing another royalty unto the
    world.   [414]

The eagle is reinstated as sacrifice bringer. It is hardly poetry; rather a first sketch for the hypnotic rhetoric of Don Ramon in *The Plumed Serpent*.

In the American poems the male self reasserts itself, no longer submitting to the primacy of the dark female underworld, where a man must be 'soft-footed' and sensitive as a tendril, but stridently asserting an exclusively male kinship with the sun of power, in accordance with the programme Lawrence had set out at the end of *Fantasia*:

The next relation has got to be a relationship of men towards men in a spirit of unfathomable trust and responsibility, service and leadership, obedience and pure authority. Men have got to choose their leaders, and obey them to the death. And it must be a system of culminating aristocracy, society tapering like a pyramid to the supreme leader . . . The intense passionate yearning of the soul towards the soul of a stronger, greater individual, and the passionate blood-belief in the fulfilment of this yearning, will give men the next motive for life.   [F 182–3]

The delicacy and sensitivity and balance of the best of the European poems has gone, as if burned out by the harsher climate, the vastness and obduracy of the American Southwest, where god is the savage Pan of the lightning and cactus-spine, rather than Dionysos of the tendrilled vine. It is as though, the initiation rites of the Mediterranean world completed, Lawrence's journey to the New World is also his assumption of priesthood and leadership, the apotheosis of his demon.

SEVEN

THE MONK AND THE BEAST: *ST MAWR*

One day when Lawrence was a boy, he and his friend Mabel Thurlby were standing at Moorgreen crossing waiting for a train to pass. The crossing-keeper was Mabel's father, who had lost an arm in a pit accident. He had closed the gates, though the small colliery engine clanking laboriously towards them was still some distance away. At that moment Thomas Philip Barber, owner of the mine, rode up and demanded to be let through. Mr Thurlby refused, and, as Major Barber forced his horse to the gates, said: 'Are you going to make that horse's mouth bleed?' The incident fixed itself in Lawrence's mind. Some fifteen years later he vividly recreated it in *Women in Love*.

The image of horse and rider became for him a symbol of the human will bullying the body, or the instincts, or the life of nature, long before he knew what a symbol was. He would meet the same symbol often in his early reading; in the Bible, for example: 'Be ye not as the horse, or as the mule, which have no understanding: whose mouth must be held in with bit and bridle' [Psalms 32:9]; or in the dialogues of Plato. Discussing Plato's *Phaedrus* with her husband, Connie Chatterley says: 'Don't you think it's rather cruel, the way Socrates drives his black horse – jerking him back till his mouth and tongue are full of blood, and bruising his haunches?' [FLC 37]. In the passage to which Connie refers, Socrates, developing his myth of the soul as a charioteer (will or intellect) driving a team of horses, one white and compliant (spirit), the other black and 'hardly controllable' (passion or instinct), reaches a point where the black horse, long frustrated and reined in, 'takes the bit between his teeth and pulls shamelessly':

> The driver . . . falls back like a racing charioteer at the barrier, and with a still more violent backward pull, jerks the bit from between the teeth of the lustful horse, drenches his abusive tongue and jaws with blood,

and forcing his legs and haunches against the ground reduces him to
torment.   [PH 63]

It is unlikely that Lawrence had a copy of the *Phaedrus* to hand while
writing *The First Lady Chatterley* at the Villa Mirenda in 1926, yet his
recollection of this passage is vivid. It is not known when he had first
read the *Phaedrus*, but certainly not later than the beginning of 1913.
His famous letter to Ernest Collings, 17 January 1913, reads like a
violent reaction to it, such as we often get from Lawrence to something he has just read – a reaction to the opposite extreme:

> My great religion is a belief in the blood, the flesh, as being wiser than
> the intellect. We can go wrong in our minds. But what our blood feels
> and believes and says, is always true. The intellect is only a bit and a
> bridle.   [LI 503]

Socrates' myth is, of course, a logical expression of his fundamental
dualism and its concomitant puritanism:

> Pure was the light and pure were we from the pollution of the walking
> sepulchre which we call a body, to which we are bound like an oyster to
> its shell.   [PH 57]

Gradually Lawrence was coming to see all cruelty, all perversity
and pollution and sterility, as a direct result of such blasphemous
and suicidal conceit as that of Socrates and Plato. Consequently he
was driven, for most of his life, to enlist on the other side, thereby
perpetuating a dualism in which he did not really believe. Of *Lady
Chatterley's Lover* he wrote to the Brewsters:

> As I say, it's a novel of the phallic Consciousness: or the phallic
> Consciousness versus the mental-spiritual Consciousness: and of course
> you know which side I take. The *versus* is not my fault: there should be no
> *versus*. The two things must be reconciled in us. But now they're daggers
> drawn.   [RC 166]

Lawrence had known for a long time, and in an acute form, the
torment of baffled desire. Frieda had released him from that; she
had also introduced him to the ideas of Freud. It was inevitable
that he should translate Plato's myth into Freudian terms, and
conclude, writing to Edward Garnett in November 1912, that
'cruelty is a form of perverted sex' [L I 469]. That is certainly
suggested in the cruelty of Gerald Crich to his red Arab mare in
Women in Love, prefiguring his subsequent relationship with the
watching Gudrun:

> He bit himself down on the mare like a keen edge biting home, and
> *forced* her round. She roared as she breathed, her nostrils were two wide,
> hot holes, her mouth was apart, her eyes frenzied. It was a repulsive sight.

But he held on her unrelaxed, with an almost mechanical relentlessness, keen as a sword pressing into her . . .

Gudrun looked and saw the trickles of blood on the sides of the mare, and she turned white. And then on the very wound the bright spurs came down, pressing relentlessly. The world reeled and passed into nothingness for Gudrun, she could not know any more.　　　　　　　　　[WL 169–70]

One model for this scene is clearly Vronsky's killing of his mare in *Anna Karenina*. But it is Gerald himself, not Gudrun, who is destroyed in *Women in Love*. Connie Chatterley thought Socrates stupid for not realizing that the black horse could not be broken by cruelty, but would ultimately overturn the chariot. What Gerald is doing to his mare represents something he is doing simultaneously to that part of himself which corresponds to her sensitivity and spontaneity. His willingness to subject her to the 'frightful strident concussions' of the colliery train is of a piece with his willingness to subject his employees to the mangling of the great machine. The crossing-keeper's wooden leg testifies to the human cost. But ultimately he is crueller to himself than to horse, woman or men. The horse – his own affective life – becomes 'convulsed', threatening to 'fall backwards on top of him'.

*

Horses figure prominently in *The Rainbow* (written after the scene from *Women in Love* we have been discussing). The book begins and ends with horses. At the beginning horses represent no problem or threat to the Brangwen patriarchs:

They mounted their horses, and held life between the grip of their knees, they harnessed their horses at the wagon, and, with hand on the bridle-rings, drew the heaving of the horses after their will.

There was no need for cruelty. They were not in conflict with the life of the body or of the earth. Men, animals, earth, weather, season, birth, marriage, death – all are caught up in a rich, fertile interrelatedness, continuity and harmony – a way of life scarcely possible since the Industrial Revolution. But a way of life perhaps not fully human, since it lacks the adventure in consciousness which it is the privilege and the curse of humanity to pursue. The thought-adventurer must be free; yet freedom means rootlessness and danger. When there is no consciousness, the unconscious is untroubled, the horses are docile. But in spite of his admiration for the unconsciousness of the Italians, Lawrence had to admit that 'it is better to go forward into error than to stay fixed inextricably in the past' [TI 60]. The Brangwen farmers, having finished their work, had no further life; they 'sat by the fire and their brains were inert, as their blood flowed heavy with the accumulation from the living day' [R 42]. Ursula, on the other hand, goes forward into error, and loses that easy unity of being. She looks into the outer darkness, which is also her own inner darkness, and it is 'passionate and breathing with immense, unperceived heaving' [364], and the body of the earth, like a great horse, 'seemed to stir its powerful flank beneath her as she stood' [370]. I have already discussed at length Ursula's final encounter with the horses, which almost kills her, purges her error, and makes possible her rebirth. We have also discussed the several kinds of light, including the 'massive fire that was locked within' the flanks of the horses, which must come together in balance and harmony to make a rainbow. The rainbow is the saving vision, the healing of the dualistic split between mind and body, male and female, self and not-self, god and nature. The image had derived partly from *Howards End.* Forster had taken his rainbow bridge from Wagner:

the rainbow bridge that should connect the prose in us with the passion. Without it we are meaningless fragments, half monks, half beasts, unconnected arches that have never joined into a man.   [HE 174]

Forster's use of the symbol is crude and confused. He considers the monk and the beast to be mere aberrations; when the bridge of love is built they will both die. But Lawrence knows that life itself depends upon, *is*, the tension between these two opposite imperatives, the absolute need to reach out for the life of the spirit, the absolute need to fulfil the life of the body. We cannot live without the monk and the beast, but the chasm between them must indeed be bridged by a rainbow arch, in the light of which they will be seen to be interdependent parts of a single whole.

*

In November 1918 Lawrence borrowed from Koteliansky a book by Jung which he then re-lent to Katherine Mansfield with this warning:

Beware of it – this Mother-incest idea can become an obsession. But it seems to me there is this much truth in it: that at certain periods the man has a desire and a tendency to return unto the woman, make her his goal and end, find his justification in her. In this way he casts himself as it were into her womb, and she, the Magna Mater, receives him with gratification. This is a kind of incest . . . I have done it, and now struggle all my might to get out. In a way, Frieda is the devouring mother.
                                                                    [L III 302]

Later he wrote: 'Jung is very interesting, in his own sort of fat muddled mystical way' [CL 938]. The book was almost certainly *Psychology of the Unconscious* (now called *Symbols of Transformation*), published in England in 1917. In it, especially in the chapter called 'The Battle for Deliverance from the Mother', Lawrence would have found a great deal about horses:

> Legend attributes properties to the horse which psychologically belong to the unconscious of man: there are clairvoyant and clairaudient horses, path-finding horses who show the way when the wanderer is lost, horses with mantic powers . . . Horses also see ghosts. All these things are typical manifestations of the unconscious. We can therefore see why the horse, as a symbol of the animal component in man, has numerous connections with the devil . . . The sexual nature of the devil is imparted to the horse as well, so that this symbol is found in contexts where the sexual interpretation is the only one that fits . . . Lightning, too, is represented theriomorphically as a horse.　　　　　　　　　　　　　[ST 277]

A great deal of Jung went into *Fantasia of the Unconscious* in 1921. But there Lawrence shies away from Jung's insistence on placing horse symbolism in a context of incest. Rather, Lawrence offers his own interpretation in which he tries to relate what he has taken from Jung to his own earlier use of horse symbolism and to his growing sense of his own father as prototype of the repressed sensual male:

> For example, a man has a persistent passionate fear-dream about horses. He suddenly finds himself among great, physical horses, which may suddenly go wild. Their great bodies surge madly round him, they rear above him, threatening to destroy him . . . Examining the emotional reference we find that the feeling is sensual, there is a great impression of the powerful, almost beautiful physical bodies of the horses, the nearness, the rounded haunches, the rearing . . . The horse is presented as an object of terror, which means that to the man's automatic dream-soul, which loves automatism, the great sensual male activity is the greatest menace. The automatic pseudo-soul, which has got the sensual nature repressed, would like to keep it repressed. Whereas the greatest desire of the living spontaneous soul is that this very male sensual nature, represented as a menace, shall be actually accomplished in life . . . The dream may mean a love of the dreamer for the sensual male who is his father. But it has nothing to do with *incest*. The love is probably a just love.　　　[F 170–71]

The father as miner is also the devil, once Pan, now condemned to an underworld repressed existence.

*

Despite his gentle mockery of Jung's muddled mysticism, Lawrence was captivated by the much more muddled mysticism of Apocalypse. Images from the Book of Revelation had been implanted in his mind since boyhood. By the beginning of 1918 he had already begun the analysis of that book which was to result in his final completed work, *Apocalypse*. The first version of Lawrence's essay on Fenimore Cooper's Anglo-American novels begins with a virtual synopsis of that book:

It is quite certain that the pre-Christian priesthoods understood the processes of *dynamic* consciousness, which is pre-cerebral consciousness. It is certain that St John gives us in the Apocalypse a cypher-account of the process of the conquest of the lower or sensual dynamic centres by the upper or spiritual dynamic consciousness. [SM 75]

This essay was published in the *English Review* in 1919. It was probably a reading of it which prompted Frederick Carter to write to Lawrence in December 1922 about his own work along these lines, and to send him, the following April, the manuscript of his as yet unpublished *Dragon of the Alchemists*. Lawrence was in Chapala at the time, working on the first draft of his own dragon book, *The Plumed Serpent*. In December he returned to England, and took the opportunity to visit Carter at Pontesbury in Shropshire to discuss Apocalyptic symbols. According to Carter: 'From this came the landscape background of *St Mawr* and the red horse itself' [CB II 515]. The drift of their conversation can be inferred from *Apocalypse*:

Horses, always horses! How the horse dominated the mind of the early races, especially of the Mediterranean! You were a lord if you had a horse. Far back, far back in our dark soul the horse prances. He is a dominant symbol: he gives us lordship: he links us, the first palpable and throbbing link with the ruddy-glowing Almighty of potency: he is the beginning even of our godhead in the flesh. And as a symbol he roams the dark underworld meadows of the soul . . . Within the last fifty years man has lost the horse. Now man is lost. Man is lost to life and power – an underling and a wastrel. While horses thrashed the streets of London, London lived . . . The red horse is choler: not mere anger, but natural fieryness, what we call passion. [A 101–2]

From Pontesbury Lawrence returned to a dead and horseless London. From there, a week later, on 9 January 1924, he wrote to thank 'Spud' Johnson for the latest number of Spud's magazine, *The Laughing Horse*. The air had smelled smoky to Lawrence even on the Welsh border. In London he could hardly breathe. The *Horse* was a lifeline, and his London letter is a cri de cœur for everything the horse had come to mean to him – for life itself. He associates the horse with the centaur, and with Pan, dead in Europe, but alive and kicking in the blue air of the Rockies:

> In modern symbolism, the Horse is supposed to stand for the passions. Passions be blowed. What does the Centaur stand for, Chiron or any other of that quondam four-footed gentry? Sense! Horse-sense! Sound, powerful, four-footed *sense*, that's what the Horse stands for. Horse-sense, I tell you. That's the Centaur. That's the blue Horse of the ancient Mediterranean, before the pale Galilean or the extra-pale German or Nordic gentleman conquered. First of all, Sense, Good Sense, Sound Sense, Horse Sense. And then, a laugh, a loud, sensible Horse Laugh. After that, these same passions, glossy and dangerous in the flanks. And after these again, hoofs, irresistible, splintering hoofs, that can kick the walls of the world down. [CL 769]

In March Lawrence escaped from the 'dreadful mummy sarcophagus' of Europe, back to New Mexico, where he knew the horse in us was not dead:

> In Lobo, in Taos, in Santa Fe the Turquoise Horse is waving snow out of his tail, and trotting gaily to the blue mountains of the far distance. And in Mexico his mane is bright yellow on his blue body, so streaming with sun, and he's lashing out again like the devil, till his hoofs are red. [769]

*

It can be seen from this account of the genesis of *St Mawr* how the horse came to focus and embody so many of Lawrence's deepest and most lasting preoccupations; how, with a minimum of overt reference to mythology or psychology or any abstract ideas imported from outside the novel, rather through vivid scenes and the perfect control of evocative language, he is able to endow his stallion with such a range and depth of significance. Yet this account is blinkered; it has left out a whole cluster of themes just as central to the novel as the horse. It is a measure of the complexity of the novel that its genesis could be described equally convincingly in terms which have nothing to do with horses. It could be described, for example, in terms of Lawrence's deepening interest in Celtic and North American Indian mythology.[1] But what I want to do here is to describe it in terms of the lasting attraction for Lawrence of monasticism.

Lawrence's allegiance to the beast (almost any beast would serve, but horse and snake are the most important) and to the body might lead us to expect that the monk would be cast in the role of villain, the opposite, negative pole. But in Lawrence's dualistic scheme, most fully set out in 'The Crown', there is no positive and negative. Who is to say that in all the great pairs of opposites whose interplay makes up existence – life and death, light and dark, male and female, hot and cold, wet and dry – one is to be preferred to the other? The monk, like the beast, is in all of us, and has as valid a claim.

Lawrence nowhere thinks of the monk as a life-denier, rather as a guardian of the sacred and the life of the spirit within a human world which would deny these things. Lawrence's hatred of the human world which plunged into war in 1914 led him to explore various possibilities of withdrawing from it. On 18 January 1915 he wrote to Willie Hopkin:

> I want to gather together about twenty souls and sail away from this world of war and squalor and found a little colony where there shall be no money but a sort of communism as far as necessaries of life go, and some real decency. [L II 259]

A few days later the Lawrences moved to Viola Meynell's cottage at Greatham. Thanking her for the loan of it six months later, Lawrence wrote:

> I feel as if I had been born afresh there, got a new, sure, separate soul: as a monk in a monastery, or St John in the wilderness. Now we must go back into the world to fight. I don't want to, they are so many and they have so many roots. But we must set about cleaning the face of the earth a bit, or everything will perish. [374]

After the collapse, in March 1915, of his attempt to form a new revolutionary party, Lawrence turned again to his 'Island idea' – Rananim. But now it was to be located in England. Philip Morrell offered to adapt an old 'monastic building' at Garsington for the purpose; but the project had to be dropped because of the estimated costs of the conversion. When, in March 1916, the Lawrences moved to Zennor, in Cornwall, Lawrence wrote excitedly to Murry that the group of cottages at Higher Tregerthen could be 'like a little monastery' – 'our Rananim' [564]. Again the project failed, with the defection of the first recruits, Murry and Katherine Mansfield. The imagined location of Rananim receded to the far West, and the language in which Lawrence spoke of it became the language of wish-fulfilment:

> The only way is my far-off wilderness place which shall become a school and a monastery and an Eden and a Hesperides – a seed of a new heaven, and a new earth. [L III 71–2]

Lawrence can hardly mention Rananim without using the word 'monastery', and he does not use it lightly. The same period saw a radical revision of his formerly hostile attitude to Christianity:

I have been reading S. Bernard's *Letters*, and I realise that the greatest thing the world has seen, is Christianity, and one must be endlessly thankful for it, and weep that the world has learned the lesson so badly.   [L II 633]

St Bernard was a bigot and heresy-hunter, a member of an order (the Cistercians) which believed that all beauty was the devil's work. And Lawrence still felt that 'Christianity is based on re-action, on negation really':

It says 'renounce all worldly desires, and live for heaven'. Whereas I think people ought to fulfil sacredly their desires. And this means fulfilling the deepest desire, which is a desire to live unhampered by things which are extraneous, a desire for pure relationships and living truth.   [633]

Nevertheless, Lawrence recognized St Bernard as a kindred spirit, fighting uncompromisingly to save the human spirit from disintegration.

In February 1920 Lawrence had an opportunity to clarify his thoughts and feelings about monasticism when he was invited to visit Maurice Magnus at Monte Cassino, the birthplace of European monasticism. There he talked at length with the monk whom he calls, in his Introduction to *Memoirs of the Foreign Legion*, Don Bernardo, and parted from him with 'real regret'. Looking down from the mountain top to the plain below Lawrence felt himself torn between two worlds:

There swarmed the *ferrovieri* like ants. There was democracy, industrialism, socialism, the red flag of the communists and the red, white and green tricolor of the fascisti. That was another world. And how bitter, how barren a world! Barren like the black cinder-track of the railway, with its two steel lines. And here above, sitting with the little stretch of pale, dry thistles around us, our back to a warm rock, we were in the Middle Ages. Both worlds were agony to me. But here, on the mountain top was worst: the past, the poignancy of the not-quite-dead past.   [P II 325]

Gradually Lawrence realized that the sense of sacredness and continuity he felt so strongly there was not specifically Christian or Medieval; it was an emanation, rather, of the spirit of place. It was a 'quick spot of earth':

The peaks of those Italian mountains in the sunset, the extinguishing twinkle of the plain away below, as the sun declined and grew yellow; the intensely powerful mediaeval spirit lingering on this wild hill summit, all the wonder of the mediaeval past; and then the huge mossy stones in the wintry wood, that was once a sacred grove; the ancient path through the wood, that led from temple to temple on the hill summit, before Christ was born; and then the great Cyclopean wall one passes at the bend of the

road, built even before the pagan temples; all this overcame me so powerfully this afternoon, that I was almost speechless. That hill-top must have been one of man's intense sacred places for three thousand years.
[325–6]

So strongly did Monte Cassino affect Lawrence, and embody ideas hitherto vague and unattached to experience, that he came close to using Monte Cassino to provide him with a resolution of the stalemate he had reached after struggling for over two years with *Aaron's Rod.* In the spring of 1921 Lawrence met the Brewsters:

He told us that he was writing *Aaron's Rod*, and began outlining the story. It seemed more beautiful as he narrated it in his low sonorous voice with the quiet gesture of his hands, than it ever could written in a book. Suddenly he stopped, after Aaron had left his wife and home and broken with his past, gravely asking what he should do with him now. We ventured that only two possible courses were left to a man in his straits – either to go to Monte Cassino and repent, or else to go through the whole cycle of experience. He gave a quiet chuckle of surprise and added that those were the very possibilities he had seen, that first he had intended sending him to Monte Cassino, but found instead Aaron had to go to destruction to find his way through from the lowest depths. [RC 243]

*

By 1921 Lawrence's intention had crystallized to locate his community in the New World:

My plan is, ultimately, to get a little farm somewhere by myself, in Mexico, New Mexico, Rocky Mountains, or British Columbia. The desire to be away from the body of mankind – to be a bit of a hermit – is paramount. [29]

The hermit life was never a serious alternative to the monastic community; in the very next sentence Lawrence is inviting the Brewsters to join him on his 'little farm'. He could justify withdrawal alone, or with Frieda, only as a temporary expedient:

I think one must for the moment withdraw from the world, away towards the inner realities that *are* real: and return, maybe, to the world later, when one is quiet and sure. [CL 687]

When Lawrence finally arrived in New Mexico in September 1922, his first reaction to Taos Pueblo was in terms of 'the old monasteries'; here he sensed another of those 'choice spots of earth, where the spirit dwelt':

To me it is important to remember that when Rome collapsed, when the great Roman Empire fell into smoking ruins, and bears roamed in the streets of Lyon and wolves howled in the deserted streets of Rome, and

Europe really was a dark ruin, then, it was not in castles or manors or cottages that life remained vivid. Then those whose souls were still alive withdrew together and gradually built monasteries, and these monasteries and convents, little communities of quiet labour and courage, isolated, helpless, and yet never overcome in a world flooded with devastation, these alone kept the human spirit from disintegration, from going quite dark, in the Dark Ages. These men made the Church, which again made Europe, inspiring the martial faith of the Middle Ages.

Taos pueblo affects me rather like one of the old monasteries. When you get there you feel something final. There is an arrival. The nodality still holds good.   [P 100]

It is an increasingly subjective reading of European history. Isolated and helpless in a cabin on the side of Lobo Mountain (like Noah and his wife on Ararat), contemplating the detritus of a civilization, the Christian era, which, for Lawrence, had essentially come to an end in 1916, Lawrence desperately wanted to be one of those brave men who would start a little community from which a whole new faith and new civilization would slowly emerge. This is the common theme of a whole set of remarkable essays which Lawrence began at the end of 1923: 'On Being Religious', 'On Human Destiny', 'On Being a Man', 'On Taking the Next Step' and 'Books'. These essays constitute a complete theoretical framework for *St Mawr*.

'On Taking the Next Step' asks what it was that came to an end in the First World War:

Why, the end of democracy, the end of the ideal of liberty and freedom, the end of the brotherhood of man, the end of the idea of the perfectibility of man, the end of the belief in the reign of love, the end of the belief that man desires peace, harmony, tranquility, love, and lovingkindness all the while. The end of Christianity, the end of the Church of Jesus. The end of idealism, the end of the idealistic ethic. The end of Plato and Kant, as well as Jesus. The end of science, as an absolute knowledge. The end of the absolute power of the Word. The end, the end, the end.   [DB 206]

In 'Books' Lawrence takes up the question of why our civilization has effectively come to an end, and what men should do in such a historical situation:

Man finds that his head and his spirit have led him wrong. We are at present terribly off the track, following our spirit, which says how nice it would be if everything was perfect, and listening to our head, which says we might have everything perfect if we would only eliminate the tiresome reality of our obstinate blood-being. We are sadly off the track, and we're in a bad temper, like a man who has lost his way. And we say: I'm not going to bother. Fate must work it out. Fate doesn't work things out. Man

256

is a thought-adventurer, and only his adventuring in thought rediscovers a way. [P 732]

Things go from bad to worse if we adopt the attitude of *après moi le déluge*; 'but a deluge presupposes a Noah and an Ark':

Now we've got the sulks, and are waiting for the flood to come and wash out our world and our civilization. All right, let it come. But somebody's got to be ready with Noah's Ark. [733]

We should take our example from what happened last time a great civilization died in Europe, after the fall of Rome:

The flood of barbarism rose and covered Europe from end to end. But, bless your life, there was Noah in his Ark with the animals. There was young Christianity. There were the lonely fortified monasteries, like little arks floating and keeping the adventure afloat. There is no break in the great adventure in consciousness. Throughout the howlingest deluge, some few brave souls are steering the ark under the rainbow . . . If I had lived in the year 400, pray God, I should have been a true and passionate Christian. The adventurer. But now I live in 1924, and the Christian venture is done. The adventure is gone out of Christianity. We must start on a new venture towards God.

Lawrence never published 'Books', for it was superseded by 'On Human Destiny', where he takes the argument further:

In the howling wilderness of slaughter and debacle, tiny monasteries of monks, too obscure and poor to plunder, kept the eternal light of man's undying effort at consciousness alive. A few poor bishops wandering through the chaos, linking up the courage of these men of thought and prayer. A scattered, tiny minority of men who had found a new way to God, to the life-source, glad to get again into touch with the Great God, glad to know the way and to keep the knowledge burningly alive . . .

As a thinking being, man is destined to seek God and to form some conception of Life. And since the invisible God *cannot* be conceived, and since Life is always more than any idea, behold, from the human conception of God and of Life, a great deal of necessity is left out. And this God whom we have left out and this Life that we have shut out from our living, must in the end turn against us and rend us. It is our destiny. Nothing will alter it. When the Unknown God whom we ignore turns savagely to rend us, from the darkness of oblivion, and when the Life that we exclude from our living turns to poison and madness in our veins, then there is only one thing left to do. We have to struggle down to the heart of things, where the everlasting flame is, and kindle ourselves another beam of light. In short, we have to make another bitter adventure in pulsating thought, far, far to the one central pole of energy. We have to germinate inside us, between our undaunted mind and our reckless, genuine passions, a new germ. The germ of a new idea. A new germ of God-knowledge, or Life-knowledge. But a new germ . . .

Man fights for a new conception of life and God, as he fights to plant seeds in the spring . . . But you have to fight even to plant seed. To plant seed you've got to kill a great deal of weeds and break much ground.

[P II 627–9]

'On Being Religious' completes the argument:

From time to time, the Great God sends a new saviour. Christians will no longer have the pettiness to assert that Jesus is the only Saviour ever sent by the everlasting God. There have been other saviours, in other lands, at other times, with other messages. And all of them Sons of God. All of them sharing the Godhead with the Father. All of them showing the Way of Salvation and of Right. Different Saviours. Different Ways of Salvation. Different pole-stars, in the great wandering Cosmos of time. And the Infinite God, always changing, and always the same infinite God, at the end of the different Ways. [P 729]

Just underneath all this is running more and more clearly and strongly the thought that the ranch itself, deep in these sacred mountains, might be just such a centre, a node, a germ of the new way; and, however much he may lighten his tone to protect himself (for it is symptomatic of our culture that no writer can make such a claim in all earnestness[2]), the thought that he himself might be just such a new saviour:

We go in search of God, following the Holy Ghost, and depending on the Holy Ghost. There is no Way. There is no Word. There is no Light. The Holy Ghost is ghostly and invisible. The Holy Ghost is nothing, if you like. Yet we hear His strange calling, the strange calling like a hound on the scent, away in the unmapped wilderness. And it seems great fun to follow. Oh, great fun, God's own good fun.

Myself, I believe in God. But I'm off on a different road. Adios! and, if you like, au revoir! [729–30]

*

Though they were probably begun in Mexico in the autumn, most of the work on these essays was done in London in December 1923. Lawrence had gone to London specifically to recruit candidates for Rananim at the ranch. After yet another betrayal by Middleton Murry, and the failure of nerve of most of his other friends, Lawrence returned to the ranch in March with only one recruit, Dorothy Brett. But the return to England, painful as it was for Lawrence, had been by no means a waste of time, for he returned also with the germ of *St Mawr* within him.

It was during the brief visit to Frederick Carter at Pontesbury that Lawrence's imagination began unconsciously to work upon experiences which seemed to offer themselves with magical aptness both by providing ready-made symbols and by fleshing out the framework of ideas we have just been discussing:

He was delighted with that wild Shropshire countryside, picturesque and broken with small hills rising to greater ones beyond. England was his own and he felt it within him deeply enough. Of course, even as he looked upon it he would hardly admit his liking. Still, he later wrote a novel about its landscape, with place-names from it, too, and the house in the churchyard with its front windows cheek by jowl with the gravestones came in besides other local matters.

Only a little of my enthusiasm about the beauty and interest of that countryside would he accept. And the people he could hardly tolerate. The good-natured curate, fat, hail-fellow-well-met, a helpful and simple-minded gossip for all the world, him he blasted with a few words. Of course the man was bovine, red-faced and naive. What else would serve in such an outlying land on the edge of two countries? Religion in Lawrence's sense meant little enough to such a man. [CB II 316]

In the essay 'On Being a Man', probably written within a fortnight of the Pontesbury visit, we can see the beginning of the process of converting this harmless curate into the far-from-harmless Dean Vyner of the novel:

He knows he's not a man. Hence his creed of harmlessness. He knows he is not a man of living red earth, to live onward through strange weather into new springtime. He knows there is extinction ahead: for nothing but extinction lies in wait for the conscious ego. Hence his creed of harmlessness, or relentless kindness. A little less than kin, and more than kind. There should be no danger in life *at all*, even no friction. This he asserts, while all the time he is slowly, malignantly undermining the tree of life. [P II 622]

Religion in Lawrence's sense was no longer to be found in churches; but it was to be found still at such places as the Devil's Chair:

Lawrence liked the name – the Devil's Chair – for the stone on which we stood. And there we talked of the great hilltop rocks with similar names that are found all over Europe as seats of the changeful gods . . . And besides, as these rocks marked the highest point of the hills in the vicinity, the point where the cloudbursts gathered that sent down floods to the valleys below, this huge mass of stone justified its title in the popular view. It was the place of power and storm – formidable. [CB II 318]

And, of course, the devil would mean something very different to Lawrence from what it meant to the curate; not the Christian embodiment of wickedness, but the pagan fertility god, Cernunnos, the Celtic horned god of the beasts, who can also be identified with

Pan. The crisis of the novel is to take place at the Devil's Chair, looking west towards Wales:

> It was one of those places where the spirit of aboriginal England still lingers, the old savage England, whose last blood flows still in a few Englishmen, Welshmen, Cornishmen. [STM 73; CSN 335]

*

The Lawrences, with Brett, returned to Taos in March. Frieda had acquired a new ranch, 2,000 feet higher up Lobo Mountain, from Mabel Luhan, and the three of them had to stay with Mabel for six weeks while it was made ready. There, with or without his community, Lawrence would embark on his new venture towards God. The essential clues, he felt, were to be found in mythology, and the three mythologies which interested him most now were Greek, Celtic and Indian.[1] Mabel had another house-guest, Jaime de Angulo, an expert on Indian mythology whom she had brought from California to meet Lawrence. They talked at length. De Angulo knew, and must have told Lawrence, the myth of Lu-Wit. According to Keith Brown, Lu-Wit (or Loo-Wit) is 'the central figure of the best-known of the American Indian volcano-myths':

> This seems doubly noteworthy, since Lawrence's fascination with the image of the volcano is well-attested throughout this period; and *St Mawr* itself is full of images of fire. The heroine of the Indian legend was set by the Great Spirit to be the keeper of the Bridge of the Gods. The Bridge lay between the domains of two mighty brothers, who eventually woke into furious anger, hurling fire, so that the bridge was broken and Lu-Wit herself badly hurt. But the Great Spirit took pity on her, and as recompense transformed her into a beautiful young woman, although she remained an ancient being within herself . . . just as Lawrence's heroine looks at once 'so much younger, and so many thousands of years older'. [163]

It cannot be chance that Lawrence chose to call his heroine Lou Witt.

From this time Lawrence began to take a much more sympathetic interest in Indian rituals and dances. In April he produced two fine essays, 'Indians and Entertainment' and 'Dance of the Sprouting Corn':

> To the Indian there is no conception of a defined God. Creation is a great flood, for ever flowing, in lovely and terrible waves. In everything, the shimmer of creation, and never the finality of the created. Never the distinction between God and God's creation, or between Spirit and Matter. Everything, everything is the wonderful shimmer of creation, it may be a deadly shimmer like lightning or the anger in the little eyes of the bear, it may be the beautiful shimmer of the moving deer, or the pine-boughs

softly swaying under snow. Creation contains the unspeakably terrifying
enemy, the unspeakably lovely friend, as the maiden who brings us our
food in dead of winter, by her passion of tender wistfulness. Yet even this
tender wistfulness is the fearful danger of the wild creatures, deer and
bear and buffalo, which find their death in it.   [MM 61]

The first thing Lawrence wrote at the new ranch was an essay
called 'Pan in America', where he defines pantheism as 'a vivid
relatedness between the man and the living universe that sur-
rounds him' [P 27]. It is not simply nature-worship, for Pan is
fierce and bristling, sometimes malevolent, with the power to blast;
and 'among the creatures of Pan there is an eternal struggle for life,
between lives' [29]. There was indeed real danger up there. Three
of the Hawks' horses from the Del Monte ranch below were killed
by lightning. The very pine tree in front of Lawrence's cabin that
much of 'Pan in America' is about, was terribly scarred by it.

Lawrence finds that the God we have left out of our God-concept
in the Christian era is the common element in all three mythologies
– Greek, Celtic and Indian. He calls this God Pan: 'And still, in
America, among the Indians, the oldest Pan is alive' [P 31]. In the
novel, Cartwright, who is based on Frederick Carter, defines Pan
in terms identical with Lawrence's:

I should say he was the God that is hidden in everything . . . Pan was
the hidden mystery – the hidden cause. That's how it was a great God.
Pan wasn't *he* at all: not even a great God. He was Pan, All: what you see
when you see in full. In the daytime you see the thing. But if your third
eye is open, which sees only the things that can't be seen, you may see
Pan within the thing, hidden: you may see with your third eye, which is
darkness.   [STM 65; CSN 326]

'The third eye' is another way of expressing what Blake calls
'fourfold vision' – the vision with which we perceive that everything that lives is holy. Lawrence uses the term again in *Apocalypse*
in describing the resurrection or second birth which takes place at
the end of the ritual of the Mysteries of Isis:

The initiate is dead, and alive again in a new body. He is sealed in the
forehead, like a Buddhist monk, as a sign that he has died the death, and
that his seventh self is fulfilled, he is twice-born, his mystic eye or 'third
eye' is now open. He sees in two worlds.   [A 107]

In 'The Woman Who Rode Away', which Lawrence probably wrote
immediately before *St Mawr*, the unnamed heroine undergoes a
kind of forced opening of the third eye by means of drugs
administered to her by primitive Indians:

This at length became the only state of consciousness she really recognized: this exquisite sense of bleeding out into the higher beauty and harmony of things. Then she could actually hear the great stars in heaven, which she saw through her door, speaking from their motion and brightness, saying things perfectly to the cosmos, as they trod in perfect ripples, like bells on the floor of heaven, passing one another and grouping in the timeless dance, with the spaces of dark between . . . With refined and heightened senses she could hear the sound of the earth winging on its journey, like a shot arrow, the ripple-rustling of the air, and the boom of the great arrow-string.   [SSS 414–16]

This woman is not an initiate undergoing a rebirth. This conscious-ness is not really her own, rather that of her Indian captors. She is allowed to experience it in such a pure form because she is not going to have to live with it – it is part of her purification for sacrifice. In *St Mawr* Lou is the voluntary initiate who has to die to her old consciousness and acquire a new one much more slowly and painfully. She must accept full responsibility for her changing consciousness in her daily living.

There is one character in *St Mawr*, Lewis the groom, in whom Pan has never quite died. Hence his understanding of St Mawr, to whom he speaks in Welsh. He has managed to hold on to folk beliefs from his childhood in Merioneth:

The world has its own life, the sky has a life of its own, and never is it like stones rolling down a rubbish heap and falling into a pond. Many things twitch and twitter within the sky, and many things happen beyond us.   [STM 110; CSN 376]

It follows, of course, that in order to be able to describe this kind of consciousness so inwardly, Lawrence himself possessed it to a high degree. It is a religious sense, but it is also the poetic imagination working at its fullest pitch, seeing into the life of things. Such vision is less difficult to sustain in poems or paragraphs. Lawrence was working up to his most sustained display of it in fiction.

*

Little is known about the first version of *St Mawr*, not even that it was called *St Mawr*. The manuscript was burned in a fire at Aldous Huxley's home in 1961. It was probably shorter than the novel we have, possibly as short as 58 pages.[3] It was apparently written very quickly in mid-June. By 18 June 1924 Lawrence was already rewriting it. Work went slowly, for Lawrence. In July Brett recorded:

You are full of your new story, of Mrs Witt. You sit down in your place, and between bites you read out to us the pages you have just written. You are still twinkling with amusement, and you are still living more with them than with us. You read out the scene of the tea-party, of the tart Mrs Witt, the scandalized Dean and his wife, and the determined Lou. You laugh so much over it, that you have to stop – and we are laughing too. Then you read out Mrs Witt's defence of the horse when Rico pulls him over and the horse kicks Rico in the face. You read it with such keen joy and pleasure at the final downfall of Rico and the terrible revenge of the horse, that Frieda is horrified; she says that you are cruel and that you frighten her.   [LB 137]

On 30 July Lawrence wrote to Nancy Pearn that he was 'just winding up *St Mawr*, a story which has turned into a novelette nearly as long as *The Captain's Doll*' [STM xxv]. The holograph manuscript of *The Captain's Doll* is 77 pages; that of *St Mawr* was 129! The most likely explanation of this anomaly (which would also make less surprising Brett's description of *St Mawr* as 'the story of Mrs Witt') is Brian Finney's: 'At this time he did not envisage continuing the story by following Lou Carrington and Mrs Witt to America. He still conceived of *St Mawr* as a satire on English society' [STM xxv].

Since his return to America, Lawrence had been more aware than ever before of the spirit of place in the Southwest: 'There is something savage, unbreakable in the spirit of place out here – the Indians drumming and yelling at our camp-fire at evening' [CL 791]. On 4 July he wrote to Rolf Gardiner, an enthusiast of international youth movements:

Here, where we have the camp just above the cabin, under the hanging stars, and we sit with the Indians round the fire, and they sing till late into the night, and sometimes we all dance the Indian tread-dance – then what is it to me, world unison and peace and all that? I am essentially a fighter – to wish me peace is bad luck – except the fighter's peace. And I have known many things, that may never be unified: Ceylon, the Buddha temples, Australian bush, Mexico and Teotihuacan, Sicily, London, New York, Paris, Munich – don't talk to me of unison. No more unison among man than among the wild animals – coyotes and chipmunks and porcupines and deer and rattlesnakes. They all live in these hills – in the unison of avoiding one another.   [796]

In mid-August, while *St Mawr* lay wound up in a form which must have realized only a fraction of its potential, Lawrence went off for ten days with the Luhans to Arizona to see the Hopi Snake Dance. His subsequent struggle to understand what he had seen there brought him as far as he was ever to get, possibly as far as a white man can get, towards understanding the Indians, their consciousness, their relationship with the place, its creatures and climate, and its gods. 'The Hopi Snake Dance' must be quoted at length, for it is Lawrence's fullest and finest description of 'animistic vision':

> The American-Indian sees no division into Spirit and Matter, God and not-God. Everything is alive, though not personally so. Thunder is neither Thor nor Zeus. Thunder is the vast living thunder asserting itself like some incomprehensible monster, or some huge reptile-bird of the pristine cosmos. How to conquer the dragon-mouthed thunder! How to capture the feathered rain! . . .
>
> The Potencies are not Gods. They are Dragons. The Sun of Creation itself is a dragon most terrible, vast, and most powerful, yet even so, less in being than we. The only gods on earth are men. For gods, like man, do not exist beforehand. They are created and evolved gradually, with aeons of effort, out of the fire and smelting of life. They are the highest thing created, smelted between the furnace of the Life-Sun, and beaten on the anvil of the rain, with hammers of thunder and bellows of rushing wind. The cosmos is a great furnace, a dragon's den, where the heroes and demi-gods, men, forge themselves into being. It is a vast and violent matrix, where souls form like diamonds in earth, under extreme pressure.
>
> So that gods are the outcome, not the origin. And the best gods that have resulted, so far, are men. But gods frail as flowers. Man is as a flower, rain can kill him or succour him, heat can flick him with a bright tail, and destroy him: or, on the other hand, it can softly call him into existence, out of the egg of chaos. Man is delicate as a flower, godly beyond flowers, and his lordship is a ticklish business.   [MM 75–6]

On 30 August, the same day on which he sent 'The Hopi Snake Dance' to his agent, Lawrence wrote to Murry: 'This animistic religion is the only live one, ours is a corpse of a religion' [H 610]. On the following day he sent his niece Margaret a detailed description of the ranch and its history:

> Forty years ago a man came out looking for gold, and staked here. There was some gold in the mountains. Then he got poor, and a man called McClure had the place. He had 500 white goats here, raised alfalfa, and let his goats feed wild in the mountains. But the water supply is too bad, and we are too far from anywhere. So he gave up . . . So we leave the ranch quite wild – only there's abundant feed for the five horses. And if we wanted to take the trouble, we could bring the water here as McClure did, and have a little farm . . . We went to get Frieda's grey horse – the Azul – shod. They call him in Spanish *el Azul* – the Blue . . . I want a Mexican to come and live here while we are away, to keep the place from going wild, squirrels and bushy-tailed pack-rats from coming in, and to see the water doesn't freeze for the horses.   [CL 805]

In the absence of the manuscript we shall probably never know, but it may well be, as Brian Finney suggests, that it was the Snake Dance experience which served as the catalyst in Lawrence's imagination, inducing the belated realization that the necessary ending of *St Mawr* was here at the ranch. Only by bringing Lou here could he take her through with what St Mawr had only prepared her for. Only here, in the crucible of the New Mexico Rockies, could he bring together and fuse *all* his preoccupations, needs and insights. The new ranch had already acquired for Lawrence a symbolic significance the old one never had. His two greatest needs (the two great needs of the species he would say), which had hitherto been kept apart, running strangely parallel courses through his work, the need for bodily, earthly, fulfilment, as symbolized by the horse, and the need for spiritual experience, to find God and worship him apart from 'the world', flowed together here at the ranch and met in Pan.

The Indians had rituals to enable them to handle the potent, potentially destructive, energies of Pan. The white man had lost them. For him there must be a death to the old consciousness followed by a resurrection, equally painful, to a new reality – the stark, sordid, beautiful, awe-inspiring reality of Pan, which he wrestled with every day on this pack-rat infested, lightning-scarred, but certainly not god-forsaken ranch.

*

The first problem confronting the reader of *St Mawr* is the title. Anyone who has taken a perfunctory interest in Welsh place-names will know that *mawr* means 'great' (it is the masculine form, the feminine being *fawr*). Is St Mawr then an obscure Welsh saint or a fictitious one? After several pages we discover that St Mawr is in fact a horse. We first meet the name when the horse is directly addressed by his owner in the language of the stable: '*Cup! my boy! Cup my beauty! Cup then! St Mawr!*' [STM 28; CSN 284]. The name comes with a deep shock; the reverberations run through the whole story. It jars on the reader's consciousness because it is so difficult, such a violation of our preconceptions, to have to bring together such polar images as saint and horse, to bridge our widely separated associations with these words. They belong to different worlds of experience; all the more so if we have become attuned to their implications in earlier Lawrence works.

Here in the name, in the title, is encapsulated Lawrence's supreme effort in this story to bridge that gap, to connect the monk and the beast, to alter our perception of the sacred and the animal to the point where they become identical. The first purpose of the name is to issue that great challenge. The second is to indicate the importance of Welshness.

St Mawr's owner pronounces the name 'with a slight Welsh twist': ' "He's from the Welsh borders, belonging to a Welsh gentleman, Mr Griffith Edwards" ' [28; 284]. He has a Welsh groom, Lewis, who speaks to him in Welsh, an exile from Welsh Wales (Merioneth) whose consciousness still retains flickers of the old animistic vision which was the vision of the druids and of pre-Christian Celtic religion; whose very name is an anglicized dilution of names which take us to the heart of Welsh history and mythology – Llewelyn, Llew and Lugus.[1] (It is also, as Keith Brown reminds us, the masculine equivalent of Louise.)

St Mawr embodies, in a pure, concentrated, blazing form, the light which in Lewis has dwindled into a Celtic twilight. St Mawr is the living reality of something we are normally aware of only as ghosts and shadows.

Though there is no St Mawr, there is, of course, a St Maur or Maurus. On the only occasion she mentions the name of the story she was typing, Dorothy Brett spells it *St Maur* [LB 123], and this may, indeed, have been Lawrence's spelling before he thought of Welshifying it. According to Brett, Lawrence pronounced the name Seymour.[4] This seemed highly unlikely to me, despite coming, as it were, from the horse's mouth, until I looked up Seymour in a book of surnames, and found that it derives from the Norman French de St Maur.

Lawrence probably first came upon St Maurus in the Prologue to the *Canterbury Tales*,[5] which was in the *International Library of Famous Literature* in the Lawrence home. There Chaucer describes the monk as a worldly man more interested in horses and hunting than study and the life of the spirit:

> The reule of seint Maure and of seint Beneit,
> Because that it was old and somdel streit,
> This ilke monk let oldë thingës pace,
> And held after the newe world the trace.   [IL IV 1790]

Lawrence has Ursula study Chaucer at college in *The Rainbow*, and probably did so himself. St Benedict, the father of Western monasticism, founded his great monastery at Monte Cassino in 529; St Maurus was his disciple and successor. It seems that in Chaucer's day their names had become by-words for the strict monastic life, withdrawal from the world to cultivate the life of the spirit. Lawrence may well have learned more of St Maurus from the monk he befriended during his visit to Monte Cassino in 1920,

whom he calls Don Bernardo in the Introduction to the memoirs of
Maurice Magnus, and to whom he later sent a copy of *The Lost Girl*!
Don Bernardo's real name was Don Mauro Iguanez.

*

The first challenge to Lawrence's art is to establish the saintliness,
sacredness, of St Mawr. He does it in two ways, each having its
distinct style and tone. The tone of the opening is flippant, ironic,
or bitingly sardonic when it expresses the views of Mrs Witt. It
evokes a world which cannot be taken seriously, cannot be lived
in, only drifted through – 'from Paris to Palermo, Biarritz to Vienna
and back via Munich to London, then down again to Rome'
[STM 21, CSN 276]. None of these unreal cities engages the soul.
They are interchangeable because equally devoid of spiritual
significance; the 'life' offered by each the same round of frivolous
pursuits, the same striking of attitudes. Nor do Lou's personal
relationships offer her anything better. Her marriage is the most
artificial attitude of all, that of the 'charming married couple'.

For several pages Lawrence keeps the style thin, superficial,
insubstantial, in order that the other style, that enters with St
Mawr, shall be the more striking in its poetic resonance, substance
and vitality:

In the inner dark she saw a handsome bay horse with his clean ears
pricked like daggers from his naked head as he swung handsomely round
to stare at the open doorway. He had big, black, brilliant eyes, with a
sharp questioning glint, and that air of tense, alert quietness which betrays
an animal that can be dangerous . . . He was of such a lovely red-gold
colour, and a dark, invisible fire seemed to come out of him . . .

She looked at the glowing bay horse, that stood there with his ears back,
his face averted, but attending as if he were some lightning conductor. He
was a stallion . . .

Dimly, in her weary young-woman's soul, an ancient understanding
seemed to flood in . . . For some reason the sight of him, his power, his alive,
alert intensity, his unyieldingness, made her want to cry. She never did
cry . . . But now, as if that mysterious fire of the horse's body had split some
rock in her, she went home and hid herself in her room, and just cried. The
wild, brilliant, alert head of St Mawr seemed to look at her out of another
world. It was as if she had had a vision, as if the walls of her own world had
suddenly melted away, leaving her in a great darkness, in the midst of which
the large, brilliant eyes of that horse looked at her with demonish question,
while his naked ears stood up like daggers from the naked lines of his
inhuman head, and his great body glowed red with power.

What was it? Almost like a god looking at her terribly out of the
everlasting dark, she had felt the eyes of that horse; great, glowing,

fearsome eyes, arched with a question, and containing a white blade of light like a threat. What was his non-human question, and his uncanny threat? She didn't know. He was some splendid demon, and she must worship him. [28–30; 284–7]

Perhaps, in writing these passages, Lawrence was drawing on one of his favourite sections of 'Song of Myself', where Whitman, asserting that animals bring him tokens of himself, goes on to describe

A gigantic beauty of a stallion, fresh and responsive to my caresses,
Head high in the forehead, wide between the ears,
Limbs glossy and supple, tail dusting the ground,
Eyes full of sparkling wickedness, ears finely cut, flexibly moving.
['Song of Myself' 32]

The question St Mawr asks Lou can be articulated in many ways: 'If I am real, what are you?'; 'What in you can answer to my godhead?'; 'Can you cross into my world?' It is a threat because she senses that what is required of her is her death to her former self and life.

Lou's vision of St Mawr is, strictly, a hierophany, 'the only thing that was real' [32; 288]. Eliade defines a hierophany in these terms:

For it is the break effected in space that allows the world to be constituted, because it reveals the fixed point, the central axis for all future orientation. When the sacred manifests itself in any hierophany, there is not only a break in the homogeneity of space; there is also revelation of an absolute reality, opposed to the nonreality of the vast surrounding expanse. The manifestation of the sacred ontologically founds the world. In the homogeneous and infinite expanse, in which no point of reference is possible and hence no *orientation* can be established, the hierophany reveals an absolute fixed point, a centre. [SAP 21]

St Mawr provides Lou henceforth with such a point, an orientation, a direction for her life. And what has hitherto constituted her world she is now able to recognize as unreal, in spite of the almost universal conspiracy to pretend that it is reality:

the talk, the eating and drinking, the flirtation, the endless dancing: it all seemed far more bodiless and, in a strange way, wraith-like, than any fairy story. She seemed to be eating Barmecide food, that had been conjured up out of thin air, by the power of words. She seemed to be talking to handsome young bare-faced unrealities, not men at all: as she slid about with them, in the perpetual dance, they too seemed to have been conjured up out of air, merely for this soaring, slithering dance-business. And she could not believe that, when the lights went out, they wouldn't melt back into thin air again, and complete nonentity.
[STM 42; CSN 300]

The form of *St Mawr* is that of the religious quest, the quest for union with God. And the fictional religious quest which stands most directly behind it is *Pilgrim's Progress*. Lawrence may have thought that *Pilgrim's Progress* was bad art, but Bunyan's images stuck like burrs. At the beginning, Lou's soul, like Christian's, is crying 'What shall I do to be saved?' But Christian lacks orientation – 'he could not tell which way to go' – until the arrival of Evangelist, who provides him with a fixed point – 'yonder shining light' – at which to aim. Christian runs towards it crying 'Life, life, eternal life'. Worldly-Wiseman (Dean Vyner) tries to persuade Christian that salvation can be attained much more safely and modestly through Morality and Civility:

> Thou art like to meet with in the way which thou goest, wearisomeness, painfulness, hunger, perils, nakedness, sword, lions, dragons, darkness, and in a word, death, and what not? [JB 49]

But Evangelist insists on danger and death, and the total rejection of everything and everybody associated with the old false life:

> The King of Glory hath told thee, that he that will save his life shall lose it: and *he that comes after him, and hates not his father and mother, and wife, and children, and brethren, and sisters; yea, and his own life also, he cannot be my disciple.* [54]

After this orientation Christian has no difficulty in recognizing Vanity Fair for what it is. Bunyan's description of the streets of that fair reminds us of Lou's reaction to Rotten Row and its equivalent in the other major capitals of Europe:

> Here is the Britain Row, the French Row, the Italian Row, the Spanish Row, the German Row, where several sorts of vanities are to be sold. [125]

I am suggesting that St Mawr corresponds not to Christ (for it is possible to live in Christ, but not in St Mawr), but to Evangelist. He is a messenger, not a goal. He brings Lou 'the intimation of other worlds' [L III 40], towards which she feels she must set out:

> Only St Mawr gave her some hint of the possibility. He was so powerful, and so dangerous. But in his dark eye, that looked, with its cloudy brown pupil, a cloud within a dark fire, like a world beyond our world, there was a dark vitality glowing, and within the fire, another sort of wisdom . . . When he reared his head and neighed from his deep chest, like deep wind-bells resounding, she seemed to hear the echoes of another, darker, more spacious, more dangerous, more splendid world than ours, that was beyond her. And there she wanted to go. [STM 41; CSN 299]

In the *Mabinogion* Math's vestigial divinity is indicated by his superhumanly acute hearing. St Mawr's most characteristic posture is head raised, ears pricked, listening to sounds from across the gulf.

But at first St Mawr's world seems so alien from her own that Lou can see it only as non-human. It seems a world of horses, of long-dead heroes like centaurs, of long-dead gods or demons like satyrs. How can she hope to enter 'that terrific equine twilight'? She needs both Lewis and Phoenix as intermediaries. Each is, in his way, a centaur: 'Phoenix looked as if he and the horse were all one piece' [36; 293]; and Mrs Witt says of Lewis: 'He seems to sink himself in the horse. When I speak to him, I'm not sure whether I'm speaking to a man or a horse' [38; 296]. Later Lewis comes to have much the same effect on her that St Mawr had had on her daughter:

> And yet, what made him perhaps the only real entity to her, his seeming to inhabit another world than hers. A world dark and still, where language never ruffled the growing leaves, and seared their edges like a bad wind. . . .
> But then, when she saw Phoenix and Lewis silently together, she knew there *was* another communion, silent, excluding her. And sometimes when Lewis was alone with St Mawr: and once, when she saw him pick up a bird that had stunned itself against a wire: she had realized another world, silent, where each creature is alone in its own aura of silence, the mystery of power: as Lewis had power with St Mawr, and even with Phoenix.
> The visible world, and the invisible. Or rather, the audible and the inaudible. She had lived so long, and so completely, in the visible, audible world. She would not easily admit that other, inaudible.   [104; 369–70]

But Lewis is a figure of the Hermit, not the Monk. He withdraws behind his beard into a private, rather childish world, inhabited by pale ghosts from the past, his own childhood in Wales, and the dim past of Wales itself. His world is as lacking in substance as Lou's, in a very different way. It has none of the robustness of Celtic mythology; and it can only be preserved by nursing it in secret, by denying human responsibility and relationship. If Pan has become a goat in Cartwright, he has become a ghost in Lewis.

Phoenix has more to offer. He represents the consciousness of the north American Indian, also in an exiled and degraded form. At the personal level he is impossible, impossible as a mate or lover for Lou, under, his integrity gone, the Pan in him reduced to the sexual opportunist. Nevertheless, the alternative vision which flickers in him, though it seems but a mirage in the context of

English 'reality', is grounded in the spirit of a real, if distant, place; a place one might actually go to; a place where God burns in every bush:

> He was watching the pale deserts of Arizona shimmer with moving light, the long mirage of a shallow lake ripple, the great pallid concave of earth and sky expanding with interchanged light. And a horse-shape loom large and portentous in the mirage, like some pre-historic beast. That was real to him: the phantasm of Arizona. But this London was something his eye passed over, as a false mirage.   [36; 293]

That horse-shape is Pan in one of his many manifestations. St Mawr is but a token and messenger from that infinitely vaster reality. It is Phoenix who sows in Lou's mind the idea of taking a ranch in Arizona. He translates the challenge of St Mawr into an orientation and a practical proposition. Once Lou is embarked on her quest towards the American Southwest, Lawrence's Delectable Mountains, St Mawr's role is fulfilled, and he drops from the story as naturally as Evangelist from *Pilgrim's Progress*.

*

It is not St Mawr's only role in the novel to play Evangelist to Lou's pilgrim. He has another, more negative role in relation to Rico. This is indicated at the very beginning of the novel, when we are told, of Rico:

> You had only to see the uneasy backward glance at her, from his big blue eyes: just like a horse that is edging away from its master: to know how completely he was mastered.   [21; 276]

The uneasy backward glance and edging away are characteristic also of St Mawr:

> Something told her that the horse was not quite happy: that somewhere deep in his animal consciousness lived a dangerous, half-revealed resentment, a diffused sense of hostility. She realized that he was sensitive, in spite of his flaming, healthy strength, and nervous with a touchy uneasiness that might make him vindictive . . . He looked like something finely bred and passionate, that has been judged and condemned.
>   [28–9; 285–6]

He had been treated cruelly in the past, and has twice 'made a break', killing two men, in one case by smashing a young man's head against an oak.

St Mawr is representative of Nature herself at her most sensitive and vulnerable, yet capable of terrible revenge when injured or denied; and of man's own deepest nature which turns upon him and rears against him when denied. Rico is representative of a civilization which had found its spokesman in H. G. Wells, whose *Outline of History* (1920) had equated human history with progress. In 1925 Lawrence was to write: 'Hadn't somebody better write Mr Wells' History backwards, to prove how we've degenerated, in our stupid visionlessness, since the cave-men?' [P II 434].[6] Mrs Witt accuses Lou of wanting a cave man who would knock her on the head with a club. She is voicing the Wellsian stereotype of early man as brute. But for Lawrence

> The pictures in the cave represent moments of purity which are the quick of civilisation. The pure relation between the cave-man and the deer: fifty per cent. man, and fifty per cent. bison, or mammoth, or deer. It is not ninety-nine per cent. man, and one per cent. horse.   [434]

Lou puts it more poetically:

> A pure animal man would be as lovely as a deer or a leopard, burning like a flame fed straight from underneath. And he'd be part of the unseen, like a mouse is, even. And he'd never cease to wonder, he'd breathe silence and unseen wonder, as the partridges do, running in the stubble. He'd be all the animals in turn, instead of one, fixed, automatic thing, which he is now, grinding on the nerves.   [STM 62; CSN 322]

Rico, on the other hand, has tried to extirpate his own animal nature: 'He had composed this little *tableau vivant* with great effort. He didn't want to erupt like some suddenly wicked horse' [27; 283]. This *tableau vivant* of his marriage and other relationships is no more life than one of his painted 'compositions'. His denial of life is, in Lawrence's terms, irreligious:

> If it is to be life, then it is fifty per cent. me, fifty per cent. thee: and the third thing, the spark, which springs from out of the balance, is timeless. Jesus, who saw it a bit vaguely, called it the Holy Ghost.   [P II 434–5]

That spark, which Rico has extinguished in himself, blazes in St Mawr; but Rico, in his visionlessness, cannot see it. He can only see that St Mawr would be 'marvellous in a composition' [STM 33; CSN 289]. It is the spark of intuitive sympathy and of creativity. Without it Rico becomes representative of 'our whole eunuch civilization, nasty-minded as eunuchs are, with their kind of sneaking, sterilizing cruelty' [96; 361].

It is inevitable that Rico, on St Mawr, should provoke a catastrophe. In conceiving the exact form the catastrophe should take, perhaps Lawrence remembered Genesis 44:17:

> Dan shall be a serpent by the way, an adder in the path, that biteth the horse heels, so that his rider shall fall backward.

St Mawr, alert in all his senses, knows there is some danger round the next bend in the path. Rico, denying the possibility of such awareness, tries to bully him to go on, like Gerald forcing his sensitive Arab mare to the crossing. Rico is not only bullying another creature, he is violating an essential part of himself. Deny creative energy and it turns savagely destructive. St Mawr becomes 'reversed, and purely evil'. But the two grooms and the two women all know where the blame lay. Phoenix, anticipating Connie Chatterley's objections to Plato's myth, says:

> That horse don't want to fall back on you, if you don't make him. If you know how to ride him. – That horse want his own way sometime. If you don't let him, you got to fight him. Then look out! [85; 348]

Around the next bend in the path there had been a dead adder, crushed by stones while drinking at a reedy pool – another victim of man's hatred of any life beyond the control of his own mind. Another violation of a lord of life. Another crime to be expiated.

If man, in trying to destroy Pan, merely turns him into the devil, then Lawrence will be of the devil's party: 'He's lashing out again like the devil, till his hoofs are red. Good old Horse!' [CL 769].

*

The concluding section of *St Mawr*, after the protagonists have left England, is a piece of marvellously sustained vision and complex art, as Lawrence puts to the test, with profound sensitivity and the clearest intelligence, the claim of New Mexico both to offer literally and to symbolize an answer to Lou's need and a viable alternative faith to the sterile visionlessness of Europe.

Lou has now cut herself off from all her former attachments. She has, in effect, emptied herself. And what rushes in to fill the vacuum is beauty, 'the marvellous beauty and fascination of natural wild things' in contrast with 'the horror of man's unnatural life, his heaped-up civilization':

> The flying-fishes burst out of the sea in clouds of silvery, transparent motion. Blue above and below, the Gulf seemed a silent, empty, timeless place where man did not really reach. And Lou was again fascinated by the glamour of the universe. [129; 398]

But the difference between 'beauty' and 'glamour' is that 'glamour' implies that the fascination is superficial, and, ultimately, delusory. If Lou's quest is for the 'roots of reality' [131; 399], she must not allow herself to be dazzled by the glamour that awaits her in New Mexico.

On the day Lou first drives out to see the ranch, it almost seems that the place is disguising its true nature the better to seduce her:

For the moment, the brief moment, the great desert-and-mountain landscape had lost its certain cruelty, and looked tender, dreamy. And many, many birds were flickering around.   [134; 403]

Lou is lured into the fantasy of herself as Vestal Virgin 'turning to the unseen gods, the unseen spirits, the hidden fire, and devoting herself to that, and that alone. Receiving thence her pacification and her fulfilment':

'I want my temple and my loneliness and my Apollo mystery of the inner fire' . . . She felt a great peace inside her as she made this realization. And a thankfulness. Because, after all, it seemed to her that the hidden fire was alive and burning in this sky, over the desert, in the mountains. She felt a certain latent holiness in the very atmosphere, a young, spring-fire of latent holiness, such as she had never felt in Europe, or in the East. 'For me,' she said, as she looked away at the mountains in shadow and the pale-warm desert beneath, with wings of shadow upon it: 'For me, this place is sacred. It is blessed.'   [138–40; 408–9]

Already, before she has even arrived at the ranch, she has projected all her tender dreams upon it. Her easy identification of the gods of this place with Apollo, the god of light, is naive. Her sense of what constitutes holiness is going to have to go into the crucible of bitter experience. The beauty of a landscape, its grandeur and sublimity, is not the same thing as its spirit, may even mask its essential spirit. Already, Lou must turn a blind eye to the real spirit of the place in order to preserve the purity of her dream:

She realized that the latent fire of the vast landscape struggled under a great weight of dirt-like inertia. She had to mind the dirt, most carefully and vividly avoid it and keep it away from her, here in this place that at last seemed sacred to her.   [140; 409–10]

The admission which will have to be wrung from her is that the dirt is also god.

It is at this point, at the very moment Lou says to herself '*This is the place*', that Lawrence gives us the history of the ranch, the reality of this place which Lou proposes as the temple where she shall 'serve the most perfect service', the nature of the gods she proposes to serve there. For Lou was not the first woman who had stood on that spot, looking out over the vast sweep of the desert, falling in love with the soul-stirring beauty of it, and wishing only to serve it. For the woman from New England it had been just the same:

Ah, that was beauty! – perhaps the most beautiful thing in the world. It was pure beauty, *absolute* beauty! There! That was it. To the little woman from New England, with her tense fierce soul and her egoistic passion of service, this beauty was absolute, a *ne plus ultra* . . . So it was, when you watched the vast and living landscape. The landscape lived, and lived as the world of the gods, unsullied and unconcerned. The great circling landscape lived its own life, sumptuous and uncaring. Man did not exist for it.

And if it had been a question simply of living through the eyes, into the *distance*, then this would have been Paradise, and the little New England woman on her ranch would have found what she was always looking for, the earthly paradise of the spirit.

But even a woman cannot live only into the distance, the beyond . . . While she revelled in the beauty of the luminous world that wheeled around and below her, the grey, rat-like spirit of the inner mountains was attacking her from behind.   [145–7; 416–18]

The pack-rats which come down out of the hills and bounce on her ceiling 'like hippopotamuses in the night' are 'symbols of the curious debasing malevolence that was in the spirit of the place'. The guardian of the place is a great pine-tree in her yard: 'But a bristling, almost demonish guardian, from the far-off crude ages of the world'. And the place is fenced in with a 'circling guard' of pine-trees:

Never sympathetic, always watchfully on their guard, and resistant, they hedged one in with the aroma and the power and the slight horror of the pre-sexual primeval world. The world where each creature was crudely limited to its own ego, crude and bristling and cold, and then crowding in packs like pine-trees and wolves.   [145; 415]

The woman is driven to the final admission: 'There is no Almighty loving God. The God there is shaggy as the pine-trees, and horrible as the lightning'. And the woman's deeper self glories in the destruction of her illusions: 'What nonsense about Jesus and a God of Love, in a place like this! This is more awful and more splendid. I like it better' [148; 418].

There follows some of Lawrence's finest prose, as he describes the 'bristling, hair-raising tussle' which characterizes 'even the life of the trees and flowers'. The flowers are fierce and dragonish, each one fighting for its ground: 'A battle, a battle, with banners of bright scarlet and yellow'. Glamour is cancelled by sordidness and savagery. But here Lawrence evokes a more robust beauty which is a marriage of heaven and hell:

The roses of the desert are the cactus flowers, crystal of translucent yellow or of rose-colour. But set among spines the devil himself must have conceived in a moment of sheer ecstasy.   [149; 420]

And if man, too, tries to live in this place, he too must expect a battle, not least against 'the animosity of the spirit of place: the crude half-created spirit of place, like some serpent-bird forever attacking man, in a hatred of man's onward-struggle towards further creation'; and against the gods of the place, who were 'grim and invidious and relentless, huger than man, and lower than man' [150; 421–2]. It is unthinkable that man should relate to them in terms of 'service'. They must be fought, 'to win from the crude wild nature the victory and the power to make another start' [151; 422].

A civilization which has lost 'its inward vision and its cleaner energy' is sordid; and 'all savagery is half-sordid'; but the fight with savage nature is rousing, energizing. It is a great reservoir of latent energy. And the struggle to draw upon it for his creative purposes is what defines a man.

The New England woman was ultimately defeated. Lou is going to have to relearn her lessons, through bitter experience. At the end of the story she is still speaking in terms of love and service:

It's my mission to keep myself for the spirit that is wild, and has waited so long here: even waited for such as me. Now I've come! Now I'm here. Now I am where I want to be: with the spirit that wants me.   [155; 427]

Mrs Witt is highly sceptical of Lou's 'something bigger':

Girls in my generation occasionally entered convents, for *something bigger*. I always wondered if they found it. They seemed to me inclined in the imbecile direction, but perhaps that was because I was *something less –*   [154; 426]

With her 'stony indifference', 'like a pillar of salt', 'crystallized into neutrality', she seems indeed something less than her daughter. However romantically Lou still conceives her mission, it does at least save her from cheapness. Lou looks at her ranch and sees beauty and hope; Mrs Witt sees nothing but 'so much hopelessness and so many rats' [152; 424]. Doomed romanticism and sterile cynicism.

Mrs Witt seems to have the last word, with her sneer at the name of the ranch – Las Chivas, the She-Goats. We remember Cartwright's account of the decline of the Great God Pan into the Great Goat Pan in the Christian centuries. Perhaps Keith Brown is right in suggesting that the name also echoes khiva, the holy place where the Indians, after centuries of imposed Christianity, still performed their secret rituals and communed with their mysterious ancient gods, their equivalent of Pan.

*

Lawrence's search for god, and his search for the vivid life of the body here on earth, both led him to Pan. But Pantheism, in Lawrence's day, in England, had come to mean little more than the Wordsworthian pieties. It had nothing to do with the realities of modern life. It was not a serious option as a religion for the twentieth century. Lawrence took it upon himself to make it so; not just an option, but a necessity for sanity and survival. It was a Herculean undertaking in 1924, when nature seemed to be disappearing under the 'century-deep deposits of layer upon layer of refuse: even of tin cans' [151; 422]; when the machine seemed to have triumphed utterly; when H. G. Wells and the majority for whom he spoke could complacently assume that history was the story of man's progress towards the triumph of mind over both nature and human nature.

Lawrence was exhausted when he finally completed the novel. He wrote to Secker on 13 September 1924:

Yes, the novelette *St Mawr* is finished and Brett is typing it out. It's good – a bit bitter – takes place in England, then moves to this ranch – some beautiful creation of this locale and landscape here. But thank God I don't have to write it again. It took it out of me.   [MS 60]

The greatness of the story depends upon the difficulty and the bitterness, upon his capacity to resist the temptation to create for his heroine a 'pure animal man', a man in whom Pan was not dead, a Centaur:

I like the Centaur as a symbol: would like to write a Centaur story: but can't in these white countries, where the lower half of man is an automobile, not a horse. – I just finished a novelette *St Mawr* – more or less a horse story. I wanted it to be a Centaur story – but – la mala suerte – impossible.   [C 15]

The following month he summed up to Catherine Carswell the experience and achievement of that summer:

The summer has gone. It was very beautiful up here. We worked hard, and spent very little money. And we had the place all to ourselves, and our horses the same. It was good to be alone and responsible. But also it is very *hard* living up against these savage Rockies. The savage things are a bit gruesome, and they try to down one. – But far better they than the white disintegration. – I did a long novelette – about 60,000 words – about 2 women and a horse – 'St Mawr'. But it may be called 'Two Women and a Horse'. And two shorter novelettes, about 15,000 words: 'The Woman Who Rode Away' and 'The Princess'. 'St Mawr' ends here. They are all about this country more or less . . . They are all sad. After all, they're true to what is.   [CL 814]

EIGHT

'THE SECRET OF THE ETRUSCANS': THE GENESIS OF *THE ESCAPED COCK*

Lawrence's deep lifelong sense of his own Englishness involved a strong sense of community. So did his concept of the artist as a discoverer and healer working 'for the race'. Hence his brief involvement with revolutionary political activity in 1915, and his persistent attempts to set up an ideal community, Rananim, preferably in the New World. For all his emphasis on individual fulfilment, he knew that 'this selfsame "accomplishment" of the fulfilled being is only a preparation for new responsibilities ahead, new unison in effort and conflict, the effort to make, with other men, a little new way into the future' [F 138]. Man is essentially a social animal, and all isolation is 'meaningless'. The isolation into which Lawrence was driven during the war, and from which he was never subsequently to escape, was a perpetual torment to him.

Lawrence knew that one man is no man, and that a good marriage is sterile if it does not release new energies in a man for his struggle to make a world. All Lawrence's visions of the good life are communal. It was a vision he was never able to accomplish in real life. Perhaps the nearest he came was the winter of 1922–3, when the two Danes, Knud Merrild and Kai Götzsche, shared the simple life of the Lawrences at the Del Monte ranch.

Of course, Lawrence's concept of the good life, an ideal community, a new world, was essentially religious rather than political. All around him he saw the evidence of what Birkin calls 'blasphemous living', the result of the original sin of falling into exclusively 'mental and spiritual consciousness', which is also the beginning of man's fatal awareness of himself as distinct from and independent of the rest of life. Lawrence sought 'to regain the naive or innocent soul', 'the pre-cognitive flow', 'the honest state before the apple' [CL 994]. It is not surprising that his descriptions of Rananim often make it sound like a cry for lost prelapsarian innocence, a dream of Paradise regained:

The only way is the way of my far-off wilderness place which shall become a school and a monastery and an Eden and a Hesperides – a seed of a new heaven and a new Earth. [H 393]

And his reason for choosing America is little more than that Fenimore Cooper and Thoreau had made it seem just such a 'far-off wilderness place' in his imagination.

But Lawrence assumed that such myths were not mere wish-fulfilment or escapism; they actually reflected some aboriginal state of man, which, if it had ever existed, might be regained. Perhaps certain races, in their rituals and religious symbolism, still retained vestiges of an ancient world-wide knowledge derived from that pre-cognitive mode. Lawrence had almost certainly got this idea from Leo Frobenius, whose *The Voice of Africa* he read in April 1918. There Frobenius claimed that the ancient religion of Yoruba was 'definitely linked to the perfected system of a primeval age'. There was a 'great and significant idea of the universe' and a 'high-toned philosophy, which once girdled the world at its earliest dawn'. Frobenius even argued that the Etruscans were the last European guardians of that philosophy, and that the Yoruban method of divination was still practised by the Pueblo Indians of Arizona – propositions Lawrence was to spend the next ten years of his life putting to the test. These quotations from *The Voice of Africa* assembled by Daniel J. Schneider [DHLR 16, 183–93] are very close to a whole cluster of ideas, including the spirit of place itself, which Lawrence first expressed in 'The Spirit of Place' in the summer of 1918:

The occultists say that once there was a universal mystic language, known to the initiated, or to the adept, or to the priesthood of the whole world, whether Chinese or Atlantean or Maya or Druid – a language that was universal over the globe at some period, perhaps before the Flood . . . It is conceivable, perhaps even probable, that at one time the priesthoods of all the world – Asiatic, African, European, American, Polynesian – held some common idea of the creation of the Cosmic universe, and expressed this idea in the same symbols or graphs. [SM 18]

Lawrence embarked on his world-wide pilgrimage in 1919 partly in the hope of meeting the living descendants of those priesthoods, or at least discovering some evidence of their former existence. It was in this spirit that he first encountered the Etruscans.

*

In January 1920 Lawrence's friend Rosalind Popham had settled in the ancient Villa Canovaia at San Gervasio, near Fiesole. In August a nearby explosion blew out all the windows; Lawrence asked if he could stay in the abandoned villa, and spent most of September there.

> Sometimes he came up to Fiesole where I was now living, climbing by a steep track up through the olives and along under the remains of Fiesole's Etruscan walls, and arriving rather jauntily, carrying something peculiar and humorous – a salamander or a little baby duck as a pet for the children. Or he came and cooked the Sunday dinner – an English Sunday dinner with roast beef and batter pudding. And there were tea parties with friends up from Florence, and evenings when we sat on the terrace high above the lights of the city, having our supper of mortadella and marsala. It was here several other poems were suggested – 'Cypresses', for example.
>
> [CB II 49–50]

Is it coincidence that the first contact we know of between Lawrence and the Etruscans should be in a context of jauntiness and humour? 'There seems to have been in the Etruscan instinct a real desire to preserve the natural humour of life' [MM 123]. Perhaps it was at this time also that Lawrence first visited the Archaeological Museum in Florence, where he would have seen many of the finest Etruscan artifacts, and read Dennis's *Cities and Cemeteries of Etruria*. 'Cypresses' implies some knowledge of the Etruscans, and years later Lawrence was to say that he had read only Dennis.

Lawrence could have chosen no better guide to the Etruscans than George Dennis. Dennis was not an academic but an explorer, motivated not by the ambition to become a professor by amassing dead facts, like the young German archaeologist Lawrence met in Tarquinia, but by a spirit of adventure, by natural curiosity and enthusiasm. He was as interested in the people and places he met on the way as in the remains themselves, and always approached the remains as evidence of a living people. His classic study of the Etruscans is also, like *Etruscan Places*, a very personal and lively travel book, full of vitality and humour.

Lawrence saw the Tuscan cypresses as hieroglyphs of a language, like Etruscan, to which we have lost the key. The 'supple, brooding, softly-swaying pillars of dark flame', the cypresses, are said to be monumental to the 'long-nosed, sensitive-footed, subtly-smiling Etruscans', silently speaking the lost language, darkly exuding the lost life, sinuous and flame-tall, a home still for the spirits of the lost whom Lawrence invokes

> To bring their meaning back into life again,
> Which they have taken away
> And wrapt inviolable in soft cypress-trees,
> Etruscan cypresses.   [CP 297]

We have buried, with the Etruscans, 'so much of the delicate magic of life'.

Lawrence does not offer to interpret the cypresses. They are silent tongues to him too. The poem is a series of unanswered questions, a dialogue of one. From other trees, from fruits, flowers and beasts, Lawrence was able to draw 'little living myths', and penetrate their symbolic secrets, most triumphantly in 'Tortoises', also written at the Villa Canovaia, and in 'Almond Blossom' four months later. But the cypresses resist him. The primary sexual symbols, the phallus and the ark, dominated Etruscan consciousness, and stood at the entrance to the tombs. They are also dominant symbols in *Birds, Beasts and Flowers*. Yet the phallic nature of cypresses, though hinted at in the poem, is not developed.

The nearest Lawrence comes to solving the mystery is in a stanza mysteriously missing from all texts except that printed by Murry in the *Adelphi* in October 1923 (though Murry took his text from Secker's proofs for *Birds, Beasts and Flowers*):

Among the cypresses
To sit with pure, slim, long-nosed,
Evil-called, sensitive Etruscans, naked except for their boots;
To be able to smile back at them
And exchange the lost kiss
And come to dark connection.

That last word gives the clue to the secret, and is at the heart of *Etruscan Places*; but not until after he had visited the Etruscan places was Lawrence able to take it any further, or even to realize how central it was.

In September 1921 Lawrence arranged to meet the Carswells in Siena in order to visit Perugia with them. He arrived in Siena before them, and hated it so much that he could not bear to stay, and returned to Florence. The Carswells went to Perugia without him. Apparently Catherine wrote to him that she had discovered the secret of the Etruscans there, for on 25 October Lawrence wrote to her:

Also, will you tell me *what* then was the secret of the Etruscans, which you saw written so plainly in the place you went to? Please don't forget to tell me, as they really do rather puzzle me, the Etruscans.   [CL 668]

We do not know what reply he received. But if Lawrence had not disliked Siena, or if they had met in Perugia instead, *Etruscan Places* might have been advanced by several years, for it was Lawrence's visit to the University Museum in Perugia with Millicent Beveridge and Mabel Harrison in March 1926 which set him planning his tour of the major Etruscan sites.

*

In the same month as his letter to Catherine Carswell, Lawrence developed his idea of a world before the flood in his Foreword to *Fantasia of the Unconscious*:

> In that world men lived and taught and knew, and were in one complete correspondence over all the earth. Men wandered back and forth from Atlantis to the Polynesian Continent as men now sail from Europe to America. The interchange was complete, and knowledge, science was universal over the earth, cosmopolitan as it is today. Then came the melting of the glaciers, and the world flood. The refugees from the drowned continents fled to the high places of America, Europe, Asia, and the Pacific Isles. And some degenerated naturally into cave men, neolithic and paleolithic creatures, and some retained their marvellous innate beauty and life-perception, as the South Sea Islanders, and some wandered savage in Africa, and some, like Druids or Etruscans or Chaldeans or Amerindians or Chinese, refused to forget, but taught the old wisdom, only in its half-forgotten, symbolic forms. More or less forgotten, as knowledge: remembered as ritual, gesture and myth-story. [F 13]

A few months later Lawrence turned his back on the Etruscans, their secret still intact, to search for that lost world at the far corners of the earth, going East, but intending, ultimately, to go West; afraid of America, perhaps, because he expected so much of it. The South Sea Islands were certainly not what he had hoped:

> There is a sort of sickliness about them, smell of cocoa-nut oil and sort of palm-tree, reptile nausea . . . These are supposed to be the earthly paradises: these South Sea Isles. You can have 'em . . . Travel seems to me a splendid lesson in disillusion – chiefly that. [CL 713]

As for the Amerindians, Lawrence was at first disappointed in them too. They were nothing like Cooper's noble savages. Their chants had no message for him:

> The voice out of the far-off time was not for my ears. Its language was unknown to me. And I did not wish to know . . . I don't want to go back to them, ah, never. I never want to deny them or break with them. But there is no going back. Always onward, still further. The great devious onward-flowing stream of conscious human blood. From them to me, and from me on. [P 99]

He was soon to modify this position:

> Let us try to adjust ourselves again to the Indian outlook, to take up an

old dark thread from their vision, and see again as they see, without for-
getting we are ourselves. [P II 243]

But it took him a year and a half to begin to 'see again as they see'.
Here, he recognized at last, was a community held together by a
common deeply religious consciousness. And for Lawrence it was
the only true religion – a religion not of theology or morality, but
simply of contact with everything else that lives:

> For the whole life-effort of man was to get his life into direct contact
> with the elemental life of the cosmos, mountain-life, cloud-life, thunder-
> life, air-life, earth-life, sun-life. To come into immediate *felt* contact, and
> so derive energy, power, and a dark sort of joy. This effort into sheer naked
> contact, *without an intermediary or mediator*, is the root meaning of reli-
> gion, and at the sacred races the runners hurled themselves in a terrible
> cumulative effort, through the air, to come at last into naked contact with
> the very life of the air, which is the life of the clouds, and so of the
> rain. [P 146–7]

Yet even here, where Lawrence goes as far as he was able to go in
entering the spirit of the Indian dances, there are still hints, in the
'dark' joy and 'terrible' effort, of a final step Lawrence was never
able or willing to take into total identification with them, still a
residue of the categorical statement he had made in 'Indians and
Entertainment' that 'there is no bridge, no canal of connection', no
possibility of reconciliation, between the Indian way of consciousness and our own. Though he tried hard to do so, especially in *The
Plumed Serpent*, he never quite overcame his initial spontaneous
recoil from certain overtones in the Indian dances:

> Just the antithesis of what I understand by jolliness: ridicule. Comic sort
> of bullying. No jolly, free laughter . . . and the diabolical, pre-human, pine-
> tree fun of cutting dusky throats and letting the blood spurt out
> unconfined. [95–6]

*

Kangaroo is essentially a sequel to *Women in Love*. Richard Lovat
Somers and his wife Harriet (who are very close to the Lawrences)
have no sooner arrived in Australia than Somers begins to involve
himself in Australian politics. Harriet reacts just as Ursula would
have done:

> 'And why couldn't we be happy in this wonderful new country, living
> to ourselves. We could have a cow, and chickens – and then the Pacific,
> and this marvellous new country. Surely that is enough for any man. Why
> must you have more?'
> 'Because I feel I *must* fight out something with mankind yet. I haven't
> finished with my fellow-men . . . I intend to move with men and get men

to move with me before I die . . . I have the roots of my life with you. But I want if possible to send out a new shoot in the life of mankind – the effort man makes forever, to grow into new forms.' [K 77–8]

Somers' need to ally himself with other men is frustrated by his even stronger need for self-protective isolation lest he be, in Harriet's words, nipped in the bud. Comradeship, like love, is finally a threat to his individual integrity and autonomy. In reaction he feels he must leave the rest of the world to its fate and 'turn to the gods' [180]. The gods he has in mind are 'the source of passions and strange motives':

> To be pure in heart, man must listen to the dark gods as well as to the white gods, to the call to blood-sacrifice as well as to the eucharist. [296]

And the call of these 'non-human gods' will be answered by the 'non-human human being' [375]. Somers, like Lawrence, answers the call by buying a ticket to America.

The closeness of Somers and Lawrence is evident from one of the first pieces Lawrence wrote in New Mexico, his review of Ben Hecht's *Fantazius Mallare*:

> The old, dark religions understood. 'God enters from below,' said the Egyptians, and that's right . . . Why don't you seek again the unknown and invisible gods who step sometimes into your arteries, and down the blood vessels to the phallos, to the vagina, and have strange meetings there? . . . And turn again to the dark gods, which are the dark promptings and passion-motions inside you, and have reverence again and be grateful for life. [CL 726]

In parts of America, particularly in Old Mexico, Lawrence found such gods: and his next heroine, Kate Leslie, turns to them:

> Sometimes, in America, the shadow of that old pre-Flood world was so strong, that the day of historic humanity would melt out of Kate's consciousness, and she would begin to approximate to the old mode of consciousness, the old, dark will, the unconcern for death, the subtle, dark consciousness, non-cerebral, but vertebrate. When the mind and the power of man was in his blood and his back-bone, and there was the strange, dark inter-communication between man and man and man and beast, from the powerful spine. The Mexicans were still this. That which is aboriginal in America still belongs to the way of the world before the Flood, before the mental-spiritual world came into being. [PS 452]

Mexico also provided Lawrence with a setting of a volatile, endemically unstable and revolutionary society, where regimes are frequently overturned and replaced with their opposite. This gave Lawrence the opportunity to depict the kind of society he wanted, not as a prelapsarian nostalgia or Utopian dream, but as a practical proposition here and now. In *The Plumed Serpent* he is able to make Don Ramon's revolution perfectly credible. Such things were even happening in Europe, with a different set of insignia. Only a few months before Lawrence began *The Plumed Serpent* Mussolini had marched on Rome and founded a fascist government. And while Lawrence was writing *The Plumed Serpent* Hitler was writing *Mein Kampf*.

In the first version of the novel, *Quetzalcoatl*, Don Ramon is a native Indian, his concern is solely with an indigenous Mexican renaissance, and his methods include a reorganization of village life in communes, each with its chieftain and chieftainess of peace, and with economic self-sufficiency. But in the final version, Ramon, now a white man, imposes a much more synthetic system on Mexico, aggrandizes himself from merely First Man of Quetzalcoatl to the Living Quetzalcoatl, and is clearly presented by Lawrence as both preaching and embodying ultimate truths equally applicable to Europeans: 'I *do* mean what Ramon means – for all of us' [CL 859]. The bulk of the novel is an attempt to vindicate Ramon's ideas rather than to test them. We can contrast the way in which Ursula in *Women in Love* was able to challenge and modify Birkin's position with the inability of Kate to do anything but submit to Cipriano, and the imperviousness of Don Ramon to any kind of influence from others. Birkin is struggling towards a set of beliefs adequate to live by; Ramon is assumed to have found it, so that there is nothing for others to do but be for him or against him. To be for him is to be a follower merely, as Cipriano and Kate are followers even though given the names of gods. To be against him is to be against life and to deserve death.

But Lawrence was too honest a writer not to put his own reservations into the novel. Kate detects a certain malevolence in the Mexicans, 'something dark, heavy and reptilian in their silence and their softness . . . They did not belong to the realm of that which comes forth' [PS 155]. She feels that she belongs, as they do not, to 'the upper world of daylight and fresh air' [182]. Lawrence felt the same. In the very letter in which he claims that *The Plumed Serpent* is his 'chief novel so far', he admits that he has had enough of America, particularly of Mexico:

America is so eternally and everlastingly tough: very good for one, for a bit; but after too long, it makes one feel leathery in one's soul. Continual leathery resistance all the time. Mexico more so. I think it's time I was softened down a bit, with a little oil of Europe.   [C 20]

The desire for comradeship having been frustrated during the war,

Lawrence had almost been seduced by the ideal of leadership in *Aaron's Rod* and *Kangaroo*, where he rejects it only in favour of lordship, which is leadership with a religious sanction; and in the changes he made from *Quetzalcoatl* to *The Plumed Serpent*, the lord, the non-human man who is also the incarnation of a non-human god, unaccountable to anyone but himself, with the absolute power of life and death, is dangerously close to being Lawrence himself.

On the very day he finished *The Plumed Serpent*, 29 January 1925, Lawrence was struck down with malaria, and came near to death. The doctor told Frieda that he had tuberculosis in the third degree, and but a year or two to live. Lawrence's instinct was to return to England, but he was told that the voyage would be bad for him, so he returned to New Mexico to recuperate at the ranch.

That near-fatal illness of February 1925 marks the beginning of a new phase, the final phase, of Lawrence's life. The first fruit of it was 'The Flying Fish', of which Lawrence later said: 'It was written so near the borderline of death, that I never have been able to carry it through, in the cold light of day' [RC 288]. The hero, Gethin Day, has almost died of malaria in Mexico, and is returning home to England. The ordinary day has lost its reality to him:

> It had cracked like some great bubble, and to his uneasiness and terror, he had seemed to see through the fissures the deeper blue of that other Greater Day where moved the other sun shaking its dark blue wings. Perhaps it was the malaria; perhaps it was his own inevitable development; perhaps it was the presence of those handsome, dangerous, wide-eyed men left over from the ages before the flood in Mexico, which caused his old connections and his accustomed world to break for him. He was ill, and he felt as if at the very middle of him, beneath his navel, some membrane were torn, some membrane which had connected him with the world and its day.   [P 782]

Gethin Day sees the flying fish and dolphins which accompany his ship as creatures of the Greater Day. The dolphins seem to hold in perfect balance instinct and consciousness, individuality and togetherness. The flying fish, when they return to their element, dive 'under the belly of death' [786]. Lawrence told the Brewsters that the last part of 'The Flying Fish' would have been 'regenerate man, a real life in this Garden of Eden' [RC 288]. Gethin Day's vision of life in the Greater Day is a prevision of the ending of 'The Escaped Cock':

> For death is not in dying, but in the fear. Cease then the struggle of thy flight, and fall back into the deep element where death is and is not, and life is not a fleeing away. It is a beauteous thing to live and to be alive. Live then in the Greater Day, and let the waters carry thee, and the flood

bear thee along, and live, only live, no more of this hurrying away.

[P 788]

In the spring at the ranch Lawrence made a splendid recovery, was himself resurrected. As his health returned, everything 'assumed the radiance of new life' [NI 168]. Just being alive in the phenomenal world became so miraculous to him that the desire for lordship fell from him. As he was to say of his own Man Who Had Died, having died he knew his own limits, and the life of his self-importance was over. He realized as never before that human life 'consists in a relation with all things: stone, earth, trees, flowers, water, insects, fishes, birds, creatures, sun, rainbow, children, women, other men', with his black cow Susan and his white cock Moses.

This essay, 'Aristocracy', written in July 1925, gives us the cock with exactly the religious and phallic significance it is to have in 'The Escaped Cock':

And as the white cock calls in the doorway, who calls? Merely a barnyard rooster, worth a dollar-and-a-half. But listen! Under the old dawns of creation the Holy Ghost, the Mediator, shouts aloud in the twilight. And every time I hear him, a fountain of vitality gushes up in my body. It is life.

So it is! Degree after degree after degree widens out the relation between man and his universe, till it reaches the sun and the night . . .

When the white cock crows, I do not hear myself, or some anthropomorphic conceit, crowing. I hear the not-me, the voice of the Holy Ghost. And when I see the hard, solid, longish green cones thrusting up at blue heaven from the high bluish tips of the balsam pine, I say: 'Behold! Look at the strong, fertile silence of the thrusting tree! God is in the bush like a clenched dark fist, or a thrust phallus.' [P II 481]

It was a relief to get back to the Mediterranean, in November 1925, 'and gradually let the tight coils inside oneself come slack'. There Lawrence discovered 'a deep insouciance, which really is the clue to faith' [P 118]. Four years later, thinking of the American pioneers, but drawing, clearly, on his own experience of America, he wrote:

The spirit and the will survived: but something in the soul perished: the softness, the floweriness, the natural tenderness. How could it survive the sheer brutality of the fight with that American wilderness, which is so big, vast, and obdurate! [267]

In the floweriness of Tuscany (with Mussolini installed in Rome), in the greenness of England, the leadership principle, which had seemed so right for Mexico, began to seem more and more 'would-be', what Frieda had called it all along: 'dessicated swelled head' [*sic* FL 235]. Here it seemed rather that hope lay in 'some sort of tenderness, sensitive, between men and men and men and women, and not the one up one down, lead on I follow, *ich dien* sort of business' [CL 1045]. He proposed to call his next novel *Tenderness*.

The American Indians had not quite embodied Lawrence's dream. His attempt to adapt their religion and culture to the needs of a modern state with white leaders in *The Plumed Serpent* had led him into horrors. The Indian way, he reluctantly decided, though it was a true way, was simply not available to a European, saddled with so different a consciousness, history, and adjustment to the spirit of such different places. He abandoned the leadership principle. He abandoned Rananim. Yet he continued to travel, and travelling itself implies a residual hope:

> We do not travel in order to go from one hotel to another, and see a few side-shows. We travel, perhaps, with a secret and absurd hope of setting foot on the Hesperides, of running our boat up a little creek and landing in the Garden of Eden.   [P 343]

*

In November 1925 the Lawrences returned to Italy. In April 1926 Lawrence wrote to Martin Secker from Spotorno:

> We might go to Perugia, and I might do a book on Umbria and the Etruscan remains. What do you think? It would be half a travel book – of the region round Perugia, Assisi, Spoleto, Cortona, and the Maremma – and half a book about the Etruscan things, which interest me very much. If you happen to know any good book, modern, on Etruscan things, I wish you'd order it for me. I've only read that old work, Dennis' – *Cities and Cemeteries of Etruria*. There will be some lectures in Perugia.   [MS 72]

Later that month Lawrence told Secker that he was 'reading Italian books on the Etruscans – very interesting indeed. I'll join Vieusseux's library here – they will have more things' [73]. One of these Italian books was certainly Pericle Ducati's *Etruria Antica*, which, according to Richard Aldington, Lawrence carried about with him during the summer of 1926.[1]

A week later, and three days before moving into the Villa Mirenda five miles south of Florence in the Tuscan hills, Lawrence wrote to his niece Margaret that he had taken the Mirenda specifically to use it as a centre for travelling round to 'quite a number of places in Tuscany and Umbria, where the best remains are. At present I'm supposed to be reading up about my precious Etruschi!' [CL 908]. One of the books he read was by Theodor Mommsen, probably *The Earliest Inhabitants of Italy*, for at the end of the month he wrote to his sister-in-law Else Jaffe:

Mommsen hated everything Etruscan, said the germ of all degeneracy was in the race. But the bronzes and terracottas are fascinating, so alive with physical life, with a powerful physicality which surely is as great, or sacred, ultimately, as the *ideal* of the Greeks and Germans.   [NI 223]

On 21 May Lawrence wrote:

I have been reading up the ancient Etruscans. I thought perhaps in July, if the weather will clear up, I might go to Cortona and Chiusi and Volterra and Tarquinia and Orvieto, the old Etruscan places, and look at all the remains, and perhaps write a light Etruscan travel book, with many photo-graphic reproductions. I think I might like it – if only the weather would be fine and hot.   [CL 916]

But in the summer heat Lawrence did not feel like travelling, or embarking on any large-scale work. It was idyllic at the Mirenda:

In the real summer, I always lose interest in literature and publications. The cicadas rattle away all day in the trees, the girls sing, cutting the corn with sickles, the sheaves of wheat lie all the afternoon like people dead asleep in the heat. E più non si frega. I don't work, except at an occasional scrap of an article. I don't much feel like doing a book, of any sort.   [923]

He did, however, write one of his most important stories, 'The Man Who Loved Islands'.

Despite his strong sense of community, Lawrence had frequently, since 1916, been tempted by the attractions of the hermit life. In December 1916 he had tried to rationalize his sense of isolation:

I have been in Cornwall for twelve months now, never out of it, so I feel a stranger to the world. I find myself divested of all my friends, and much more confident and free, having no connections anywhere. Why should one seek intimacies – they are only a net about one. It is one's business to stand quite apart and single, in one's soul.   [L III 48]

It was often hard for him to hold on to the 'law of life and creation, from which we cannot escape', which is that 'Man doth not live by bread alone. He lives even more essentially from the nourishing creative flow between himself and another or others . . . between the individual and the outer universe' [F 246].

In 1920 Compton Mackenzie, with whom Lawrence was friendly at the time, leased from the Crown the islands of Herm and Jethou in the Channel Islands. His wife, Faith, wrote of it:

There was no doubt about it – Herm was the perfect retreat for a man who wanted to get away from everything and work in peace. Besides, there was a capital farm which could be run for profit, and probably in time the island would pay its way. Jethou had not been visited. It was tiny and derelict, but it was a nice shape and had two attendant islets, Crevichon and Fauconnaire.   [C B II 22]

Lawrence wrote to Mackenzie: 'What is this I hear about Channel Isles? The Lord of the Isles. I shall write a skit on you one day' [L III 594]. Lawrence had met Faith Mackenzie again on Capri in March 1926, and she had told him that her husband 'had been forced by farming losses to abandon Herm (and many of his retainers there) for Jethou in 1923. She also informed him of her husband's purchase of the Shiant Islands in the Outer Hebrides the previous October' [SSS 538]. This gave Lawrence his fable. He hoped Mackenzie wouldn't mind: 'He only *suggests* the idea – it's no portrait' [MS 88]. In 1950 Mackenzie told Harry T. Moore that Lawrence 'had a trick of describing a person's setting or background vividly, and then putting into the setting an ectoplasm entirely of his own creation' [PL 284]; but in 1927 he did object very strongly to 'The Man Who Loved Islands', and persuaded Secker not to publish it. Lawrence wrote to Secker that 'though the circumstances are some of them his, the man is no more he than I am' [SSS 538].

'The Man Who Loved Islands' is certainly not *about* Compton Mackenzie. Nor is it a skit. The protagonist, Cathcart, is not there to be pilloried, like Sir Clifford Chatterley, nor to be dismissed by irony, like Rico Carrington. There is no animus against him. The tone is meticulously dispassionate, objective. The tale has the true autonomy of fable. Cathcart is not Lawrence either. Lawrence would never have worn a white suit or compiled a reference book of all the flowers in Classical literature. But Lawrence was a man who loved islands. It was of his alter ego Rupert Birkin that he had written, ten years previously:

> What a dread he had of mankind, of other people! It amounted almost to horror, to a sort of dream terror – his horror of being observed by some other people. If he were on an island like Alexander Selkirk, with only the creatures and the trees, he would be free and glad, there would be none of this heaviness, this misgiving. He could love the vegetation and be quite happy and unquestioned, by himself. [WL 166–7]

And in the worst years only his unbroken faith in the non-human world had saved him from a fate like Cathcart's.

The title and opening sentences clearly characterize the story as a moral fable, almost a cautionary tale:

> There was a man who loved islands . . . He was born on one, but it didn't suit him, as there were too many other people on it besides himself. He wanted an island all of his own: not necessarily to be alone on it, but to make it a world of his own.
>
> An island, if it is big enough, is no better than a continent. It has to be really quite small, before it *feels like* an island; and this story will show how

tiny it has to be, before you can presume to fill it with your own personality. [SSS 458]

In a realistic story Cathcart would be a mere eccentric with a unique obsession. But in terms of the fable we can recognize him as embodying in an extreme and very pure form a common, almost normal condition. We are all would-be solipsists. The force of Donne's 'No man is an Island, entire of itself; every man is a piece of the Continent, a part of the main' derives from the fact that most of us behave as if we were islands. Cathcart gets his wish, but, as is the way with fables, everything implied by that wish is taken to its logical conclusion, which is annihilation. Cathcart is an idealist. Idealism, for Lawrence, is a form of egotism. Nothing beyond the self is allowed a life of its own. Creatures are reduced to ideas, to words, so that they can be manipulated and contained. The story shows that to be a fully fledged idealist is to be a nihilist. It enacts a willed reduction of the varied colours of experience to a flat white, a gradual withdrawal from all relationships until the self disintegrates. The self is granted a void to live in, but cannot survive there; for that is Lawrence's definition of *real* death – a loss of contact with the flow of life through relationships.

Cathcart is at the opposite end of the spectrum of human possibilities from the Etruscans. The ascetic, idealistic discipline which masks his egotism is the opposite of the *disciplina etrusca*, which, according to Werner Keller:

reflects a sense of close union with the cosmos, the Etruscan belief in the profound interconnection of all elements, in the mystic unity that joined the celestial and terrestrial worlds with the underworld. Everything on earth, the life of the individual as well as that of the nation, is integrated in the unalterable rhythm of creation . . . It was as though the human ego had surrendered, was resigned to the divine will, and set its sole hope in a belief in the magical efficacy of ritual. [E 81]

In August and September of 1926 Lawrence made his last visit to England. He spent a long weekend with Richard Aldington in Berkshire:

As I knew he was contemplating a book on the Etruscans, I had a dozen standard works on the subject sent down from the London Library; and we spent a good deal of time turning them over and discussing Etruria, which was very important at that time in Lawrence's private mythology. [CB III 84–5]

Unfortunately, the only book Aldington specifies is *Villanovans and Early Etruscans* by D. Randall-Macivers. It is clear, however, that

Lawrence prepared himself very assiduously before making his Etruscan tour.

From Lincolnshire Lawrence wrote to Earl Brewster:

Curiously, I like England again, now I am up in my own regions. It braces me up: and there seems a queer, odd sort of potentiality in the people, especially the common people. One feels in them some odd, unaccustomed sort of plasm twinkling and nascent. They are not finished. And they have a funny sort of purity and gentleness, and at the same time, unbreakableness, that attracts one.   [CL 933]

But Lincolnshire was hardly his own region. When he actually went 'home' for three days in mid-September, he felt 'at once a devouring nostalgia and an infinite repulsion' [P II 257]. It was the time of the great coal strike, with families 'living on bread and margarine and potatoes', and the once-proud miners scouring the countryside for blackberries to sell for fourpence a pound. In his sister's car he made the same depressing tour of north-west Derbyshire that Connie Chatterley was later to make:

And now, this last time, I feel a doom over the country, and a shadow of despair over the hearts of the men, which leaves me no rest. Because the same doom is over me, wherever I go, and the same despair touches my heart.   [264]

On his return to Italy he wrote to Rolf Gardiner:

I was at my sister's in September, and we drove round – I saw the miners – and pickets – and policemen – it was like a spear through one's heart. I tell you, we'd better buck up and do something for the England to come, for they've pushed the spear through the side of *my* England.   [CL 952]

Lawrence's contribution was to embark on the 'English novel' [MS 76] we now know as *The First Lady Chatterley*. His programme for the novel was laid down in 'Return to Bestwood':

One is driven back to search one's own soul, for a way out into a new destiny . . . I know that we could, if we would, establish little by little a true democracy in England: we could nationalise the land and industries and means of transport, and make the whole thing work infinitely better than at present, *if we would*. It all depends on the spirit in which the thing is done. I know we are on the brink of a class war . . . I know we must take up responsibility for the future, now. A great change is coming, and must come. What we need is some glimmer of a vision of a world that shall be, beyond the change. Otherwise we shall be in for a great débâcle . . . What we should live for is life and the beauty of aliveness, imagination, awareness, and contact.   [P II 264–6]

The task of finding such a vision proved, at this stage, too much for Lawrence. The sexual relationship between Lady Chatterley and

Parkin is intended to be a means to a larger end, the healing of the class divide, the establishment of a new physical basis for social relationships. It is, therefore, as Lawrence insisted, a phallic rather than a sexual novel: 'The phallos is the point at which man is broken off from his context, and at which he can be re-joined' [A 181]. That context is both religious and social. Parkin's relationship with Connie is supposed to release in him new creative energies for his constructive activity in the world of men. But Lawrence can give that activity no more convincing substance in the novel than Parkin's vague involvement with the communist party. At the end of the novel Lawrence is aware that he has not been able to do enough with communism, and makes a last desperate attempt to inflate its significance by putting his own hopes directly and quite inappropriately into the mouth of Duncan Forbes:

Do you know what I think the English *really* want? . . . Contact! Some sort of passionate human contact among themselves. And perhaps if the Communists *did* smash the famous 'system' there might emerge a new relationship between men: *really* not caring about money, *really* caring for life, and the life-flow with one another. [FLC 242]

It is evident that Lawrence did not believe this sufficiently to be able to incorporate it into the body of the novel. Indeed, so honest is his handling of the distance between Parkin and Lady Chatterley in terms of class and culture that he is not even sure that there is any future for their relationship. His confidence is further undermined by his doubts of finding a sympathetic hearing, or any hearing at all, from either side in the impending class war:

And what is the good of saying these things, to men whose whole education consists in the fact that twice two are four? – which, being interpreted, means that twice tuppence is fourpence. [P II 266]

The First Lady Chatterley, then, does not take Lawrence where he wants to go. Rather than struggle with the recalcitrant elements, and, if no resolution emerges, leave them openly unresolved, as in earlier novels, Lawrence simply rewrites this novel, leaving them out. The most obvious instance is in the problems caused by the class-chasm between Connie and Parkin. The second version, now known as *John Thomas and Lady Jane*, flatly denies that the problem exists:

Class is an anachronism. It finished in 1914. Nothing remains but a vast proletariat, including kings, aristocrats, squires, millionaires and working-people, men and women alike. And then a few individuals who have not been proletarianised. [JT 294]

Mellors is such an individual. But the class problems which had been so inescapable between Connie and Parkin disappear because Mellors is given all the credentials of a 'gentleman', including an education and culture which, like Lawrence's, enables him to move freely through all classes.

In the final version, Mellors fears entering upon a relationship with Connie because he sees it as a threat to his hard-won isolation, his hermit life, the first connection which will inevitably lead to further connections and responsibilities until he is caught again in the social web. And in a realistic novel this would have to happen. But here it does not. On the contrary, their relationship is justified precisely as an escape route from a fallen and damned world, a saving of their souls in a secret renewal of paganism in whatever remote corner of the world they can find, their own private Paradise Regained. The idea of communal life is now reduced to a few perfunctory gestures borrowed from Rolf Gardiner, a Utopian dream tacked on to the novel in Mellors' concluding letter to Connie.

Lawrence drops his original social theme in order to concentrate on what he is sure he can do, to go through with the role he had chosen years before as a priest of love. The novel concentrates, in its final version, on a mythic interpretation of love as communion with the fecund but vulnerable gods of the English countryside, gods not of fear, darkness, passion and silence, as in Australia or Mexico, but of tenderness, sunshine, desire, bird-song, and sacred relatedness. This Lawrence could do supremely well. But the novel by this stage had also acquired another purpose, to shock the castrated sensibilities of English readers by treating the subject of sex more explicitly than ever before (a purpose arising from the new freedom given him by the decision to publish privately). Inevitably, this became the overriding characteristic of the novel (and even of Lawrence himself) for generations of readers, both admirers such as Richard Aldington, who thought it a feather in the cap of the twentieth century, and Shaw, who thought it should be compulsory reading for every sixteen-year-old girl, and those who found it a landmark in evil. Some of the purposes Lawrence outlined in his fine subsequent essays 'A Propos of *Lady Chatterley's Lover*' and 'Pornography and Obscenity' have subsequently been realized, but they have continued to obscure the larger religious purpose. That purpose is also obscured by a radical uncertainty of mode in the novel. A good deal of the realism of the first version survives into the third, and prevents it from becoming wholly myth like *The Escaped Cock*.

For all the celebration of sex, Connie and Mellors get no further in any direction than Ursula and Birkin. For all its incidental virtues, *Lady Chatterley's Lover* does not seem to me to constitute a significant advance or breakthrough in Lawrence's vision.

*

The second version of *Lady C.* was probably finished in February 1927. The following month Frieda was planning to go to Germany, so Lawrence invited himself to stay with the Brewsters, who had just moved to Ravello. His plan was to stay in Ravello for a week or ten days, then set out from there with Earl Brewster on the long-planned Etruscan pilgrimage:

> What *I* should most like to do, for the trip, would be to do the western half of the Etruscans – the Rome museums – then Veii and Civita Castellana and Cerveteri – which one does from Rome – then Corneto, just beyond Civita Vecchia in Maremma – then the Maremma coast-line – and Volterra. Do you know any of these places? I should like to do them very much. If there were time, we might get to Chiusi and Orvieto – we could see. I have a real feeling for the Etruscans. [RC 119]

The trip went much as Lawrence had planned. He and Earl Brewster arrived in Rome on 4 April. They began with the museum of the Villa di Papa Giulia – 'With what lively interest Lawrence studied its treasures!' Brewster recalled. On 6 April Lawrence saw his first Etruscan necropolis, at Cerveteri. This time there was no disillusion. The spirit of this place was more congenial to him than anywhere else he had been. At Cerveteri he found 'a queer stillness and a curious peaceful repose . . . quite different from the weirdness of Celtic places, the slightly repellent feeling of Rome and the old Campagna, and the rather horrible feeling of the great pyramid places in Mexico, Teotihuacan and Cholula, and Mitla in the south; or the amiably idolatrous Buddha places in Ceylon':

> There is a stillness and a softness in these great grassy mounds with their ancient stone girdles, and down the central walk there lingers still a kind of homeliness and happiness. True, it was a still and sunny afternoon in April, and larks rose from the soft grass of the tombs. But there was a stillness and a soothingness in all the air, in that sunken place, and a feeling that it was good for one's soul to be there. [MM 105]

The next day they reached Tarquinia, and this was the high spot of the tour. In the afternoon they walked with a guide out to the necropolis. The first of the painted tombs Lawrence entered was the Tomb of Hunting and Fishing. To enter that tomb today is to recapture Lawrence's joy:

> It is all small and gay and quick with life, spontaneous as only young

life can be. If only it were not so much damaged, one would be happy, because here is the real Etruscan liveliness and naturalness. It is not impressive or grand. But if you are content with just a sense of the quick ripple of life, then here it is.   [133]

And the scene at one end, of the dead man banqueting in the underworld, confirmed Lawrence's belief that 'the underworld of the Etruscans was a gay place . . . For the life on earth was so good, the life below could but be a continuance of it' [134]. Next, they were taken to the Tomb of the Leopards:

The walls of this little tomb are a dance of real delight. The room seems inhabited still by Etruscans of the sixth century before Christ, a vivid, life-accepting people, who must have lived with real fullness . . . All is colour, and we do not seem to be underground at all, but in some gay chamber of the past.   [136]

In these dark underground chambers, Lawrence found colour and daylight and fresh air. In these Etruscan tombs he felt he had come face to face with unfallen man:

You cannot think of art, but only of life itself, as if this were the very life of the Etruscans, dancing in their coloured wraps with massive yet exuberant naked limbs, ruddy from the air and the sea-light, dancing and fluting along through the little olive-trees, out in the fresh day.   [136]

Earl Brewster recalled:

How happy were our days at Tarquinia! The tombs are on a high plateau back a few miles from the sea. They number about a hundred and cover the area of a small city. We were thrilled by the freshness and beauty of their mural paintings. I felt Lawrence truly maintained Etruscan art has a certain sensitive quality not found in the Greek. The symbolism, as he explained it, seemed so convincing that I could but wonder at the variety of explanations archaeologists give to it. From the jewelled splendour of those dark tombs we came forth into the brightness of an April day and a blue sky, broken by hurrying white clouds: the fields through which we walked were gay with red poppies: our guide unlocked the door leading to another tomb and we would descend again to behold the joyous scenes with which the Etruscans, of such a distant world, chose to decorate the homes of their dead.   [RC 123]

After visiting more Etruscan museums and tombs at Vulci and Volterra, Lawrence returned to the Villa Mirenda on 11 April. The next day he wrote:

But I was really happy looking at Etruscan tombs by the coast north of Rome – Cerveteri, Tarquinia etc. No rush there! Even the ass brays slowly and leisurely, and the tombs are far more twinkling and alive than the houses of men.   [C 29]

296

Two days later he wrote to his mother-in-law:

> The Etruscan tombs are very interesting and so nice and lovable. They were a living, fresh, jolly people, lived their lives without wanting to dominate the lives of others. I am fond of my Etruscans – they had life in themselves, so they had no need to govern others. I want to write some sketches of these Etruscan places, not scientifically, but only as they are now and the impression they make. [CB III 137]

One might have expected Lawrence to throw himself into this work at once; but a fortnight later we find him writing to Kot that he has yet to begin these sketches [Q 311]. He had not, however, been idle, for in the interim he had written 'a story of the Resurrection – what sort of a man "rose up", after all that other pretty little experience' [EC 65].

Later Lawrence gave Earl Brewster a fuller account:

> I wrote a story of the Resurrection, where Jesus gets up and feels very sick about everything, and can't stand the old crowd any more – so cuts out – and as he heals up, he begins to find what an astonishing place the phenomenal world is, far more marvellous than any salvation or heaven – and thanks his stars he needn't have a 'mission' any more. It's called *The Escaped Cock*, from that toy in Volterra. [CL 975]

Lawrence later explained this incident in a note to the publisher Harry Crosby which accompanied the MS.:

> MS. of the story afterward called The Escaped Cock – Part I – written in the Villa Mirenda near Florence in 1927, Easter, & suggested by a little Easter toy of a cock escaping from a man, seen in a shop window – in Volterra the week before Easter – after looking at Etruscan tombs. [EC 136]

If Lawrence at this time was thinking of *Etruscan Places* as no more than a collection of impressionistic sketches, it is, perhaps, not surprising that he should be willing to set it aside in favour of imaginative work. His decision to do so is still less surprising when we realize the extent to which *The Escaped Cock* grew not only from the incident in Volterra, but from the whole Etruscan experience.

*

At college Lawrence read many rationalist texts, including Renan's *The Life of Jesus*, and lost his faith in the divinity of Christ.[2] According to Jessie Chambers, he disliked Renan because 'It is Jesus according to the likeness of Ernest Renan' [PR 112]. Lawrence was probably thinking of passages such as that in which Renan comments on Christ's 'profound words': 'Render therefore unto Caesar the things that are Caesar's; and unto God the things that are God's':

Words of the most profound spirituality, and of marvellous justice, which established the separation of the spiritual from the temporal, and laid the foundation of true liberalism and true civilization!

[IL XVII 8478]

Lawrence must already have felt that it was just such a separation which made Christ, as he said many years later, 'profoundly, disastrously wrong' [CL 829]. But Renan's sympathetic account of Jesus in Jerusalem, a small-town provincial and lover of nature, always constrained by the big city and the reactionary establishment which was hypocritical, petty, deaf to his words, blind to his 'great moral grandeur', anxious to do him down, driving him into bitterness and 'perpetual self-assertion' [IL XVII 8474–6], sounds very like Jesus in the likeness of D. H. Lawrence, Lawrence in London.

Again and again from 1915 onwards, Lawrence was driven by his extremity to compare himself, directly or by implication, with Christ. On the last day of January 1915 he wrote to Lady Cynthia Asquith:

And now, I feel very sick and corpse-cold, too newly risen to share yet with anybody, having the smell of the grave in my nostrils, and a feel of grave clothes about me.

The War finished me: it was the spear through the side of all sorrows and hopes.   [L II 267–8]

It was during those 'five months in the tomb' that Lawrence grew a beard, which made him actually look like Christ for the rest of his life. In 1921 Achsah Brewster saw him as both Christ and Pan:

His mouth was curiously unmodelled like those the Greeks assigned to Pan and the satyrs. A trick of drooping the head pensively; his gentle expression; the dignity of his pose; the way the beard grew from his delicate, high cheek-bones; the fall of his hair over the forehead; all made him look like the Christ figure on many a carved crucifix.   [RC 241]

(How closely Lawrence had described those very crucifixes in *Twilight in Italy*.) In New Mexico the Indians called him 'Creeping Jesus' [CB III 104], and in Mexico they called 'Cristo! Cristo!' after him [LB 170].

Brett, too, saw in Lawrence the double image of Christ and Pan. Early in 1926, while staying with the Brewsters on Capri, she painted it:

The picture is of a crucifixion. The pale yellow Christ hangs on the Cross, against an orange sunset. With that final spurt of strength before death, he is staring at the vision of the figure in front of him. His eyes are visionary, his figure tense and aware. Before him, straddled across a rock, half curious, half smiling, is the figure of Pan, holding up a bunch of grapes to the dying Christ: a dark, reddish-gold figure with horns and hoofs. The heads of Pan and Christ are both your head. Behind lies the sea. [288]

In March Lawrence visited Capri, and Brett showed him the picture:

'It's too like me,' you repeat abruptly. 'You will have to change it.' . . . 'It is you,' I say. 'Perhaps,' you answer grimly. [288]

Brett's perception and its graphic expression clearly struck home and troubled Lawrence deeply. He would have liked to deny the identification with Christ. Only five months earlier he had written: 'Jesus becomes more *unsympatisch* to me, the longer I live: crosses and nails and tears and all that stuff! I think he showed us into a nice *cul de sac*' [CL 861]. In *The Plumed Serpent* he had shown the deposition of Christ in Mexico, to be replaced by the resurrected Quetzalcoatl, the plumed serpent god, who had thrown himself, phoenix-like, into a volcano when Christ came to Mexico, and so ascended in smoke to the place behind the sun where the gods live, there to sleep the great sleep of regeneration until his cycle should come round. Now the malevolent dragon of the Aztecs is reborn as a man of great stature, dark and bearded, who rises naked from a lake. The Quetzalcoatl symbol is a snake with his tail in his mouth, the markings on his back forming the rays of the sun within which an eagle spreads his wings. This signifies the creative intercourse between the powers of the earth and those of the sky. The rituals of Quetzalcoatl centre on the coming of the rains, and the men of Quetzalcoatl call themselves Lords of the Two Ways, of heaven and earth, fire and water, day and night. Quetzalcoatl is also Lord of the Morning Star, because he stands between the day and the night, in the creative twilight, time of rebirth. His return is the return of Pan, who is also reputed to have died at the advent of Christ, or Lucifer in all his pristine brightness:

Lucifer is brighter now than tarnished Michael or shabby Gabriel. All things fall in their turn, now Michael goes down, and whispering Gabriel, and the Son of the Morning will laugh at them all. Yes, I am all for Lucifer, who is really the Morning Star. [NI 252]

To Don Ramon, the perpetrator of all this in the novel, Quetzalcoatl is 'the Quick of all beings and existence' [PS 290]; he is 'only the symbol of the best man may be, in the next days' [309].

As we have seen, Lawrence, on his return to Europe, was to change his ideas about 'the best man may be'. In January 1925 he had written to Brett: 'We are creatures of two halves, spiritual and sensual – and each half is as important as the other' [CL 828]. In her painting Brett showed Lawrence a truth-telling mirror, vividly embodying those words. Her insistence that Lawrence was both the faun-like Pan and the crucified Christ elicited a grim 'Perhaps'. A year later, when Lawrence painted his *Resurrection*, the face of the newly risen Christ is clearly his own.

*

Justifying the need for religious symbolism, Don Ramon says: 'A man's blood can't beat in the abstract' [PS 309]. The names of the gods will be different in every culture; what they symbolize will be much the same:

> So if I want Mexicans to learn the name of Quetzalcoatl, it is because I want them to speak with the tongues of their own blood. I wish the Teutonic world would once more think in terms of Thor and Wotan, and the tree Igdrasil. And I wish the Druidic world would see, honestly, that in the mistletoe is their mystery, and that they themselves are the Tuatha De Danaan, alive, but submerged. And a new Hermes should come back to the Mediterranean, and a new Ashtaroth to Tunis; and Mithras again to Persia, and Brahma unbroken to India, and the oldest of dragons to China. [285]

But when Lawrence spoke with the tongues of his own blood, or at least of his own inheritance, he spoke in the symbolism of the Judaeo-Christian tradition. When he first felt the need to formulate his own in some ways anti-Christian metaphysic, he knew no other. The incoherence of the Foreword to *Sons and Lovers* and the difficulty of 'Le Gai Savaire' are attributable partly to the fact that he felt obliged to reinterpret rather than reject Christian symbolism in order to make it fit his heterodox ideas.

Long after Lawrence had ceased to believe in Christianity, he still needed its potent symbolism as a means of understanding himself in relation to the Whole. In December 1914 he wrote:

> The Crucifix, and Christ, are only symbols. They do not mean a man who suffered his life out as I suffer mine. They mean a moment in the history of my soul, if I must be personal. [L II 248]

Of all the Christian symbols, the one which meant most to Lawrence at this time was the Resurrection. He felt that the greatest mistake the Christian church had made was to attach so much importance to the Crucifixion and so little to the Resurrection. Christianity had become so otherworldly and hostile to the life of the body that it seemed to find the idea of the resurrection of the flesh an embarrassment:

> In the mediaeval period, Christianity did *not* insist on the Cross: but on the Resurrection: churches were built to the glorious hope of resurrection.

Now we think we are very great, whilst we enumerate the smarts of the Crucifixion. We are too mean to get any further . . .

But Christianity should teach us now, that after our Crucifixion, and the darkness of the tomb, we shall rise again in the flesh, you, I, as we are today, resurrected in the bodies, and acknowledging the Father, and glorying in his power, like Job. [248–9]

Lawrence is, of course, using these terms symbolically. What he understands by Crucifixion is what we should call an ego-death, and by Resurrection, the psychic reintegration which follows it. In the following month, January 1915, Lawrence wrote to Forster:

I do feel every man must have the devil of a struggle before he can have stuffed himself full enough to have satisfied all his immediate needs, and can give up, cease, and withdraw himself, yield himself up to his metamorphosis, his crucifixion, and so come to his new issuing, his wings, his resurrection, his whole flesh shining like a mote in the sunshine, fulfilled and now taking part in the fulfilment of the Whole. [266]

It was about this time that Lawrence reached the end of the tenth chapter of *The Rainbow*. He is discussing what Easter meant to the Brangwen children, but the subject of resurrection is so important to him that he cannot resist embarking on a brief essay or prose poem which is a remarkable synopsis of the story he was to begin twelve years later. I give the passage in full:

For from the grave, after the passion and the trial of anguish, the body rose torn and chill and colourless. Did not Christ say 'Mary!' and when she turned with outstretched hands to him, did he not hasten to add 'Touch me not; for I am not yet ascended to my father.'

Then how could the hands rejoice, or the heart be glad, seeing themselves repulsed. Alas, for the resurrection of the dead body! Alas, for the wavering, glimmering appearance of the risen Christ. Alas, for the Ascension into heaven, which is a shadow within death, a complete passing away.

Alas, that so soon the drama is over; that life is ended at thirty-three; that the half of the year of the soul is cold and historiless! Alas, that a risen Christ has no place with us! Alas, that the memory of the passion of Sorrow and Death and the Grave holds triumph over the pale fact of Resurrection!

But why? Why shall I not rise with my body whole and perfect, shining with strong life? Why, when Mary says: Rabboni, shall I not take her in my arms and kiss her and hold her to my breast? Why is the risen body deadly, and abhorrent with wounds?

The Resurrection is to life, not to death. Shall I not see those who have risen again walk here among men perfect in body and spirit, whole and glad in the flesh, living in the flesh, loving in the flesh, begetting children in the flesh, arrived at last to wholeness, perfect without scar or blemish, healthy without fear of ill-health? Is this not the period of manhood and joy and fulfilment, after the Resurrection? Who shall be shadowed by Death and the Cross, being risen, and who shall fear the mystic, perfect flesh that belongs to heaven?

Can I not, then, walk this earth in gladness, being risen from sorrow? Can I not eat with my brother happily, and with joy kiss my beloved, after my resurrection, celebrate my marriage in the flesh with feastings, go about my business eagerly, in the joy of my fellows? Is heaven impatient for me, and bitter against this earth, that I should hurry off, or that I should linger pale and untouched? Is the flesh which was crucified become as poison to the crowds in the street, or is it as a strong gladness and hope to them, as the first flower blossoming out of the earth's humus? [R 326–7]

Six months later, after reading Burnet's *Early Greek Philosophy*, Lawrence made his resolution to come 'out of the Christian Camp' [L II 367], and we hear little more of Christ for several years. At the end of 1915, Lawrence's reading of Frazer made available to him an older tradition of resurrection symbolism which had none of Christianity's bitterness against the earth and fear of the flesh. Christ is subsumed in the larger tradition of torn and regenerated fertility gods. Insofar as, within that tradition, it is the underworld rather than the tomb in which the exiled or dormant god spends his period of absence from the earth, Lucifer was a better candidate than Christ for the role. 'When Jesus was born, the spirits wailed round the Mediterranean: *Pan is dead. Great Pan is dead*' [CL 768]. Lucifer is only the Christian repudiation of the horned fertility god.

Early in January 1925, while in the middle of the final version of *The Plumed Serpent*, Lawrence wrote his essay 'Resurrection'. It repeats the novel's assertion that the Christian era is over:

It is time for the Lord in us to arise. With the stigmata healed up, and the eyes full open. Rise as the Lord. No longer the man of Sorrows. The Crucified uncrucified. The Crown of Thorns removed, and the tongues of fire round the brows. The Risen Lord. [P 737]

Lawrence did a great deal of walking on his Etruscan tour. According to Earl Brewster, these were the last long walks he was ever strong enough to make. He arrived back at the Mirenda tired out. Among his accumulated mail was a letter from Mabel Luhan complaining about the change of life. Lawrence replied four days later, on Good Friday:

Myself, I'm in just the same way – just simply suffering from a change of life, and a queer sort of recoil, as if one's whole soul were drawing back from connection with everything. This is the day they put Jesus in the tomb – and really, those three days in the tomb begin to have a terrible significance and reality to me. And the resurrection is an unsatisfactory business – just *noli me tangere* and no more. [LT 326]

Behind this change in Lawrence and this reidentification with Christ it is not hard to see the dawning knowledge in his heart of hearts that he was entering the last phase of his life, that death, real not symbolic death, was not far ahead of him, and that he must prepare his soul to meet it.

By one of those remarkable coincidences which frequently confirmed Lawrence's belief that there is no such thing as an accident, his accumulated mail also contained a parcel from Koteliansky containing Kot's new translation of V. V. Rozanov's *Solitaria*. Lawrence, too tired to embark on any major work, read it at once, and was so excited by it that he immediately wrote a brief review. *Solitaria* itself did not interest him much. But Kot had also included twenty pages of extracts from Rozanov's *The Apocalypse of Our Times*, and that was a different matter. Here, it seemed to Lawrence, 'Rozanov has more or less recovered the genuine pagan vision, the phallic vision, and with those eyes he looks, in amazement and consternation, on the mess of Christianity':

> He is the first [Russian] to see that immortality is in the vividness of life, not in the loss of life. The butterfly becomes a whole revelation to him: and to us. When Rozanov is wholly awake, and a new man, a risen man, the living and resurrected pagan, then he is a great man and a great seer, and perhaps, as he says himself, the first Russian to emerge. [P 369]

Lawrence does not attempt, here, to explain to us what Rozanov's butterfly reveals: it needed both *The Escaped Cock* and *Etruscan Places* to make that 'whole revelation' his own. But the immediate reference has been explained by George Zytaruk.[3] Rozanov is discussing with two friends, Kapterev, a naturalist, and Florensky, a priest, the question 'in a caterpillar, chrysalis, and butterfly – which is the "I"?' Florensky quotes Aristotle: 'the soul is the intelechy of the body'. Rozanov continues:

> Then it became suddenly clear to me – from Florensky's answer (and what else could Florensky have said, if not this?) – that the 'butterfly' is *really*, mysteriously, and metaphysically, the soul of the caterpillar and chrysalis. Thus happened this, cosmogonically overwhelming, discovery ... Kapterev mused for a while and said: Observations show that in a caterpillar wrapped up in a cocoon and appearing as though dead, there actually begins after this a reconstruction of the tissues of the body. So that it does not only appear dead, but actually dies ... And if you were to pierce the caterpillar, say, with a pin, then no butterfly will come out of it, nothing will come out of it, and the grave will remain a grave, and the body will not 'come to life again'.

Rozanov goes on to speculate that 'the burial ritual of the Egyptians sprang from imitating the phases of the caterpillar'. Thus Rozanov gave Lawrence the final clue he needed to conceive *The Escaped Cock*, and to transform *Etruscan Places* into so much more than a collection of light travel sketches.

So we see, at Easter 1927, the confluence of several streams in Lawrence's life and thought, the sudden concurrence of several potent images. His own change of life and nearness to death force him to seek a less metaphorical concept of resurrection than hitherto, a concept which would allow him to confront death with gladness and to reconcile within himself the figures of Christ and Pan. The dolphins watched by Gethin Day merge with those still leaping gaily in the frescoes of Tarquinia. The white cock Moses, symbol of assertive life with the voice of the Holy Ghost, merges with the escaping cock in the shop window in Volterra. Earl Brewster remembered that rooster as escaping from an egg, not a man. Whether or not, the egg, the Easter egg, was a symbol which had struck Lawrence particularly in the tombs. The man who has died 'holds up the egg of resurrection, within which the germ sleeps as the soul sleeps in the tomb, before it breaks the shell and emerges again' [MM 142]. The image of the egg merges with that of the chrysalis, the tomb of the caterpillar, which is also the womb from which the butterfly will emerge. It is as though these themes and images were only latent, unfertilized, until they came together. The emergence of *The Escaped Cock* is itself an intelechy – 'a condition in which a potentiality has become an actuality' [*OED*].

It did not, however, emerge all at once. The first version was apparently conceived as a complete short story. It was published as such in *The Forum* in February 1928. This corresponds to Part I of the final version.

*

The cock in the story is tied by the leg. 'Body, soul, and spirit were tied by that string. Underneath, however, the life in him was grimly unbroken' [EC 104]. He represents the dauntless life-urge – 'resplendent with arched and orange neck by the time the fig trees were letting out leaves from their end-tips' – denied its full expression. He crows for the kingdom, power and glory which are his birthright. His crow wakes the man who had died. He crows from the world the man had denied, as he had denied 'the greater life of the body':

> The world, the same as ever, the natural world, thronging with greenness, a nightingale singing winsomely, wistfully, coaxingly calling from the bushes beside a runnel of water, in the world, the natural world of morning and evening, forever undying, from which he had died. [106]

The cock, herald of a new day, is already risen. The man, recognizing in the cock 'the assertion of life, the loud outcry of the cock's petty triumph in life', must rediscover and re-establish his connection with the phenomenal world, must learn to ride the 'wave of life of which the bird was the crest' [109].

The cock justifies its prominence in the story in these terms. But it is, perhaps, surprising that Lawrence wished to retain the title *The Escaped Cock* even after he had added the longer and more important second part in which the cock does not appear. Also we may wonder why a toy of a rooster escaping from a man should suggest to Lawrence a story of the Crucifixion. And what does the man mean when, asked why he carries a cock, he replies: 'I am a healer, and the bird hath virtue' [33]?

Lawrence would be familiar, from Frazer, with the cock as corn-spirit. Frazer tells of several rituals where a live cock, associated with the last sheaf to be gathered, is released, chased, caught and sacrificed:

> By keeping its feathers till spring, then mixing them with the seed-corn taken from the very sheaf in which the bird had been bound, and scattering the feathers together with the seed over the field, the identity of the bird with the corn is again emphasised, and its quickening and fertilizing power, as an embodiment of the corn-spirit, is intimated in the plainest manner. Thus the corn-spirit, in the form of a cock, is killed at harvest, but rises to fresh life and activity in spring.   [GB 594]

The word 'virtue' means, no doubt, just this 'quickening and fertilizing power'.

Robert Graves tells us that 'the creation of the world, according to the Orphics, resulted from the sexual act performed between the Great Goddess and the World-Snake Ophion':

> The Goddess then laid the world-egg, which contained infinite potentiality but which was nothing in itself until it was split open by the Demiurge. The Demiurge was Helios, the Sun, with whom the Orphics identified the God Apollo – which was natural, because the Sun does hatch snakes' eggs – and the hatching-out of the world was celebrated each year at the Spring festival of the Sun . . . Since the cock was the Orphic bird of resurrection, sacred to Apollo's son Aesculapius the healer, hens' eggs took the place of snakes' in the later Druidic mysteries and were coloured scarlet in the Sun's honour; and became Easter eggs.   [WG 248–9]

The image of a healer with a cock under his arm certainly suggests Aesculapius. Perhaps Lawrence knew the story of Aesculapius, newborn, abandoned on a mountain and found there by a peasant who proposes to take him home, but, being afraid of the radiance which suggests that the child might be divine, dare not do so. The child indeed grew up to be a remarkable physician, not only curing the sick but raising the dead, became a god, was himself killed and resurrected, his image set among the stars holding a serpent.

The man's questioners assume that he is a pagan: 'You are not a believer?' He replies, mocking their 'narrow belief': 'Yea! I believe the bird is full of life and virtue' [EC 33]. It is as though, as a stage in his transformation into Osiris, the man who had died becomes Aesculapius, the divine but humane Saviour-Healer of the Greeks.[4]

But Lawrence, at this first attempt, was not able to take his hero convincingly beyond his 'noli me tangere'. His disgust with other men is expressed much more strongly than in the final version:

I cannot touch my fellow men because they smell of greed and fear. It is fear of death that hampers them. Why don't they die, to be rid of their staleness and their littleness, covered up as they are and gnawed by the weariness of their greed and the compulsion of their fear?   [116–17]

So strong is this repulsion that we can hardly imagine him following his calling as a physician. His hope of recovering touch is vague and tentative: 'Perhaps within the inner air I shall meet other men, perhaps women, and we shall be in touch'. What he means by the 'inner air' is close to what Gethin Day meant by the Greater Day, but much less adequately rendered. It is, we are told, 'within the Father', and the Father is the 'essential body' of the phenomenal world, which presumably contains the outer air also. The story ends, as in the final version, with an affirmation that the phenomenal world 'is a vast complexity of wonders', and the 'last question': 'From what, and to what, could this infinite whirl be saved?' [120]. But the question hardly disposes of his earlier perception of that whirl as an absurdity:

And this mad insistence of chaotic life, everything insisting against everything else, was repellent to the man who had died. He looked on, relieved that it was no longer his affair.   [110]

The hero of this version is very much the Jesus of Lawrence's *Resurrection* painting, Jesus 'stepping up, rather grey in the face, from the tomb'. In his more misanthropic moments, he is not unlike Henry the Hermit, the protagonist of 'The Man Who Was Through with the World', probably written in May. On 12 April Lawrence had written: 'I only want to retire away into the hills here, and be a hermit' [C 30]. And on 19 May:

I feel like turning hermit and hiding away the rest of my days away from everybody. But I suppose it is a phase, a sort of psychic change of life many men go through after forty. I wish it would hurry up and get over.

[EL 157]

'The Man Who Was Through with the World' was probably an attempt to speed the process by satirizing the hermit life. Without the clearly satirical tone of the context we should hardly know how to take Henry's misanthropy:

The hermit always hurried back to his hermitage in disgust. Absence from his fellow-men did not make him love them any more. On the contrary, they seemed more repulsive and smelly, when he came among them, after his isolation among the chestnut trees, and their weird sort of greed about money, tiny sums of money, made them seem like a plague of caterpillars to him. 'People badly need to have souls, to hatch out with wings after death,' he thought to himself, 'for they really are repulsive pale grubs in this life.' [POS 151]

It seems that Henry had also been reading Rozanov.

The purpose of the hermit life, according to Earl Brewster, a Buddhist, would have been to arrive at holiness by meditation. But Henry cannot get beyond the limits of his own body:

He didn't mind not being able to meditate nor to concentrate, and not having any holiness to bless himself with. The sun on his body seemed to do all the meditating and concentrating he needed. [152]

Perhaps Brewster had also introduced Lawrence to the Hindu *Srimad Bhagavadgita*, where he would have read:

He who, restraining the organs of action, sits revolving in the mind the objects of the senses, he, of deluded understanding, is called a hypocrite.

The satire worked as auto-therapy, for on 28 May Lawrence wrote to Brewster:

I shall go out into the world again, to kick it and stub my toes. It's no good my thinking of retreat: I rouse up, and feel I don't want to. My business is a fight, and I've got to keep it up. [CL 980]

This is the spirit of Part II of *The Escaped Cock*, though Lawrence was not to begin that for over a year.

*

After finishing the first version of *The Escaped Cock*, Lawrence still did not begin *Etruscan Places*. He wrote next the essay 'Making Love to Music'. After expounding the theory that 'we are such stuff as our grandmothers' dreams were made on, and our little life is rounded by a band' [P 162], he asks what the modern young woman, condemned by her grandmother's dream to make love to

music, dreams of. She dreams, he answers ('the thought occurred
to me suddenly when I was looking at the remains of paintings
on the walls of Etruscan tombs at Tarquinia'), of rediscovering
the Etruscan secret, though she may never have heard of the
Etruscans, of becoming herself one of those gaily dancing Etruscan
women:

> The Etruscan young woman is going gaily at it, after two thousand five
> hundred years. She is not making love to music, nor is the dark-limbed
> youth, her partner. She is just dancing her very soul into existence, having
> made an offering on one hand to the lively phallus of man, on the other
> hand, to the shut womb-symbol of woman, and put herself on real good
> terms with both of them. So she is quite serene, and dancing herself as a
> very fountain of motion and of life, the young man opposite her dancing
> himself the same, in contrast and balance, with just the double flute to
> whistle round their naked heels.   [166]

On 27 April Lawrence wrote to Kot: 'I liked my trip to Cerveteri
and Tarquinia and Vulci so much, I'd like to jot them down while
they are fresh' [Q 311]. Within the next day or two he began to do
so, but almost immediately broke off to write more essays, including 'Flowery Tuscany'. In all of these it is evident that what Lawrence is thinking about is the ways in which the Etruscan spirit has
lived on in Italy:

> Italy today is far more Etruscan in its pulse than Roman; and will always
> be so. The Etruscan element is like the grass of the field and the sprouting
> of corn, in Italy: it will always be so.   [MM 126]

In 'Flowery Tuscany' he sees the very landscape of Italy as a manifestation of the Etruscan spirit:

> Man *can* live on the earth and by the earth. It has been done here, on all
> these sculptured hills and softly, sensitively terraced slopes.   [P 46]

He identifies the 'Etruscan element' as essentially non-tragic, for
tragedy is a resistance, typically Northern, to the passing of things.
Hardy's Little Father Time is typical of the Northern consciousness:
flowers upset him because he cannot look at them without thinking
that they will all be withered in a few days. But in a permanently
sunny climate, such thoughts become morbid:

> Where are the little yellow aconites of eight weeks ago? I neither know
> nor care. They were sunny and the sun shines, and sunniness means
> change, and petals passing and coming. The winter aconites sunnily came
> and sunnily went. What more? The sun always shines. It is our fault if we
> don't think so.   [58]

The Etruscans themselves lived like flowers, and apparently died like them – totally without morbidity. Their little wooden temples were 'small, dainty, fragile, and evanescent as flowers' [MM 122].

In May Lawrence was not well. It was 'lazy weather' and 'not a working season' [MS 88]. He pottered about with stories and other 'trifles'. By the end of the month he had done only the first three Etruscan essays. It took him until the last week in June to finish them, so that the essay on Volterra was written some ten weeks after the actual visit – and without notes.

On 25 June Lawrence wrote to Earl Brewster:

> One day we will really go after more Etruscans together. Meanwhile I think I shall go to Arezzo and Cortona, Chiusi, Orvieto, Perugia with Frieda, towards the end of next week. I'd like to do those places before we leave. With Cerveteri and Tarquinia, Vulci and Volterra, that makes nine of the great cities – the twelve. – But it leaves a whole bookful of little places – Veii, Civita Castellana, Norchia, Vetulonia, Cosa, Populonia, Bieda – we might do those, and make a second vol. – after. [CL 986]

A few days before the planned excursion with Frieda, Lawrence bathed in the sea at Forte dei Marmi and brought on a bronchial haemorrhage. The trip had to be abandoned. For Lawrence the completion of the book was contin████ upon seeing those other sites. He continued to plan the trip f█████other two years, but it was never made, and so the book was never published in his lifetime, though four of the essays appeared in *Travel* and *World Today*.

*

It was a great temptation to Lawrence to interpret the Etruscan remains to fit his dream. He ignored some of the facts he perfectly well knew, for example, that the Etruscans were a colonizing and trading people who used slave labour in the mines of Populonia and did not spend their whole lives dancing and fluting. But on the whole his scholarship is sound, and many of his new insights have been verified by subsequent scholarship. The books he had read had no answers to the questions which really interest us about the Etruscans – the meaning of their language, their art, their religious symbols and rituals, the quality of their daily lives. Lawrence felt free to interpret the surviving artifacts imaginatively, resurrecting a race of which he felt himself to be a lost survivor. His long pilgrimage brought him at last to these tombs, and in them he found the vivid human life he had been seeking, a life of perfect awareness and relatedness, without the crippling dualism of body versus spirit, human versus non-human, life versus death. The whole Etruscan ambience was balm to his soul:

There is a simplicity, combined with a most peculiar, free-breasted naturalness and spontaneity, in the shapes and movements of the underworld walls and spaces, that at once reassures the spirit . . . They leave the breast breathing freely and pleasantly, with a certain fullness of life. Even the tombs. And that is the true Etruscan quality: ease, naturalness, and an abundance of life, no need to force the mind or the soul in any direction.   [MM 108–9]

The imagery of the breast 'breathing freely and pleasantly' suggests a Lawrence cured of his consumption, as if that were a symptom of the disease of modern life, the body's protest against its deprivation and desacralization: 'it is our being cut off that is our ailment, and out of this ailment everything bad arises' [CL 993].

During the war Lawrence had begun to formulate a theory that the real is an inner, not an outer reality; that truth resides in the human spirit rather than in facts. But the gap between life as it is and life as it should be was painfully wide. His assertion that his dreams were truer than facts would not prevent those dreams being dismissed by others as merely escapist or wishful. He strove to bridge that gap between what is and what should be by writing always of what *could* be, or what had been and therefore might be again. Before he went to America, he had been obliged to express his dream in the symbolism of myth, including the myth of Eden or the Golden Age. Half-way between such myths and our world is the ancient world at the point where it emerges into history and bequeaths us the evidence of its artifacts. It was an important breakthrough for Lawrence when he found himself able to claim that life, in Europe, was once the incarnation of his dream. We can test Lawrence's recreation of the life of the Etruscans against our own response to their remains. He articulates our own spontaneous response to them. After reading Lawrence's interpretation of them, no other seems tenable. It really does seem, as we descend into the Etruscan underworld, that it is 'more real than the above day of the afternoon' [MM 138].

The most striking characteristic of the Etruscans, for Lawrence, was their 'profound belief in life, acceptance of life'. And this involved also an acceptance of death, with no heaven or hell:

For the life on earth was so good, the life below could but be a continuance of it.   [134]

This belief in life was so profound as to constitute a religion, a religion the very opposite of the life-denying puritanism of Lawrence's childhood:

As the pagan old writer says: 'For no part of us nor of our bodies shall be, which doth not feel religion: and let there be no lack of singing for the soul, no lack of leaping and of dancing for the knees and heart; for all these know the gods.' [144]

It is the culmination of what Rupert Birkin called 'the old effort at serious living', where seriousness has nothing to do with moral intensity, but is an essential element in gaiety – a total commitment to life in the body and in this world:

Behind all the Etruscan liveliness was a religion of life, which the chief men were seriously responsible for. Behind all the dancing was a vision, and even a science of life, a conception of the universe and man's place in the universe which made men live to the depth of their capacity. To the Etruscan all was alive; the whole universe lived; and the business of man was himself to live amid it all. He had to draw life into himself, out of the wandering huge vitalities of the world. The cosmos was alive, like a vast creature. The whole thing breathed and stirred. [146–7]

Modern science is at last catching up with the simple fact, self-evident to pagan man, that the universe can only be understood and lived in when it is seen to be 'a single aliveness with a single soul'.

Biochemistry tells us that each cell contains all the information necessary to reconstitute the entire organism. Pagan thought knew that the whole could always be inferred from any of its parts, that there was no distinction between macrocosm and microcosm, inner and outer, above and below, physical and metaphysical. Thus there was nothing of childish, primitive superstition in the discipline of the augur, who looked for signs in the flights of birds, or the haruspex, who examined entrails for portents:

In their flight the suddenly roused birds, or the steady, far-coming birds, moved wrapped in a deeper consciousness, in the complex destiny of all things. And since all things corresponded in the ancient world, and man's bosom mirrored itself in the bosom of the sky, or *vice versa*, the birds were flying to a portentous goal, in the man's breast who watched, as well as flying their own way in the bosom of the sky. If the augur could see the birds flying *in his heart*, then he would know which way destiny too was flying for him . . .

Prayer, or thought, or studying the stars, or watching the flight of birds, or studying the entrails of the sacrifice, it is all the same process, ultimately: of divination. All it depends on is the amount of *true*, sincere, religious concentration you can bring to bear on your object. An act of pure attention, if you are capable of it, will bring its own answer. And you choose that object to concentrate upon which will best focus your consciousness. Every real discovery made, every serious and significant decision ever reached, was reached and made by divination. The soul stirs, and makes an act of pure attention, and that is a discovery.

The science of the augur and the haruspex was not so foolish as our modern science of political economy. If the hot liver of the victim cleared the soul of the haruspex, and made him capable of that ultimate inward attention, which alone tells us the last thing we need to know, then why quarrel with the haruspex? To him, the universe was alive, and in quivering *rapport*. To him, the blood was conscious: he thought with his heart. [152–3]

This is also, clearly, an account of the operation of the creative imagination, and of the unified sensibility which alone is capable of real thinking, for thought, as Lawrence was later to define it, is 'a man in his wholeness, wholly attending'.

The old knowledge has survived as poetic symbolism: 'We can know the living world only symbolically' [168]. This 'old Etruscan symbolic thought' is what Blake called 'fourfold vision'. It differs from our ordinary, exclusively rational, thinking ('single vision and Newton's sleep') by releasing the Energies, opening up the circuits of vitality ('twofold vision'), by recapturing innocence on the far side of experience ('threefold vision'), and by the resacralization of the world, the recognition that *everything* is miraculous, 'everything that lives is holy' ('fourfold vision').

Lawrence's terminology for these things is very like that of the Existentialists. In the essay on Galsworthy, almost the last thing Lawrence wrote before making his Etruscan trip, he had written:

While a man remains a man, a true human individual, there is at the core of him a certain innocence or naïveté which defies all analysis, and which you cannot bargain with, you can only deal with it, in good faith, from your own corresponding innocence or naïveté. . . .

It is the essential innocence and naïveté of the human being, the sense of being at one with the great universe-continuum of space-time-life, which is vivid in a great man, and a pure nuclear spark in every man who is still free. [STH 210–11]

It is the openness of the child to the world:

The ancients saw, consciously, as children now see unconsciously, the everlasting *wonder* in things . . . They were like children: but they had the force, the power and the sensual *knowledge* of true adults. They had a world of valuable knowledge, which is utterly lost to us. Where they were true adults, we are children; and vice versa. [MM 168]

Blake used Newton and Locke as representatives of single vision. Lawrence uses Socrates:

Later, when scepticism came over all the civilized world, as it did after Socrates, the Etruscan religion began to die, Greeks and Greek rationalism flooded in, and Greek stories more or less took the place of the old Etruscan symbolic thought. [150]

To allow one's being to be reduced to single vision is to live in bad faith, or, in Lawrence's phrase, with impure heart:

> But all attempt at divination, even prayer and reason and research itself, lapses into jugglery when the heart loses its purity. In the impurity of his heart, Socrates often juggled logic unpleasantly. [154]

This murder of 'symbolic thought' was fatal not only for the Etruscans, but condemned Western civilization to over two thousand years of increasingly blasphemous living:

> The old religion of the profound attempt of man to harmonize himself with nature, and hold his own and come to flower in the great seething of life, changed with the Greeks and Romans into a desire to resist nature, to produce a mental cunning and a mechanical force that would outwit Nature and chain her down completely, completely, till at last there should be nothing free in nature at all, all should be controlled, domesticated, put to man's meaner uses. [174]

Aldous Huxley was one of Lawrence's most sympathetic critics, but in his review of *Etruscan Places*[5] he completely misunderstood what the Etruscans meant to Lawrence:

> For the sake of the double flute and all that it stands for, he [Lawrence] was prepared to sacrifice most of the activities upon which, for the last two thousand years or thereabouts, humanity, at any rate in the West, has set the highest value. The philosophy and the practice of non-acceptance have made it possible for man to become, in some respects, more than human. But in the process he has had to sacrifice much of his former happiness; and while he has become spiritually and intellectually more, emotionally and physically he has, too often, degenerated and become less than human.

This would be an accurate enough account of Lawrence's position in, say, 1913. But it is a travesty of his position in 1927. The crude choice between the spiritual and intellectual on the one side and the emotional and physical on the other is no longer to be found in Lawrence's writings at this date. Nor is he searching for happiness – that is a desirable but not inevitable by-product of what he is seeking, which is wholeness. He wishes to reinstate the body and its emotions not because he values it higher than the life of the spirit and of consciousness, but because he now knows that to pursue the life of the spirit or of the mind in opposition to the life of the body and to Nature, is to alienate, stultify or pervert the spirit and to turn the mind into a sterile mechanism or juggling act. It is because they had a rich physical life that the Etruscans were able to have a rich spiritual life, or vice versa, since to distinguish between them at all is part of the Socratic sickness.

Lawrence's effort, in these last years, is to respiritualize the

world. The Etruscans confirmed for him what he had always
known, that it is futile hubristic perversity to seek the life of the
spirit apart from the given world; for God is in everything that lives
and nowhere else. The Etruscans had their symbol for this divine
spark at the centre, the patera or mundum:

It stands for the plasm, also, of the living cell, with its nucleus, which is
the indivisible God of the beginning, and which remains alive and unbroken to the end, the eternal quick of all things, which yet divides and sub-
divides, so that it becomes the sun of the firmament and the lotus of the
waters under the earth, and the rose of all existence upon the earth: and
the sun maintains its own quick, unbroken for ever; and there is a living
quick of the sea, and of all the waters; and every living created thing has
its own unfailing quick.   [127]

All our modern knowledge is knowledge of the self-apart-from-
God. In his last poems and many other late writings Lawrence seeks
and finds the assurance that he is in the hands of the unknown
God, in death as in life.

                                        *

There remained, of course, a yawning gap between the life of the
Etruscans and Lawrence's life in 1927. In July he wrote to Dr Trigant
Burrow complaining 'What ails me is the absolute frustration of
my primeval societal instinct . . . I think societal instinct much
deeper than sex instinct – and societal repression much more dev-
astating' [CL 989–90]. Lawrence is now thinking of resurrection
specifically as the re-establishing of touch, not only with the 'phenomenal world', but, even more urgently, with one's fellow men.
In Burrow he had met someone even more utopian than himself:

And then there will *never* be a millennium. There will *never* be a 'true
societal flow' – all things are relative. Men were never, in the past, fully
societal – and they never will be in the future. But more so, more than now.
Now is the time between Good Friday and Easter. We're absolutely in the
tomb.   [993]

The same day, Lawrence reviewed Burrow's book *The Social Basis
of Consciousness*. How apt was Burrow's analysis to his own condition:

Helplessly he must strive for more consciousness, which means, also, a
more intensified aloneness, or individuality; and at the same time he has
a horror of his own aloneness, and a blind, dim yearning for the old
togetherness of the far past, what Dr Burrow calls the preconscious state . . .
Men must get back into *touch*. And to do so they must forfeit the vanity
and the *noli me tangere* of their own absoluteness.   [P 379, 382]

Lawrence's own immediate effort to 'utterly break the present great picture of a normal humanity: shatter that mirror in which we all live grimacing: and fall again into true relatedness' was the unfinished and untitled story which I have called 'A Dream of Life'.

Here Lawrence's quest reveals itself as essentially shamanistic. He sees his function as an artist as a healing function on behalf of his people. The purpose of his pilgrimage is to discover healing truths and then make them available to his people through his writing. 'A Dream of Life' is a vision of what the community which bore him would be like once healed and whole. The Etruscans were not by any means primitives, nor Arcadian shepherds and shepherdesses, but citizens in a sophisticated manufacturing as well as agricultural community. The lovely hill towns of Etruria reminded him of what Eastwood and the mining countryside might have been, might still be if everything could be swept away and a new start made, building up from the contours of the land not just villages, but splendid cities 'which would make us unite in pride and dignity in the bigger gesture of the citizen, not the cottager' and which would fulfil the 'instinct of community' [139].

On his last visit home, a year previously, Lawrence had detected 'a queer, odd sort of potentiality in the people, especially the common people. One feels in them some odd, unaccustomed sort of plasm twinkling and nascent. They are not finished' [CL 933]. Now he sought to combine the best potentialities of his own people with those elements he most admired in the Etruscan way of life.

In the story, he visits a quarry, a favourite haunt of his when a boy, and sees a landslide, which discloses a crevice of Blue John spar. He creeps into this 'womb of quartz', falls asleep, and dreams that he wakes a thousand years hence. The local people find him and take him to their city. Later he watches their evening dance, which echoes the Etruscan dance – 'a dance that surges from within, like a current in the sea' [MM 146] – and also the movements of Gethin Day's porpoises, as though Lawrence were now attempting to answer Gethin Day's question: 'What civilization will bring us to such a pitch of swift laughing togetherness, as these fish have reached?' [STM 222]:

> The dance swept into swifter and swifter rhythm, with the most extraordinary incalculable unison. I do not believe there was any outside control of the dance. The thing happened by instinct, like the wheeling and flashing of a shoal of fish or of a flock of birds dipping and spreading in the sky . . . They were dancing the sun down, and dancing as birds wheel and dance, and fishes in shoals, controlled by some strange unanimous instinct. It was at once terrifying and magnificent, I wanted to die, so as not to see

it, and I wanted to rush down, to be one of them. To be a drop in that wave
of life.   [P 832; POS 175]

It had seemed to the man at first that these people had realized the
fullest potential of human beings:

> That was the quality of all the people: an inner stillness and ease, like
> plants that come to flower and fruit. The individual was like a whole fruit,
> body and mind and spirit, without split.   [830; 173]

Why, then, should the dance be 'terrible'?

> I was afraid: afraid for myself. These people, it seemed to me, were not
> people, not human beings in my sense of the word. They had the stillness
> and the completeness of plants. And see how they could melt into one
> amazing instinctive thing, a human flock of motion.   [833; 177]

Much as he admires this degree of unison and completeness, Lawrence has to recognize that he is not finally very interested in people
who are as indistinguishable from each other as fishes or birds.

'A Dream of Life'* is clearly intended to be another resurrection
story. One of the men, perhaps a priest, says to the reborn man:

> You went to sleep, like a chrysalis: in one of the earth's little chrysalis
> wombs: and your clothes turned to dust, yet they left the buttons: and you
> woke up like a butterfly. Why are you afraid to be a butterfly that wakes
> up out of the dark for a little while, beautiful?   [836; 180]

At this point the manuscript breaks off. Perhaps Lawrence was not
yet able, or unable within this context of a community, to create his
'regenerate man'. The concept of individual freedom and development, the 'life-adventure', becomes meaningless within a perfect
undifferentiated community. The perfect community turns out to
be as much of a dead end for the novelist as the hermit life.

*

The whole of December and the first week of the new year were
spent writing the final version of *Lady Chatterley's Lover*. Here,
partly, no doubt, in response to the frank sexuality of the Etruscans,
partly to the phallic vision of Rozanov, he stressed as never before
the regenerative potential of that closest form of togetherness and
being in touch which is sexual love.

On 6 March Lawrence told Brett that he had had the idea of
adding 'perhaps another 5000 words' [EC 68] to 'The Escaped
Cock'. A few days later he described this to Curtis Brown as 'the
phallic second half I always intended to add to it' [H 709]. Most of
Lawrence's energies in the ensuing weeks went into seeing *Lady
Chatterley's Lover* through the press. He was finally free of it on 7

June. Since his haemorrhages the previous June, Lawrence's health had continued to decline, despite spending several weeks at high altitude in Switzerland in the winter. Now, accompanied by the Brewsters, the Lawrences headed for Switzerland again. The first three weeks they spent in the Grand Hotel, Chexbres-sur-Vevey. There, by the waters of Leman, Lawrence wrote the last works of fiction he was ever to write, the second half of *The Escaped Cock* and 'The Blue Moccasins'.

The continuing relationship with the Brewsters meant that Buddhism was a frequent topic of conversation. Lawrence's own attraction to the hermit life and ultimate rejection of it mirrors his attitude to Buddhism. In *Etruscan Places* Lawrence had coupled Christ and Buddha:

And before Buddha or Jesus spoke the nightingale sang, and long after the words of Jesus and Buddha are gone into oblivion the nightingale still will sing. Because it is neither preaching nor teaching nor commanding nor urging. It is just singing. And in the beginning was not a Word, but a chirrup. [MM 126]

In *The Escaped Cock*, as in *Etruscan Places*, the villains are the Romans, who understand nothing but power, who trample on everything they do not understand, and burden the earth with their monuments:

Because a fool kills a nightingale with a stone, is he therefore greater than the nightingale? Because the Roman took the life out of the Etruscan, was he therefore greater than the Etruscan? Not he! Rome fell, and the Roman phenomenon with it. Italy today is far more Etruscan in its pulse than Roman; and will always be so. [126]

The Etruscans, according to Lawrence, were a people who 'lived their own lives without wanting to dominate the lives of others' [CB III 137]. Both Jesus and Buddha had wanted to do that as much as the Romans, since saving is as much a form of domination as conquering. Both sought to lift man above greed and desire, yet themselves fell into the greed of the saviour. Lawrence had to rewrite 'The Escaped Cock' to make his resurrected man recognize and reject this form of greed also. He added this passage:

I have outlived my mission, and know no more of it. It is my triumph. I have survived the day and the death of my interference, and am still a man . . . The teacher and the saviour are dead in me; now I can go about my own business, into my own single life . . . My public life is over, the life of my conviction and my mission, the life of my self-importance . . . Now I can live without striving to sway others any more. For my reach ends in my finger-tips, and my stride is no longer than the ends of my toes. Yet I would embrace multitudes, I who have never truly embraced even one woman, or one man.   [EC 24]

He is discovering the Etruscan insouciance, as Lawrence had discovered it. (The essay 'Insouciance' was also written at Chexbres.) The Etruscans knew the gods 'in their very finger-tips'; they danced to the very ends of their fingers and toes; they entered into the flow of touch which comes not from pawing and laying hold, but 'from the middle of the human being' [MM 143–4]. In the revised version the man is much more aware that his earlier denial of the world, including the world of men, was a denial of the life-issue, leading to betrayal and crucifixion as inevitably as, in 'The Man Who Loved Islands', Cathcart's loathing 'with profound revulsion the whole of the animal creation' had led to his physical and spiritual dissolution.

The Escaped Cock is the story of how Christ became an Etruscan. It is also the story of how Buddha stood up. Earl Brewster tells us that Lawrence 'used often to say of the seated Buddha: "Oh I wish he would *stand up!*" ' [RC 49]. In November 1927, Lawrence had read a book on the Bagh Caves from which he learned that the original Buddha figure had been standing, and had replaced the *stupa*:

> Now it looks to me as if this *stupa* was just the monumental phallic symbol, like the Etruscan *'cippus'*. And the standing Buddha has still a phallic quality.   [CL 1018]

As Gerald Doherty has suggested, this gives Lawrence's deeply serious pun 'I am risen' a still wider reference.[6]

At the end of Part I the cock had fulfilled his role as pointer of the way. It remained to show the man moving beyond his *noli me tangere* and into his atonement with his own body, with the woman of his choice, and with the wider world. Rozanov's challenge had been to 'remove' Christ, with all the accretions of the centuries, from human consciousness. Knowing the impossibility of this, Lawrence sought rather to transform a caterpillar Christ into a butterfly Osiris. As he tries to restore the ur-Buddha, the phallic Buddha, so he tries to detach Christ from the life-denying Christianity of St Paul or St Augustine and to restore him to the company of the torn and resurrected fertility gods. Frazer had trod warily here, but allowed himself to comment that 'Christians and pagans alike were struck by the remarkable coincidence between the death and resurrection of their respective deities' [GB 475]. Lawrence completed the identification of Christ with Osiris: Christ is crucified, and resurrected as a young fertility god at the hands of the priestess of Isis in Search.

The fragmented man, fragmented, he now realizes, as much by his own theoretical rejection of his body as by the violation of it by others who shared his lack of respect for it, now recovers wholeness through the healing power of the woman, through reintegration with the eternal female, the human embodiment of the regenerative power of the earth itself, and the waters under the earth:

suddenly she put her breast against the wound in his left side, and her arms round him, folding over the wound in his right side, and she pressed him to her, in a power of living warmth, like in the folds of a river.

[EC 56]

She is the source, but she needs the missing Osiris, the risen man, the renewed sun of spring, before she can release her power in new life. Insofar as she is a single woman, her creative power issues in the resurrection of the man and the conceiving of his son and successor. Insofar as she is the goddess she is the oceanic mother of that whole phenomenal world the unrisen man of Part I had looked upon as an outsider:

The man who had died looked nakedly onto life, and saw a vast resoluteness everywhere flinging itself up in stormy or subtle wave-crests, foam-tips emerging out of the blue invisible, a black-and-orange cock, or the green flame tongues out of the extremes of the fig-tree. They came forth, these things and creatures of spring, glowing with desire and with assertion. They came like crests of foam, out of the blue flood of the invisible desire, out of the vast invisible sea of strength, and they came coloured and tangible, evanescent, yet deathless in their coming.   [21]

The exclusion of the man is emphasized by the inclusiveness, interconnectedness, of everything else, in a matrix of living relationships indicated largely by highly sexual metaphors: flowers, waves, tips, ends, crests, tongues. In Robert MacDonald's words:

The rich, complex imagery itself must demonstrate the cosmic harmony: the sun must be in the flower, the cock in the sun, the force that makes the tree bud must move in the crest of the wave. All must be different yet all must be one; image must vary yet repeat. The actual language of the story, far from being merely decorative, is part of the precise orchestration of the whole: rhetorical, poetic, but to a purpose, a necessary part of the creative achievement.   [DHLR 10 35–6]

The priestess of Isis is able to draw the man back into the unfallen state, 'nakedly breast to breast with the cosmos' [A 181]. Frazer speaks of Osiris 'diffusing the blessings of civilization and agriculture wherever he went'. But agriculture is impossible and civilization is not a blessing unless grounded in the fecundity of the goddess.

The story ends:

> The man who had died rowed slowly on, with the current, and laughed to himself: I have sowed the seed of my life and my resurrection, and put my touch forever upon the choice woman of this day, and I carry her perfume in my flesh like essence of roses. She is dear to me in the middle of my being. But the gold and flowing serpent is coiling up again, to sleep at the root of my tree. So let the boat carry me. Tomorrow is another day.   [EC 61]

This clear and serene prose brings together many strands. The sun sinks into the sea each day, but rises refreshed on the morrow. 'The suns come back in their seasons. And I shall come again.' The seed is 'the eternal quick of all things, which yet divides and sub-divides, so that it becomes the sun of the firmament and the lotus of the waters under the earth, and the rose of all existence upon the earth' [MM 127]. So the man, who is sun-god and corn-god, as he commits himself once more to the waters of potentiality, takes with him in the perfume of the woman the 'essence' of all existence upon the earth, and leaves her pregnant with himself, as Horus was believed to be the resurrected Osiris.

We find in *Etruscan Places* and *The Escaped Cock* a willingness new in Lawrence to associate resurrection with procreation. The phallus is no longer simply a bridge between the self and the not-self, the innermost and the outermost; its sacredness is specifically that it 'carries the fiery spark of procreation' [151]. This was very much the emphasis of Rozanov's phallic vision:

> It means then the 'world of the future age' is pre-eminently determined by 'copulation'; and then light is thrown on its irresistibility, on its insatiability, and – 'alas!' or 'not alas!' – on its 'sacredness,' and that it is a 'mystery' (the mystery of marriage). The further, the more discoveries. But it is obvious that in insects, cows, everywhere in the animal and vegetable world, and not only in man alone, it is a 'mystery, heavenly and sacred.' And, indeed, it is so, in its central point, *in copulation*. Then we understand 'the shame that attaches to sexual organs'; it is the 'life of the future age,' through which we enter into 'life beyond the grave,' into 'life of the future age.'[3]

The serpent had gradually accumulated more and more meanings for Lawrence. For the Etruscans 'the serpent represented the vivid powers of the inner earth, not only such powers as volcanic and earthquake, but the quick powers that run up the roots of plants and establish the great body of the tree, the tree of life, and run up the feet and legs of man, to establish the heart' [MM 207]. Lawrence knew that in yoga this power is called *kundalini*:

> A hero was a hero, in the great past, when he had conquered the hostile dragon, when he had the power of the dragon *with him* in his limbs and breast . . . the liberation within the self of the gleaming bright serpent of gold, golden fluid life within the body . . . For in his good aspect, the dragon is the great vivifier, the great enhancer of the whole universe . . . It is the same dragon which, according to the Hindus, coils quiescent at the base of the spine of a man, and unfolds sometimes lashing along the spinal way. [A 124–5]

The serpent is phallic because of its shape. It is a resurrection symbol because of its ability to emerge renewed from its own sloughed skin. It is the sacred symbol of Aesculapius. It is also central to some versions of the Osiris myth:

> The Goddess . . . had a lover who was alternatively the beneficent Serpent of Wisdom, and the beneficent Star of Life, her son . . . The Son, who was also called Lucifer or Phosphorus ('bringer of light') because as evening-star he led in the light of the Moon, was reborn every year, grew up as the year advanced, destroyed the Serpent, and won the Goddess's love. Her love destroyed him, but from his ashes was born another Serpent which, at Easter, laid the *glain* or red egg which she ate; so that the Son was reborn to her as a child once more. Osiris was a Star-son, and though after his death he looped himself around the world like a serpent, yet when his fifty-yard long phallus was carried in procession it was topped with a golden star; this stood for himself renewed as the Child Horus, son of Isis, who had been both his bride and his layer-out and was now his mother once again. [WG 387–8]

Lawrence knew all this from his reading of such books as Petrie's *The Religions of Egypt*, Pryse's *The Apocalypse Unsealed*, and Madame Blavatsky's *Isis Unveiled*. But he was not interested in displaying his knowledge of mythology, anthropology and Oriental religions, nor in quarrying them for fragments to shore against his ruins. The last paragraph of *The Escaped Cock* needs no notes. What we happen to know of its sources and antecedents and parallels will make fertile connections for us. Words such as 'boat', 'current', 'night', 'seed', 'resurrection', 'roses', 'serpent' and 'tree' are bound to make such connections without our being aware of it, independently of any mythic context. The passage works as simple poetic prose, creating a sense of atonement between the innermost needs and powers of the man and the woman of his choice, his unborn child, the currents and seasons of life itself, the larger world of the distance and the future for him to adventure into, even the Romans, against whom he sharpens his wits and his weapons. The scene in its wholeness is the very opposite of a crucifixion. We imagine this Christ escaping into the Greater Day with the enigmatic Etruscan smile on his lips.

One wonders whether Lawrence knew an already famous poem also written on Lake Leman just seven years earlier – 'The Waste Land'. There, at the end, Eliot also uses a boat to express the poem's strongest affirmation, that control which is the opposite of death by water:

> *Damyata*: The boat responded
> Gaily, to the hand expert with sail and oar.
> The sea was calm, your heart would have responded
> Gaily, when invited, beating obedient
> To controlling hands

The image is, surely, not very satisfactory. Those 'controlling hands' are too reminiscent of the assured 'young man carbuncular' whose 'exploring hands encounter no defence'. The woman's heart, like the sea, is supposed to respond to and obey the expert handling of the man. Control, in this sense, becomes the imposition of one man's will upon woman and nature, a variant of Plato's chariot driver. Lawrence calls this greed. His Christ, in Gerald Doherty's words, 'dies to "greed" and rises to "desire" ' [DHLR 15 63]. His boat is controlled partly by him and partly by the current: 'So let the boat carry me'.

Eliot reprimanded Lawrence for 'using the terminology of Christian faith to set forth some philosophy or religion which is fundamentally non-Christian or anti-Christian' [CH 361]. Lawrence might have responded, with Blake, that he was seeking to rescue Christ from the Christians. It was a daring undertaking in 1928, and caused much outrage at the time. Lawrence was called a traitor to the human race. But such is the tact and sensitivity with which he carried it through that many Christians have subsequently responded warmly to it as a corrective to the tendency of orthodox Christianity to be life-denying, and to evade the implications of the phrase 'the resurrection of the body'.

One might wish that Lawrence had been able to follow his regenerate man still further, and imagine a life for him wherever he is heading. We can get a hint of that from 'The Risen Lord', an essay Lawrence wrote in August 1929, which might almost be regarded as an outline for a third part to *The Escaped Cock*:

> If Jesus rose in the full flesh, He rose to know the tenderness of a woman, and the great pleasure of her, and to have children by her. He rose to know the responsibility and the peculiar delight of children, and also the exas-

peration and nuisance of them. If Jesus rose as a full man, in the flesh, He rose to have friends, to have a man-friend who He would hold sometimes to His breast, in strong affection, and who would be dearer to Him than a brother, just out of the sheer mystery of sympathy. And how much more wonderful, this, than having disciples! If Jesus rose a full man in the flesh, He rose to do His share in the world's work, something he really liked doing. And if He remembered His first life, it would be neither teaching nor preaching, but probably carpentering again, with joy, among the shavings. If Jesus rose a full man in the flesh, He rose to continue His fight with the hard-boiled conventionalists like Roman judges and Jewish priests and money-makers of every sort. But this time, it would no longer be the fight of self-sacrifice that would end in crucifixion. This time it would be a freed man fighting to shelter the rose of life from being trampled on by the pigs.   [P II 575]

When he wrote that, Lawrence had only six months to live, and would write no more fiction.

We could say that Lawrence is here merely recreating Jesus in his own image. With equal justice and more generosity, we might say that he is redefining Jesus as a hero he can whole-heartedly imitate. One man-friend of these last years, whom Lawrence never tried to turn into a disciple, was the novelist Rhys Davies, who could not say what Lawrence had meant to him without reference to Christ:

He was a Christ of an earthly estate, and those about him knew the Godhead he had found in himself, and were warmed by it. His humanity was so purely aristocratic and undefiled. Here was the complete flowering of the spirit in flesh. Let me not be misunderstood: Lawrence was a man and no Jesus in rapt love with the Heaven that is to come; but a Christ of himself as every man can become who has once found the pure centre of his being and keeps it uncontaminated.   [C B III 316]

NINE

'NEW, STRANGE FLOWERS': PANSIES, NETTLES, AND LAST POEMS

Between the beginning of 1923 and the end of 1928 Lawrence wrote only a handful of poems. When he resumed, it was to write a very different kind of poetry from *Birds, Beasts and Flowers*. Whatever reservations we may have about *The Plumed Serpent*, the American fiction certainly engaged the whole of Lawrence's imaginative effort in a way the fiction of the immediate post-war years had not. The return to Europe in 1925 coincided with a restoration of Lawrence's concern with and for the human world, and that concern expressed itself in fiction (and in the imaginative prose of *Etruscan Places*) up to the completion of *The Escaped Cock* in July 1928.

Lawrence had never fully recovered from the haemorrhages of July 1927. Neither inhalation treatment at Baden nor six weeks at Les Diablerets at four thousand feet had done any good. In July 1928 he wrote his last works of fiction. From this time forth he had the strength to produce only short newspaper articles, essays, poems, paintings, and the unfinished *Apocalypse*.

In October the Lawrences went to the island of Port-Cros to stay with the Aldingtons, who had a fortress there, La Vigie. Frieda had brought a raging cold from Italy and gave it to Lawrence, who struggled up to the Vigie but was too ill to go out again. The following week he had haemorrhages again, and stayed in bed reading the deeply hurtful reviews of *Lady Chatterley's Lover*, 'the most evil outpouring that has ever besmirched the literature of our country', according to *John Bull* [CH 278]. Aldington recalled:

> It seems to me one up to Lawrence that he went tranquilly on with his writing although he was so ill, and was angry and bitter about the attacks on him in England. Every morning he sat up in bed, wearing an old hat as protection against an imaginary draught, and produced a short story or one of the little essays of *Assorted Articles* . . . He must also have been working secretly on *Pansies*, for two of them were inspired by books he read on the island. One was Aldous Huxley's *Point Counter Point* and the other a book on Attila. [CB III 254]

In fact, Lawrence wrote no short stories there, though he did finish

324

his translation of Il Lasca's *The Story of Dr Manente*, corrected the proofs of 'The Blue Moccasins', and lengthened 'Rawdon's Roof' by five pages. The essays were 'Is England Still a Man's Country?', 'Sex Versus Loveliness' and 'Do Women Change?'

Lawrence actually blamed Aldington and Huxley for his illness on Port Cros. On 28 October he wrote to Huxley:

. . . if you can only palpitate to murder, suicide, and rape, in their various degrees – and you state plainly that it is so – *caro*, however are we going to live through the days? Preparing still another murder, suicide, and rape? But it becomes of a phantasmal boredom and produces ultimately inertia, inertia, inertia and final atrophy of the feelings. Till, I suppose, comes a final super-war, and murder, suicide, rape sweeps away the vast bulk of mankind. It is as you say – intellectual appreciation does not amount to so much, it's what you thrill to. And if murder, suicide, rape is what you thrill to, and nothing else, then it's your destiny – you can't change it *mentally*. You live by what you thrill to, and there's the end of it. Still for all that it's a *perverse* courage which makes the man accept the slow suicide of inertia and sterility: the perverseness of a perverse child. – It's amazing how men are like that. Richard Aldington is exactly the same inside, murder, suicide, rape – with a desire to *be* raped very strong – same thing really – just like you – only he doesn't face it, and gilds his perverseness. It makes me feel ill, I've had more hemorrhage here and been in bed this week. [CL 1096]

The first draft of *Pansies*[1] must have been started at this time. The second poem, 'What Matters', is very close to this letter:

As one of our brightest young intellectuals said to me:
                    . . .
What matters is what we thrill to.
We are ultimately determined by what we thrill to
And, of course, thrilling is like loving, you have no choice about it.
                    . . .
No, when it comes to thrills, there are really very few.
Judging from the fiction it is possible to read, I should say rape was
            rather thrilling
or being raped, either way, so long as it was consciously done, and
            slightly subtle.   [CP 531]

The poem goes on to discuss murder and suicide. The first poem, 'The Noble Englishman', is also a savage attack on Aldington, as are several others. It is not surprising that Lawrence kept his poems to himself on Port Cros.

'What Matters' is not a bad poem, but any reader must be aware at once of the superiority of the letter. It is the depth of Lawrence's personal commitment and caring which gives the informal prose of the letter its irresistible sweep and urgency. The poem attempts to take the matter out of the area of the personal, but there is not a sharp enough edge to the satire to make up for the loss of weight, of total seriousness.

The first poem to achieve that simplicity of pure perception which is to be characteristic of the best pansies is the fifth poem in the manuscript, 'Roses', which Lawrence chose to discard:

> Nature responds so beautifully.
> Roses are only once-wild roses, that were given an extra chance,
> So they bloomed out and filled themselves with coloured fulness
> Out of sheer desire to be splendid, and more splendid.   [831]

There soon followed several more beautiful tiny poems, of four or five lines. 'The Gazelle Calf' and 'Little Fish' are well known. 'New Moon' is equally fine:

> The new moon, of no importance
> lingers behind as the yellow sun glares and is gone beyond the sea's
>   edge;
> earth smokes blue;
> the new moon, in cool height above the blushes,
> brings a fresh fragrance of heaven to our senses.   [467]

Here, perhaps, is the first faint hint of the theme of death. In *Last Poems* the yellow sun of life will again sink into the sea, and a full moon will preside over the passage through blue darkness to renewed life.

The nineteenth and twentieth poems, 'The Mess of Love' and 'Fidelity', seem to be by-products of the essay 'Do Women Change?' (written between 5 and 8 November). The essay ends with the statement that love is a flow; it flowers and fades: 'If flowers didn't fade they wouldn't be flowers, they'd be artificial things. But there are roots to faded flowers and in the root the flow continues and continues' [P II 542]. 'The Mess of Love' goes no further than the essay. 'Fidelity' reaches the conclusion of the essay by its mid-point:

> Embalmed flowers are not flowers, immortelles are not flowers;
> flowers are just a motion, a swift motion, a coloured gesture;
> that is their loveliness. And that is love.   [476]

(The poems themselves are to be just such transient coloured gestures.) But the poem goes deeper. All life is a flow, not only that which seems, by the human time-scale, ephemeral. At the opposite pole is the slow flowing of a sapphire

> the sapphire of fidelity.
> The gem of mutual peace emerging from the wild chaos of love.   [477]

Richard Hoggart has characterized Lawrence's distinctive voice in *Pansies* as 'the voice of a down-to-earth, tight, bright, witty Midlander . . . slangy, quick, flat and direct, lively, laconic, sceptical, nonconforming, nicely bloody-minded' [15]. Indeed, that voice is often heard; but so are many others. Often, and we have heard it already, there is the tender voice of true feeling, the naked voice of the man without a mask. At the other extreme, there are the voices not his own, in poems where he exercises his great gift of mimicry, as, for example, in 'What Ails Thee?', a dialogue, as it might be, between a gamekeeper and his uncompliant mistress, impervious to the 'Robbie Burns touch' [540].

The first title Lawrence intended to use for his new poems was *Pensées*. Some of Pascal's *Pensées* are like sharp little poems: 'Le nez de Cléopâtre: s'il eût été plus court, toute la face de la terre aurait changé'. But, rather than any sense of debt to or affinity with Pascal, it was probably more his need to write what could be produced without taxing imaginative effort, his desire to communicate with a larger audience than that which 'art' poetry commands, and his need, time being short now, to encapsulate his ideas, which led him to jot down loosely versified thoughts, the poetic equivalent of the newspaper articles he was writing at the same time. And the possibility of the pun on pansies must have occurred to him at an early stage. The pansy was a perfect flower for his purpose. He needed something unpretentious and unselfconscious and ephemeral. He wanted his poems to have the quality which had so attracted him in Etruscan art:

> Myself, I like to think of the little wooden temples of the early Greeks and of the Etruscans: small, dainty, fragile, and evanescent as flowers . . . all vivid and fresh and unimposing. The whole thing small and dainty in proportion, and fresh, somehow charming instead of impressive.
>
> [MM 122]

Poems such as the man who had died, smiling to himself, might have casually jotted down. Most of all he wanted to avoid the kind of art which seems 'too much cooked in the artistic consciousness' [206].

The word pansy in fact derives from the French *pensée*. But by analogy with daisy, which means day's eye, Lawrence may have also thought of the false derivation of pansy from Pan's eye. Each pansy is intended to be 'a true thought, which comes as much from the heart and the genitals as from the head. A thought, with its own blood of emotion and instinct running in it like the fire in a fire-opal' [CP 417]. They are therefore the thoughts of the demon, at their best as subversive of ordinary thinking as Blake's 'Proverbs of Hell'. The 'Retort to Jesus', for example, is the demon's retort:

And whoever forces himself to love anybody
begets a murderer in his own body.   [653]

At the end of *More Pansies* the demon announces himself in 'Demon Justice' and 'Be a Demon!'

Lawrence's demonic or 'true thought' is very different from Pascal's. He defined it in the later poem 'Thought':

Thought is the welling up of unknown life into consciousness,
Thought is the testing of statements on the touchstone of the
    conscience,
Thought is gazing on to the face of life, and reading what can be read,
Thought is pondering over experience, and coming to a conclusion.
Thought is not a trick, or an exercise, or a set of dodges,
Thought is a man in his wholeness wholly attending.   [673]

Four times in three consecutive poems comes the imperative 'think!', as if Lawrence were giving us a crash course in this kind of thinking. The first of these is called 'Think – !':

Imagine what it must have been to have existence
in the wild days when life was sliding whirlwinds, blue-hot weights,
in the days called chaos, which left us rocks, and gems!
Think that the sapphire is only alumina, like kitchen pans
crushed utterly, and breathed through and through
with fiery weight and wild life, and coming out
clear and flowery blue!   [529–30]

To think is to imagine. These poems are exercises for the atrophied imagination, little acts of pure attention producing fragments of life-knowledge.

Lawrence's own life-knowledge, acquired by this means, he confidently opposes to orthodox scientific knowledge in, for example, 'Self-Protection'. This is the first of many poems, most of them in *Last Poems*, where a scientific or philosophical theory is wittily undermined, and then replaced by a theory which Lawrence makes to seem like the merest common sense, though in fact a product of his own uncommon sensibility. Here it is the theory of 'protective coloration' in animals, which makes 'self-protection the first law of existence'. The vulgar error to be demolished is deliberately expressed in lifeless and abstract formulary prose. As it turns to look at living creatures, the language comes alive:

A tiger is striped and golden for his own glory.
He would certainly be much more invisible if he were grey-green.

Sheer vivacity of language almost guarantees the validity of Lawrence's alternative theory:

> As a matter of fact, the only creatures that seem to survive
> Are those that give themselves away in flash and sparkle
> and gay flicker of joyful life;
> those that go glittering abroad
> with a bit of splendour. [523]

The Lawrences left Port Cros ('that poky island') on 17 November for Bandol. Lawrence's room at the Hotel Beau Rivage looked south over the sea. Four days later he wrote to Maria Huxley:

> It is incredibly lovely weather, and the place very lovely, swimming with milky gold light at sunset, and white boats half melted on the white twilight sea . . . [H 762]

The world seemed simplified down to its elements, sun, moon and sea:

> We don't know how lovely the elements are.
> Why trouble about people?
> The sun is so lovely.
> If a man looked at me for one moment as the sun does
> I could accept men.
> If twilight came in the eyes of women
> As it comes over the milk-blue sea, hinting at gold and darkness,
> Oh lovely women! [CP 840]

As sometimes happens in *Pansies*, the freshness and simplicity of the original perception in the first draft is lost as Lawrence later 'develops' it into something more like conventional thoughts. Neither 'Elemental' nor 'I Wish I Knew a Woman' can preserve the freshness of their source-poem 'The Elements'.

Gazing every day out to sea at the setting sun of November, Lawrence felt his own affinity with it:

> A few gold rays thickening down to red
> as the sun of my soul is setting
> setting fierce and undaunted, wintry
> but setting, setting behind the sounding sea between my ribs.
>
> The wide sea wins, and the dark
> winter, and the great day-sun, and the sun in my soul
> sinks, sinks to setting and the winter solstice
> downward, they race in decline
> my sun, and the great gold sun. [455]

Many of the poems in *Pansies* fall into clusters of several variations on the same theme. A group which Lawrence may have begun on 23 November is typical.[2] The theme is 'peace', especially that inward peace which comes from roots that go 'deep beyond the world of man', bringing him a 'natural abundance' and nobility which Lawrence contrasts with mere riches [499]. Within each group there are usually some poems of bald, prosaic assertion which fall flat:

> I would rather sit still in a state of peace on a stone
> than ride in the motorcar of a multimillionaire
> and feel the peacelessness of the multimillionaire
> poisoning me. [498]

Others develop from the same basic thought towards real poems in two distinct directions. Some are amusing, mocking or self-mocking, colloquial, with deft manipulation of tone and rhythm ('What Would you Fight For'). Some, beginning flatly, become real poems, new efforts of attention and discovery, as soon as they become concrete and metaphorical. 'Poverty', for example, is nothing until the tenth line, when Lawrence ceases to assert in the abstract and looks at 'this pine tree near the sea, / that grows out of rock, and plumes forth, plumes forth':

> With its roots it has a grand grip on its daily bread,
> and its plumes look like green cups held up to the sun and air
> and full of wine. [498]

The best poem in this group is, perhaps, 'Glory':

> Glory is of the sun, too, and the sun of suns,
> and down the shafts of his splendid pinions
> run tiny rivers of peace.
>
> Most of his time, the tiger pads and slouches in a burning peace.
> And the small hawk high up turns round on the slow pivot of peace.
> Peace comes from behind the sun, with the peregrine falcon, and the
> owl.
> Yet all of these drink blood. [496]

The young Welsh novelist Rhys Davies stayed with the Lawrences for the last weekend in November:

At this time in Bandol he was writing the satirical poems to be called *Pansies* and also painting one or two pictures. He told me he would write no more novels; *Lady Chatterley's Lover* was to be his last long work of fiction, the last large attempt to tell men and women how to live. For all his fury and rages, he got immense fun out of writing *Pansies*. He would write them in bed in the mornings, cheerful and chirpy, the meek sea air blowing in from the enchanting little bay outside his window . . . There was something perky and bird-like about him thus, and he was intensely happy and proud of the *Pansies*; he would read out the newest ones with delight, accentuating the wicked sharp little pecks in them.

[CB III 273-4]

The poems Lawrence read to Davies may well have included some further attacks on Huxley and Aldington, such as 'Little-Boy Brilliant' (a poem omitted from *Pansies* as, perhaps, too 'wicked'). The modern woman, Lawrence says, thinks it wonderful in a man to have 'such a subtle destroying mind':

> So she marries one of these little-boy brilliants
> and finds that the subtle destructive cynicism is only a small-boy's
>   compensation
> for his own deficiency, most mawkish in its inverted sentimentalism
> and when she has most unsatisfactorily shared his little-boy bed for a
>   year or two
> and born him a son or so, who at the age of seven is so infinitely the
>   better man of the two,
> why, the modern young wife of the little-boy brilliant begins to feel
>   cynical even about cynicism
> and wonders if a parrot hasn't more to it.   [CP 842]

It would, however, be a mistake to think of *Pansies* as merely 'satirical'. One of the paintings Lawrence was doing at the time of Davies's visit was probably *Leda*. The group of poems which relates to that painting is apocalyptic (as are many other poems in *Pansies*, for example 'Dies Irae', 'Dies Illa' and 'The Death of Our Era'). It would have been helpful to the reader if the group had been introduced by the earlier poem 'Nemesis':

> If we do not rapidly open all the doors of consciousness
> and freshen the putrid little space in which we are cribbed
> the sky-blue walls of our unventilated heaven
> will be bright red with blood.   [515]

Nemesis was a daughter of primeval Night. Her name means 'anger' – anger against any violation of *themis*, the law of Nature. *Themis* means, particularly, the proper relations between men and gods, and between men and women. Many poems in *Pansies* are about the breakdown of both those relations. Nemesis was winged, and is depicted accompanied by swans. When Zeus pursued her, she turned herself into a goose, but Zeus, in the form of a swan, caught and mounted her. In later versions of this myth she becomes Leda, which is not a Greek name, and probably means simply 'the woman', Nemesis being the first female on earth.

The poem immediately preceding 'Swan' in the manuscript is an early version of 'To Let Go or to Hold On', a poem which holds in perfect balance the two alternatives, to hold on 'and go ahead with what is human nature / and make a new job of the human world' (that is, to restore human life to *themis*), or to let go 'leaving it to the vast revolutions of creative chaos / to bring forth creatures that are an improvement on humans' [429].

In 'Swan' Lawrence imagines the energy 'within vast chaos, within the electron' as 'the great swan upon the waters of all endings' [435], a swan which no longer goes about its own business but, angered by our violation of *themis*, stoops upon us in the dark, discarding men, but using women to initiate a new era of creation.

'Give Us Gods' is the fullest statement of the theme. Here Lawrence recapitulates, backwards, the images, human and animal, in which man has conceived his gods. Now scientific man conceives no gods at all, just mists of random atomic energy. But from those very mists emerges, for Lawrence, the oldest image of god:

Look then
where the father of all things swims in a mist of atoms
electrons and energies, quantums and relativities
mists, wreathing mists,
like a wild swan, or a goose, whose honk goes through my bladder.

And in the dark unscientific I feel the drum-winds of his wings
and the drip of his cold, webbed feet, mud-black
brush over my face as he goes
to seek the women in the dark, our women, our weird women whom
        he treads
with dreams and thrusts that make them cry in their sleep.

Gods, do you ask for gods?
Where there is woman there is swan.   [438]

The 'marshy flesh' of woman is for ever the birth place, the homing place of the swan, the father of all things, the vivifier:

The vivifier exists, but for me is neither man-like nor woman-like
nor even like an animal, bull, ram, or lion, or lamb.
Yet when I think of the wild swan, or the ripple-marked black-headed
        goose
far off upon the misty waters of the depths of space
silently swimming and sleeping, and pressing the flood
with webbed fecundity, plunging the seed of life in the wet wilderness
and honking with a horn-like annunciation of life from the marshes of
        chaos
something thrills in me, and I know
the next day is the day of the goose, the wild swan's day.   [841]

Man has, apparently, forfeited his right to woman. If he questions her about the fatherhood of the 'little beast' she bears

will there be a whistle of wings in the air, and an icy draught?
will the singing of swans, high up, high up, invisible
break the drums of his ears
and leave him forever listening for the answer? [439]

According to the painting *Singing of Swans*, it will leave him worse than that. There angry swans swoop over men who are insanely destroying each other; dies irae, the swan-song of the race.

Most of the subsequent poems in the manuscript, the December poems, are satirical. A major breakthrough comes with Lawrence's discovery of the satirical value of rhyme. 'In Nottingham' seems merely petulant and small-minded in its original near-prose. Rhythm and rhyme transform it into the twinkling but cutting comedy of 'Nottingham's New University'. 'Red Herring' brings a new gusto into the collection:

My mother was a superior soul
a superior soul was she
cut out to play a superior role
in the god-damn bourgeoisie. [490]

In 'No! Mr Lawrence' the dull thud of the final rhyme undermines the speaker's would-be sophistication. In 'The Little Wowser' Lawrence turns his wit wryly against himself:

I think of all the little brutes
as ever was invented
that little cod's the holy worst.
I've chucked him, I've repented. [493]

On 15 December Lawrence described these poems to Maria Huxley:

I have been doing a book of *Pensées* which I call pansies, a sort of loose little poem form; Frieda says with joy: real doggerel. [CL 1106]

The first draft was finished by 23 December: 164 poems in two months. Immediately Lawrence wrote a little foreword defending his pansies:

If some are only in bud, and some are a bit shrivelled-looking, c'est la vie, mon cher! That's how life is! And if there is no system, think of pansies pansily marching one after the other, still as wooden soldiers forming fours around a general! It's enough system for pansies that they all turn to the sun, and droop when they feel like it.[3]

And if they have a 'peppery sort of little smell' that makes the reader sneeze, that too is part of the whole living flower:

Live beauty will always be a bit 'shocking', and pansies will always have their roots in dung and humus.

Within a few days Lawrence wrote a much longer foreword, making bolder claims. Most of this foreword is a defence against the charge of obscenity. Prophetically, Lawrence wrote: 'Obscene means today that the policeman thinks he has a right to arrest you, nothing else' [CP 418]. By 7 January Lawrence had typed out the poems, revising and adding to them. Both copies of the typescript were sent to Pollinger on that date, and were seized by the police. At the beginning of February Lawrence 'typed them all out afresh – and revised many of course' [CL 1130]. Secker refused to print fourteen of the more outspoken poems, so Lawrence arranged for a private edition which would include them, together with the longer foreword. For the Secker trade edition he produced in April yet a third version of the foreword, close to the original one, and 'perfectly proper'.

The reviewers were predictably worried by the general hatred of modern life expressed in the poems, but most were prepared to take the poems on Lawrence's terms. The anonymous review in the *Times Literary Supplement* ended:

And, while there is much modern poetry which does not seem to express anything that the poet greatly wished to say, there is scarcely a line of Mr. Lawrence's verses which does not sound like a piece of the author's mind, in both the obvious and the idiomatic sense of the phrase.

[CH 311]

*

In March 1929 Lawrence went to Paris to arrange for the publication of a popular edition of *Lady Chatterley's Lover*. There he succumbed to big-city 'grippe':

I haven't been well in Paris. Sometimes one feels as if one were drifting out of life altogether – and not terribly sorry to go. These big cities take away my real will to live. [CL 1140]

By the end of April the Lawrences were settled in Majorca, which gave Lawrence just the relaxation he needed:

I agree this isn't a good place for work. I have tried to paint two pictures – and each time it's been a failure and made me all on edge. So I accept the decree of destiny, and shall make no further attempt to work at all while I am in Spain. [1152]

But Lawrence did write fifty or sixty more pansies before leaving Majorca on 18 June.

In the seven months from May to November 1929, Lawrence wrote over three hundred poems. Except for those he prepared for publication, the twenty-seven in *Nettles*, the six which appeared in the 1930 *Imagist Anthology*, and the two published by the *London Mercury* in 1930 ('Bells' and 'The Triumph of the Machine'), none of these received their final revision, and many would undoubtedly have been discarded.

The demon has two distinct voices, the mischievous or jeering voice he uses to needle his enemies, and the lyrical voice, sometimes sparkling, sometimes intense and quietly rhapsodic, of his own true thinking. *More Pansies* (to adopt Aldington's title) opens with a dozen poems in the first voice, attacking various kinds of self-important people. Then, in the second voice, comes 'Andraitx – Pomegranate Flowers', a glimpse of people who are not at all self-important, insistent or self-advertising, but whose flame of life is all the brighter for being cupped in silence and darkness, like the pomegranate's 'short gasps of flame in the green of night', 'small sharp red fires in the night of leaves':

> And noon is suddenly dark, is lustrous, is silent and dark
> men are unseen, beneath the shading hats;
> only, from out the foliage of the secret loins
> red flamelets here and there reveal
> a man, a woman there.   [CP 606]

The demon speaks from that dark interior of man where 'flow the heart's rivers of fulness, desire and distress' [607]. The demon is a man's naked self, when he has cast off his moral clothing:

> And if stark naked I approach a fellow-man or fellow-woman
> they must be naked too,
> and none of us must expect morality of each other:
> I am that I am, take it or leave it.
> Offer me nothing but that which you are, stark and strange.
> Let there be no accommodation at this issue.   [608]

A man's demon is what keeps him 'in the rooted connection with the centre of all things' [610]. One of the names of the demon is Lucifer, who lost none of his brightness in falling, and is now due to replace the orthodox angels 'tarnished with centuries of conventionality' [614].

Frieda's sister Else called Lawrence's paintings *Satanisch*. Lawrence replied:

> Perhaps you are right; Lucifer is brighter now than tarnished Michael or shabby Gabriel. All things fall in their turn, now Michael goes down, and whispering Gabriel, and the Son of the Morning will laugh at them all. Yes, I am for Lucifer, who is really the Morning Star. The real principle

of Evil is not anti-Christ or anti-Jehovah, but anti-life. I agree with you, in a sense, that I am with the antichrist. Only I am not anti-life.   [NI 286]

Another of the demon's names is the Holy Ghost:

> The Holy Ghost is the deepest part of our consciousness
> wherein we know ourselves for what we are
> and know our dependence on the creative beyond.   [CP 621]

But modern life is a sinning against the Holy Ghost, repudiating and persecuting the demon until 'we destroy the most essential self in us'. For these self-inflicted wounds 'there is no remedy'.

In his introduction to *Pansies* Lawrence stressed the healing function of these poems:

> Or, if you will have the other derivation of pansy, from *panser*, to dress or soothe a wound; these are my tender administrations to the mental and emotional wounds we suffer from. Or you can have heartsease if you like, since the modern heart could certainly do with it.   [CP 417]

(Did he know that the Elizabethans first cultivated the pansy because they believed it to contain a cure for inflammation of the lungs?)

The wound that most concerns him here is the broken connection between man and the living cosmos. In 'Fatality', he suggests that the only healing of that wound might be death:

> Death alone, through the long processes of disintegration
> can melt the detached life back
> through the dark Hades at the roots of the tree
> into the circulating sap, once more, of the tree of life.   [617]

In 'Healing', he is less fatalistic. Here Lawrence sees himself as the patient as well as the healer:

> I am ill because of wounds to the soul, to the deep emotional self
> and the wounds to the soul take a long, long time, only time can help
> and patience, and a certain difficult repentance
> long, difficult repentance, realisation of life's mistake, and the freeing
>   oneself
> from the endless repetition of the mistake
> which mankind at large has chosen to sanctify.   [620]

One form that mistake has taken has been to substitute for 'dependence on the creative beyond' dependence on the machine. In 'The Triumph of the Machine', 'the man in the machine', that is the perverse will endlessly, mechanically repeating the same mistake, persecutes 'the native creatures of the soul' until they rebel and drive him mad. Then 'the edifice of our life will rock in the shock of the mad machine, and the house will come down' [624].

It is a vision of holocaust, for 'over the middle of the earth will be the smoky ruin of iron'. The 'native creatures' will survive, but only 'in the ultimate, remote places'. It is difficult to know from the first version of the poem whether the swan, the lark and the lambs of the poem's ending are still symbols of the demon within the hearts of those men who never capitulated to the machine, or whether the catastrophe eliminates man, and releases them into their animal being to begin a new day without men in the far places.

The revised version of the poem drops the apocalyptic ending completely. Now Lawrence asserts that so long as one heart harbours them, the wild creatures cannot die. 'And at last . . . they will hear a silence fall . . . as the machine breaks finally down.' It is the demon who triumphs now, in the form of a sprout of hornbeam rending the asphalt roads.

> And then at last
> all the creatures that were driven back into the uttermost corners of the
>   soul
> they will peep forth. [958]

*

The Lawrences left Majorca on 18 June, Lawrence to visit the Huxleys at Forte dei Marmi, Frieda to London to see the exhibition of Lawrence's paintings at the Warren Gallery. On 5 July the police raided the gallery and confiscated thirteen pictures deemed obscene because of the depiction of pubic hair. On the same day Lawrence was struck down in Forte with stomach pains. He travelled to Florence the following day, but was so ill that Orioli put him to bed in his own flat and sent for Frieda.

As we can see from such titles as the Blakean 'Dark Satanic Mills', 'What have they done to you?' and 'Cry of the masses', several of the poems written at Forte had expressed feelings of outraged and tender fellow-feeling:

> And though the pomegranate has red flowers outside the window
> and oleander is hot with perfume under the afternoon sun
> and I am 'il Signore' and they love me here,
> yet I am a mill-hand in Leeds
> and the death of the Black Country is upon me
> and I am wrapped in the lead of a coffin-lining, the living death of my
>   fellow men. [630]

But Lawrence was so deeply hurt by the raid ('The dirty swine would like to think they made you weep' [EL 194]) that he repudiated his fellow men with almost incoherent disgust:

I love my neighbour
but
are these things my neighbours?
these two-legged things that walk and talk
and eat and cachinnate, and even seem to smile
seem to smile, ye gods!

Am I told that these things are my neighbours?

All I can say then is Nay! nay! nay! nay! nay!   [CP 644]

Later that month, in Baden, Lawrence seems to be returning to his preoccupation with leadership. He defines true democracy as 'demos serving life', which means that 'the many must obey the few that look into the eyes of the gods' [650]. But when he turns to look himself into the eyes of the gods, a group of lovely poems follows. He sees a woman, shy and alone, washing herself under a tap, 'and the glimmer of the presence of the gods was like lilies,/and like water-lilies' [651]. The tall white corn, as it yields to the scythe, is 'the fallen stillness of god', 'the pale-gold flesh of Priapus dropping asleep'. Alone, their presence makes the air still and lovely to him:

And I fall asleep with the gods, the gods
that are not, or that are
according to the soul's desire,
like a pool into which we plunge, or do not plunge.   [652]

This sequence of twenty-eight poems about the gods, and what happens to us if we deny them ('your sensual atrophy/will at last send you insane' [655]), ends with a return to the image of the pansy, now yielding its essential heartsease:

There is nothing to save, now all is lost,
but a tiny core of stillness in the heart
like the eye of a violet.   [658]

Lawrence's effort in these poems 'to save the streaked pansy of the heart from being trampled to mud' carried over into the splendid essay 'The Risen Lord', where the risen Christ faces his greatest test, 'to be a man on earth':

Now comes the true life, man living his full life on earth, as flowers live their full life, without rhyme or reason except the magnificence of coming forth into fulness . . . But this time, it would no longer be the fight of self-sacrifice that would end in crucifixion. This time it would be a freed man fighting to shelter the rose of life from being trampled on by the pigs.
[P II 575]

One of the attributes of the risen Lord is 'the accomplished acceptance of His own death'. Lawrence's own health had declined to the point where he allowed himself to be persuaded to go with his mother-in-law to the Kurhaus Plattig. The Baroness had not accepted her death:

> She is 78, and is in a mad terror for fear she might die; and she would see me or anyone else die ten times over, to give her a bit more strength to drag on a few more meaningless years. It is so ugly and so awful, I nearly faint. I have never felt so down, so depressed and ill, as I have here these ten days: awful! [CL 1172]

Such resistance to death implies also 'a rancid resistance/to life':

> Old men, old obstinate men and women
> dare not die, because in death
> their hardened souls are washed with fire, and washed and seared
> till they are softened back to the life-stuff again, against which they
>   hardened themselves. [CP 663]

For Lawrence, closeness to death enhanced his appreciation of life:

> we can but touch, and wonder, and ponder, and make our effort
> and dangle in a last fastidious fine delight
> as the fuchsia does, dangling her reckless drop
> of purple after so much putting forth
> and slow mounting marvel of a little tree. [667]

By the end of July, Lawrence had rallied enough to write 'some nice stinging nettles, and let's hope they'll sting the arses of all the Meads and Persians of slimy London' [CL 1174].[4] Frederick Mead was the eighty-two-year-old magistrate before whom Lawrence's paintings were to be tried on 8 August. In 'Innocent England' Lawrence takes up the fight against the 'hard-boiled conventionalists' with a comic verve which suggests that he is writing now not with the helpless savagery of a man at bay, but from a position of inner strength, like the twinkling mockery of the gods:

> A wreath of mist is the usual thing
> in the north, to hide where the turtles sing.
>
> Though they never sing, they never sing,
> don't you dare to suggest such a thing
>
> or Mr Mead will be after you.
> – But what a pity I never knew
>
> A wreath of English mist would do
> as a cache-sexe! I'd have put a whole fog. [CP 580]

But the improvement in Lawrence's health was short-lived. At the end of August, Lawrence and Frieda went to Rottach, in

Bavaria, to be near Lawrence's friend Max Mohr, who was a doctor as well as a writer. Lawrence spent the first week in bed. Max Mohr brought three doctors from Munich. They prescribed a diet which included arsenic, and made Lawrence worse. 11 September was his forty-fourth birthday. In his heart of hearts he knew it would be his last.

As early as 1916, Lawrence had affirmed a very positive attitude towards death:

Do I fear the strange approach of the creative unknown to my door? I fear it only with pain and with unspeakable joy. And do I fear the invisible dark hand of death plucking me into the darkness, gathering me blossom by blossom from the stem of my life into the unknown of my afterwards? I fear it only in reverence and with strange satisfaction. For this is my final satisfaction, to be gathered blossom by blossom, all my life long, into the finality of the unknown which is my end. [P 698]

Now that courage was to be put to the ultimate test. Could it be maintained through the process of actual dying? At the Kurhaus he had written of turning 'to the adventure of death, in eagerness':

I have always wanted to be as the flowers are
so unhampered in their living and dying,
and in death I believe I shall be as the flowers are.

I shall blossom like a dark pansy, and be delighted
there among the dark sun-rays of death.
I can feel myself unfolding in the dark sunshine of death
to something flowery and fulfilled, and with a strange sweet perfume.

Men prevent one another from being men
but in the great spaces of death
the winds of the afterwards kiss us into blossom of manhood. [CP 677]

Death, he believes, will call out from him whatever in him can answer to the perfume of the pansy, the blueness of the gentian. And that will be his essential manhood. Did Lawrence literally believe that after death he would in some sense retain his humanity, manhood and identity? He could only discover what he truly believed by giving his whole attention to whatever images of death life brought him.

Frieda recalled:

I remember some autumn nights when the end seemed to have come. I listened for his breath through the open door, all night long, an owl hooting ominously from the walnut tree outside. In the dim dawn an enormous bunch of gentians I had put on the floor by his bed seemed the only living thing in the room. [NI 213]

Four drafts having survived, we can follow the process by which Lawrence explored deeper and deeper levels of meaning in these Bavarian gentians.[5] The first draft was called 'The State of Grace' [PP 228]. The idea of the poem is similar to that of the next poem in the manuscript, 'Flowers and Men', which begins 'Flowers achieve their own floweriness and it is a miracle' [CP 683]. By recognizing that miracle, a man's soul can enter and share the 'dark-blue godhead' of the gentian. The poem is largely descriptive. In spite of the perception that the gentians make a 'dark-blue gloom / in the sunny room', there is no image of the gentians as torches. Nor, in spite of the line 'How deep I have gone', is there any journey. But the first revision (interlinear) seized on that opportunity, cancelling 'in your marvellous dark-blue godhead' in favour of 'since I embarked on your dark blue fringes', and changing 'What a baptism for / my soul' to 'What a journey . . .'. The Christian terminology having disappeared, the title becomes 'Glory of darkness'. The next revision (marginal) opens up a new mythic dimension with the perception of the gentian as a dark doorway to Hades, through which Persephone has just gone back to her bridegroom, and to her 'wedding in the winter dark' [PP 229]. But in developing this idea, the theme of the journey of the poet's soul into darkness is completely lost. This he takes up in a different context in 'Ship of Death', leaving the unrealized potentialities of the 'Glory of darkness' drafts to be developed later.

On 30 August Lawrence wrote describing Rottach to Orioli: 'It is quite beautiful, and very peaceful, cows and haymaking and apples on tall apple trees, dropping so suddenly' [CL 1188]. Three days later he was visited by his sister-in-law Else and her lover Alfred Weber. According to Frieda, when Lawrence was alone with Weber, he said to him: 'Do you see those leaves falling from the apple tree? When the leaves want to fall you must let them fall' [NI 213]. Obviously she misremembered, since no leaves would have been falling so early. It was the apples themselves Lawrence had spoken of. They provided him with the opening of 'Ship of Death':

> I sing of autumn and the falling fruit
> and the long journey towards oblivion
>
> The apples falling like great drops of dew
> to bruise themselves an exit from themselves.   [PP 221]

Years earlier, he had responded in a similar way to medlars and sorb apples:

The fibres of the heart parting one after the other
And yet the soul continuing, naked-footed, ever more vividly
    embodied
Like a flame blown whiter and whiter
In a deeper and deeper darkness
Ever more exquisite, distilled in separation.   [CP 281]

Now, however, there is a new, more deeply personal urgency. The image of the falling apples is abruptly dropped, with no further development, in this draft, as Lawrence moves on to what will be, the title tells us, the controlling image:

Have you built your ship of death, oh, have you?
Build then your ship of death, for you will need it!   [PP 221]

We hear nothing more of the ship for the moment, as the poem considers the plight of the soul for which no ship has been built, 'thrust out onto the grey grey beaches of shadow / the long marginal stretches of existence crowded with lost souls'.

Pity the poor gaunt dead that cannot die . . .
but must roam like outcast dogs on the margins of life.   [222]

This long section of 'Ship of Death' is later to be dropped from 'The Ship of Death' and become four separate poems, 'Difficult Death', 'All Souls' Day', 'The Houseless Dead' and 'Beware the Unhappy Dead'.

Now Lawrence turns to the ship he must build for his own soul 'with oars and food / and little dishes, and all accoutrements / dainty and ready for the departing soul'. The primary source of this image is the 'little bronze ship of death' [MM 107] which symbolized, for the Etruscans, 'the mystery of the journey out of life, and into death; the death-journey, and the sojourn in the after-life' [150]. This, not only to the Etruscans, but to all the 'peoples of the great natural religions', was but 'a continuing of the great wonder-journey of life' [174]. Another important source, and a conscious one, given the Whitmanesque opening 'I sing of autumn . . .', was Whitman's 'Passage to India', from which these lines must have come strongly back to him:

O we can wait no longer,
We too take ship O soul,
Joyous we too launch out on trackless seas,
Fearless for unknown shores on waves of ecstasy to sail,
Amid the wafting winds, (thou pressing me to thee, I thee to me, O
    soul,)
Caroling free, singing our song of God,
Chanting our chant of pleasant exploration.   [WW 434–5]

At last the 'shirt of the spirit's experience' melts away, the boat 'dissolves like pearl', and the soul slips into 'the womb of silence in the living night' [PP 223]. How literally we are to take the word 'womb' is indicated by the cancelled phrase 'sperm-like', and the question with which the poem ends: can it be that the 'last lapse of death, into pure oblivion' is also 'procreation' [224]? In the later version of the poem, the idea of procreation is replaced by that of resurrection; but if we think of the Buddhist concept of the soul re-entering the womb-door after death, the two concepts cease to be distinct.

In spite of, or perhaps because of, his closeness to death at Rottach, Lawrence also wrote there, just before 'Glory of darkness' and 'Ship of Death', the most life-affirming poem in *More Pansies*, 'God is Born'. It is also a triumph of mimetic art. The poem derives from Lawrence's response to the Etruscan idea of 'the vitality of the cosmos':

> The universe, which was a single aliveness with a single soul, instantly changed, the moment you thought of it, and became a dual creature with two souls, fiery and watery, for ever mingling and rushing apart, and held by the great aliveness of the universe in an ultimate equilibrium. But they rushed together and they rushed apart, and immediately they became myriad: volcanoes and seas, then streams and mountains, trees, creatures, men.   [MM 147]

The opening lines of the poem mime the straining of chaos to bring forth identities:

> The history of the cosmos
> is the history of the struggle of becoming.
> When the dim flux of unformed life
> struggled, convulsed back and forth upon itself,
> and broke at last into light and dark
> came into existence as light,
> came into existence as cold shadow . . .   [CP 682]

The verse itself struggles towards the phrase 'light and dark', thrusting them to their polar extremes with that resistant phrase 'came into existence as'. The separation of light and dark in turn creates the opposites of hot and cold, which in turn generate the next pair, condensation and evaporation – the birth of the waters and the atmosphere. Gradually all the constituents of chaos are polarized, the whole process witnessed by and participated in by the delighted atoms. It is the permanent rocking balance between these pairs of mighty opposites which *is* life. If that were lost, all would collapse again into chaos. The words embody the ideas, ultra-tangible, as if the poem were giving them their very first incarnation. Each stanza ends with the recognition and celebration of miracle.

> Throughout the aeons, as the lizard swirls his tail finer than water,
> as the peacock turns to the sun, and could not be more splendid,
> as the leopard smites the small calf with a spangled paw, perfect,
> the universe trembles: God is born! God is here!

Lizard, peacock and leopard have one line each, but are there, splendid and perfect, with only one descriptive adjective between them, 'spangled'; for it is action, a distinctive life-mode, which conveys identity, not merely appearance. Even a flower, the narcissus, is itself for what it does: it 'lifted a tuft of five-point stars / and dangled them in the atmosphere'. How, after these, can the emergence of man be rendered as anything but an anti-climax? The greatest poetry is very simple. Here Lawrence goes with striking simplicity to the heart of the matter:

> And when at last man stood on two legs and wondered,
> then there was a hush of suspense at the core of every electron:
> Behold, now very God is born!
> God Himself is born!

We know how crucial a moment that was in evolution, when man, by standing upright, freed his hands for all sorts of creative purposes, and somehow also freed his spirit to perceive and worship the wonder of the universe. The verb to wonder can carry all the weight it needs to carry because Lawrence has already so vividly demonstrated in this poem, and in so many others, what it means.

At Rottach Lawrence heard from Frederick Carter, and resumed the relationship that was to lead to the writing of his last book, *Apocalypse*. When Carter tried, years later, to sum up Lawrence's essential beliefs, he concentrated particularly on Lawrence's deep belief in man's capacity for wonder and worship before the fall:

> Man, he asserted, then mastered things not by thought of the conscious kind only, or so much, as by the thrust of the under-conscious will and desire in him. Thence came the pure physical mastery that set him upright on his two legs in defiance of nature's rule for the animal creation. Man has a pure physical poise that no other creature possesses, the power of balance, a sense of positive and negative, of good and evil – the beginnings of things as they are. [BM 54]

It was because he held so high an estimate of man's capacities, and man's place in the natural order, that Lawrence was so outraged by what men had done to themselves and to each other. The desire to hurt, in *Nettles* and the more satirical *Pansies*, is only a desire to pierce the hard shell of the modern ego, which must be done before the healing process can begin. To sting was also, perhaps, an end in itself, Lawrence's only means of defending himself against those who had persecuted *Lady Chatterley* and the paintings. But it was not simply a matter of revenge, since, through Lawrence, these men were, he knew, doing dirt on life itself, denying the gods in themselves and other men.

When he left Rottach in mid-September, Lawrence was physically no better, but had purged himself of anger. His next collection of poems, he told the Brewsters, would be called *Dead Nettles* 'because they were to have no sting in them' [RC 309]. All his strength and attention would be needed now to build that ship of death we know as *Last Poems*.

*

For months Lawrence had longed for the Mediterranean. It did not disappoint him. Ten days after his arrival in Bandol, he wrote to Else on 4 October:

> I still love the Mediterranean, it still seems young as Odysseus, in the morning . . . When the morning comes, and the sea runs silvery and the distant islands are delicate and clear, then I feel again, only man is vile. [CL 1205–6]

In this spirit Lawrence wrote the opening poems of *Last Poems*. In the spirit, also, of the beginning of 'Passage to India':

> The Past – the dark unfathom'd restrospect!
> The teeming gulf – the sleepers and the shadows!
> The past – the infinite greatness of the past!
> For what is the present after all but a growth out of the past?

So Lawrence in these poems, as in *Apocalypse*, which he worked on in parallel with them, discovers 'a new vision in harmony with the memories of old, far-off, far, far-off experience that lie within us' [A 54]. In this sense, the pagan gods and heroes of the ancient Mediterranean (in more than one sense Middle of the World) were more alive to Lawrence than the smoking liners which 'cross like clock-work the Minoan distance' [CP 688].

Though these are bright morning poems, with all the freshness of the dawn of our civilization, they are also poignantly autumnal, equally aware of the waning of the year. The sun 'goes slowly down the hill', while the ascending moon looks down on him like a queen. But the moon is no longer, for Lawrence, 'cursed Syrea Dea', the maleficent all-consuming female. She is now the goddess who 'gives men glistening bodies', and 'only cares/that we should be lovely in the flesh, with bright, crescent feet' [687]. He has now recovered 'the grand pagan calm which can see the woman of the cosmos wrapped in her warm gleam like the sun, and having her feet upon the moon, the moon who gives us our white flesh' [A 121]. On 29 October Lawrence wrote to Carter:

> In my opinion the great pagan religions of the Aegean, and Egypt and Babylon, must have conceived of the 'descent' [of the soul into the body] as a great triumph, and each Easter of the clothing in flesh as a supreme glory, and the Mother Moon who gives us our body as the supreme giver of the great gift, hence the very ancient Magna Mater in the East. [15]

In 'Invocation to the Moon' Lawrence, at the gate of her mansion, begs that gift. Many of these poems speak of a gate or door. They are rites of passage for the soul. Hermes stands at the gate because he is the messenger or herald who moves freely between the worlds of men and gods. As psychopomp he brings back to this world the souls which are to be born again.

In *Apocalypse* Lawrence tells us that the Twins, the Kabiri, are 'the ancient gods of gateposts', 'guardians of the gate'. Their function is to open the gates 'that birth may come through between them' [116]. According to Lawrence's understanding of pagan religion, the purpose of spirit, its raison d'être, is to animate the physical world. Consequently, its separation from the body can only be temporary, a transition (experienced by the soul as oblivion) from a worn-out body to a new incarnation. The moon symbolizes this transition because she herself waxes and wanes, passes through a brief period of total eclipse, then renews herself. Her 'garden' is of silver bells and cockle-shells, magical transformations of living flora and fauna ('Of his bones are coral made') quite contrary to the vividly coloured but ephemeral flowers and creatures in the garden of the sun. The moon's garden holds beautiful representations and relics of life which serve to preserve the soul's attachment to the physical world by memory through the period of its withdrawal from that world:

> Now, lady of the Moon, now open the gate of your silvery house
> and let me come past the silver bells of your flowers, and the cockle-
>   shells
> into your house, garmentless lady of the last great gift:
> who will give me back my lost limbs
> and my lost white fearless breast
> and set me again on moon-remembering feet
> a healed, whole man, O Moon! [CP 696]

This strong desire to re-enter the womb-door is the opposite of Buddhism, whose spiritual disciplines are designed to strengthen the soul in its efforts to close the womb-door and resist the pull back into the great wheel of Karma. In *Apocalypse* Lawrence claims that 'with the Orphics the tedious idea of "escaping the wheel of birth" had begun to abstract men from life' [A 131]. On the contrary, Lawrence wishes his soul to remain as long as possible 'wrapped in the dark-red mantle of the body's memories' [PP 223], and to emerge from brief oblivion back on the shores of life.

Several of the best of *Last Poems* have a common strategy. They begin with some widely held, seriously taken belief or proposition, which seems to Lawrence specious or absurd, and proceed, wittily and passionately, to demolish it, not by mere counter-argument or analysis, but simply by making us see the reality through his own direct perception of it. 'Demiurge' is the first of these. The vulgar error is Platonic idealism:

They say that reality exists only in the spirit
that corporal existence is a kind of death
that pure being is bodiless
that the idea of the form precedes the form substantial.

But what nonsense it is!
as if any Mind could have imagined a lobster
dozing in the under-deeps, then reaching out a savage and iron claw!

Even the mind of God can only imagine
those things that have become themselves:
bodies and presences, here and now, creatures with a foothold in
     creation
even if it is only a lobster on tip-toe. [CP 689]

In 'Red Geranium and Godly Mignonette' the same idea generates wicked but genial comedy:

You can't imagine the Holy Ghost sniffing at cherry-pie heliotrope.
Or the Most High, during the coal age, cudgelling his mighty brains
even if he had any brains: straining his mighty mind
to think, among the moss and mud of lizards and mastodons
to think out, in the abstract, when all was twilit green and muddy:
'Now there shall be tum-tiddly-um, and tum-tiddly-um,
hey-presto! scarlet geranium!'
We know it couldn't be done. [690]

Lawrence knew also, modulating to total seriousness, how it could be done:

But imagine, among the mud and the mastodons
God sighing and yearning with tremendous creative yearning, in that
     dark green mess

oh, for some other beauty, some other beauty
that blossomed at last, red geranium, and mignonette.

He knows by analogy with the creative process within himself:

Even an artist knows that his work was never in his mind,
he could never have *thought* it before it happened.
A strange ache possessed him, and he entered the struggle,
and out of the struggle with his material, in the spell of the urge
his work took place, it came to pass, it stood up and saluted his mind.

[690]

A later example of this type of poem is 'Anaxagoras'. Anaxagoras claimed that since all things are mixed, even pure white snow must contain an element of blackness:

That they call science, and reality.
I call it mental conceit and mystification
and nonsense, for pure snow is white to us
white and white and only white
with the lovely bloom of whiteness upon white
in which the soul delights and the senses
have an experience of bliss.

[708]

At first glance it might seem that Lawrence is proceeding by mere contradiction. What is in fact happening in such poems is that Lawrence is demonstrating the difference between the thinking of fallen and unfallen man. Thinking which is abstract, conceptual, mechanical, which has lost its hold on phenomena and sensory experience, which is no longer informed by man's many other ways of knowing, is the thinking of fallen man which can bring only ungodly knowledge and corruption. Lawrence submits himself wholly to the experience of snow, and is faithful in his thinking to that incontrovertible reality.

In 'The Man of Tyre', the proposition to be tested and found wanting is 'that God is one and all alone and ever more shall be so' [692], a proposition already mischievously undermined by the nursery language in which it is stated, so out of keeping with the serious philosophical 'pondering' which is supposed to have generated it. To go 'down to the sea' is to confront and be cut down to size by a vast reality anterior to all human attempts to reduce it to intellectual propositions, the sea 'where God is also love, but without words' [695]. The man of Tyre is not mocked, or only very gently, for he is at least open to that reality, and to the human revelation of the divine he is granted in the form of a naked woman wading shorewards 'with her back to the evening sky':

both breasts dim and mysterious, with the glamorous kindness of
    twilight between them
and the dim blotch of black maidenhair like an indicator,
giving a message to the man –
So in the cane-brake he clasped his hands in delight
that could only be god-given, and murmured:
Lo! God is one god! But here in the twilight
godly and lovely comes Aphrodite out of the sea
towards me!

As Michael Kirkham has pointed out,[6] the man's delight is more
than sexual. She is, like the moon in her nakedness, 'more wonderful than anything we can stroke' [695]. Her divinity is also
bound up with her relation to sea and sky, the ebb and flow of her
movements. At first sight she is purely of the workaday world, a
woman washing clothes in a pool. But as she lays her shift on the
shore and wades out to 'the pale green sea of evening', away from
the watcher, she suggests the body detaching itself from the world,
committing itself to the deep and the dark. But the woman does
not drown or disappear. 'Pouring sea-water over herself', like a
baptism, she turns and returns shorewards, transfigured by 'the
glamorous kindness of twilight', re-enacting the birth of Venus
from the foam. Her intimation of renewal cannot be separated from
her sexuality. The unspoken message to the man indicated by her
maidenhair is that the source of new life is within her. It is through
the eternal female and only through her that man has access to the
'bath of life' which the sea symbolizes.

The poem itself, in keeping with its delicacy and muted tones,
makes no such overt statement. We sympathize with the puzzle-
ment of the man, unable to reconcile revelation with doctrine. 'Lo!
God is one god! But . . .' Is he admitting that doctrine must be hived
off from experience? Is he admitting exceptions to his rule? Or is
he wondering whether, if God is one god, the name of that one god
might be Aphrodite?

Between 'The Man of Tyre' and 'Invocation to the Moon' come
two more poems about the sea, answers to the false proposition
that the sea is loveless. The dolphin is another token of the capacity
of the cold sea to create new warm life, the sea as the womb of life.
But such births can only follow a meeting and mingling of opposites, symbolized by the rainbow. The Etruscans, according to Lawrence, knew the sea in this way:

The dolphin leaps in and out of it suddenly, as a creature that suddenly
exists, out of nowhere. He was not: and lo! there he is! The dolphin which
gives up the sea's rainbows only when he dies. Out he leaps; then, with

a head-dive, back again he plunges into the sea. He is so much alive, he is like the phallus carrying the fiery spark of procreation down into the wet darkness of the womb. [MM 151]

The poems, with their perfect control of rhythm, their flexibility and athleticism, their exuberance, are themselves like dolphins, leaping gaily between the elements of reality and myth:

> and up they come with the purple dark of rainbows
> and flip! they go! with the nose-dive of sheer delight;
> and the sea is making love to Dionysos
> in the bouncing of these small and happy whales. [CP 693]

It is amazing that Lawrence could write such poems on days after, in all probability, he had been kept awake all night by incessant coughing. Frieda recalled such days:

> But then at dawn I believe he felt grateful that another day had been given him. 'Come when the sun rises,' he said, and when I came he was glad, so very glad, as if he would say: 'See, another day is given me.'
> The sun rose magnificently opposite his bed in red and gold across the bay and the fishermen standing up in their boats looked like eternal mythological figures dark and alive against the lit-up splendour of the sea and sky.
> His courage and unflinching spirit doing their level best to live as long as he possibly could in this world he loved so much, gave me courage too. [NI 302]

Nor did he flinch from the effort to imagine his departure to another world. He took up again the 'Glory of darkness' drafts. At first the crucial idea of the gentians as torches still did not come, despite the 'smoking blueness of Pluto's gloom' [PP 229]. First they were 'sheaf-like', an image which could lead nowhere, then

> many cups sharp-lipped, erect, oh very erect
> long and erect and fathomless, dark sharp cups of pure blue darkness,
> and burning with dark-blue power.

The cups were no better than the sheaves. But the word 'burning' surely brought with it the image Lawrence needed. He went back over the preceding lines, changing them to:

> Bavarian gentians, big and dark, only dark
> darkening the day-time, torch-like with the smoking blueness of
>   Pluto's gloom,
> ribbed and torch-like, with their blaze of darkness spread blue
> down flattening into points, flattened under the sweep of white day
> torch-flower of the blue-smoking darkness, Pluto's dark-blue daze

and so on to the now familiar ending, where the torches guide him

to the sightless realm where darkness is awake upon the dark
and Persephone herself is but a voice
or a darkness invisible enfolded in the deeper dark
of the arms Plutonic, and pierced with the passion of dense gloom,
among the splendour of torches of darkness, shedding darkness
on the lost bride and her groom.

But there are implications of the Persephone story not followed through here. If she is pierced with passion on this her wedding night, does not that imply her renewal and return journey? Nor is it clear what the marriage of Persephone has to do with the poet's own soul-journey, which the ending loses sight of. Also, with those jettisoned lines, Lawrence had thrown out a crucial word, 'erect'.

On the next page of the notebook, he starts again, and now, for the first time, releases all the poem's potentialities, follows through its images with the boldness of a great metaphysical poem. Outwardly the gentians are phallic – 'ribbed hellish flowers erect'; inwardly they are womb-like. They are both Pluto and Persephone. Persephone, the life of the vegetation, and, here, of the body, is no longer 'the lost bride'. She goes to her marriage, to be 'ravished' by Pluto, pierced once more by his 'passion of the utter dark'. To be pierced by that darkness is to be violated and to die, yet at the same moment to be fertilized. Death is a nuptial to which the gentians summon and guide the poet. As wedding-guest he is himself to witness and perhaps participate in this process:

> Give me a flower on a tall stem, and three dark flames,
> for I will go to the wedding, and be wedding-guest
> at the marriage of the living dark.

At the time he wrote this, Lawrence was studying, and attempting to reconstruct, 'the mystery of the individual adventure into Hades' which, it seemed to him, must have been the pagan source for the business of the seven seals in the Book of Revelation. The 'three dark flames' reveal that 'Bavarian Gentians' in its final form has become Lawrence's personal re-enactment of this mystery:

> The initiate [the wedding-guest] . . . is bodily dead. There remains, however, the journey through the underworld, where the living 'I' must divest itself of soul and spirit, before it can at last emerge naked from the far gate of hell into the new day. For the soul, the spirit, and the living 'I' are the three divine natures of man [the 'three dark flames']. The four bodily natures are put off on earth. The *two* divine natures can be divested in Hades. And the last is a stark flame which, on the new day, is clothed anew and successively by the spiritual body, the soul-body, and then the 'garment' of flesh, with its fourfold terrestrial natures.   [A 104]

'Bavarian Gentians' can only enact the early stages of this mystery. It stops short of the re-emergence and the new day. The remaining stages need further poems to work through, culminating in the final version of 'The Ship of Death'.

In 'Bavarian Gentians' the bride was enfolded in deepest darkness. In 'Silence', the poet wishes to be enveloped in Silence, 'great bride of all creation', 'embedded in a shell of Silence . . . the silence of the last of the seven great laughs of God' [CP 698]. These 'seven creative thunders' are described in *Apocalypse*. They are also 'seven new words' which will 'bring the new cosmos into being', but the seer is forbidden to write them down: 'We must wait for the actuality' [A 114]. The holy silence, then, is the 'silence of passing through doors', the 'great hush of going from this into that':

> Lift up your heads, O ye Gates!
> for the silence of the last great thundrous laugh
> screens us purely, and we can slip through.

At the end of October, Lawrence turned again to 'The Ship of Death'. The long first draft is broken down now into several poems. In particular, the sections of concern for the fate of those who have no ship of the soul are stripped away, leaving a much clearer narrative line – the need to build the ship of death, the preparations, and the journey – and this is then filled out with new material. It is clearly stated at the outset that the journey is a metaphor for 'the long and painful death/ that lies between the old self and the new' [PP 225]. The ship is now described as a 'little ark', suggesting both Noah's ark ('already the flood is upon us') and the ark of the covenant ('the ark of faith'). The image of the flood allows Lawrence to extend the threat of death to 'all of us': 'and soon it will rise on the world, on the outside world'. This brings the poem into accord with *Apocalypse*, where he speaks of two simultaneous processes, 'the destruction of the old Adam and the creation of new man', and the 'general or universal message of the destruction of the old world and creation of the new' [A 114]. Whether the individual is literally dying or not, he will be unable to cope with life and change unless he has accepted death. Otherwise, instead of slipping through the gateway to new life, he will 'slip entirely through the fingers of the hands of god/into the abyss of self-knowledge/knowledge of the self-apart-from-god' [CP 701], or join the hosts of the walking dead in the 'bursten cities' [704].

Much more dramatically, with much more conviction and immediacy than before, Lawrence now describes the disappearance of the ship into utter darkness:

> And everything is gone, the body is gone
> completely under, gone, entirely gone.
> The upper darkness is heavy on the lower,
> between them the little ship
> is gone
> she is gone.
>
> It is the end, it is oblivion.   [PP 226]

New too is the moving imagery of dawn which follows:

> A flush of rose, and the whole thing starts again.
>
> The flood subsides, and the body, like a worn sea-shell
> emerges strange and lovely.
> And the little ship wings home, faltering and lapsing
> on the pink flood,
> and the frail soul steps out, into her house again
> filling the heart with peace.   [227]

It is very wistful and poignant. It seems cruel to probe something so tender. Yet it seems to me too wishful and imprecise, like a fairy-tale. There is no attempt to find imagery that will give any clue as to how the renewal is brought about. Is it the same soul stepping into the same body in the same world? If so, the imagery is more appropriate to healing than to rebirth. All the sexual and procreative imagery of the earlier version has been dropped, imagery which had equated the process he describes with familiar processes of nature. In the last analysis, there seems a reluctance to let go of the self, the 'living "I" ', the last 'stark flame'; a reluctance understandable enough were it not for Lawrence's insistence, in so many other poems in this collection, that abandonment of self is a prerequisite for rebirth. It can be argued that a willingness to enter oblivion is itself an abandonment of self. But if, in oblivion, the soul loses irrecoverably all memory of body, self and world, what sense does it make to speak of it as the 'living "I" ', or to suggest that it is still the same soul? How do 'the body' and 'the heart', implying the same body and heart, become habitable again after death? The image of the 'worn sea-shell' does not help.

It may be that Lawrence himself was not happy with this version of 'The Ship of Death', since there exists another, apparently later, version, reduced to less than a quarter of its length. The journey itself is given in a mere four lines:

> Rigging its mast with the silent, invisible sail
> That will spread in death to the breeze
> Of the kindness of the cosmos, that will waft
> The little ship with its soul to the wonder-goal.   [CP 965]

Perhaps he regretted his attempt to spell out the mystery, for, as he says in 'Know-All':

> Man knows nothing
> till he knows how not-to-know. [726]

Only the silent soul can sink into God:

> But anyone who shall ascribe attributes to God or oblivion
> let him be cast out, for blasphemy.
> For God is a deeper forgetting far than sleep
> and all description is a blasphemy. [726]

There follows Lawrence's last important poem on death, and best, 'Shadows', with no description of God or oblivion, no attempt to use myth or esoteric lore as a key, no imagery beyond that of 'earth's lapse and renewal'. Each section of the poem begins 'And if . . .', laying claim to no knowledge, no certainties:

> And if, in the changing phases of man's life
> I fall in sickness and in misery
> my wrists seem broken and my heart seems dead
> and strength is gone, and my life
> is only the leavings of a life:
>
> and still, among it all, snatches of lovely oblivion, and snatches of
>   renewal
> odd, wintry flowers upon the withered stem, yet new, strange flowers
> such as my life has not brought forth before, new blossoms of me –
> [727]

We have ourselves been witness to this miracle. Out of this chronic sickness and wasted body (he had less than four months to live) have come such a profusion of new, strange flowers, *Pansies* and *Last Poems*:

> then I must know that still
> I am in the hands of the unknown God,
> he is breaking me down to his own oblivion
> to send me forth on a new morning, a new man. [727]

*

What he had seen and felt and known he gave in his writing to his fellow men, the splendour of living, the hope of more and more life he had given them, a heroic and immeasurable gift.   Frieda Lawrence

NOTES

CHAPTER 1. THE YOUNG MAN AND THE DEMON

1. These poems and the early drafts I discuss later in this chapter are all in a Nottingham University College notebook [B E317] now at Nottingham University Library. In *A Personal Record* Jessie recalled:

He was writing poems too, in a small thick note-book with the college arms on the cover. He passed all his writings on to me, secretly, and insisted upon a criticism, or at least, I was to tell him what I thought of them.

There are markings in pencil on some of the poems in the notebook, including 'Guelder Roses', which may well have been made by Jessie. Thus the revised ending of 'Guelder Roses' cannot have been written until after September 1906, when Lawrence began his course at Nottingham University College.
2. The fullest account of this early version and the story's subsequent metamorphoses is in Keith Cushman, *D. H. Lawrence at Work: the Emergence of the 'Prussian Officer' Stories*, Virginia U.P. and Harvester Press 1978, pp. 148–66.
3. See Cushman 47–76; James T. Boulton, 'D. H. Lawrence's "Odour of Chrysanthemums": An Early Version', *Renaissance and Modern Studies* 13 (1969), 5–11; Mara Kalnins, 'D. H. Lawrence's "Odour of Chrysanthemums": The Three Endings', *Studies in Short Fiction* 13 (1976), 471–9.
4. In page references to *The White Peacock*, the first is to the Cambridge edition, the second to the Penguin English Library edition.
5. He also wanted Garnett's help in choosing a title. Lawrence had already rejected 'The Harassed Angel' and could not decide between 'The Right Thing to Do' and 'The Only Thing to be Done'. It was only when revising the typescript in March that he thought of the title 'The Soiled Rose', under which the story was published in the *Forum* in March 1913, and the *Blue Review* in May 1913 (to which the BR references refer).
6. He has 'an artist's impersonal, observant gaze' [BR 7]: his full name, John Adderley Syson, may be intended to suggest the aestheticism of John Addington Symonds, the Victorian poet and authority on Renaissance art.
7. For an interesting intermediate version of this paragraph see PO 262.

CHAPTER 2. THE BIRTH AND EARLY DEATH OF A DRAMATIST

1. O'Casey's review, 'A Miner's Dream of Home', appeared in the *New Statesman* on 28 July 1934; it is reprinted in his *Blasts and Benedictions*, ed. Ayling, Macmillan 1967, pp. 222–5.
2. John Millington Synge, *Plays, Poems and Prose*, Dent 1968, pp. 265–6.
3. In an article in DHLR 16 133–63 Cecil Davies convincingly argues that the uncut

text can be made to work in the theatre if played non-realistically – as 'high comedy' or farce. His case is based on a production at the Octagon Theatre, Bolton, in 1980, which unfortunately I did not see.
4. For a fuller account see 'The Strange History of *The Daughter-in-Law*' by Keith Sagar, DHLR 11 175–84.
5. See George Panichas, *Adventures in Consciousness, The Meaning of D. H. Lawrence's Religious Quest*, Mouton, The Hague, 1964, pp. 136–50.

CHAPTER 3. 'A GREAT TRAGEDY': THE GENESIS OF *SONS AND LOVERS*

1. B E373d. References to the manuscript, which is titled *Paul Morel*, are given as PM.
2. See, for example, 'Son and Lover', J. F. C. Littlewood, *Cambridge Quarterly* 4 (1969–70), 323–61; MW 118–21.
3. CB III 562–620.
4. F. R. Leavis's studies of *The Rainbow, Women in Love* and *St Mawr* appeared in *Scrutiny* in 1950 and 1951 in a series called 'The Novel as Dramatic Poem'; Dorothy van Ghent's excellent essay on *Sons and Lovers* appeared in her book *The English Novel: Form and Function* in 1953; Mark Spilka's *The Love Ethic of D. H. Lawrence* was published in 1955.
5. I have described these in *The Art of D. H. Lawrence*, Cambridge 1966, 30–31.
6. In *Stephen Hero*, Joyce defines an epiphany as a 'sudden spiritual manifestation', the moment when a spiritual eye manages 'to adjust its vision to an exact focus . . . The soul of the commonest object, the structure of which is so adjusted, seems to us radiant. The object achieves its epiphany' [*Stephen Hero*, Cape 1944, 216–18].

CHAPTER 4. 'NEW HEAVEN AND EARTH': THE GENESIS OF *THE RAINBOW*

1. See p. 83.
2. Letters 576 and 577 are clearly reversed in L I. Possibly Lawrence misdated the latter, which should have been 17 May and therefore belongs with the envelope here assigned to 576.
3. One of these figures is reproduced in Sagar, *The Life of D. H. Lawrence*, Methuen 1980, p. 70.
4. The balance of Lawrence's sympathy gradually swung away from Anna and towards Will. In the final MS. Anna relinquishes her adventure into the unknown 'with a pang' rather than with satisfaction, and Will is blamed for holding her back. In his proof revisions Lawrence made Anna herself responsible. See CR 66; and below.
5. Here again Lawrence's proof revisions favoured Will. The final MS. had, not 'set another man in him free', but merely 'left a superficial man in him disengaged'. In the published text, though Will's achievement may be limited, it is not therefore to be disparaged. See CR 51–2.
6. See above, p. 100.
7. B E331a should read 711 pages, not 811.
8. See 'Keynes, Lawrence, and Cambridge Revisited', S. P. Rosenbaum, *Cambridge Quarterly* 11, No. i (1982), 252–64.

CHAPTER 5. 'BLASPHEMOUS LIVING': THE GENESIS OF *WOMEN IN LOVE*

1. The evidence is primarily in the unpublished manuscript [B E441a] discussed below. The similarity between the names Loerke and Gertler must have been fortuitous, since Lawrence did not meet Gertler until the summer of 1914. Lawrence later told Gertler: 'We knew a man, a german, who did these big reliefs for great, fine factories in Cologne' [L III 46].

2. See Mark Gorton, 'Some Say in Ice: The Apocalyptic Fears in *Women in Love*', *Foundation* 28, 56–60.

3. Since this was only the second 1916 draft, Lawrence must have been counting the two 1913 drafts of *The Sisters*.

4. CR 112.

5. The novel was to be extensively revised in November 1916, September 1917, August/September 1919 and November 1920. See Herbert Davis, '*Women in Love*: A Corrected Typescript', *University of Toronto Quarterly* 27, 34–53; IW; CR; Pierre Vitoux, 'The Chapter "Excurse" in *Women in Love*: Its Genesis and the Critical Problem', *Texas Studies in Literature and Language* 17, 821–36, and '*Women in Love*: From Typescripts into Print', *TSLL* 23, 577–93.

6. The painting is reproduced in Carrington, *Gertler: Selected Letters*, facing p. 129; and in MW, facing p. 161.

7. Lawrence, familiar as he was with Greek tragedy, and studies of it by Jane Harrison and Gilbert Murray, would not use the word 'agonizing' without an awareness of the meaning of *agon*. As Charles Ross observes: 'An *agon* is not simply the spirited dialogue or clash of opinion common to all dramatic literature. It is a contest between opposed attitudes to life or world-views that achieves a representative or symbolic comprehensiveness . . . Lawrence strives to endow his *agons* with great symbolic weight, so that, in several climactic scenes, the many aspects of the novel's world are embodied in action' [DHLR 10 10].

8. This dedication appears on an early draft of the poem (called 'Eden').

9. Lawrence would have known the Dies Irae from the same volume of the *International Library of Famous Literature* which had first introduced him to Dante:

> Where thy sheep go, turn my way:
> Drive me ne'er with goats astray:
> Nigh thy right hand make me stay.
>
> Ere the accursed their fate shall know,
> Doomed to burn in flames of woe,
> Call me where thy sainted go.   [IL IV 1610]

The division into sheep and goats was presumably a central theme in the lost *Goats and Compasses*, and was carried over into the 'Reality of Peace' essays, though there Lawrence reverses the Biblical scheme by damning the sheep.

10. Four of the essays are collected in *Phoenix* under that title. 'Whistling of Birds' is a fifth. The other two are lost.

11. All published texts of *Women in Love* read: 'he knew he did not want a further sensual experience . . .' There is no sign of this 'not' in Lawrence's perfectly clear revision of the definitive typescript. There are two possible explanations. Lawrence may have added the 'not' in the proofs. This is highly unlikely, since it makes no sense. 'Suddenly he found himself face to face with a situation.' Lawrence means that Birkin was in a dilemma. 'On the one hand, he knew he did want a further

sensual experience . . .' 'On the other hand' never follows in so many words; but what is clearly implied is that Birkin does not, on the other hand, want to 'fall into the long, long African process of purely sensual understanding, knowledge in the mystery of dissolution'. Birkin subsequently resolves the dilemma by taking 'another way, the way of freedom' [331], freedom which includes a 'further sensual experience' with Ursula, but does not involve falling 'from the connection with life and hope', lapsing 'from pure integral being'. The other explanation is that the 'not' was a compositor's error which Lawrence failed to spot in his proof-correcting – as he failed to spot a great many more.

CHAPTER 6. 'LITTLE LIVING MYTHS': *BIRDS, BEASTS AND FLOWERS*

1. These 'Mystical Notes', drawing heavily on Burnet, were written by Lawrence in November 1929 for the 1930 illustrated edition of *Birds, Beasts and Flowers* [B A27c]. He was, however, already familiar with Burnet when the poems were written.
2. See Richard P. Blackmur, 'D. H. Lawrence and Expressive Form' in *Language as Gesture*, Allen & Unwin 1954. Lawrence is defended against Blackmur's formalist attack by, among many others, Harold Bloom, 'Lawrence, Blackmur, Eliot and the Tortoise' in *A D. H. Lawrence Miscellany*, ed. Harry T. Moore, Southern Illinois 1959; and Vivian de Sola Pinto in his Introduction to the *Complete Poems*.
3. Lawrence's poetic wit is well described by A. Alvarez, 'D. H. Lawrence: The Single State of Man' in *The Shaping Spirit*, Chatto 1958; also reprinted in *A D. H. Lawrence Miscellany*.

CHAPTER 7. THE MONK AND THE BEAST: *ST MAWR*

1. See Keith Brown, 'Welsh Red Indians: D. H. Lawrence and *St Mawr*', *Essays in Criticism* 32 (1982), 158–79.
2. 'Poets usually refuse the call. How are they to accept it? How can a poet become a medicine man and fly to the source and come back and heal or pronounce oracles? Everything among us is against it.' Ted Hughes in Faas, *The Unaccommodated Universe*, Black Sparrow Press 1980, p. 206.
3. Lawrence Clark Powell, *The Manuscripts of D. H. Lawrence*, p. 12, describes an incomplete manuscript of an early version of *St Mawr* numbered 17–58. It is not clear, however, whether the ending of this manuscript was the conclusion of that draft of the story.
4. Brett told me this in conversation, about 1973.
5. I owe this suggestion to Polly Whitney.
6. This suggestion was subsequently taken up by William Golding in *The Inheritors*.

CHAPTER 8. 'THE SECRET OF THE ETRUSCANS':
THE GENESIS OF *THE ESCAPED COCK*

1. According to Billy T. Tracy, ' "Reading up the Ancient Etruscans": Lawrence's Debt to George Dennis', *Twentieth Century Literature* 23 (1977), 437–50, Lawrence also read something by A. L. Milani.
2. Lawrence had probably been familiar with the chapters quoted below earlier than the rest of the book, since they were in Richard Garnett's *International Library of Famous Literature* in the Lawrence home.

3. See 'The Phallic Vision: D. H. Lawrence and V. V. Rozanov' in *D. H. Lawrence's Response to Russian Literature* by George J. Zytaruk, Mouton 1971.
4. See Evelyn J. Hinz and John J. Teunissen, 'Savior and Cock: Allusion and Icon in Lawrence's *The Man Who Died*', *Journal of Modern Literature* 5 (1976), 279–96.
5. 'Lawrence in Etruria', *Spectator*, 4 November 1932.
6. Gerald Doherty, 'The Nirvana Dimension: D. H. Lawrence's Quarrel with Buddhism', DHLR 15 51–67.

CHAPTER 9. 'NEW, STRANGE FLOWERS': *PANSIES, NETTLES* AND *LAST POEMS*

1. B E302d. The manuscript is described and the poems listed in DB 104–12. I have used this manuscript only as a guide to the order and date of composition, quoting those poems which were published in *Pansies* [B A47c] in the often revised form in which they appeared there and in CP. Since I have space to discuss these revisions in relation to only a handful of the 231 poems in *Pansies*, it would have been confusing to confront the reader with unfamiliar unrevised texts of the remainder.
2. B E192a. According to Richard Aldington's description of MS. B of *Last Poems* (which he called *More Pansies*), the inside cover of the notebook bears the date 23 November 1928. It does not. But the front free endpaper is missing now; perhaps, when he examined it, the inscription was there. The first nineteen poems in the notebook, which is headed *Pensées*, are early drafts of poems which went into *Pansies*, except for five which were rejected. For further details see CW 179.
3. B C258. *Review of English Studies* 21 (1970), 183.
4. In CL, Moore mistakenly transcribes this as 'shiny London'.
5. The early drafts of 'Bavarian Gentians' and 'The Ship of Death' which I discuss here are also in CP 958–64. I have directed the reader rather to PP because Mandell gives all the interlinear revisions not given in CP, and avoids such misprints or mistranscriptions as 'skirt' for 'shirt' [CP 964].
6. 'D. H. Lawrence's *Last Poems*', DHLR 5 110–12.

BIBLIOGRAPHY
AND REFERENCE KEY

This does not attempt to be a comprehensive or even selective bibliography – merely a list of books cited or directly used.

1. WORKS OF D. H. LAWRENCE

THE CAMBRIDGE EDITION

A   *Apocalypse and the Writings on Revelation*, ed. Mara Kalnins
L I   *Letters*: Vol. I, ed. James T. Boulton
L II   *Letters*: Vol. II, ed. George J. Zytaruk and James T. Boulton
L III   *Letters*: Vol. III, ed. James T. Boulton and Andrew Robertson
LG   *The Lost Girl*, ed. John Worthen
MN   *Mr Noon*, ed. Lindeth Vasey
PO   *The Prussian Officer and Other Stories*, ed. John Worthen
STH   *Study of Thomas Hardy*, ed. Bruce Steele
STM   *St Mawr and Other Stories*, ed. Brian Finney
T   *The Trespasser*, ed. Elizabeth Mansfield
WP   *The White Peacock*, ed. Andrew Robertson

THE PENGUIN ENGLISH LIBRARY

CSN   *The Complete Short Novels*, ed. Keith Sagar and Melissa Partridge
PS   *The Plumed Serpent*, ed. Ronald G. Walker
R   *The Rainbow*, ed. John Worthen
SSS   *Selected Short Stories*, ed. Brian Finney
SL   *Sons and Lovers*, ed. Keith Sagar
WP   *The White Peacock*, ed. Alan Newton
WL   *Women in Love*, ed. Charles Ross

OTHER PENGUINS

AR   *Aaron's Rod*
CP   *The Complete Poems*, ed. Vivian de Sola Pinto and F. Warren Roberts
F   *Fantasia of the Unconscious and Psychoanalysis and the Unconscious*
FLC   *The First Lady Chatterley*
JT   *John Thomas and Lady Jane*
K   *Kangaroo*
LC   *Lady Chatterley's Lover*
MC   *The Mortal Coil and Other Stories*
MM   *Mornings in Mexico and Etruscan Places*
POS   *The Princess and Other Stories*

S   *Studies in Classic American Literature*
SS   *Sea and Sardinia*
TI   *Twilight in Italy*
TP   *Three Plays: A Collier's Friday Night; The Daughter-in-Law; The Widowing of Mrs Holroyd*
WWR   *The Woman Who Rode Away*

OTHER EDITIONS

C   *The Centaur Letters*, University of Texas 1970
CL   *The Collected Letters*, ed. Harry T. Moore, Heinemann 1962
CPL   *The Complete Plays*, Heinemann 1965
EC   *The Escaped Cock*, ed. Gerald M. Lacy, Black Sparrow Press 1973
H   *The Letters*, ed. Aldous Huxley, Heinemann 1932
M   *Movements in European History*, ed. James T. Boulton, Oxford 1971
MS   *Letters from D. H. Lawrence to Martin Secker 1911–1930*, ed. Martin Secker, Bridgefoot, Iver, 1970
P   *Phoenix: The Posthumous Papers of D. H. Lawrence*, ed. Edward D. McDonald, Heinemann 1936
P II   *Phoenix II: Uncollected, Unpublished and Other Prose Works*, ed. Warren Roberts and Harry T. Moore, Heinemann 1968
        (P and P II are published as Penguins in the U.S.A. only; the pages references are the same.)
Q   *The Quest for Rananim: D. H. Lawrence's Letters to S. S. Koteliansky 1914–1930*, ed. George J. Zytaruk, McGill-Queen's 1970
SLF   *D. H. Lawrence: Sons and Lovers: A Facsimile of the Manuscript*, ed. Mark Schorer, California 1977
SM   *The Symbolic Meaning: The Uncollected Versions of Studies in Classic American Literature*, ed. Armin Arnold, Centaur 1962
TS   *Letters to Thomas and Adele Seltzer*, ed. Gerald M. Lacy, Black Sparrow Press 1976

2. BOOKS ABOUT LAWRENCE

References to articles in periodicals other than DHLR are in the Notes.

AA   *Acts of Attention: The Poems of D. H. Lawrence*, Sandra Gilbert, Cornell 1972
        The Dark Night of the Body: D. H. Lawrence's The Plumed Serpent, L. D. Clark, Texas 1964
B   *A Bibliography of D. H. Lawrence* (Second Edition), Warren Roberts, Cambridge 1982
BM   *D. H. Lawrence and the Body Mystical*, Frederick Carter, Denis Archer 1932
BTW   *Between Two Worlds*, John Middleton Murry, Cape 1935
CB   *D. H. Lawrence: A Composite Biography*, 3 vols., Edward Nehls, Wisconsin 1957–9
CH   *D. H. Lawrence: The Critical Heritage*, ed. R. P. Draper, Routledge 1979
CR   *The Composition of The Rainbow and Women in Love*, Charles Ross, Virginia 1979
CS   *D. H. Lawrence: A Critical Study of the Major Novels and Other Writings*, ed. A. H. Gomme, Harvester 1978
CW   *D. H. Lawrence: A Calendar of his Works*, Keith Sagar, Manchester 1979

DB   The Frieda Lawrence Collection of D. H. Lawrence Manuscripts: A Descriptive Bibliography, E. W. Tedlock, New Mexico 1948
DHLR   The D. H. Lawrence Review, ed. James C. Cowan, University of Arkansas
EL   The Early Life of D. H. Lawrence, Ada Lawrence and G. Stuart Gelder, Secker 1932
FL   Frieda Lawrence: The Memoirs and Correspondence, ed. E. W. Tedlock, Heinemann 1961
FS   D. H. Lawrence: A First Study, Stephen Potter, Cape 1930
HC   In Our Infancy, Helen Corke, Cambridge 1975
IN   The Idea of the Novel, John Worthen, Macmillan 1979
IW   Imagined Worlds, ed. Maynard Mack and Ian Gregor, Methuen 1968
LB   Lawrence and Brett, Dorothy Brett, Sunstone Press 1974
LH   A D. H. Lawrence Handbook, ed. Keith Sagar, Manchester 1982
LT   Lorenzo in Taos, Mabel Dodge Luhan, Secker 1933
KM   The Letters and Journals of Katherine Mansfield, ed. C. K. Stead, Penguin 1977
MD   The Minoan Distance: The Symbolism of Travel in D. H. Lawrence, L. D. Clark, Arizona 1980
MT   Modern Tragedy, Raymond Williams, Chatto 1966
MW   D. H. Lawrence: The Man and His Work, Emile Delavenay, Heinemann 1972
MWL   D. H. Lawrence: The Man Who Lived, ed. Robert J. Partlow and Harry T. Moore, Southern Illinois 1980
NI   Not I, But the Wind, Frieda Lawrence, Heinemann 1935
O   Ottoline: the Early Memoirs of Lady Ottoline Morrell, ed. Robert Gathorne-Hardy, Faber 1963
OG   Ottoline at Garsington: Memoirs of Lady Ottoline Morrell, 1915–1918, ed. Robert Gathorne-Hardy, Faber 1974
PL   The Priest of Love, Harry T. Moore, Penguin 1976
PP   The Phoenix Paradox: A Study of Renewal Through Change in the Collected Poems and Last Poems of D. H. Lawrence, Gail Porter Mandell, Northern Illinois 1984
PR   D. H. Lawrence: A Personal Record, Jessie Chambers, Cass 1965, Cambridge 1980
RC   D. H. Lawrence: Reminiscences and Correspondence, Earl and Achsah Brewster, Secker 1934
RL   Reminiscences of D. H. Lawrence, John Middleton Murry, Cape 1933
SK   The Plays of D. H. Lawrence: A Biographical and Critical Study, Sylvia Sklar, Vision Press 1975
SP   The Savage Pilgrimage, Catherine Carswell, Chatto 1932, Cambridge 1981

3. OTHER BOOKS CITED

AAR   Ancient Art and Ritual, Jane Harrison, Williams and Norgate 1913
CE   Creative Evolution, Henri Bergson, tr. A. Mitchell, London 1911
CS   Christian Symbolism, Mrs Henry Jenner, Methuen 1910
CSS   Collected Short Stories, E. M. Forster, Penguin 1954
D   Dionysos, C. Kerenyi, Routledge 1976
DCH   The Divine Comedy: Hell, Dante, Penguin 1949

E   *The Etruscans*, Werner Keller, Cape 1975
EGP   *Early Greek Philosophy*, John Burnet, A. & C. Black 1930
         Five Stages of Greek Religion, Gilbert Murray, Oxford 1925
FA   *Far Away and Long Ago*, W. H. Hudson, Dent 1923
GB   *The Golden Bough*, J. G. Frazer, Macmillan 1957
HE   *Howards End*, E. M. Forster, Penguin 1941
IL   *International Library of Famous Literature*, ed. Richard Garnett, Edward
         Lloyd 1899
JB   *The Pilgrim's Progress*, John Bunyan, Penguin 1965
JW   *The Joyful Wisdom*, F. Nietzsche, tr. Thomas Common, Vol. 10 in *The
         Complete Works of Friedrich Nietzsche*, ed. Oscar Levy, London 1909–13
PA   *Portrait of the Artist as a Young Man*, James Joyce, Penguin 1960
PC   *Primitive Culture*, E. B. Tylor, London 1871
PH   *Phaedrus*, Plato, Penguin 1973
RU   *The Riddle of the Universe*, Ernst Haeckel, tr. J. McCabe, London 1906
SAP   *The Sacred and the Profane*, Mircea Eliade, Harcourt Brace 1959
ST   *Symbols of Transformation*, Carl Jung, Pantheon 1956
WBY   *W. B. Yeats: The Poems*, ed. R. J. Finneran, Macmillan 1984
WG   *The White Goddess*, Robert Graves, Faber 1961
WW   *Walt Whitman: The Complete Poems*, ed. Francis Murphy, Penguin 1977
U   *Ulysses*, James Joyce, Penguin 1969

INDEXES

WORKS OF D. H. LAWRENCE
(Main entries in heavy type)

GENERAL INDEX